BROWN WATERS OF AFRICA

PORTUGUESE RIVERINE WARFARE 1961-1974

John P. Cann

Helion Studies in Military History Number 17

Helion & Company Ltd

Helion & Company Limited
26 Willow Road
Solihull
West Midlands
B91 1UE
England
Tel. 0121 705 3393
Fax 0121 711 4075
Email: info@helion.co.uk
Website: www.helion.co.uk

Published by Helion & Company 2013

Designed and typeset by Farr out Publications, Wokingham, Berkshire
Cover designed by Euan Carter, Leicester (www.euancarter.com)
Printed by Lightning Source Ltd, Milton Keynes, Buckinghamshire

Front cover: African *fuzileiros* in Guiné. Author's photo.
Rear cover: *Fuzileiros* aboard LFG *Sagitario* (P 1131) in the Cacheu River. Photograph courtesy private collection of Admiral Nuno Vieira Matias.

ISBN 978-1-908916-56-3

British Library Cataloguing-in-Publication Data.
A catalogue record for this book is available from the British Library.

For my dear friend
VICE ADMIRAL ANTÓNIO EMÍLIO FERRAZ SACCHETTI

Contents

List of photographs

List of maps

List of tables

Preface

The origin of my interest the Portuguese campaigns in Africa began during the period between 1987 and 1992. It was during this time that, as a naval officer, I was assigned as an occasional augmentee to the staff of the NATO command, Commander-in-Chief Iberian Atlantic Area, in Oeiras, Portugal, for its various maritime exercises. All of the Portuguese officers with whom I worked had fought in Africa during the Portuguese campaign to retain its Empire between 1961 and 1974. The stories of their experiences during this lengthy thirteen-year war fascinated me, and even today it remains a conflict that is not well known or understood outside of Portugal and of which little has been written in English. My subsequent assignments generated an interest in insurgency, and as a consequence, I naturally returned to the Portuguese African campaigns when I had the opportunity to do so.

My first book, *Counterinsurgency in Africa: The Portuguese Way of War, 1961–1974*, was originally published in 1997 and gave a broad overview of the war. It focused largely on the land campaign, as people live ashore, and such wars are fought for the loyalty of the population. There are, however, two other important mediums in the conflict, the naval and air dimensions. Each has its own perspective and merits an account.

This volume addresses the naval component in counterinsurgency and specifically traces how the Portuguese Navy anticipated the conflict, prepared for it, and fought on its rivers in Africa during this war. It explores the imaginative thinking behind the development of the Portuguese "brown water" navy and shows how this conceptualization led to the successful development of a well-considered plan. It called for the integration of a trained and competent cadre of sailors and marines or *fuzileiros* and a blend of equipment to execute national and theater strategy in support of the land effort in neutralizing the insurgent threat. An important ingredient was the elasticity of the plan, a flexibility that was able to accommodate needed adjustments in both the construction and employment of the riverine launches and the necessary modifications in the training and deployment of personnel to adjust to the enemy, the fighting environment, and the constriction on resources. In the end, the navy accomplished exactly what it had originally sought to achieve. The weaknesses in its use can be attributed to the primacy of the army and a lack of understanding on the part of its leaders as to how a riverine navy can be most effectively used to support a land campaign in counterinsurgency. In the two theaters where variations of this disconnect occurred, Guiné and Mozambique, there were difficulties in containing the insurgent advance. In the case of Angola, where naval operations complemented the land campaign well, success was clearly achieved, and the nationalist movements were completely stalemated. The depth and thoughtfulness of Portuguese Navy thinking in building and deploying a substantial riverine capability in the hostile remoteness of a distant continent remains a relevant model. It is one that continues to influence the shape of current and future navies that want to move inshore where new enemies hide and to seize the opportunity to influence events.

Acknowledgments

This book would not have been possible without the unstinting support of Admiral Nuno Gonçalo Vieira Matias, former Chief of Staff of the Portuguese Navy, and his successor, Admiral Francisco António Torres Vidal Abreu, for which I am most thankful. They made virtually every resource at their disposal available to me and for that I am most appreciative. Rear Admiral José Luís Ferreira Leiria Pinto and his predecessor, Rear Admiral Luís Joel Alves de Azevedo Pascoal, both Presidents of the Cultural Commission of the Navy and Directors of the Central Library of the Navy, provided their personal support and took an active interest in the project. I am indebted to their very professional archive and library staffs and most particularly to Captain José António Rodrigues Pereira, Doctor Isabel Beato and *Comandante* Ferreira Pinto, all of whom spent many hours helping me with my research and gave generously of their time. Additionally, I am indebted to Rear Admiral Luís Augusto Roque Martins, the Director of *Revista da Armada* for his advice and support, and to *Comandante* Luís Jorge Rodrigues Semedo de Matos for his help on *fuzileiro* history.

My deep appreciation goes to Vice Admiral António Emílio Ferraz Sacchetti, former President of the Academia de Marinha, who took a personal interest in the success of this volume from its inception until his untimely death. His hospitality and support proved indispensable.

Vice Admiral António Carlos Rebelo Duarte, Director of the Instituto Superior Naval de Guerra, and his predecessor, Vice Admiral Carlos Magalhães Queiroz, were most helpful in making the resources of the Instituto available.

This is a story that could not have been told without the assistance and interest of the many veteran "brown water sailors" who took time from their busy schedules to share their experiences. I am indebted to Vice Admiral José Deolindo Torres Sobral and his friend of many years *Comandante* Raul Patrício Leitão, who spent some considerable time describing operations on Lake Niassa. Rear Admiral Joaquim Manuel Barreiros Espadinha Galo and the former Governor of Niassa, Carlos Augusto Pereira da Costa Matos, likewise provided a valuable appraisal of life on the Lake. With respect to Guiné, I owe much to Rear Admiral Luiz Casimiro de Mesquita Dias for his reflections on the naval shipyard there, to Vice Admiral José Alberto Lopes Carvalheira and to *Comandantes* Guilherme Almor de Alpoim Calvão, José Manuel Malhão Pereira, Eurico Nelson de Campos Marques Pinto, and Carlos Encaração Gomes for their appraisal of operations.

The Naval Reserve played a vital role in the conflict, and as one admiral put it, the war could not have been fought without it. Its veterans today vividly remember their experiences, and I am most grateful of the time that they took to share them with me. I am particularly indebted to António de Castro Moreira, Manuel Lema Santos, J.D. Pires Branco, José Augusto Pires de Lima, António Luís Marinho de Castro, Ricardo Manuel Migães de Campos, Paulo Lowndes Marques, and Vasco Quevedo Pessanha, all members of the Associação dos Oficiais da Reserva Naval.

Funding of the initial research for this work was received from the Marine Corps University Foundation in conjunction with a sabbatical granted by the Marine Corps

University, for which I am most grateful.

Finally, I owe a particular debt to my wife Anne, who lived patiently with the domestic chaos of this work.

Maps

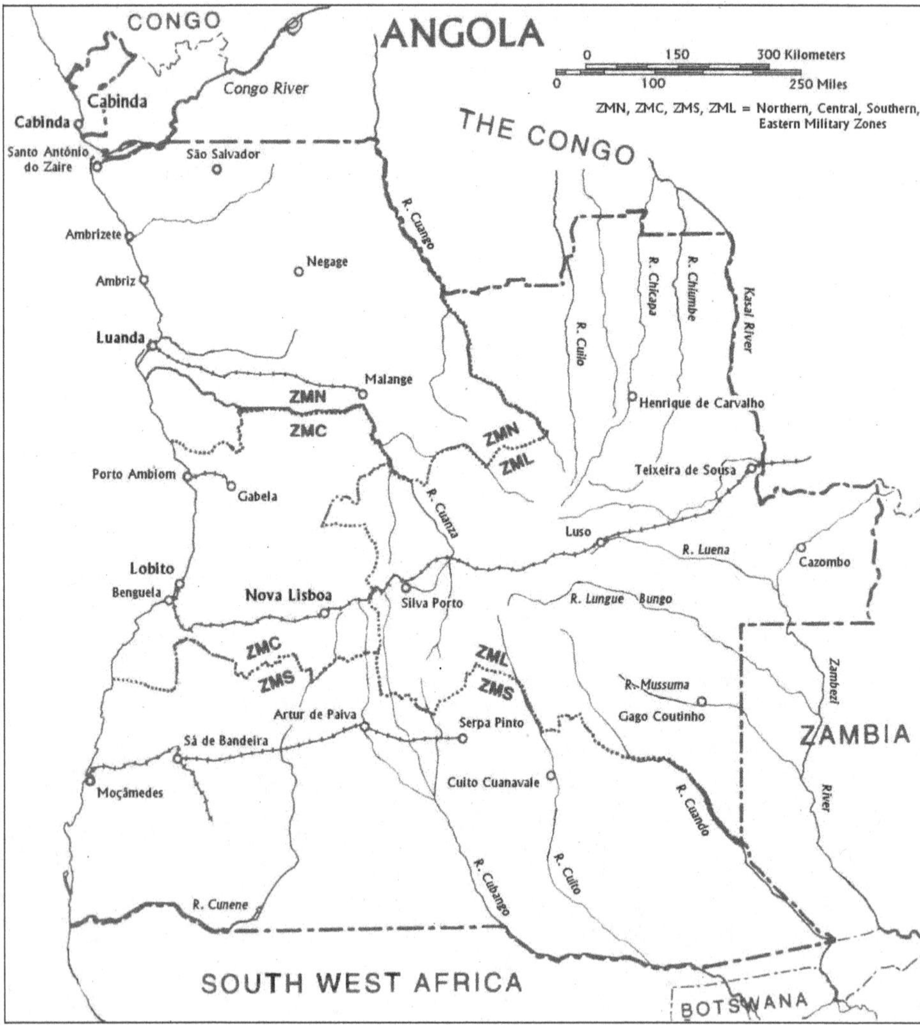

Map of Angola

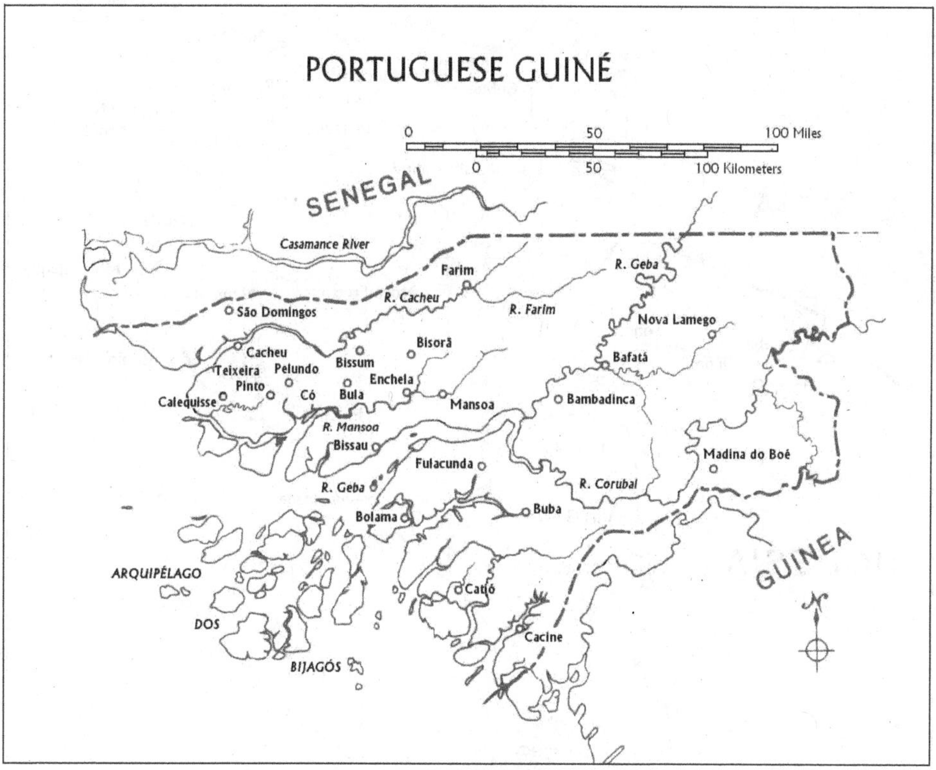
PORTUGUESE GUINÉ
0
50
100 Miles
0
50
100 Kilometers
SENEGAL
Casamance River
Farim
R. Cacheu
São Domingos
R. Farim
R. Geba
Nova Lamego
Bisorã
Cacheu
Bissum
Bafatá
Teixeira
Pelundo
Enchela
Pinto
Calequisse
Có
Bula
Mansoa
Bambadinca
R. Mansoa
Bissau
Fulacunda
Madina do Boé
R. Geba
R. Corubal
Bolama
Buba
ARQUIPÉLAGO
DOS
BIJAGÓS
Catió
Cacine
GUINEA

Map of Guiné

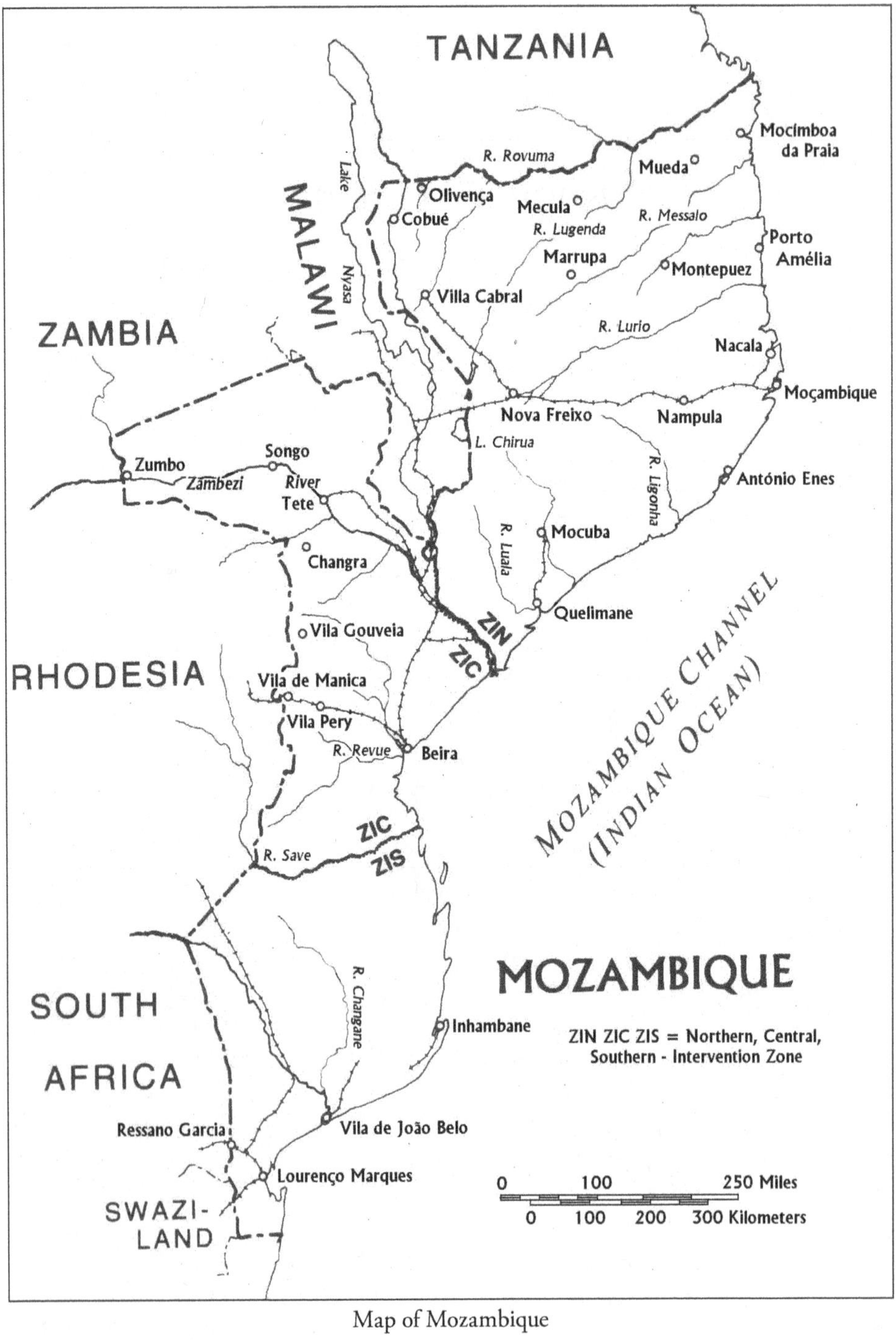

Map of Mozambique

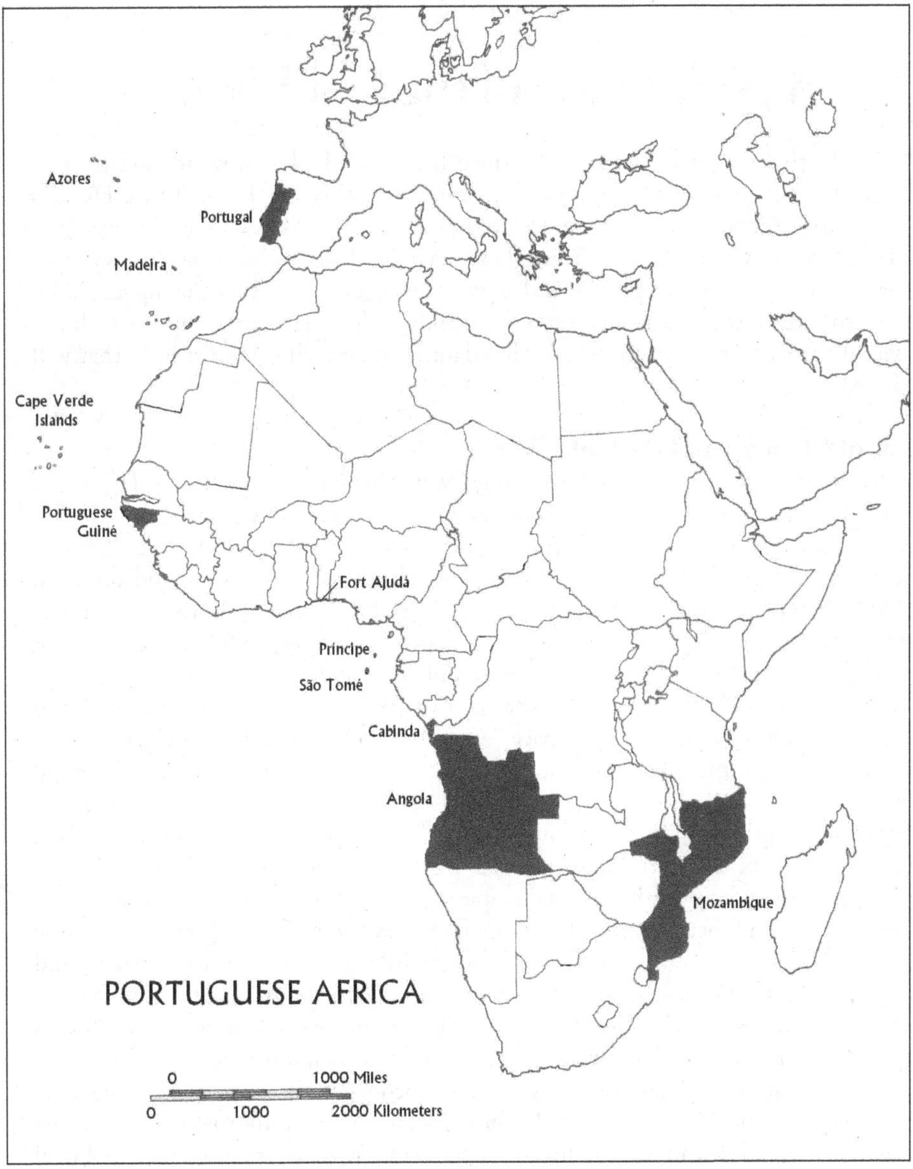

Map of Portuguese Africa

1

A New Phase of the Cold War

From the time of the Discoveries, Portugal has always looked seaward, and thus its navy has always played a key role in its maritime successes. From Prince Henry's innovative development of the caravel to the creation of its "brown water" navy of the 1961–1974 African Campaign, the Portuguese Navy has had an illustrious history. This latter campaign was shaped by geopolitical as well as local events, and the Portuguese Navy was asked to address the associated tasks at both ends of this spectrum. In Africa its duties were very different from those in the North Atlantic, and it is this African story that will be explored here.

"Winds of Change" and the Cold War

In the decade of the 1950s, the "winds of change" were blowing through Africa. The largest colonial power, Britain, was freeing its colonies at a regular pace in step with its reluctant promise made to the United States during World War II. Following the independence of British India in August 1947, its empire wound steadily down, and by the mid-1960s all of its African possessions were independent countries for all practical purposes. France, despite its reduced circumstances, remained adamant in retaining its colonies and fought two losing conflicts, Indochina between 1946 and 1954 and Algeria between 1954 and 1963. During the Algerian conflict, an exhausted France began to grant independence to the remainder of its colonies at a rapid pace. With the 1959 débâcle in the Belgian Congo and its independence the following year, Portugal then possessed the last intact colonial empire.

Following World War II, the colonial troops of both Britain and France who had helped their masters defeat the two imperial regimes of the Axis Powers returned to their role as lesser citizens in the colonial empires of their mother countries. There was a conflict in their minds between the ideals for which they had fought and their continuing underprivileged "native" status. They had difficulty in reconciling this discrepancy, and this led to the notion that perhaps their colonial home should be an independent country with the political freedoms that they were currently being denied. The answer to this search for equal status in the face of intransigent regimes was to form resistance movements. As the British, French, and Belgian colonies gained independence, the indigenous movements became political parties in the bequeathed nominal democracies. While these were generally short-lived and rapidly became oligarchies or dictatorships with fewer economic or political freedoms than before, they were, nevertheless, now independent states and comprised a large part of Africa. Their national and foreign policies reflected their heritage of resistance to colonialism. Portugal thus found itself surrounded in Africa by ideologically hostile countries that would readily serve as guerrilla sanctuaries and provide other practical support for resistance movements within its colonies. Angola initially faced such regimes in the Congo to the north and later Zambia to the east. Guiné was sandwiched between and indeed besieged by the former French Guinée to its south and a compliant Senegal to its north. Mozambique had Tanzania to its north and an ambivalent Malawi to the northwest. All of these neighbors were either sources or avenues of armed incursions.

In the context of the Cold War, the Soviet Union, the Peoples Republic of China, and their various satellites were ready to provide important support to guerrilla movements hostile to Portugal and other colonial powers in the direct form of military training, advice, and weapons and indirectly in the moral dimension. Their encouragement to Portugal's colonial opponents developed across a broad spectrum from armed conflict in the field to support in the diplomatic arenas of the United Nations (UN), the Organization of African States (OAS), and numerous other international fora. This hostile environment was clearly developing in line with the solidarity that the newly independent former colonies, now largely despotic regimes, felt with each other and the uncritical tyrannical communist bloc. Portugal, one of the early members of NATO, was staunchly anticommunist, and so there was now an additional dimension to the philosophical divergence with its African neighbors.

This development reflected the competing forces of the Cold War, which lasted some forty-four years from the end of World War II in 1945 to the fall of the Berlin Wall in 1989 and pitted the largely former Western Allies against the Soviet Union, communist China, and their satellite states. The initial of several phases ran until 1960 and was characterized by the creation of the Western and Eastern Blocs in a simple and starkly contrasting international bipolar system, with various states aligning themselves largely through alliances with either the principal "free world" or "communist" powers. The Western Bloc led by the United States followed a long-term policy of containment towards its Eastern counterpart and managed to extend and consolidate its Western system in this context. This consolidation was made through such vehicles as the Marshall Plan, the Atlantic Alliance, the Rio Pact, the Japanese-American Alliance, and the creation of the Federal Republic of Germany. In a very short time the United States had marshaled the forces of the developed world against its communist bloc foes in support of this containment policy.[1] The Soviet Union in response to this increased encirclement initiated two crises during the period in an attempt to increase its hegemony, the Berlin Blockade of 1948–1949 and the Korean War of 1950–1952. In the first instance the United States organized the Berlin Airlift as a response to a Soviet rail and road blockade of the city. This response avoided an obvious Allied ground confrontation, one that had the potential to be a messy troop encounter without solving the problem of sustaining an Allied presence. The Soviets lifted their blockade once the success of the airlift became obvious and demonstrated Allied determination to remain.

In the second instance, the Soviet Union tried the less direct method of using a proxy force to gain communist hegemony on the Korean peninsula. The Allies had demobilized their forces substantially following the war and were clearly vulnerable in peripheral areas, such as Korea. The Soviet Union and China encouraged and supported North Korea in its desire to unify the Korean peninsula under a communist regime and in a surprise attack on the South to achieve this aim. The Allies again scrambled to counter this aggression and under a UN resolution fielded a force that eventually restored South Korea under its legitimate government. The naïve post-war notion in many quarters that communists were "simple peace-loving people" was forever dispelled here.[2] The effect of this realization was a serious rearmament in the West, an unfortunate and debilitatingly expensive development for the Soviets.

The second "rearmament" phase ran from 1960 to 1973 and corresponded to the period of the Portuguese wars in Africa, which were directly affected by the U.S.-Soviet superpower confrontation. Following an established pattern, the Soviet Union initiated two crises during this period, the Berlin Crisis of 1961 and the Cuban Missile Crisis of 1962. These crises followed on the heels and, in the latter instance, were a direct result of the Pay of Pigs fiasco. This disaster had its origins in a failed plan that was developed during the last months of the Eisenhower and the first weeks of the Kennedy administration by the Central Intelligence Agency (CIA) to invade Cuba with about one thousand Cuban expatriates and overthrow its dictator Fidel Castro, a continuing thorn to the United States. It was based on the hopeful premise that the unhappy Cuban population would rally around the U.S.-trained and -armed invaders and help defeat Castro and his 200,000-man militia. When the CIA put the force ashore in April 1961, it was smothered by the militia.[3] Later that summer, Berlin was thrown into crisis with the building of the Berlin Wall by its communist East to isolate it as part of Soviet premier Nikita Khrushchev's continuing efforts to intimidate the Allies into abandoning the city. Things were not proceeding well for the new Kennedy administration.

Khrushchev had twice in 1960 pledged to defend Cuba from U.S. aggression, and after the Bay of Pigs threat, took this commitment to heart. Instead of simply installing defensive hardware there, he decided to use Cuba as an opportunity to bring much of the United States within reliable nuclear range of Soviet attack by deploying both 1,000-mile medium-range and 2,200-mile intermediate-range missiles and 700-mile range Illyushin-28 (IL-28) *Beagle* jet bombers. While strategically it would hardly matter whether the United States was struck by an attack from Cuba or an intercontinental ballistic missile from the Soviet Union proper, the now off-balance Kennedy administration could accept neither the domestic nor the international political consequences of Soviet-Cuban fortification. Kennedy consequently instituted a naval blockade of Cuba to prevent any further Soviet build-up after publicly revealing the existence of the missiles and generating diplomatic support for their removal. He directly threatened the island with a U.S. invasion, an option that the Soviets could not counter successfully so far from home. Khrushchev had thus gambled and lost. The Soviet troops and matériel were removed, and two years later Khrushchev paid the price with his fall from power. This military humiliation and the compensation that the Soviet armed forces extracted for it marked the beginning of the accelerated advance in Soviet naval power over the next decade. It was to develop into a force formidable enough to challenge the free hand that the U.S. and Allied navies had previously enjoyed. By the 1970s, Soviet fleets were a significant presence in every ocean of the world. For Portugal this increased presence meant that communist influence could be extended to remote peripheral areas and that outside support could now be delivered more readily to subversive, anti-Western resistance movements and their guerrilla elements.

A second development stemming from the rise of Soviet power was a diffusion of the Atlantic Alliance. In this post-war era the United States had been presiding over world affairs in a way not previously available to any nation. It possessed only a relatively small portion of the global population and natural resources but had proceeded to dominate military and commercial power with a vast margin of superiority over both its friends and foes. With the relative economic recovery of Europe after the war and the birth of the European Economic Community (EEC), many European nations had begun to chafe at the U.S. direction and now sought greater autonomy. U.S. leaders took for granted the uniformity of interests among members of the Alliance and appeared to forget in their position of dominance the long history of European dynamism, political philosophy, and style of diplomacy. This heritage was bound to reassert itself, and no one felt this need more than Charles de Gaulle, the President of France. In an attempt to give new stature to his country, one that was suffering from a deep sense of failure and vulnerability after its devastation in both world wars and defeat in Indochina and Algeria, he took France on its own course. As he was unable to bridge the psychological gulf between his country and the United States, he first ordered the removal of all nuclear weapons from French soil, then withdrew the French fleet from the integrated NATO command, and finally in 1966 separated France from the NATO military structure altogether. In a turnabout France began to seek stronger collaboration with the Federal Republic of Germany. De Gaulle wanted France to be perceived by Germany as a more reliable ally than the United States and over time to displace U.S. with French leadership. The deviation from U.S. influence by these two countries was to give Portugal two critical allies in the prosecution of its wars in Africa.

This crack in the bipolar solidarity was not restricted to the West. China developed a far deeper breach with its Soviet neighbor, so much so in fact that forty Soviet divisions faced the Chinese army across the 4,000 mile Sino-Soviet border from 1969 until the Soviet Union in its economic distress unilaterally abandoned the arms race in 1988. The potentially violent and confrontational nature of this breach played into Allied hands and was fully exploited in the U.S. pursuit of its containment policy. Immediately the United States sought to open contacts with China and in February 1972 signed the Shanghai Communiqué formalizing relations with this formerly hostile state.

There were other divergences and crosscurrents in the bipolar concept, and none were more apparent than the behavior of the nonaligned nations. In 1955 a group of Asian, African and European nonaligned and communist countries met in Indonesia at the Bandung Conference and passed a resolution condemning colonialism "in all its manifestations" and declaring that "the subjection of peoples to alien domination and exploitation constitutes a denial of fundamental human rights, is contrary to the Charter of the United Nations, and is an impediment to the promotion of world peace and cooperation."[4] This declaration signaled a new offensive against the Western powers and was greatly encouraged by the retreat of Britain and France from Suez in 1956. This retreat not only destroyed the Great Power status of these two and presaged the wholesale abandonment of their colonies but also left the United States alone outside of Europe to man the ramparts of the Cold War. The Egyptian leader, Gamal Abdel Nasser, who had forced the British and French to abandon the Suez Canal to Egypt, proceeded to play U.S. and Soviet offers against each other to his benefit. This pattern of raising the ante with each overture and seeking to siphon further benefits from both sides was to become a familiar pattern in the nonaligned world to the extent the superpowers could be manipulated, and we shall see this in the case of Ahmed Sékou Touré and the Republic of Guinée.

This anti-colonial momentum was reflected in a further targeting of Portugal, as it increasingly assumed the role of sole colonial power. The Organization of African Unity (OAU) was formed in 1963 with its genesis in the Bandung Conference and held its first meeting in Addis Ababa. It approved a resolution there authorizing armed violence to overthrow existing colonial regimes. In the following year it specifically advocated the expulsion of Portugal from Africa by force, and in 1968 at its Algerian meeting endorsed concrete military support for all liberation movements.[5] This Third World rhetoric gained added legitimacy through its treatment in the United Nations.

Portugal had joined the United Nations in 1955 following a number of vetoes by the Soviet Union, and as if these Soviet rejections were not enough, was immediately made to feel isolated by the international community over its colonies. There had been noisy pressure from a contingent of UN members for Portugal to grant its colonies self-rule. This agitation had been fed by the newly independent states joining the United Nations and by the writings of a number of authors exposing the human abuses in the policy of Lisbon toward its colonies, most notably the Galvão report. Henrique Galvão, an army captain, was chief inspector of the Colonial Administration and had authored a report in 1947 describing labor conditions in Angola and cautioning against their continuance.[6] In a rather obtuse decision considering the developing international climate, António de Oliveira Salazar, the Portuguese prime minister, had the report banned and in 1952 arrested Galvão on charges of treason. With this reaction, the incident gained international notoriety and fueled the opponents' case. Additionally, Portugal refused to submit the periodic technical reports on its colonies that were requested by the United Nations for non-selfgoverning territories. While other colonial powers were unhappy about this requirement, they complied. Portugal managed to attract additional unwanted attention in its refusal. So Portugal, in fighting the highly vocal anti-colonial lobby, seemed to play into its hands with these ill-conceived decisions.

Likewise in 1955, a group of UN members advocating colonial independence managed to pass a resolution with the help of the Soviet Union condemning colonialism as a violation of human rights and the UN Charter. In response, Portugal claimed that it had no colonies and that all of its overseas provinces were part of a single state with one constitution. It likewise claimed that the United Nations had neither jurisdiction nor competence in this matter, as it was an internal affair. The issue festered in debate for four years, and finally in December 1960, the UN General Assembly, pushed by this group and the Soviet Union, voted against Portugal. While Portugal was to an extent a victim of its own intransigence, it saw itself as targeted and refused to accept the resolution. Its NATO allies rallied to prevent a catastrophe; however, this support began to fray by 1961.[7] To maintain its position successfully as a colonial power, Portugal would have to become more flexible and imaginative both in its international and domestic approaches to the problem.

By 1961, the Portuguese colonies or *ultramar* had become an important and integral part of the country's overall economic health. Its economy by that time had shifted from a partial autarky under orthodox economic practices to a fledgling but rapidly growing industrialized one. The shift away from an agriculturally based economy in both the *metrópole,* or continental Portugal, and the *ultramar* meant that there was a decreasing dependence on peasant labor and its attendant policies. As the *metrópole* developed in this direction, so the first moves were made to foster complementary development in the colonies. Mining, oil exploration and refining, textiles, and cashew processing were in place by 1961, and other basic industries were in the planning stages. These activities reflected a break with the past and a new Salazar policy fueled by colonial promise. Education received renewed and expanded attention, as literate workers with skills were in increasing demand. The paranoia regarding foreign investment had evaporated, and French, German, U.S., Rhodesian, and South African participation in the economy was welcomed. The gathering momentum of the colonial economies continued to accelerate well past 1961 and became a welcome support for the political element in the counterinsurgency campaigns. The colonies were thus developing into substantial economic engines in their own right, and not only were their citizens beginning to benefit individually, but Portugal itself was also reaping substantial rewards from this growing prosperity. The historic potential of the colonies was being realized, a fact that reinforced their long-time importance to Portugal and Salazar's commitment of the nation to their defense.

Colonial Resistance

At the time when Portugal's colonial commitment was being strengthened, local resistance within its African population was increasing. During this period the democratized European powers in Africa were freeing their colonial possessions in step with the post-World War II trend. This development put increasing pressure on Salazar to move in line with the Western European forms of government and to allow the Portuguese colonies to do so as well. Revolts and the war enabled Salazar to exploit a tide of Portuguese nationalist fervor in preserving the *status quo* and his personal regime, the *Estado Novo* or New State. Consequently, the nationalist resistance and its challenge to his colonial vision had the effect of reinforcing the Portuguese commitment rather than the opposite. While the economy was deemed important, Salazar's personal position of authority was overriding.[8] Further, his hatred and mistrust of communism played an important role. He was mindful of the Western powers' impotence to contain the economically bankrupt but politically ascendant communism.[9] In a speech to army and naval officers on 6 July 1936, Salazar described communism as "systems of ideals which are literally systems of crime" and was so convinced of the threat of this ideology that he believed "Western civilization is at stake."[10] His worst fears were realized when Daniel Semenovich Solod, the "brilliant organizer and expert in the tactics of infiltration and subversion," was assigned to the neighboring former French colony, the Republic of Guinée, in 1960.[11] Ambassador Solod had established an impressive reputation for increasing Soviet influence in the Middle East and North Africa, and now began to work on the Portuguese colonies and to nurture their long-standing dissident undercurrent of nationalism.

The nationalist movements and their military wings of insurgents that challenged Portugal's ownership of its colonies had their origins in the 1930s. The emergence of modern-day black opposition to Portuguese rule began with the repressive practices of Salazar's *Estado Novo* toward any form of dissent, particularly political. This attitude extended from the *metrópole* to the colonies. Resistance began slowly, as there was a practical barrier to any such opposition in the ethnic and social fragmentation of the overseas non-white community. Without strong leadership, there would be no nationalist movement able to gain the necessary momentum in reconciling these divergent viewpoints and crystallizing resistance to the Salazar regime. Local African grievances were long-standing and had come to the fore during the early twentieth century with the influx of white settlers and abusive labor practices. This indigenous resentment was publicly evident in 1932 when an independent Mozambican newspaper, *O Brado Africano* (The African Cry) slipped through Salazar's censorship and published a scathing editorial titled "Enough." Thereafter this feeling was never far below the surface, and the apparent calm was illusory.

Following World War II, nationalist sentiments grew among the *mestiços* (mixed-race peoples) and *assimilados* (mostly *mestiços* who were legally assimilated into Portuguese culture). However, these groups were largely urban and thus did not represent the greater population. As they were located in cities, they were in a hostile environment for two reasons: the majority of their opponents, the white population, lived in cities, and the national police or PIDE (*Polícia Internacional de Defesa do Estado*, or International Police for Defense of the State) operated most effectively there. Consequently, they were either short-lived or dormant.[12] By 1956, the young Marxists of the Angolan Communist Party contributed to the formation of the MPLA (*Movimento Popular de Libertação de Angola*, or Popular Movement for the Liberation of Angola). The MPLA developed roots among Luanda's urban and largely radical intellectuals, among its slum dwellers, and to a lesser extent, eastward from the capital among the Mbundu, Angola's second largest ethnolinguistic group, and the Chokwe people. These urban roots were composed largely of *mestiços*, who controlled the party. The movement had little in common with the rural peasants of the east and south of Angola and made little effort to gain their true devotion. In December 1956, the initial MPLA manifesto was openly published in a direct frontal assault on the government. Predictably the PIDE reacted adversely, and a number of the MPLA leaders were forced to flee into exile. From 1957 onward, PIDE action was so successful "that the nationalists were not able to maintain more than the most rudimentary organization inside the colonies and could not communicate with those cells that did exist."[13] The parties were forced to conduct their affairs from neighboring states and were deeply influenced by their foreign connections.

The presidential election in May 1958 gave all of Portugal some opportunity to express its dissatisfaction with the *status quo*. Elections under the Salazar regime as a rule were perfunctory, colorless, cosmetic affairs with foreseeable results. In 1958, however, General Humberto Delgado's high-profile and emotionally charged challenge to Salazar's candidate, Admiral Américo Tomás, excited all of Portugal. This taste of partial suffrage awakened dissatisfaction within the *mestiços* and *assimilados*, and a number of small parties were formed in Angola, only to be shattered through arrests in March, May, and July of 1959. As the PIDE systematically wrecked the MPLA organization, it became progressively weaker and isolated from its leadership that was now abroad. In this deteriorating position, it supported an uprising in February 1961 that stood no chance of a lasting success. It was doomed to be transient, for it occurred in Luanda, center of Portuguese police and military strength, and the MPLA had no constituency or bases elsewhere among the rural population.

The MPLA in exile established itself initially in Léopoldville and aligned itself not only with other independent African nations and their socialist philosophy but also with the communist bloc, including the Italian and French communist parties. The leadership was consequently familiar with the communist theory in wars of national liberation and organized itself accordingly. The MPLA found that it was in competition with the other prominent Angolan nationalist group at the time, the UPA (*Uniao das Populações de Angola*, or Union of Angolan Peoples), for acceptance as the leading representative of the Angolan people. In 1962 the MPLA formed its military wing, EPLA (*Exército Popular de Libertação de Angola*, or Popular Army for the Liberation of Angola), to project its influence into Angola. This nascent force numbered between 250 and 300 young men who had undergone military training in Ghana and Morocco. The EPLA sought to expand the conflict across Angola's northern border with this force and penetrate the entire country, publicizing the MPLA manifesto. Recruiting proved to be difficult because of ethnic rivalries, and military action was thwarted by the competing UPA. The UPA through its influence with the Congo leadership forced the MPLA to leave Léopoldville in 1963 and reestablish itself in Brazzaville, from which it was difficult to conduct a campaign across an unenthusiastic third country and into a now distant in Angola. As a result, northern Angola proved to be barren for the MPLA, and it was not until 1966, with the opening of its second front from Zambia, that some success would come. The most consequential development from the Portuguese perspective was the capture in July 1963 of various 35mm films that described the MPLA military doctrine of revolutionary warfare. It paralleled the Maoist creed by reiterating that the movement was a people's war and that the struggle would be protracted.[14] The first priority would be indoctrination and organization of the masses, and next the establishment of rural bases and resistance areas.[15] This pseudo-nationalistic doctrine was flawed in that the MPLA had little in common with the larger population of Angola. Nevertheless, it would serve the MPLA until 1974, and as we shall see in future chapters, the Portuguese correctly anticipated the weakness of this approach.

The UPA was formed in the mid-1950s from a number of small groups with conflicting goals by Barros Nekaka, who in 1958 passed leadership to his nephew Holden Roberto. UPA strength rested in the rural populations of the Bakongo ethnolinguistic region of Angola. These people straddled the border between the Belgian Congo and Angola and extended into Cabinda and the French Congo, the boundaries of the ancient Kongo kingdom. Roberto unequivocally held the view that not just the Bakongo kingdom or some other entity but all of Angola must be freed. An ardent anti-colonialist, Roberto had been born in Angola but had lived his adult life in the Belgian Congo. He had been educated in the Baptist Church missionaries and employed in the Belgian colonial economy as an accountant between 1941 and 1949. Northern Angola was an area that had become more politically aware in the 1950s through white settlement, Baptist missionary influence, and an easy access to the developing political activities of the Belgian Congo. Roberto thus felt a close kinship with the peoples immediately across the border. The UPA was able to develop a following there because of the relatively open frontier, and this loyal cadre became the basis for the uprising in March 1961. Portuguese presence in this area took the form of *chefes do posto* (heads of posts) and administrators, as opposed to PIDE, and these officials were so sparse that it was physically impossible for them to maintain anything but the most casual control over their districts.[16]

While Roberto was relatively well educated, he was a member of the Bakongo ethnolinguistic group, was not a *mestiço*, and consequently did not share their more European cultural perspective. He was also tribally oriented in contrast to the non-tribal declarations of the MPLA. As a result, the personality and leadership philosophy of the UPA contrasted clearly with the MPLA and its sophisticated *mestiço* leadership, which was left-wing, intellectual, and acculturalatively Portuguese. Funding and support also glaringly contrasted, the MPLA actually being linked with the Eastern bloc. The UPA received financial support from the American Committee on Africa and from various African governments, preponderantly that of Léopoldville.[17] Accordingly they were never able to resolve their differences and join forces effectively.

When the Belgian Congo became independent on 30 June 1960, its government began to give Roberto practical assistance, including permission to establish a radio station and a training camp within its borders. This sanctuary was an important facet of UPA operations in its early years. Roberto had witnessed the long series of Congolese crises that had begun with the violent political rioting on 4 January 1959 and had led to the accelerated Belgian push toward Congo self-government and independence in eighteen months. By December 1960, he believed that just as the Belgians had quickly grown weary of armed conflict, so would the Portuguese when it was initiated. He consequently used his Congo sanctuary and the porous common border to set the stage for an end to relative colonial tranquility for Portugal.

The UPA formed its military wing, the ELNA (*Exército de Libertação Nacional de Angola*, or Army of National Liberation of Angola), in June 1961 after the March attacks did not achieve a Portuguese withdrawal. Roberto was its commander-in-chief, and its other two leaders were Portuguese Army deserters, Marcos Xavier Kassanga, its chief of staff in Léopoldville, and João Batista, its operational commander in Angola with headquarters near Bembe. This leadership was ineffective. Roberto was so autocratic that he would accept little more than arms and money. Without training, the ELNA "set a demoralizing example of politico-military incompetence and indiscipline."[18] The South African Defense Force vice-consul in Luanda noted that the ELNA "involved itself in military activities in the narrowest sense ... but avoided contact with the Portuguese security forces as far as possible."[19] The training was so poor that despite the expansion of the ELNA to about 6,200 troops, their deportment at such camps as Kinkuzu in the Congo was cause for alarm.[20] Andreas Shipango, South-West Africa People's Organisation representative in Léopoldville, made an appraisal during a 1963 visit:

> With representatives from a number of other liberation movements, I visited Holden Roberto's training camps near the Angolan border with a view to sending our young men there. But the atmosphere in Roberto's training camps was very bad, and I could not recommend such a course.[21]

This lack of direction caused great rifts in the UPA leadership. Despite the UPA reorganization in March 1962 to include additional groups, to rename itself FNLA (*Frente Nacional de Libertção de Angola*, or National Front for the Liberation of Angola), and to establish a government in exile named GRAE (*Governo da República de Angola no Exílio*, or Government of the Republic of Angola in Exile), little of substance was accomplished. A frustrated Jonas Savimbi, Roberto's "foreign minister," formally broke with the UPA/FNLA in July 1964 and eventually formed the third nationalist movement in Angola, UNITA (*União Nacional para a Independência Total de Angola*, or the National Union for the Total Independence of Angola). The next year Alexandre Taty, "minister of armaments," after challenging Roberto in an unsuccessful coup, defected to the Portuguese in Cabinda with a substantial number of his followers. John Marcum described the situation as it existed in 1963: "Whether by the inaction or heavy hand of shortsighted leadership, one opportunity after another was lost, one potential source of support after another was alienated."[22] The political crosscurrents within the UPA/FNLA, the lack of training for ELNA cadres, and major competition from MPLA and UNITA activities reduced the UPA/FNLA to a spent force within two years of initiating the conflict.

Roberto followed no sophisticated guerrilla creed other than the initiation of violence in the hope that the Portuguese would become weary with it and capitulate. There was only a weak military program unsupported by political indoctrination. There was no talk of winning the population to the UPA/FNLA point of view, which was simply that Angola should be an independent country with Roberto as head of state. The approach was amateurish and ineffective alongside that of PAIGC (*Partido Africano da Independência da Guiné e Cabo Verde*, or African Party for the Independence of Guiné and Cape Verde) and the work of its founder, Amílcar Cabral.

Aside from Angola, there were nationalist movements associated with Guiné and Mozambique that prior to the events of 1961 were hoping to negotiate concessions with the Portuguese on self-determination. In Guiné efforts by local nationalists to organize began in the early 1950s. The PAIGC was founded in September 1956 by local *assimilados* and educated Cape Verdeans. Its initial political organization prompted an aggrieved dockworkers' strike on 3 August 1959, which ended in a violent disaster when it was broken with excessive military force. Fifty workers were killed, and the incident became known as the "Pidjiguiti dock massacre." PAIGC leadership quickly realized that peaceful protest would not achieve its objective of self-rule and independence. Accordingly, it shifted its strategy to one of clandestinely organizing the rural population for an insurgency.[23] The PAIGC had learned hard lessons in 1959 well ahead of the MPLA and UPA/FNLA experiences of 1961, and had shifted its approach. It was not prepared to begin guerrilla war in Guiné until January 1963, when all of the elements for success were in place, including firm sanctuaries in adjacent countries.

The driving force behind the PAIGC was Amílcar Cabral, who was born in Guiné of Cape Verdean parents. Cabral was an agronomist by profession, having been educated in Lisbon, served the Portuguese administration in Guiné (1952–1955), and worked for various agricultural institutions in the *metrópole* (1955–1959) with research trips to Angola. His political awareness came at an early age and matured during his academic time in Lisbon. While influenced by Marxist-Leninist ideas of the time, Cabral was primarily a nationalist and developed his own variant of both the PAIGC political message and its associated military dimension. In his own words:

> It is good [for all nationalist movements] to remember ... that regardless of how similar are their struggles and their enemies to one another, national liberation and social revolution cannot be exported. They are ... the products of local and national forces. While somewhat influenced by external factors, they are largely determined and tempered by the particular culture of a country's people and its unique local characteristics.[24]

It was in this context that Cabral began to prepare the political landscape for guerrilla warfare.

Following his experience in the Pidjiguiti dock demonstration, Cabral realized that the Portuguese would not negotiate and that an armed struggle was the only way to achieve PAIGC ends. Cabral had received no known military training and had little interest in such affairs prior to 1959. It is possible that he had some such exposure during his visit to China in 1960, and certainly Chinese influence was seen in the training of his guerrilla army. It was known that elements of PAIGC also underwent courses in guerrilla warfare and subversion in Algeria, the Soviet Union, and Czechoslovakia.[25] Notwithstanding this lack of military experience, the mantle of undisputed commander and tactician fitted him well, and his imagination and flexibility were evident in the conduct of his campaign.

Cabral became quite attuned to the requirement for population indoctrination and keenly aware of the need to bridge the gap between the urban intellectual and the traditional Guinean. His two-year preparation of the political battlefield was classic in its effort to draw the population together in a common ideology that would transcend tribal and ethnic divisions. His investigation into local grievances was the most thorough of any of the nationalist movements. Cabral faced a difficult task in convincing the population that they were being oppressed. The land, for instance, already belonged to the peasants and was generally village property. Guiné had no concentration of foreign settlers who were seemingly exploiting the population. In Cabral's own words:

> We were not able to mobilize the people by telling them: 'The land to him that works it.' Because here land is not lacking … . We were never able to mobilize the people on a basis of the struggle against colonialism. This yielded nothing. To speak of the struggle against imperialism yielded nothing between us … . This proved the necessity of having each peasant find his own formula to mobilize for the fight.[26]

He thus sought to couch his revolutionary message in terms that would address the daily concerns of the rural population:

> Remember always that the people do not fight for ideas, for things that only exist in the heads of individuals. The people fight and they accept the necessary sacrifices. But they do it in order to gain material advantages, to live in peace and to improve their lives, to experience progress, and to be able to guarantee a future to their children.[27]

This approach was far more fruitful than comparable activities in Angola.

Cabral met and worked closely with MPLA leaders and established his exile headquarters in Conakry, the capital of the ex-French Republic of Guinée. From here he conducted his confrontational campaign against the Portuguese. The other prominent nationalist movement in Guiné was FLING (*Frente de Luta pela Independência da Guiné*, or Front for the Struggle for the Independence of Guiné). Led by Benjamin Bull, Jonas Fernandes, and Henry Labery, it was an amalgamation of a number of smaller, more moderate movements and was given sanctuary in Senegal by its leader Léopold Sédar Senghor to operate on the northern border of Guiné. Senghor, a moderate himself, was at odds with Cabral and the PAIGC. While he did not want this movement using Senegal as a sanctuary to launch attacks into Portuguese territory, there was little that he could do about it, given the nature of the terrain and his lack of a force to prevent a PAIGC presence. Again as in Angola, the philosophies of the PAIGC and FLING leaders were so disparate that there was little common ground for agreement and cooperation, although Cabral attempted to compromise and remained in contact with Senghor.

Following the unsuccessful employment of autonomous guerrilla groups in the first year of the conflict, Cabral held the Cassacá Congress in February 1964 to reorganize the war effort and establish a national army in the FARP (*Forças Armadas Revolucionárias de Povo*, or Revolutionary Armed Forces of the People). Because the Portuguese had shown that they were not going to negotiate, Cabral's only option was to win in the field. He thoughtfully assembled and implemented the proper elements of guerrilla warfare, particularly that of political indoctrination, to achieve PAIGC ends.

In Mozambique, there were a number of very small exile nationalist organizations prior to 1961. The Portuguese government made every effort to dampen the spirit of nationalism in its formative stages; however, there were at any one time perhaps half a million Mozambicans, or about 10 percent of the population, working in neighboring countries. These expatriates were exposed to new political ideas and in the period 1958–1960 began to organize themselves into associations with the goals of social contact, self-help, and ultimately national politics. The first true nationalist organization was UDENAMO (*União Democrática Nacional de Moçambique*, or the National Democratic Union of Mozambique) and was established in Southern Rhodesia in October 1960, moving to Dar-es-Salaam in February 1961. Two additional groups of note appeared at the time, MANU or UNAM (*União Nacional Africana Moçambique*, or Mozambican African National Union), depending on the English or Portuguese conformation, founded among Makonde emigrants in Kenya and Tanzania, and UNAMI (*União Nacional do Moçambique Independente*, or National Union of Independent Mozambique), established in Malawi. Both MANU and UDENAMO set aside their differences and attended the 1961 conference in Casablanca, where the nationalist movements in the Portuguese colonies consolidated their front to become a coalition. Subsequently, in September 1962, elements of MANU, UNAMI, and UDENAMO were united in FRELIMO (*Frente de Libertação de Moçambique*, or Front for the Liberation of Mozambique) at the urging of Julius Nyerere, the Tanganyikan leader, making it the strongest and most important movement.

Eduardo Mondlane assumed its leadership. He, too, absorbed the lessons of 1961 and was not prepared to launch a guerrilla war until some three years later in September 1964, after his small army was trained. Mondlane, in coming late to the nationalist movements against Portugal, was very much influenced by the trend in Angola and Guiné. His organization initially developed similarly to the PAIGC and experienced the same sort of problems in subordinating military operations to political leadership. His doctrine paralleled that of the MPLA and particularly of the PAIGC with its emphasis on political indoctrination, and it was along these lines that he sought to conduct his military campaign. Mozambicans belonging to MANU had already tried peaceful demonstrations with the same consequences that had occurred in Angola and Guiné. At Mueda on 16 June 1960, it attempted to petition the local Portuguese administrator, who responded by using troops against unarmed peasants. Reputedly seventeen Africans were killed in this demonstration.[28] This "massacre" at Mueda politicized the Makonde and affected the development of FRELIMO and its campaign. FRELIMO now felt that armed struggle was the only answer, as Portugal would not grant self-determination and would destroy those who demonstrated for political freedom.[29]

Political expression was forbidden both in the *ultramar* and in the *metrópole* except in the narrow context of the Portuguese staged elections every four years. The airing of grievances or liberal political views attracted a heavy hand from the authorities. In the case of the 1959 strike by the Pidjiguiti dockworkers, the PAIGC had hoped that it would lead to negotiations with the authorities and a redress of grievances. When this traditional procedure failed, Cabral had no choice but to seek an alternative in guerrilla warfare with the goal of opening negotiations or ultimately of gaining control of the country. The same can be said for the MPLA and its earlier flight from Angola in 1956 and 1957.

Peasant populations are not normally a revolutionary force, and such was the case in Portuguese Africa.[30] They are conservative by nature and find security and comfort in the routine of their lives and the socioeconomic institutions that govern them. Change is resisted and outsiders are viewed with suspicion. The guerrillas of the various nationalist movements in Portuguese Africa represented change that the populations were not prepared to accept readily. Thus, despite the justified grievances of Portugal's black African citizens, overall they appeared to be loyal to Portugal and to suspect the activities of the nationalists. This apparent support reinforced Portugal's commitment to the colonies and their people. As Portugal entered 1961, its internal confidence in its position was as strong as ever. There occurred, moreover, a series of events that had the cumulative effect not only of reinforcing this attitude but of hardening it into an irreversible course of war. This series in order began with the humiliating hijacking of the Portuguese ship *Santa Maria* through a reappearance of the activist Galvão, the affront of the attacks in the north of Angola, and an attempted coup against Salazar in an effort to moderate the country's position toward the demands of the nationalist movements. This failure at moderation alongside the message from the United Nations served to silence voices of reason. The final blow was the debacle of Goa, which made any further loss unthinkable. Each of these and its role in moving Portugal to war is examined below.

Santa Maria Incident

In January 1961, the Portuguese ship *Santa Maria* was seized by a group of twenty-four men belonging to DRIL (*Directório Revolucionário Ibérico de Libertação*, or the Iberian Revolutionary Directorate of Freedom) and led by the familiar activist Galvão. Galvão was now an exile in Venezuela, after escaping from prison in 1959 and traveling through Argentina and Brazil. The *Santa Maria* was a liner carrying about 612 passengers and a crew of 350 and operating in the Caribbean. Galvão, his group, and their intentions had come to the renewed attention of Portuguese authorities as early as October 1960. Although their plans for a demonstration did not materialize then, there was significant support for their activities from the Portuguese expatriate opposition community and particularly from Delgado now residing in Brazil. On 20 January, some of the DRIL operatives boarded the *Santa Maria* in the Venezuelan port of La Guaria, and a day later Galvão and the remainder clandestinely entered the ship in Curacao. Once at sea, the ship was easily seized on the evening of 22 January, resulting in one death and one wounded crewmember.

The rather fanciful goal of the seizure was to take the ship to the West Coast of Africa and there to conduct a surprise attack on the island of Fernando Pó in Spanish Guinea, just north of the Portuguese possessions of São Tomé and Príncipe. Once taken, this island would then serve as a base for an attack on Luanda supported by undefined local rebel forces. Next Galvão would conduct a campaign to liberate part of Portuguese territory, install an opposition government in it, and from there mount a war against the Salazar regime. After Angola, he would free Mozambique and then the *metrópole*, presumably establishing his own regime.[31] The contradiction among the various elements of this plan is immediately apparent in seizing a major vessel on the high seas in a noisy and widely publicized act of piracy and then an ocean away attempting to conduct a surprise attack in which a clandestine approach was vital to any success. Despite this ridiculous plan, Galvão's more realistic goal seems to have been to show the world in a highly public way that there was an active opposition to the Salazar regime. He certainly accomplished this end.

As information on the *Santa Maria* was received in Lisbon, the Portuguese government decided on 23 January to enlist the help of the U.S. and British governments and accordingly approached both with initially favorable reactions. The United States saw the incident as one of piracy and proceeded to locate and track the errant vessel with the intent of boarding it and returning it to the nearest North American port with the use of force, if necessary. The objective was to protect the passengers and ship and to return the vessel to its rightful owners. Both navies immediately assigned destroyers and open-ocean reconnaissance aircraft to fix the *Santa Maria*.

The new Kennedy administration, having come to office on 17 January, developed second thoughts about this initial reaction. On 24 January, Galvão had made a proclamation carried on a number of national news broadcasts that DRIL was pro-democracy and anti-totalitarianism and opposed to all forms of arbitrary government. Simultaneously in Brazil, Delgado chimed in to assert his support for DRIL and to say that he had personally ordered Galvão to seize the ship.[32] This position appealed to the liberal elements of Kennedy's political party and caused his administration to do some homework on Delgado and Galvão. After three days, the Kennedy administration was not certain that a case of piracy could be made. Meanwhile the U.S. Navy was pursuing the *Santa Maria* with the authorization to intercept and board it to protect U.S. citizens and to look after the humanitarian interests of the other passengers and crewmembers. In response to the political change of heart, the U.S. Navy suddenly received orders simply to follow the ship and report its movements. The Royal Navy too relaxed its stance.

Kennedy now faced an element in his party that accused him of making a pact with the "dictator" Salazar. Anxious to please his constituency and to resolve the problem of "political piracy," Kennedy gave the navy new instructions to negotiate the return of the ship and release of the passengers and crew.[33] From 25 January substantial communications developed between the ship and the naval reconnaissance aircraft in which Galvão was persuaded to free the U.S. passengers before continuing his voyage to Africa. Eventually an agreement was reached in which a U.S. emissary would board the ship at sea and negotiate a plan to discharge the passengers at the closest Brazilian port. Following these negotiations on 27 January, Galvão agreed to take the *Santa Maria* to Recife to disembark the passengers. After feverish diplomatic work to gain assurances over current treaty obligations, the *Santa Maria* entered Recife. Even so, there remained some confusion about the conditions of departure, and Galvão continued to detain the hostages on board. This standoff was brief and ended when Admiral Dias Fernandes, the naval port commander of Recife, and 60 of his marines acted to resolve it. Galvão and his DRIL compatriots spent another day alone on the ship pondering their situation before asking for political asylum in Brazil. Again with great fanfare, they disembarked into a crowd of journalists, reporters, and fellow oppositionists led by Delgado. Several days later the *Santa Maria* was returned to the Portuguese government.

This episode served to highlight the political struggle against the Salazar regime. Galvão had succeeded in his main objective of bringing his crusade to international prominence and at the same time creating a political divide within the highest levels of the Portuguese government over his affront to the regime and insult to its leader. As we shall see, this divide within the Salazar government and the Kennedy administration's evolving position on Portuguese colonial policy will both resurface.

Angola Uprisings of 1961

The Angola uprisings and their immediate events served as a warning of things to come and prompted Portugal to think more clearly about defending its colonies. Sporadic agitation and unrest had occurred throughout 1960 at the time when Portugal began to realize the rich economic potential of Angola and Mozambique. Yet European troop strength in Angola numbered under 1,000 in early 1958, and was reinforced only to about 3,000 by mid-1960.[34] Overall strength was 8,000, of which at least 5,000 were African troops.[35] These forces, while scattered throughout Angola, were confined to garrisons in the larger towns and accustomed merely to administering subjective rule.[36] This modest order of battle was neither properly organized, nor trained, nor led, and its numbers were inadequate to face the uprisings in early 1961.

The opening challenge was instigated by the MPLA in Luanda on 4 February 1961 by a truly aggrieved group armed only with clubs and knives and driven by a frustration with their treatment. It entered the capital and attacked a number of police installations, a prison, and the radio station in an attempt to have 52 political prisoners released. Seven policemen and 40 of the group were killed. During the funeral for the policemen, shots were fired on the mourners, and whites attacked blacks in a display that incensed Portugal. The prison was suicidally attacked again on 10 February. Government forces overreacted in quelling the disturbance because of the strong emotional feelings that had accumulated in Luanda. Several hundred Africans were killed indiscriminately, their bodies being left to rot in the streets as a warning sign to aspiring revolutionaries. The events gained international attention and put Portugal firmly on the UN agenda. Race relations remained polarized in Luanda and would take years to rebuild. The MPLA instigated the mob action with little planning or consideration of the consequences. Picking the capital with its troop and national police concentration was an unfortunate choice, and the MPLA was quickly destroyed inside Angola.

These events were a prelude as well as a warning of further trouble. On 15 March 1961 shortly after the MPLA episode, the UPA seized on the confusion and launched a multipronged attack in northern Angola with a flood of 4,000 to 5,000 armed men across a 300-kilometer strip. This number is thought to have been increased to as much as 25,000 through forced recruiting.[37] Approximately 700 European farms plus additional trading settlements and government posts were overwhelmed.[38] This mob laid waste to whatever was in its path and killed men, women, black, white, young, and old. It was a senseless act of violence with only a misplaced political aim rather than a military campaign with a political goal. Roberto did not understand the difference. All of Portugal was shocked at the horror, and Roberto's belief that Portugal would act as Belgium did proved false.

This savage foray occurred in an area demarcated by the Congolese frontier, the Cuango River, the Malange-Luanda railroad, and the Atlantic Ocean. The attackers pushed nearly to Luanda. Military leaders faced a situation in which over 100 administrative posts and towns in the three districts of northern Angola from the Congo border to within 30 miles of Luanda, the capital, had been either wiped out, taken, or paralyzed by African nationalist groups. Over 1,000 Europeans and an unknown number of Africans were thought to have perished. The economy of north Angola was crippled. Communications were largely cut or damaged. Finally, thousands of Portuguese refugees were camped in Luanda or on their way back to Portugal. The chaotic internal situation in Angola was rapidly and sensationally projected to a large international audience over the succeeding several months.[39]

For a month Portugal and Angola seemed paralyzed and unable to act. Equally, the insurgents were incapable of sustained military engagement. Civil militias were formed, and loyal Africans armed. It was this patchwork of civil-military defense and its frenetic activity that brought UPA momentum to a halt. Formal military reoccupation began on

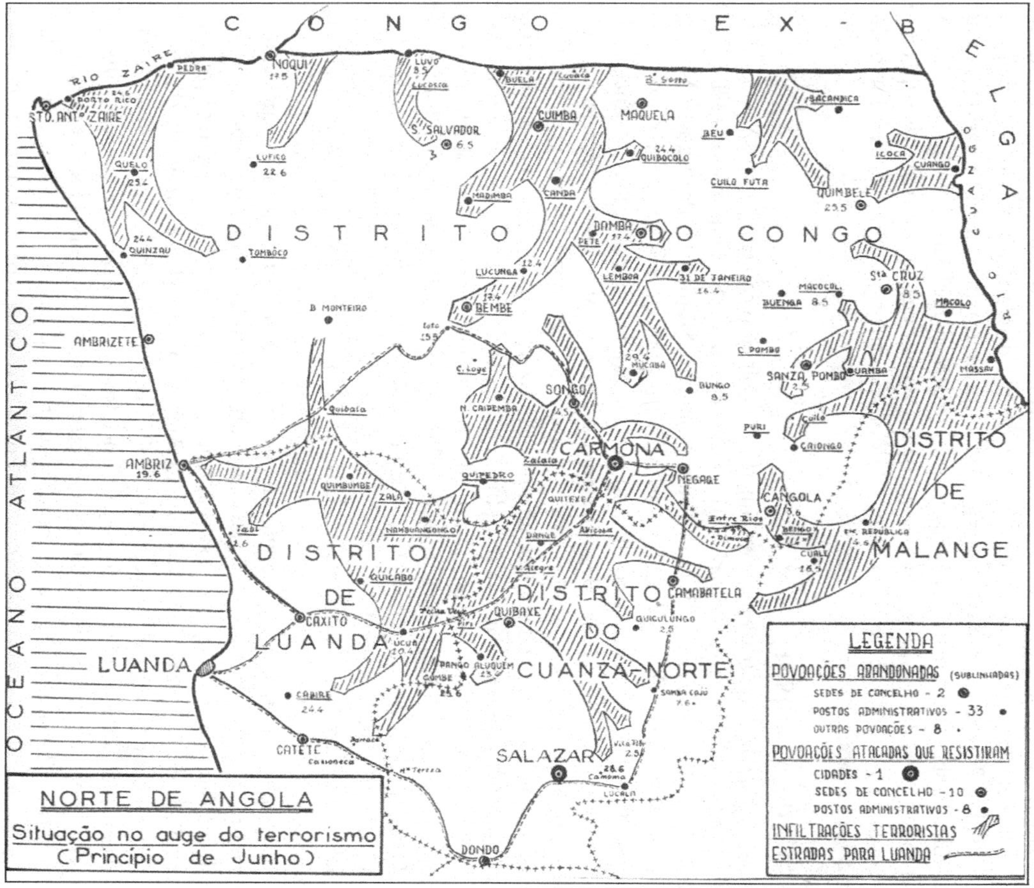

Attacks in the North of Angola at Their Height, beginning of June 1961. Map courtesy of Hélio Felgas, *Guerra em Angola* [War in Angola] (Lisbon: Livraria Clássica Editoria, 1961).

13 May and was intensified as troops arrived from the *metrópole*. During the July-August period approximately 20,000 reinforcements landed in Angola. These troops behaved emotionally as they bombed and strafed areas that had not been affected by the uprising. This indiscriminate terror did enormous damage to Portuguese credibility and to race relations, and drove over 150,000 refugees into the Congo over the next nine months.[40] On 7 October, General Venâncio Deslandes, the governor-general, announced that reoccupation was complete and that mop-up policing would begin. It has been estimated that 500 Europeans and about 20,000 local people died in this *jacquerie*.[41] It deeply shocked all of Portugal and hardened its colonial commitment to the restoration of order in Angola. To the Portuguese, it was unthinkable that such lawlessness should be tolerated, and a strong, uncompromising reaction to the nationalist behavior was widely supported. These events with their horror also diverted domestic attention from Salazar's increasing political vulnerability.

The "Abrilada" of 1961

The fissure that had been opened within the Salazar government by the *Santa Maria* incident was plainly evident when on 17 February the U.S. Ambassador to Portugal, Charles Burke Elbrick, lunched with General Botelho Moniz, the Portuguese Minister of National Defense. The ambassador recorded that the general was very frank in his criticism of the Salazar regime and the impracticable and undesirable maintenance of the *status quo* in Portuguese Africa. He indicated that action must be taken to accelerate social reforms both in the *ultramar* and the *metrópole* and to "pry loose the iron grip of the few controlling families" over Portuguese affairs.[42] Moniz here claimed that he had discussed this position with the senior members of his staff, all of whom were in agreement, and that at least 90 percent of the Portuguese armed forces supported this view. With "startling candor" he described Salazar's increasing inability to exercise true leadership and attributed this shortcoming to his advancing years.[43] Elbrick's final observation on the meeting was that Moniz was a man to watch.

Salazar's vulnerability had been revealed in the Delgado challenge of 1958 and its strong message that it was time for Portugal to move toward democracy. The colonies were seen by many as a liability in that their ownership under the current arrangement represented a major obstacle in Portugal's joining the European Economic Community and in trading with Third World nations, a direction that held great promise.[44] The strength of this view was manifested in the attempted coup of 13 April 1961, which was probably the closest that Salazar came to being removed. The 1960 débâcle in the Belgian Congo prompted heated debate in the Portuguese Supreme Council for National Defense (*Conselho Superior de Defesa Nacional*) about the security of its overseas territories. Colonel Kaúlza de Arriaga was notably vociferous in saying that the *ultramar* forces should be augmented, particularly in Angola.[45] He was opposed by Moniz and by fellow Colonels Almeida Fernandes and Costa Gomes, who advocated a dose of the "winds of change" for the colonial situation.[46] Moniz consequently undertook to write a long and formal letter to Salazar describing the concerns that he and many of his politico-military colleagues on the Council shared about a military solution to the colonial problem. They felt that success was very uncertain and that proceeding down such a road would lead Portugal to an untenable position in which it would find itself under attack with its forces dispersed on four continents. He described the military course of action as suicidal because of a lack of resources and the ability neither to win on the battlefield nor achieve a favorable political solution to colonial ownership.[47] The pursuit of such a course would generate considerable ill-will, particularly in the United Kingdom, the United States, and now Brazil, where both Delgado and Galvão had been given political asylum. From here these two continued to produce a stream of invective that drew international attention to the corruption of the Salazar regime and its exploitation of the indigenous African population that was subject to enormous abuse and forced to work for "wages of misery."[48] A change of direction, it was argued, was needed to correct the moral injustices in the *ultramar* and at home and to regain international prestige, something the current line of diplomacy seemed incapable of doing. The political shackles needed to be removed so that Portugal could expand socially and economically with the Western world.

The uprisings themselves acted to bring the differing opinions into focus. After considerable debate, virtually the entire defense staff decided that a motion of no confidence in Salazar should be made at the approaching meeting of the Council on 8 April. Salazar, tipped to the plans by Arriaga, did not attend the meeting. As an alternative, the plotters had asked President Tomás to dismiss Salazar. Tomás indicated that he would not dismiss the "greatest statesman of the century after Churchill." By then Salazar had identified the culprits, and on 13 April the relevant participants were reassigned. The inevitable reshuffle ensued in which Salazar assumed the defense portfolio, and no change in policy was brooked.

Salazar had managed over the years of his rule to control and manipulate the military through a strategy of co-optation and "divide and rule."[49] Military pay was poor, and to advance in pay and promotion, ambitious officers were removed from the immediate military environment by posting them to lucrative and prestigious special positions. Normally these were at high levels of government in both the *metrópole* and the *ultramar*, and it was these postings, promotions, and pay that Salazar oversaw. Allegiances were ambivalent. This undermining of traditional military bonds enabled Salazar to create mistrust and fear within the armed forces to his advantage. Until the 1974 revolution, when the coup participants had developed broad and determined backing, the Salazar regime would be safe from a military coup, and despite its enormous reservations and latent moral indignation, the armed forces would be forced to honor his commitment to the colonies and to fight his war in Africa.[50] With this event, it became evident that the purpose of colonial policy was now to preserve the Salazar regime. Advocates of any alternative colonial options had been neutralized, and commitment to war reinforced through destruction of the coup. These events accented Portugal's increasing international isolation.

UN Reversal

Following the uprisings and the *Santa Maria* incident, the UN Security Council convened in May and June to discuss, among other agenda items, the events of Angola. On 19 May, the UN Commission on Information on Autonomous Territories offered a resolution that denounced Portugal for not cooperating in submitting colonial reports and attempted to force Portuguese cooperation in future reporting. The United States supported this action. While other colonial powers disliked the reports requested by this UN commission; nevertheless, they complied. In the following month the Security Council approved a new resolution condemning the massacres and the excessive force used against the Angolan population, saying that it "compromised the maintenance peace and international security."[51] The United States under the new Kennedy administration reversed support in this forum and sided with the Soviet Union in condemning Portuguese African policy.[52] After the change of heart in the *Santa Maria* incident, the Kennedy administration in the spring of 1961 was torn between the "Africanists" and the "Europeanists" in crafting its policy towards Portugal. The more liberal Africanists prevailed and advocated that the United Nations in the form of a conciliation commission initiate immediate negotiations between Portugal and the nationalist movements. The ostensible aim was to obtain a cease-fire and institute reforms leading to auto-determination for the colonies. This event was an enormous blow to Salazar, who criticized the United States for voting with the Soviet Union in the face of historical opposition to Soviet diplomatic and military activity. This also called into question the NATO relationship. The U.S. position was tempered later in the summer when it was necessary to renegotiate its lease on the strategically important base in the Azores. Nevertheless, the damage between two old friends had been done. Portugal found itself a semi-pariah state, politically isolated for the moment along with its colonial neighbors South Africa and Southern Rhodesia, and was forced to fight the ensuing war hobbled by this isolation. It felt beleaguered and betrayed by its long-term ally, the United States, and viewed its position as neither understood nor appreciated. This ostracism served to harden its commitment to its colonies. Portugal believed that it was acting properly and that it had nothing of which to be ashamed. It proceeded accordingly to defend its sovereign territory and interests.

The Loss of Goa

This beleaguered colonial position was reinforced by the actual loss of the Indian colonies in what was an act of war that Portugal was powerless to prevent. The events surrounding Goa in 1961 again hardened the Portuguese position by providing Salazar with a nationally distressing event to coalesce the population for the coming African conflict. While Portuguese Indian territory was relatively small at 4,194 square kilometers, the Indian government seizure was a blatant act of aggression against another state. Portugal had three trading enclaves there: Goa, Damão, and Diu. The fledgling Indian government had threatened to take these properties in the late 1940s immediately following independence, as it considered them an affront. The British Prime Minister, Winston Churchill, along with the United States, forcefully intervened to moderate Indian ambitions. Later Indian Prime Minister Jawaharlal Nehru, emboldened by the outbreak of armed revolt in Angola, made some very peremptory demands of the Portuguese.[53] When it became clear that Salazar did not intend to relinquish the territory and refused to negotiate, India massed 30,000 troops, supported by tanks, aircraft, and warships, on the borders of the three territories. Governor-General Vassalo e Silva could defend his territory with only about 3,000 ill-equipped troops without air cover or air defense, 900 Goan police, and an old frigate. On 11 December, Salazar attempted to invoke the Anglo-Portuguese Treaty without success. Great Britain had since 1954 refused to help, saying that the 600-year-old alliance had clear limitations, particularly since a member of the Commonwealth was involved. Britain no longer needed Portuguese ports for the transit to its colonies, and Portugal no longer needed the protection of the dwindling British navy. New alliance structures, such as NATO, had clearly replaced the Anglo-Portuguese Treaty in both intent and practice.

Salazar gave instructions that resistance must last at least eight days to mobilize international support. Should that not be forthcoming, then "total sacrifice" must be made to save Portuguese honor. Indian forces invaded in the morning of 17 December, and

Vassalo e Silva capitulated in the pointless struggle on 19 December, far short of eight days and total sacrifice. Vassalo e Silva and the other officers involved were dismissed from the army in 1963 in what appeared to be an effort to shift blame for the loss of Portuguese India to the military and to set an example for officers in similar future situations, such as the approaching colonial wars. The military at large was resentful at the unjust punishment and at making soldiers the scapegoats for civilian mistakes. The armed forces carried into the African campaigns this "ominous message that the government was prepared to manipulate and sacrifice them in hopeless missions and to court-martial virtually all survivors."[54] General António de Spínola, who was to be the Commander-in-Chief of Portuguese forces in Guiné (1968–1972), the Deputy Chief of the General Staff (1972–1974), and the first President of the new government following the revolution in 1974, described in his controversial book *Portugal and the Future* the anxiety permeating the entire Portuguese military on the eve of the African wars:

> India is a clear example of what we fear. Never was its inevitable loss believed possible. And yet when the tragedy happened, the Nation's attention was immediately focused on the narrow aspect of military conduct. The Armed Forces were accused of not having defended India heroically; when, in reality, no matter how effective its defense, India would have fallen in only a matter of days.[55]

The punishment for the leaders of the Indian garrison carried the broad message that there would be no turning back from the government decision to defend the colonies. Salazar's commitment to preserving his regime was unswerving in its purpose, and the events in Goa served to push Portugal further down the road to war.

Portugal's commitment to the defense of the *ultramar* had its origins in a search for the renewed greatness of an earlier era, a vision of empire held by the Salazar government. The modern-day African colonies had largely been an irregular economic and political burden until the eve of the wars, and until after World War II, had held only a promise of economic benefit. Political opposition to Salazar was tolerated neither at home nor in the *ultramar*. The long-standing abuses of Portuguese African populations had created widespread dissatisfaction with no outlet. Between the intransigent Salazar and an aggrieved African population an explosion was inevitable. When it happened in 1961, the events in Angola along with the *Santa Maria* incident, the "*abrilada*," the isolation in the United Nations, and the seizing of Goa pushed Salazar to solidify the commitment of the Portuguese people to defend the colonies and preserve his regime. This national commitment was a reflection of his own personal commitment and his propensity to brook no opposition, particularly from seemingly upstart nationalist movements and elements of his military. So strong was this feeling that it defied any voice of reason and foreclosed any retreat or compromise over African affairs. Portugal's armed forces and treasure were thus pledged in full as the ultimate manifestation of this promise to make the colonial system work in Salazar's concept of empire.[56]

Notes

1 António José Telo, *História da Marinha Portuguesa: Doutrinas e Organização, 1924–1974* [History of the Portuguese Navy: Doctrine and Organization, 1924–1974] (Lisbon: Academia de Marinha, 1999), 515.

2 George F. Kennan, "'Long Telegram' from Moscow, February 22, 1946," *Foreign Relations of the United*

States, 1946 IV (Washington, D.C.: U.S. Government Printing Office, 1969): 666–709.

3 Russell F. Weigley, *The American Way of War* (New York: Macmillan, 1973; Indiana University Press, 1977), 450.

4 David M. Abshire and Michael A. Samuels, *Portuguese Africa, A Handbook* (New York: Praeger Publishers, 1969), 375.

5 Sérgio Augusto Margarido Lima Bacelar, *A Guerra em África 1961–1974: Estratégias Adoptadas pelas Forças Armadas* [The War in Africa 1961–1974: Strategies Adopted by the Armed Forces] (Porto: Liga dos Amigos do Museu Militar do Porto and Universidade Portucalenese Infante D. Henrique, 2000), 41.

6 Captain Henrique Galvão, *Report on Native Problems in the Portuguese Colonies* (Lisbon: Ministry of the Colonies, 1947).

7 Joaquim Moreira da Silva Cunha, *O Ultramar, a Nação e o "25 de Abril"* [The Overseas Provinces, the Nation and the "25th of April"] (Coimbra: Atlântida Editora, 1977), 13–14.

8 W. Gervase Clarence-Smith, *The Third Portuguese Empire 1825–1975: A Study in Economic Imperialism* (Manchester: Manchester University Press, 1985), 193. Internal and external pressures to democratize Portugal and put it in step with Western Europe had increased since World War II, and Salazar's rule had become tenuous in the late 1950s.

9 Hugh Kay, *Salazar and Modern Portugal* (London: Eyre and Spottswoode, 1970), 69, 133. The author argues that even in England communism had become "the rallying cry of the revolutionary instincts of our age" and had done so "by power of words, by sheer bluff, perhaps by the voluptuousness of contrast." It was largely the success of communist "evangelism" that made Salazar so suspicious of it.

10 Salazar quoted in Ibid., 133.

11 Ibid., 238.

12 John A. Marcum, *The Angolan Revolution: Volume I, The Anatomy of an Explosion (1950–1962)* (Cambridge, Mass.: MIT Press, 1969), 347–351. Marcum lists some fifty-nine groups affecting Angola alone beginning in the 1940s and either merging with one another or vanishing by 1962.

13 Malyn Newitt, *Portugal in Africa: The Last Hundred Years* (London: C. Hurst & Co., 1981), 190.

14 Willem S. van der Waals, *Portugal's War in Angola 1961–1974* (Rivonia: Ashanti Publishing, 1993), 103. Neto is quoted: "If the enemy presently possesses more forces than we do, and this is so, then it is correct that we should prepare for a protracted war. The misconception that we should be able to execute a war of rapid decisions should be removed once and for all." See also Alpoim Calvão, "Guerra Revolucionária e Guerra Subversiva" [Revolutionary War and Subversive War], *Anais do Clube Militar Naval* (October-December 1967): 713-720.

15 Região Militar de Angola, *Supintrep No. 19: Guerra Revolucionária* [Supplemental Intelligence Report No. 19: Revolutionary War], July 1963, Luanda, quoted in van der Waals, 103.

16 Douglas L. Wheeler and René Pélissier, *Angola* (London: Pall Mall Press, 1971), 167. The authors cite as an example the Congo district in 1960. For its 37,000 square miles it had fourteen *concelhos* (basic urban or semi-urban administrative unit) or *circunscrições* (basic rural administrative division) and thirty-seven posts, for an average of 725 square miles per administrative division. This presence would hardly be effective in controlling a frontier, as the posts would be dozens of miles apart. Large numbers of people could and did cross undetected.

17 Hélio Felgas, "Angola e a Evolução Política dos Territórios Vizinhos" [Angola and the Political Evolution of the Neighboring Territories], *Revista Militar* (December 1965): 706.

18 van der Waals, 96.

19 Ibid., 97. The author argues that Portuguese propaganda and social work among the refugees in Angola persuaded most of these displaced people to move into controlled settlements. This development deprived ELNA of popular support. ELNA had concentrated on military action in a human desert and

on preventing MPLA infiltration. It had neglected to indoctrinate, organize, and win recruits among refugees returning to Angola and thus missed an opportunity to undermine Portuguese authority. Consequently no ELNA internal political infrastructure was established in Angola. Portugal gained the upper hand and maintained superior momentum until 1974.

20 Neil Bruce, "Portugal's African Wars," *Conflict Studies* 34 (March 1973): 22.

21 Sue Armstrong, *In Search of Freedom* (Gibraltar: Ashanti Publishing, 1989), 71.

22 John A. Marcum, *The Angolan Revolution: Volume II, Exile Politics and Guerrilla Warfare (1962–1976)* (Cambridge, Mass.: MIT Press, 1978), 113.

23 Patrick Chabal, *Amílcar Cabral* (Cambridge: Cambridge University Press, 1983), 56–57.

24 Amílcar Cabral, *Guiné-Bissau–Nação Africana Forjada na Luta* [Guiné-Bissau–African Nation Forged in Struggle] (Lisbon: Publicações Nova Auora, 1974), 39.

25 Hélio Felgas, *Os Movimentos Terroristas* [The Terrorist Movements] (Lisbon: Privately printed, 1966), 57.

26 Amílcar Cabral, *Textos Políticos* [Political Texts] (Porto: Edições Afrontamento, 1974), 19–20.

27 Amílcar Cabral, *Palavras de Ordem Gerais* [Speeches on Overall Methods] (Bissau: PAIGC/Secretariado Geral, 1976), 34.

28 Carlos Fontes, "Moçambique: A Guerra de Libertação (1964–1974)" [Mozambique: The War of Liberation (1964–1974)], *Imigrantes Somos Todos* http://imigrantes.no.sapo.pt/page2mocGLibert.html (accessed 11 November 2011).

29 Eduardo Mondlane, *The Struggle for Mozambique* (London: Zed Press, 1969), 125.

30 Gerald J. Bender, "The Limits of Counterinsurgency: An African Case," *Comparative Politics* 4 (April 1972): 357.

31 Luís Nuno Rodrigues, *Salazar–Kennedy: A Crise de uma Aliança* [Salazar–Kennedy: The Crisis of an Alliance] (Lisbon: Editorial Notícias, 2002), 35–36.

32 Ibid., 39.

33 António José Malheiro García, "A Operação *Santa Maria*" [Operation *Santa Maria*], in the unpublished collection *Participação da Armada na Defesa das Províncias Ultramarinas* [Participation of the Navy in the Defense of the Overseas Provinces], TMs [photocopy], (Lisbon: Ministério de Marinha, 1972), 1.

34 Douglas L. Wheeler, "The Portuguese Army in Angola," *Modern African Studies* 7 (October 1969): 430.

35 Douglas L. Wheeler, "African Elements in Portugal's Armies in Africa (1961–1974)," *Armed Forces and Society* 2 (February 1976): 237.

36 Estado-Maior do Exército, *Resenha Histórico-Militar das Campanhas de África, Vol. II, Dispositivo das Nossas Forças Angola* [Historical-Military Report on the African Campaigns, Vol. II, Disposition of Our Angolan Forces] (Lisbon: Estado-Maior do Exército, 1989), 63–65.

37 Van der Waals, 64.

38 René Pélissier, *Le Naufrage des Caravelles: Etudes sur la Fin de l'Empire Portugais (1961–1975)* [The Shipwreck of the Caravels: Studies on the End of the Portuguese Empire (1961–1975)] (Orgeval: Editions Pélissier, 1979), 147.

39 Douglas L. Wheeler, "The Portuguese Army in Angola," *Modern African Studies* 7 (October 1969): 431.

40 René Pélissier, *La Colonie du Minotaure, Nationalismes et Révoltes en Angola (1926–1961)* [The Colony of the Minotaur, Nationalist Movements and Revolts in Angola (1926–1961)] (Orgeval: Editions Pélissier, 1978), 658.

41 Ibid., 657–660; van der Waals, 58–61.

42 Charles Burke Elbrick, U.S. Ambassador to Portugal, Lisbon, Telegram 508 to U.S. Secretary of State, Washington, 18 February 1961, TMs [photocopy].

43 Ibid.

44 Clarence-Smith, 193. The author argues that by 1968 the Portuguese economy was turning decisively

from the colonies toward Europe. Portugal in the course of the 1960s and early 1970s became a booming and aggressive "newly industrialized country" and was described as a "Taiwan of southern Europe."

45 António de Spínola, *País sem Rumo* [Country without Direction] (Lisbon: Editorial SCIRE, 1978), 83.

46 Douglas Porch, *The Portuguese Armed Forces and the Revolution* (Stanford: The Hoover Institution Press, 1977), 38.

47 Lima Bacelar, 39.

48 João José Brandão Ferreira, *A Evolução do Conceito Estratégico Ultramarino Português* [Evolution of the Portuguese *Ultramar* Strategic Concept] (Lisbon: Hugin Editores, 2002), 377.

49 Douglas L. Wheeler, "The Military and the Portuguese Dictatorship, 1926–1974: 'The Honor of the Army,'" in *Contemporary Portugal*, ed. Lawrence S. Graham and Harry M. Makler (Austin: University of Texas Press, 1979), 199.

50 Porch, 26.

51 Rodrigues, 92.

52 Ibid., 92–95.

53 Richard Robinson, *Contemporary Portugal* (London: George Allen & Unwin, 1979), 103. Nehru announced that India was "not prepared to tolerate the presence of the Portuguese in Goa, even if the Goans want them to be there."

54 Porch, 36.

55 António de Spínola, *Portugal e o Futuro* [Portugal and the Future] (Lisbon: Editoria Arcádia, 1974), 235.

56 Manuel Limpo Serra, "Imperativo da Continuação de Portugal em África" [The Imperative of the Continuation of Portugal in Africa], *Anais do Clube Militar Naval* (July–September 1961): 455.

2

The Naval Dimension

When the troubles in Angola began during the opening months of 1961, the Portuguese Navy had only a modest representation on hand to help restore civil order and defend the integrity of its borders.[1] While these developments began with the cotton growers in Baixa do Cassange on 4 January, the assault on the police station in Luanda on 4 February, and the UPA attack in the north on 15 March, trouble in the area can be traced to 30 June 1960, the day of Congo independence. At that time the only naval units in the theater were a frigate, two patrol boats, and a partially constructed radio station. The frigate *Pacheco Pereira* and the patrol boats *Sal* and *São Vicente* were all operating in and near the Zaire River.[2] Shortly afterwards on 11 July the hydrographic vessel *Carvalho Araújo* joined them, and as the local unrest developed over the ensuing months, an additional patrol boat, *SãoTomé*, arrived on 28 January 1961, and two additional frigates, *Nuno Tristão* and *Diogo Gomes*, on 14 February and 1 April respectively.[3] The presence of this small force and its leisurely augmentation belied a wider and carefully considered naval strategy, the consequent development of associated naval doctrine, and the construction of an appropriate naval force. Before proceeding with that story, however, a few words are necessary on activities just across the border within the new Democratic Republic of the Congo that need not detain us long.

Congo Anarchy

The Belgian Congo had prospered, since its transfer to the Belgian government from the estate of its King Leopold II in 1908. It now operated under a colonial ministry that answered to a democratically elected parliament and that had opened the heretofore crown domains to private ownership and ended the monopoly on trade. The right of the Congolese to own and work their lands had been restored. The system of forced labor had been abolished. As a consequence of these new liberalizations came new opportunities. The European population moved to take advantage of the potential in the Congo, and its numbers there had risen from about 3,000 in 1908 to more than 100,000 in 1960.[4] There occurred over this period a great rush of development in agriculture, banking, mining, and infrastructure. Despite all of this apparent progress and its attendant social benefits, there remained a strong undercurrent of resentment within the local population. No civil rights for the Congolese were thought necessary, and racial segregation was standard practice. The highest rank a Congolese could hold in the colonial administration was one of a minor clerk in the civil service or a noncommissioned officer in the Congolese army, known as the *Force Publique*. Until 1955 the Congolese were forbidden to attend college and even after that could only attend designated institutions so as not to be "corrupted." When independence came in 1960, there were fewer than 30 African university graduates. Of the 5,000 management-level positions in the civil service, only three were filled by Africans.[5]

Despite the democratic government of Belgium, the Congo since 1908 had been run by decree from Brussels through a governor-general in its capital, Léopoldville. The colony was permitted no politicians, no political parties, and no elections.[6] No Congolese or Belgians residing there had a vote on any matter. Following World War II and the subsequent political developments in the neighboring French and British colonies, Belgium was obliged in 1956 to permit the same political freedom in the Congo. Prior to that time there had been social, religious, and cultural clubs formed along regional and tribal lines. Within this framework, there were discussions on how the Congolese might improve their plight and ultimately gain independence. These clubs now became the political parties of the Congo. By late 1959 the activities of these various political movements had matured to a point of demanding independence. The MNC (*Mouvement National Congolais* or Congolese National Movement), founded in October 1958 by the charismatic postal clerk Patrice Lumumba, had grown out of a government workers' club in Stanleyville. ABAKO (*Alliance des Ba-Kongo* or Alliance of the Bacongo), the powerful cultural-political association of the Bakongo people, was led by Joseph Kasabuvu, a pudgy civil servant who became its president in 1955. CONAKAT (*Confédération des Associations Tribales du Katanga* or Confederation of the Tribal Associations of Katanga) was a former club among the Luba-Lunda tribesmen founded by Moise Tshombe. The leader of a soldiers' club in the *Force Publique* garrison at Thysville was a young sergeant-major, Joseph-Désiré Mobutu.

Beginning in January 1959, these demands for immediate independence were reinforced by rallies and strikes, many violent and bloody. This mayhem created a sense of urgency within the Belgian government and caused it to rethink its colonial policy of a five-year transition culminating in 1964. This reconsideration occurred at the February 1960 Round Table Conference in Brussels, at which it was resolved to grant the Congo its independence in June, a mere four months hence.

In that short period the Belgian government attempted to overcome the enormous obstacles of accelerating the formation of a new Congolese government, a patently impossible task. It left little time for the Congolese to organize themselves politically, hold a wide array of elections, and assume the colonial administration from the Belgians using the largely untrained and uneducated local population. The seeds of immediate trouble began during the election campaign, in which candidates made wild promises, took the opportunity to vent long-repressed hostilities toward Europeans, and stirred long-standing tribal animosities. Peter Forbath describes the scene leading to Independence Day as one of nervous excitement with crowds roaming the streets of major cities, "impatient for the miracles of freedom to begin, nursing tribal grudges, eager to become lords over the whites and take vengeance for past injustices."[7] In the 23 June elections, Lumumba's party outpolled Kasabuvu's; however, neither side could form a parliamentary coalition. Consequently, as a compromise measure they formed an uneasy partnership with Kasabuvu as president and Lumumba as prime minister. This fragile government might have survived in a benign environment; however, it stood little chance with the legacy bequeathed to it by Brussels. The mood rapidly degenerated and turned ugly during the first week of independence. Public services deteriorated with the wholesale departure of Belgian civil servants and a lack of trained Congolese to replace them. When the new civil servants were not paid, there were strikes that turned into riots when the *Force Publique* attempted to intervene. All semblance of order, however, vanished when the *Force Publique* itself mutinied.

Despite the desire to replace Belgians with Congolese at every turn, Lumumba had not done so in one important sphere. He had elected to retain the 1,000 Belgian officers who led the 24,000-man *Force Publique* as an insurance policy against the difficult times ahead. In the minds of the black noncommissioned officers and troops this policy smacked of discrimination, and on 1 July there was a demonstration against it at the Lépoldville garrison. When the demonstrators refused to return to barracks, the commanding general ordered the Thysville garrison to intervene. In such a situation it would have been unrealistic to expect sympathetic brother to attack brother, and so the Thysville garrison predictably mutinied too. In a rapid chain reaction, most garrisons around the country followed suit with the result that the soldiers went on a rampage, attacking their officers, raping officers' wives, and looting. On 6 July, Lumumba, in an attempt to quell disaffection in the *Force Publique,* replaced the Belgian officers with Congolese. This move did not stem the tide, and the mutinies spawned a widespread wave of violence. Blacks attacked whites and each other, as they vented their anti-European hatreds and intertribal rivalries.

In the midst of this crisis, Lumumba in an irresponsible statement accused Belgian army officers of instigating the mayhem in a plot to re-annex the Congo. This developing chaos prompted a mass exodus of some 40,000 Europeans. Essential services ground to a halt. Food became scarce. Epidemics threatened. The spread of disorder prompted Tshombe, the newly-elected premier of Katanga Province, to ask Lumumba to appeal to Belgium for troops to restore order. Fearing a return of Belgian rule, he refused. Tshombe then in an attempt to address his executive responsibilities and preserve his province, declared mineral-rich Katanga an independent state and seceded from the Congo on 11 July. The continuing riots prompted Belgium to deploy paratroops to protect its nationals, and it seems they landed principally in Katanga, where they helped to sustain the secessionist state by rounding up and expelling the mutinous elements of the *Force Publique*.

On 12 July, Lumumba asked the United Nations to expel the Belgian "forces of aggression" and to compel Katanga to end its secession.[8] Three days later the first of 25,000 UN troops arrived, Belgian soldiers began to depart, and Lumumba declared martial law. The political situation then degenerated completely. The people of the lower Congo, who were represented by ABAKO, took their cue from Tshombe and demanded the abolition of the central government in favor of a system of independent provincial governments. This demand was followed by a declaration of independence in Kasai Province. Lumumba's country was falling apart with good reason, and having no reliable way to enforce his will, he turned to the United Nations with a request to use its peace-keeping troops to unify the Congo by force. When it refused, he countered by appealing to the Soviet Union. It obliged with a flight of 19 Illyushin transport aircraft, thereby supplying sufficient arms and airlift capability to enable Lumumba to march on Kasai and pour the proverbial gasoline onto an already incendiary situation. In what Mike Hoar describes as a one-sided battle, Lumumba's forces massacred Kasai tribesmen by the hundreds.[9] He then turned his force toward Katanga, where it was stopped at the border. Frustrated by this stalemate, elements of the *Force Publique* turned to brutalizing the population.

At this point Lumumba was a spent force in any attempt to unify the Congo politically. While he was a persuasive orator, he proved to be an unstable diplomat and an incompetent head of state. On 5 September, Kasabuvu dismissed the prime minister. In turn Lumumba dismissed the president. Kasabuvu prevailed by placing Lumumba under house arrest with the support of Mobutu, now a colonel and head of the army. All pretense of a functioning government seems to have ended. On hearing of Lumumba's arrest and the ensuing confusion, Antoine Gizenga declared the secession of Oriental Province, Lumumba's power base with its capital in Stanleyville. Gizenga's forces attacked Mobutu's garrisons,

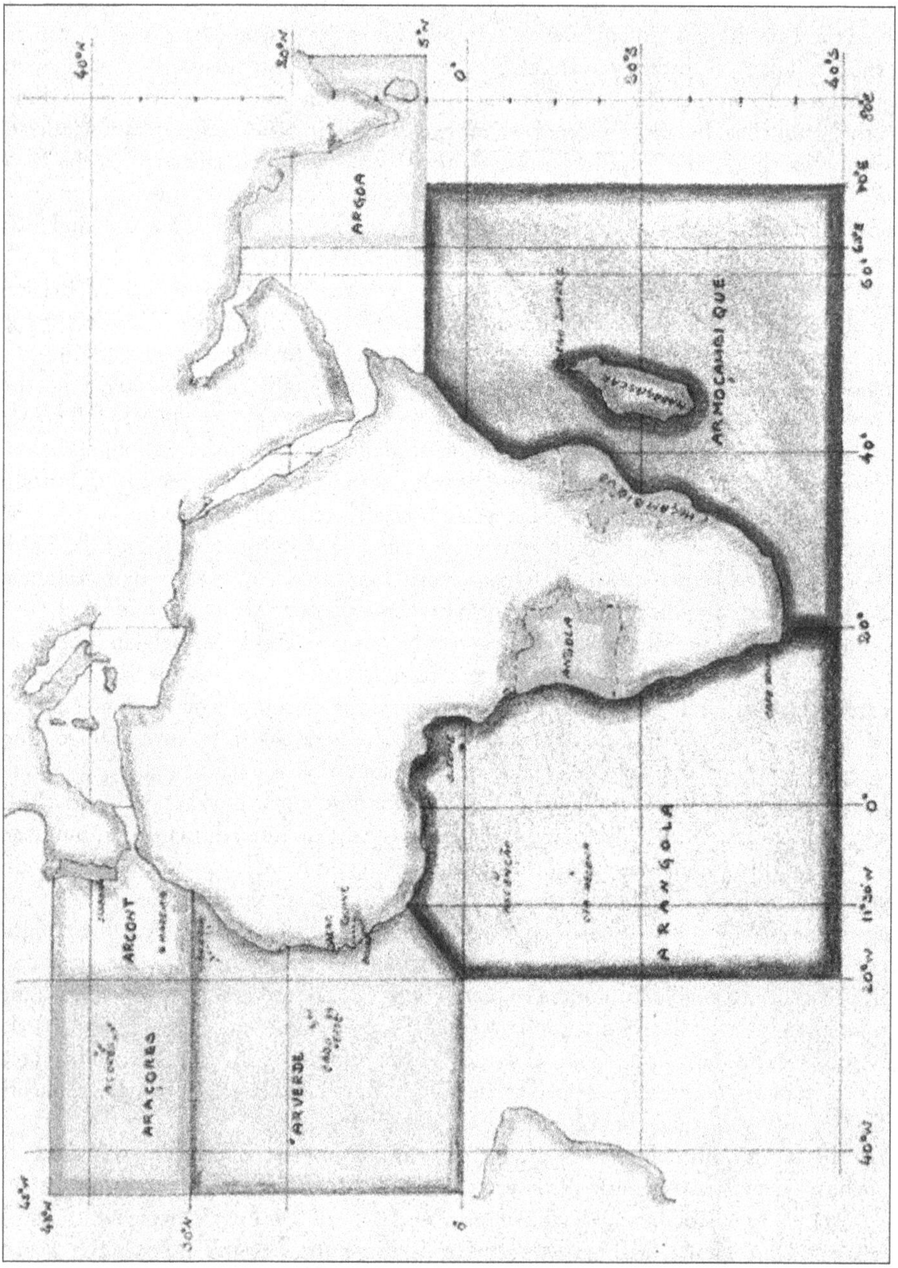

Portuguese Oceanic Operations Areas. Courtesy of António Emílio Sacchetti, "A Armada nas Campanhas de África," *Revista da Armada* (May 1997).

and a new bout of the most brutal savagery raged through the rain forests. It involved the worst sort of tribal warfare marked by wholesale massacres and cannibalism.[10] In the midst of the anarchy, Mobutu formed a "college of administrators" on 14 September and assumed the day-to-day running of the government, "neutralizing" all politicians. One of his first actions was to close the embassies of the Soviet Union and Czechoslovakia and banish their presence from the Congo.[11] The situation stabilized for a time; however, in November, Lumumba left Léopoldville, where he had enjoyed UN protection, to travel to Stanleyville, where his supporters had control. En route he was caught by Mobutu's troops on 2 December, and on 17 January 1961 was flown to Katanga, where he was reluctantly received in an apparent near-death condition by Tshombe.[12] Later in the month he was shot by Congolese or Katangese troops while allegedly trying to escape from a mud hut in which he had been held prisoner.[13] Lumumba's death caused an international outrage and raised the man to martyr-hero status. Mobutu returned the government to Kasabuvu, as his suspected hand in Lumumba's death became known, and in turn Kasabuvu made him commander-in-chief of the armed forces. The agony of the Congo continued until a now better prepared Mobutu stepped in again in 1965 and ruled for better or for worse until his downfall and death in 1997. It is estimated that over 200,000 Congolese perished in the five years between independence and the establishment of his second and final regime.[14] While these developments have been summarized loosely, it was into the fringe of this chaos that the naval presence in Angola and particularly along the Zaire River was thrust.

A Second Navy

With the development of this unhappy situation in the Belgian Congo from 1956 onward, there was a profound shift in naval thought at the highest levels of the naval staff. Portuguese military leaders had foreseen difficulty in its African colonies and had attempted to make moves to prepare their services for the coming conflict.[15] The navy had identified a number of critical tasks in this vein. First, the naval commands needed to be reorganized and properly established to effect the necessary command and control over the envisioned activities in Africa. Before the administrative reorganization of 1955 and the subsequent authorization in 1957 to establish naval commands in the *ultramar*, the navy had suffered the poverty of neglect for some forty years.[16] There was virtually no naval infrastructure in the *ultramar* before this authorization, and it represented the first serious step in establishing a permanent presence there.[17] Under this authorization, the Naval Commands of Angola and Mozambique were created, and the next year those of Goa, of Cape Verde and Guiné, and of Macao and Timor, along with a number of Maritime Defense Commands subordinate to the Naval Commands of Angola (São Tomé, Santo António do Zaire, Luanda, Lobito, and Mossâmedes) and Mozambique (Lourenço Marques, Inhambane, Beira, Quelimane, Chinde, Mozambique Island, and Porto Amélia). It was this organization of commands that oversaw the development of naval infrastructure and the return of the navy to the *ultramar*. The new Portuguese Oceanic Operations Areas of each of these *ultramar* Naval Commands plus those of the *metrópole* are depicted in the map, which was drawn by Vice Admiral António Emílio Sacchetti as a junior officer on board the frigate *Santaigo* during a voyage to Luanda in 1959. They form a contiguous zone of responsibility for the several commands extending from Latitude 43 degrees North to 40 degrees South and encompassing a great part of the Indian Ocean from the Cape of Good

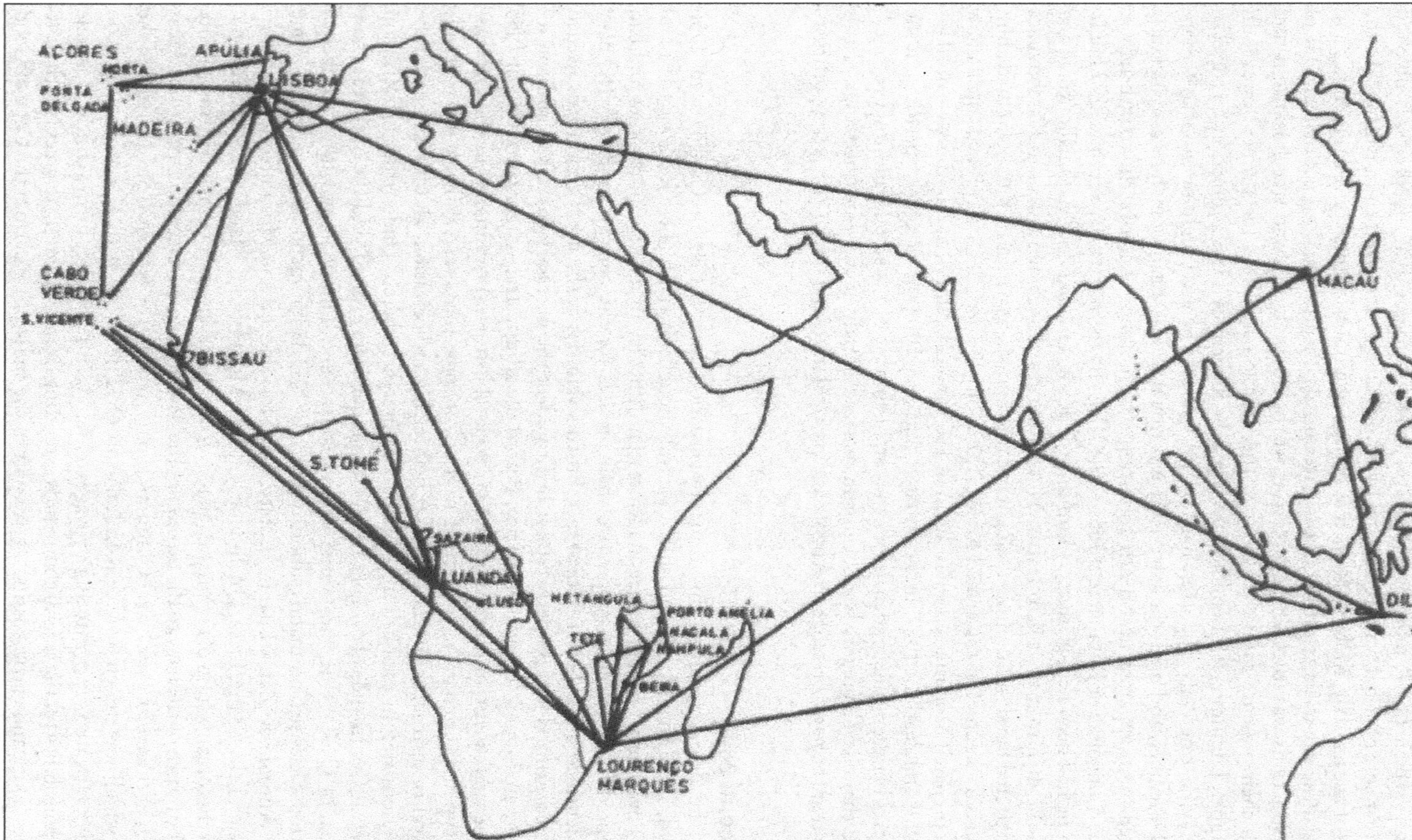

Naval Communications Network – Principal Stations. Source: José Luís Leiria Pinto, "As Comuniçõess na Marinha: Dos primórdios a 1975" [Naval Communications: From the Beginning to 1975], Presentation in the Academia de Marinha, Lisbon, 1 June 2010.

Hope to Longitude 85 degrees East.

In addition to the expansion of the facilities and capabilities of the Lisbon Naval Base, which now made it worthy of the name, support bases were established in Ponta Delgada (Azores), São Vicente (Cape Verde), Luanda, Lourenço Marques, Goa, and Macau. These installations would be the logistical support centers for the four naval regions: North Atlantic (Lisbon and Ponta Delgada), South Atlantic (Luanda and São Vicente), Indian Ocean (Lourenço Marques and Goa), and the Far East (Macau).[18] As there was no existing naval infrastructure at first, it was necessary to improvise in the case of each command during the construction of its facilities.

The exercise of command, however, presupposed the existence of a modern and reliable radio link. Improvisation was not practicable in this case, and so it was necessary to study, plan, and build a worldwide naval communications system. The project began in 1957 and expanded in scope, as from April 1958, the Ministry of National Defense assigned responsibility to the navy for communications between the *metrópole* and the *ultramar* for the three services and the local overseas governments. This new responsibility gave the project the highest priority in a claim on available resources. By 1960 the first three principal stations of Luanda, Lourenço Marques, and São Vicente were established and supported by seven more auxiliary stations to provide complete coverage (Macau, Santo António do Zaire, Nacala, Bissau, Dili, São Tomé, and Metangula).[19] The system was expanded from this beginning, and ultimately the navy operated fourteen radio stations worldwide, twelve of which were in Africa, and 60 radio posts, all of which were in Africa. This extensive system of primary radio stations and secondary posts guaranteed reliable communications throughout the Empire. The system infrastructure is identified in Table 2.1.[20]

Table 2.1: Radio Stations and Posts in the *Ultramar*

Source: José Luís Leiria Pinto, "As Comuniçóess na Marinha: Dos primórdios a 1975" [Naval Communications: From the Beginning to 1975], Presentation in the Academia de Marinha, Lisbon, 1 June 2010.

Overseas Territory	Primary stations with date of establishment and posts
Cape Verde:	São Vicente (1961) + 8 posts
Guiné:	Bissau (1961) + 3 posts
São Tomé and Príncipe:	São Tomé (1962) + 2 posts
Angola:	Luanda (1960) + 22 posts Santo António do Zaire (1960)
Mozambique:	Lourenço Marques (1960) + 25 posts Beira (1960) Nacala (1960) Porto Améila (1962) Metangula (1968) Nampula (1968) Tete (1973)
Macau:	Macau (1960)
East Timor:	Dili (1962)

This network was truly a technical and logistic effort of gigantic proportions in that it reliably assured the maintenance of a vital communications link between all of the various far-flung reaches of the Empire, 24 hours a day, day-in and day-out. The bulk of the system was created in the short two-year period between 1960 and 1962, and its success reflects exemplary planning and the flawless execution of that plan. The construction of the facilities, many in very forbidding climates that degrade communications equipment, the training of personnel to man and maintain them, and their reliable operation over a decade and a half were indispensible to protecting the Empire. It was, indeed, one of the most noteworthy accomplishments of the Navy.[21]

With the planned assignment of units to the new naval commands, it was necessary to expand the attendant base structure and complete the necessary logistical support for its projected needs. The navy had little experience in the beginning with its anticipated force of small vessels, the associated infantry detachments, and their specialized requirements.[22] Nevertheless, it proceeded with an ambitious construction program to fill what it saw as a need to strengthen the naval presence in the *ultramar* against the threat of subversive war. It acquired the capability of an inshore and riverine force complete with the specialized manpower to project power ashore. These moves were creating a very different trajectory for the navy and a departure from its traditions. It was one fraught with a new and uncertain national risk because of its unfamiliarity and cost.[23]

This sea change indeed represented a radical departure from tradition, for as far back as the Naval Plan of 1930 the course had been set for a blue water navy, that is, one with a predominantly oceanic configuration. This plan called for a light cruiser, destroyers, frigates, submarines, mine hunters, mine sweepers, and some coastal and riverine patrol boats.[24] While some progress was made in the construction of this fleet and in the recruiting and training of its personnel, a lack of national resources at the time and later the neutrality of Portugal during World War II frustrated its completion. Portugal had emerged from World War II with a modest navy of about 40,000 tons. Following the world war and the relative isolation of its neutrality, Portugal joined the Atlantic Alliance in 1949 as a charter member and began to address the rebuilding of its navy with an unfettered enthusiasm. The technology and associated tactics developed by the Allies during the war were now shared with their new NATO partner. Throughout the decade of the 1950s the navy was heavily influenced by the Cold War and the Soviet submarine threat to the sea lines of communication between Europe and the United States. It found a new orientation towards antisubmarine and mine warfare and this important niche within NATO. These newly acquired skills were in keeping with the trend of deemphasizing naval gunnery and the other traditional naval capabilities in favor of more modern technologies and weapons. The older destroyers and frigates were fitted with new and specialized arms and equipment, increasing their value in the naval mission of NATO. Personnel were reorganized in the NATO mold, and their instruction and training accelerated in the new procedures and tactical doctrine of the Alliance. This situation continued into the 1960s, and it was during this time that the support of the Alliance was critical in raising the level of technical training through its shared experience and knowledge. By 1966 the navy had more than doubled in tonnage.[25] The nature of the navy had also changed. The navy of 1946 consisted of six frigates (*fragatas*), five more heavily gunned destroyers (*contratorpedeiros*), three submarines (*submersiveis*), and an assortment of auxiliaries. By 1960 the effects of Portugal's membership in NATO and its blue water orientation were apparent. The number of frigates had doubled to a dozen.

Thirteen new corvettes (*corvetas*) had been added. Seventeen large patrol boats (*patrulhas*) and a dozen minesweepers (*draga-minas*) reflected this new posture. This support had helped the navy by the early part of the decade reach a level of proficiency in open ocean operations that until that time was unsurpassed by other emerging navies.[26]

The *quid pro quo* in this situation was that in exchange for the matériel and training received from the Allies, Portugal would commit this force to the NATO order of battle. This commitment had required the bulk of the fleet to be based in the *metrópole* for the better part of two decades. The NATO obligation had also made it increasingly difficult to maintain a naval presence in the East for the security of Timor, Macau, and Portuguese India. The Indian and Pacific Ocean mission was thus relegated to old, out-dated *avisos* or dispatch boats, small ocean-going gunboats of 1,000 to 2,000 tons (2nd class and 1st class *avisos* respectively) that were unencumbered by the NATO commitment.[27] Then too in the *ultramar* during most of the 1950s the security environment from the naval perspective was so benign as to warrant little more than the routine deployment of a hydrographic ship performing its normal charting duties.[28]

Despite the operational euphoria of NATO, the navy recognized the need to safeguard Portuguese national interests and consequently began to review the "gunboat policy" of the previous century that had served so well in the pacification of the *ultramar*.[29] This, however, was hardly adequate in light of the situation developing in Africa. So in January 1957, a new naval program was proposed that would be for Portugal as revolutionary as the shift from wooden to steel ships. It detailed the nucleus of a tailored force that would be established in the *ultramar* as an embryo for future expansion, as the security situation dictated, and that would avoid infringing on the NATO obligations.[30] The composition of this force remained under debate for two years. The first school of thought envisioned a navy centered in a force of *Fuzileiros* or marines on board aircraft carriers prepared to support ground operations with great mobility and flexibility, much as the Royal Marines or the U.S. Marines deployed on their specially configured assault landing ships. The second was more classical and affordable and supported a force of *Fuzileiros* and attendant inshore ships adapted to the African environment.[31] There was enormous and predictable opposition to the first option from both the air force and the army for the obvious parochial reason that a fleet of aircraft carriers would absorb the lion's share of the defense budget and leave little for the other services. The naval air arm, which in 1952 had been merged with the air force, would likely be resurrected and put into renewed competition for scarce aviation resources. While these two negative arguments were important, the overwhelming one was that the anticipated conflict was an insurgent war and did not require power projection from the sea. Portugal already owned the colonies, so putting men ashore in a riverine environment did not require an expensive and elaborate force. Aircraft carriers were not needed, it was argued, as the air force had an extensive airfield infrastructure in Africa and could provide aviation services and support with far more flexibility, rapidity, and cost effectiveness than a small carrier or two. The French experience in the Mekong Delta of Indochina was contemporary testimony to the effectiveness of a specialized, small, and relatively inexpensive force backed by land-based aviation.

As the debate on naval construction continued and the security situation in the Belgian Congo began to collapse, the Portuguese Navy took its first significant steps in many years to strengthen its presence in Africa. This move was reminiscent of the earlier Naval Stations (*Estações Navais*) not seen since the 1920s, and the periodic appearances of the old Colonial

Naval Division (*Divisão Naval Colonial*) not seen since the 1930s.[32] On 28 April 1959, it established Patrol Ship Group Nº 1 (*Grupo Nº 1 de Navio Patrulhas*) consisting of the ocean-going patrol boats *Santiago* and *Madeira* and ordered it to Angola. Both vessels would serve a year before being relieved by the *Sal* and *São Vicente.* Later between 22 August and 23 December, Ocean Escort Group Nº 2 (*Grupo Nº 2 de Escoltas Oceânicos*) was established with the frigates *Nuno Tristão* and *Diogo Gomes* and likewise assigned to Angola. Also in August in Bissau with the aggrieved dockworkers strike and subsequent overreaction in the "Pijiguiti dock massacre," the frigate *Pero Escobar* and patrol boat *Boavista* were dispatched to reinforce inshore and riverine security in Guiné. These developments had a substantial influence on the debate within the navy concerning its mix of ships to be built. By 22 December 1959, a consensus for the second option had been developed, and the naval staff presented its Naval Construction Plan to the Minister of the Navy defining two distinct and independent navies. The first was European and would be used to support the NATO commitment. It would consist of:

6 modern frigates of the U.S. *Dealey* class,
9 corvettes of the Italian *Airone* class,
3 submarines of the French *Daphné* class,
8 patrol craft,
18 minesweepers already operational, and various auxiliaries.
The second was the African navy and would be built from scratch. It would consist of:
6 frigates of the French *Commandant Riviére* class,
6 corvettes of the Italian *Airone* class, and
29 patrol boats of various types and sizes.

Despite the seeming agreement on the plan, there continued debate on the ideal vessel at the intermediate level between the frigates and the patrol boats. The *Airone* was small at 800 tons, having originally been a U.S. escort patrol craft design, but it was affordable. Because it was projected to be a class of fifteen, it was thought that two versions might be built, one for NATO and the other for Africa. In reality much of the deep water capability was postponed or modified because of political differences between Portugal, the United States, and the United Kingdom over the defense of Africa. Eventually in 1964 the plan was more realistically set at 7 frigates, 6 submarines, and 15 corvettes, of which the first phase would be 4 frigates, 4 submarines, and 6 corvettes. In September of that year, contracts were signed for four of the *Commandant Riviére* class frigates and four of the *Daphné* class submarines in France.[33] The United States also underwrote three of the *Dealey* class frigates to be built in Portugal but used only in a NATO role.[34] This program would essentially satisfy the frigate and submarine requirements, as it turned out, for naval strategy began to focus more and more on Africa.

The definition of the six first-phase corvettes was more difficult, as no off-the-shelf vessel seemed to fit the needs of the navy. In 1961 it was decided to undertake a national program for the corvette, and discussions were begun with a German shipyard. By yearend 1963, so many revisions had occurred that by 1965 the project had to be returned to the concept development stage. In February 1966, the corvette was presented as one featuring modular systems of sensors and arms that could be rapidly changed to give the ship either a NATO escort role or a simpler, more rudimentary African configuration. This concept was revolutionary at the time, although today it is widely accepted.[35] There was also a preoccupation with obtaining a ship that was simple, small, inexpensive, easy to maintain, and able to adapt to virtually any type of mission. The compromise was, of course, that by being a jack of all trades it could perform each of these missions only so well. To contain the cost, the proposal made use of many components already in the navy inventory, such as, the French 100mm cannon. This corvette project became one of the most prominent technical successes of Portuguese naval engineering and served as an example for other navies, most notably those of France, Germany, and Spain.[36]

The first six corvettes, now known as the new *João Coutinho* class of 1,200 tons, were built in Germany and Spain between 1970 and 1971 and were popular in Africa because of their adaptability and easy maintenance. Each had a helicopter platform and accommodation for 34 *Fuzileiros* and their equipment. The corvette was, however, limited in its traditional open ocean role, because its budget restrictions did not permit very sophisticated systems. The delay in adding the *João Coutinho* class to the fleet was such that naval plans had changed by the time of its initial delivery and only a further four with reduced armament were built in Spain between 1974 and 1976. By this time the war in Africa was effectively concluded, and Portugal was struggling with the internal upheaval of its aftermath.

The entire naval plan over its lifetime was thus beset by adjustments in policy, shifts in resource allocation dictated by the "real war" in Africa, and refinements in prosecution of the counterinsurgency campaign. With this pace of construction and delivery, the war in Africa would likely be concluded before the navy could effectively engage the enemy. Indeed, the ships designated for Africa did not respond completely to the requirement to fight in the rivers. As a result, there was a concerted push to assemble a much-needed and expanded fleet of riverine craft that could be put into the fight more quickly. The assembly of this African navy and its evolution became the most noteworthy development during the period.

What made it even more unusual was that officers proposing this course of action might be described as part of the "NATO generation" in that their careers had largely been spent solidifying the Portuguese position in NATO since its joining. For the navy, NATO had provided direction with its Eurocentric strategy, new infrastructure in an economically recovering continent, and modern warships that were compatible and complementary to those of other NATO partners. Europe was the logical direction for Portugal with its expanding economy and clear security problems developing at sea and on land to the East. After all, Portugal was a European nation and not an African one.

However, because from 1957 onward it looked more and more as if Portugal should be preparing itself for an insurgent war in its African colonies, the issue of European or African national orientation became vital in addressing the future. During the failed coup or *abrilada* of April 1961, the military hierarchy had believed that it was acting in the best interests of the country by raising the African issue with Salazar, particularly in light of what its members perceived as the direction best befitting Portugal. Despite his difference of opinion with Salazar and his subsequent ouster, Botelho Moniz had only reflected the divided opinion of the military leadership on Africa that had existed to that point and would continue throughout the conflict. He had ably directed the Ministry of National Defense and had prepared the Portuguese military well for its coming conflict in Africa.

It was Botelho Moniz, who in 1959 met with the U.S. Secretary of Defense and described how Portugal was so completely preoccupied with its defense of the *ultramar*.[37] He noted the vulnerability of Portuguese India, Guiné, and Angola with the independence of British India and French Guinée (Guinée-Conakry or the Republic of Guinée), and the brewing trouble in the Belgian Congo. The United States responded with a squadron of C-118 *Skymaster* transport aircraft, three escort destroyers, and three coastal patrol boats; however, when pressed for C-130 *Hercules* aircraft and UH-1 *Iroquois* helicopters that were proving themselves in Vietnam, landing craft, rubber boats, outboard motors, and other matériel, Portugal initially was given an ambiguous reply and later a negative one. This change in attitude not only of the United States but of Great Britain forced Portugal to seek alternative supplies in France and the Federal Republic of Germany, more colloquially known as West Germany. There were interesting reasons for the new alignments.

In the case of France, its physical proximity with Portugal and the fact that it was currently fighting an insurgency in Algeria gave the two a common touchstone. Further France under de Gaulle's leadership was at the time following an independent line regarding NATO and its own defense. It was consequently happy to align itself with those European countries that were also at odds with U.S. and NATO leadership. This liaison resulted in France becoming a substantial supplier of war matériel under generous credit terms alongside a general rise in the commercial links between the two countries. For the navy this meant that its future frigates and submarines would become the French *Comandant Riviere* and *Daphiné* classes respectively rather than continuing the U.S. and British inventory. This change was expensive for the navy, as it caused substantial technical problems with this departure from earlier acquisition patterns.

The liaison with West Germany was made for completely different reasons. In any European conflict with the Soviets it was obvious that West Germany was going to be the primary battlefield. Consequently during the late 1950s in reaction to this, the country developed a conventional arms manufacturing capability, infrastructure, and training facilities to support its forces. The single limiting resource in this development was land, and consequently a provision needed to be made for a rear area for these activities in the event of war. Because of French withdrawal from its military role in NATO, nations nearby that might serve this purpose were limited to Portugal and Italy. Portugal proved ideal with its Atlantic exposure, natural ports, and relatively mild climate. Accordingly, negotiations were opened, and in 1959 a defense agreement was signed. Between 1960 and 1962 there were more than twenty accords between the two countries initiating the construction of infrastructure, the supply of technologically advanced armaments, and the modernization of defense industries under favorable financial terms to Portugal.[38]

For the navy this development was very significant. The first river patrol boats designed especially for Africa, the *Bellatrix* class, were built in German shipyards. German Maybach diesel engines, designed for ease of maintenance in the harsh African environment, became a prime powerplant in the landing craft and river and coastal patrol boats. The German-origin MG-42 machine gun and the Walther G-3 assault rifle came into use throughout the navy. Moreover, whenever there was a shortage of munitions in the African campaign, Germany promptly and without question supplied them to Portugal.[39]

It thus developed that there would be two distinct navies very distant from one another during the 1960 to 1974 period. There would be one in Africa financed by Portugal and supported with its national resources and those of France and Germany. The other would be operating with NATO in the North Atlantic and be financed by U.S. aid and British-

U.S. technical support.[40]

The later needs of the colonial conflict not only expanded the navy but took it in an amphibious direction to address the African littoral and riverine environment. The coastal and riverine fleet in Africa grew from 15 patrol ships, 10 patrol boats, and a gunboat in 1960 to 17 patrol ships, 43 patrol boats, and no less than 83 landing craft of various types and sizes in 1970, an expansion from 26 to 143 units without any rigid plan.[41] The vessels ranged from small patrol craft of 30 tons to considerably more capable craft of 200 tons.[42] Its amphibious force of landing craft in three different sizes of increasing capability was literally created from scratch.[43] This loosely guided development rather followed the demonstrated needs of each theater commander. Unfortunately there were continuing requests from each for additional ships that resulted in an almost inexorable expansion across Africa. This constant augmentation caused the Minister of the Navy in September 1970 to declare that there would be no more ships without a "full justification." The African navy consequently stabilized, and at the end of 1973 it stood at 137 units, with which it had to provide security over approximately 920 miles of navigable rivers and 120 miles of the Lake Niassa coast.[44] While it also had to provide coastal security, this was not a substantial factor in either Angola (Atlantic Ocean) or Mozambique (Indian Ocean) because of the lack of insurgent seaborne capability and the distance of any fighting from these coasts. This was a positive development, as planners had anticipated an insurgent effort similar to that encountered by the French Navy in Algeria and Indochina and the U.S. Navy in Vietnam, in which the insurgents attempted to supply their forces by sea disguised as merchants or fishermen. This attempted logistical link necessitated a rigorous and costly coastal inspection effort by the French, South Vietnamese, and U.S. navies.

The fleet expansion also included an augmentation and shift in types of personnel. In 1946 there were 719 officers and 5,550 men.[45] By 1960 there were 887 officers and 8,583 men, a 50 percent expansion.[46] By 1974 total personnel had more than doubled to 19,500 officers and men, of whom 3,400 were *Fuzileiros*.[47] The *Fuzileiros* had their origin in the formation of the Terço da Armada Real (Royal Naval Regiment) by the Portuguese Crown in 1618. Deactivated in 1890, they remained so until 1961 except for a brief period from 1924 to 1926. Responsible for maritime and riverine security, the *Fuzileiros* played key and varying roles in all of the African theatres, of which we will hear more later.

In the 1960s Portugal faced opponents with an aggregate of 27,000 troops. The UPA had an active force of about 6,200 men based in the former Belgian Congo. The MPLA was not much of a force militarily until 1966, when it opened its eastern front from Zambia with an estimated strength of 4,700. UNITA, operating from an area within southeast Angola under terms that had been negotiated with the Portuguese, mustered about 500 men who were restricted to fighting the MPLA.[48] The PAIGC first fielded a small force in 1962 and by 1973 had 5,000 regular troops and 1,500 militia. FRELIMO by the early 1970s had an active force of 7,200 regulars and 2,400 popular militia.[49] The various insurgent units were spread across three distinct theaters of operations and carried various degrees of competence. In Angola following the 15 March 1961 *jacquerie*, the UPA and MPLA forces immediately across the northern border represented more of a policing problem than any threat of a major assault because of internal political, training, discipline, and logistic problems. Later in the east, however, the MPLA became a difficult and skilled opponent operating from the newly-available Zambian sanctuary. In Guiné, the PAIGC were always a highly motivated and formidable foe and were aided by the terrain and neighboring sanctuaries that helped to reduce the colony to a besieged enclave. In Mozambique, FRELIMO was isolated in the north of the theater and faced long distances over often open and sparsely populated terrain to engage concentrations of the population or troop formations. With some exceptions the insurgents in all theaters operated in small bands and traveled long distances to set ambushes, collect taxes, gather food, and recruit troops. Rarely did they stay and fight. The military job of the Portuguese Navy was to control the waterways in enemy areas, inhibit insurgent movement, counter these small groups through ambushes in the riverine areas, project power ashore, and supply villages and troops. Alongside this were the political duties of reassuring the population with recurring naval presence and psychosocial support and gathering intelligence. As we shall see, it did this with a well-conceived strategy that was properly executed with appropriate means.

The seemingly *ad hoc* and "make do" approach to brown water resources was characteristic of other similar conflicts, particularly the French experience in Indochina and the United States in Vietnam. The French Navy was faced with policing both the Mekong River Delta in Cochinchina and the Red River Delta in Tonkin, as these waterway systems were the principal communication routes and a major economic importance in this undeveloped country. The Mekong Delta has 1,500 miles of natural waterways and another 2,500 miles of canals.[50] The Red River in its lower reaches connects with other waterways to form a network that extends some 2,000 miles in forming the Red River Delta.[51] In 1946 the French faced a force of 30,000 Viet Minh operating in and around the Red River Delta. In the south they faced an additional 12,000 enemy.[52] These were troops operating in and for their homeland, where familiarity with the terrain, the people, and the language gave them a distinct advantage, unlike multi-ethnolinguistic Portuguese Africa. To counter this force and its use of the waterways the French devoted an inadequate flotilla of about 60 vessels of various types to the Mekong Delta and another of about 30 vessels to the Red River Delta and were always in need of additional craft to counter the enemy.[53] They were remarkably successful in adapting the available matériel, generally from U.S. surplus stocks, to the imperatives of brown water or riverine warfare. The majority of ships and craft had been originally designed and built for amphibious operations in World War II and thus had little or no armor. To these was added the necessary protection to withstand the shock of surprise encounters at short ranges. They were also armed to deliver the heavy volume of fire needed to counter an ambush and to engage all types of targets along the waterways. The French could never fully control either delta. They also never had the means to extend their brown water operations and thus project their power beyond the two deltas, but indeed these were the most important areas to control. While the force performed well as far as it went, it was limited in its combat power and radius of action. As the Viet Minh became more capable, the French brown water navy became increasingly circumscribed in its abilities.

In 1965, the United States and South Vietnam faced an estimated 80,000 Viet Cong and their sympathizers in the Mekong Delta. Of these some 30,000 were estimated to be regular troops and 50,000 part-time insurgents capable of operating in battalion-sized units.[54] A force of this size had considerable logistic requirements, and when its sea line of communication was denied, it was forced to rely completely on the canals of the Mekong from Cambodia and the "Ho Chi Minh Trail" through Cambodia and Laos. In contrast to the small French force, the U.S. Navy developed and operated a varied fleet of about 619 inshore vessels to gain control the Mekong Delta alone.[55] This fleet was over and above the approximately 600 armed seagoing junks of the Vietnamese Navy and the additional blue water forces of the Seventh Fleet operating off the coast and interdicting its use.

The U.S. Navy was ill-prepared for riverine warfare in the mid-1960s and the small-boat operations that it required. Once commenced, however, it took just three years from the spring of 1965 to the fall of 1968 for the Navy to penetrate and dominate the furthest reaches in the maze of waterways comprising the Mekong Delta. The expansion was a rushed affair that necessitated extensive improvisation of equipment, organization and tactics; however, it remains one of the strategic and tactical successes of U.S. involvement in Vietnam.[56] The initial order of 120 patrol boats, for example, was based on a modified commercial sport craft with the designation River Patrol Boat (PBR), Mark I. It weighed seven tons, had a top speed of 25 knots, a length of 10 meters, and was armed with a .50-caliber machinegun forward and three M-60 (7.62-mm) machineguns or MK-18 grenade launchers on the sides and stern. For a little *ad hoc* craft, it was very potent. The second group of 80 was ordered in March 1967 with some modifications and was designated the Mark II. The PBR force level reached 250 by late 1968. Landing Ships Tank (LST) were reactivated from the reserve fleet and converted as required into mother ships, barracks ships, and repair ships. Landing Craft Medium (LCM) were drawn from stocks and modified as armored troop carriers, command and control boats, assault support boats, and refuelers. Tactics were borrowed from earlier French operations and adjusted as needed. Aviation support was cobbled together, and several specialized aviation squadrons were formed to support riverine operations. With this virtual *ad hoc* armada developed on short notice, the U.S. Navy gained control of the Mekong and successfully and impressively denied its use to the enemy.

The forgoing broad-gauged overview is summarized in Table 2.2 as an aid in comparing the three riverine campaigns. Except for the Angola uprisings of 1961, the Portuguese faced no insurgent army, as in Indochina and Vietnam, that massed troops and employed them in conventional ways. The Portuguese dealt largely with small bands, as embodied in the PAIGC *bi-groupo* of twenty-six men. An insurgent force of as many as 200 men was rare. As the territories were sparsely inhabited, the terrain difficult and, in Angola and Mozambique, vast, finding insurgents was a considerable challenge. Where they were encountered, fights were brief affairs, as their staying power was relatively limited. Hence the African navy was tailored more specifically to this type of enemy and the threat that it posed. In contrast, the Viet Minh and North Vietnamese tended to operate in larger troop concentrations, moving clandestinely through remote countryside with relatively large and sophisticated logistic tails to effect an engagement. Consequently, when encountered by either the French or the U.S. Navy, it was going to be a heavier force applied with different intentions generally than those of the African insurgents. The French suffered a paucity of resources, and while successful as far as they went, were limited in their capabilities and could never fully destroy the enemy or deny it access to the waterways. Air and artillery support for river landings and subsequent enemy engagement were only irregularly available. In contrast, while the United States faced a heavier foe in numbers and sophistication, it was able to counter effectively with the well choreographed application of air power, waterborne armament, and infantry landings. Portuguese resources, while relatively modest in the context of the U.S. involvement in Vietnam, were always adequate to accomplish the mission of denying the enemy use of the waterways. By January 1969, the U.S. Navy literally owned the Mekong Delta, and the southern flanks of Saigon were secure. The conclusion to be drawn from Table 2.2, however approximate, is that the Portuguese and U.S. Navy each tailored their forces appropriately for both the enemy each faced and the waterways to be policed. In contrast, the French would have needed perhaps another 800 vessels to gain effective control of the Mekong and Red River Deltas in light of the determined Viet Minh and the complexity of the two waterway systems.

Table 2.2: Riverine Naval Comparison

	Portuguese Navy	French Navy	U.S. Navy
Estimated Primary Waterways (nautical miles)	1,040	6,000	4,000
Naval Units	137	90	619
Miles of Waterway per Unit	7.59	66.67	6.46
Enemy Troop Strength	27,000	42,000	80,000

Emerging Strategy

Logically speaking, one might have thought that the various naval plans would be a reflection of Portuguese national policy and strategy and the naval policy and strategy that would have naturally flowed from it. Such was not the case, as there was no formal document describing any of these.[57] Without such guidance, the proposed fleet composition became subject to any number of variables. As Sacchetti ably points out, the definition of a particular strategy and its evolution is so often the result of a subsequent analysis to explain what happened and why it happened as it did, rather than an established process to guide future activity.[58]

This problem is not uniquely Portuguese, as the history of the U.S. Navy, for instance, is replete with examples of its finding itself unprepared to fight in restricted waters and having no strategy, written or otherwise. While the U.S. Navy has routinely operated in enclosed waters, it has paid inadequate attention to fighting in this environment and has deigned to anticipate and address the strategic and operational aspects of "brown water" operations. In both world wars it was called to build vast numbers of small combat vessels and train their crews under an accelerated program. In each case at the conclusion of the conflict the forces were disbanded, the ships and craft discarded, and the lessons forgotten.[59] This process was repeated in Korea and Vietnam, and operations today in the Persian Gulf reflect a complete lack of strategy, proper force composition, and training to fight in restricted waters. So historically speaking, it was not surprising that there was no formal document establishing either national or naval strategy when the crisis of the *ultramar* occurred.[60] This vacuum left the Portuguese Naval Staff to a considerable extent feeling its way along in search of solutions to the security of its African waterways.

This ambivalence and indecision was, in all fairness, caused by a shifting national policy from one of looking toward Europe and the United States within the Atlantic Alliance membership to one of renewed concern for the *ultramar*. National policy is a statement of national interests, and in its pursuit it will create and direct war, if it has to be initiated to realize national goals. National strategy is that activity that strives directly to attain the objectives of policy and is the method of applying and coordinating all of the elements of national power, military, diplomatic, economic, and ideological, to form a cohesive effort in realizing policy. The military component of national strategy, the one that concerns us here, is the applied or threatened use of military force to impose policy.[61] It is subordinate to national strategy and should be coordinated with the use of other elements of national power. Naval policy and strategy are a further component of military strategy. With these concepts and their relationship established, it is important to put Portuguese national policy and strategy in context as a prelude to examining the resultant naval subset.

The national policy of Portugal and the rationale for the deployment and use of the Portuguese armed forces in Africa was always to attain the political objective of maintaining the integrity of the Empire. This policy reflected the Portuguese politico-strategic philosophy of holding its widely dispersed territories as an insoluble traditional empire in a geopolitical environment generally hostile to such a notion.[62] The Empire was officially seen as a heritage and a promise of a richer future. This notion was captured in an editorial by Dr. Marcello Caetano in *O Mundo Português* [Portuguese World] that appeared in 1935: "Africa is for us a moral justification and a raison d'être as a power. Without it we would be a small nation; with it, we are a great country."[63] From this perspective any fragmentation would not only betray the past but would reduce the Empire to a modest European country. This seeming catastrophe was to be avoided at all costs. Salazar was particularly sensitive to the vulnerability of Portuguese Africa to the nationalist movements that had gained ascendancy following World War II, and particularly to the local resistance within its African population. During this period, the democratized European powers in Africa were freeing their colonial possessions in step with the post-war trend. There was thus increasing pressure for Portugal to move in line with the Western European governments and to allow its colonies to become independent. The sensitivity to this pressure was likewise reinforced by a very deep and ingrained anticommunist Cold War stance by Portugal. Salazar's hatred and mistrust of communism played an important role, as he was very much aware of the impotence of the West to contain the "economically bankrupt but politically ascendant" communism.[64] Salazar was of the common view following World War II that with the German bulwark dismantled, an unchecked Soviet Union would engulf Europe. Few, he believed, understood the acquisitive and imperialistic character of Soviet leadership despite the fact that Stalin in the aftermath of World War II had annexed over 600,000 square kilometers of Eastern Europe and had brought an additional 87 million non-Russians under his rule. The place of Portugal was alongside the democratic nations that had won the war, and the collective security arrangement of NATO was the only logical way to contain the threat. This national policy had led Portugal and its armed forces into a NATO orientation at the expense of colonial policing.

When the Soviet Union found itself checked in Europe, it sought other avenues of expansion to realize its national policy of creating a world communist order directed from the Kremlin. The Soviets regarded Africa as a fruitful ground for subversion despite the Congo setback, and Portuguese Africa was one of their valued targets.[65] Characteristic of this African policy was the disturbing development from the 6 December 1960 meeting in Moscow of the "Congress of 81" communist countries. At first, little attention was paid to the Congress by the West, as its last meeting in 1957 had attracted only thirteen countries. However, in the minutes of this widely publicized recent gathering, Portugal was specifically targeted for subversive activity.[66] It was asserted that the way to topple the Salazar government, which had refused even to establish diplomatic ties with the Soviet

Union, and to replace it with one friendly to the communist sphere was through the vulnerability of its colonies. According to Soviet logic, if Portugal could be separated from its colonies in a debilitating war as well as politically undermined at home, then a weakened Salazar would topple. Nikita Khrushchev seemed to confirm the first of this two-pronged strategy in his famous and disturbing speech on "wars of national liberation" delivered at this noisy and threatening forum. This direct challenge was a clear threat to Portuguese Africa.

In countering this threat, the Portuguese national strategy devolved from the policy of maintaining the Empire with all of its promise and rested on the mobilization of national power along the following lines:

1. Military action would maintain order in the colonies and expel or defeat the insurgents in combat.
2. Diplomatic efforts would support military action by seeking to nullify the activities of Portugal's adversaries, strengthen ties with allies, and forge new alliances, and while not accepting the legitimacy of the terrorist organizations, seek to open a dialogue with them toward a peaceful solution that did not compromise Portuguese sovereignty.
3. Socioeconomic development within the colonies would improve the lot of the colonial population and make it feel ideologically a part of greater Portugal.[67]

This reasoning would have been apparent to the naval staff attempting to wrestle with the decision of resource allocation and the nature of the fleet to be built, and its members would likely have been torn between addressing the future of Portugal in Europe and in the *ultramar*.

There was an unofficial school of thought developed by Admiral Armando Júlio de Roboredo e Silva, who regularly wrote a column titled "Chronicles of the *Ultramar*" (*Crónica do Ultramar*) in the old journal *Anais de Marinha* (*Annals of the Navy*) during the 1950s. In 1956 as a commander (*capitão de frigata*), he published a seminal article in an effort to highlight a redefined naval policy in the *ultramar*, and while it was merely an expression of his opinion, it was, nevertheless, the beginning of a coherent and thoughtful look at naval policy for Africa.[68] When at the beginning of the war the now Rear Admiral Roboredo was promoted to Deputy Chief of Staff and then between 1963 and 1970 served as Chief of Staff, naval policy had crystallized under his hand into a firm operational plan with the means to execute it.

In a later article, a protégé of Roboredo, Commander Manuel Pereira Crespo, described national policy and the rationale for deployment and use of the military, and particularly the navy, to be the attainment of the political objective of maintaining the integrity of the Empire. He began an examination of the role of the navy based on the experiences of other Western militaries in encountering an insurgency.[69] He noted that there were a number of common errors committed initially in addressing the type of insurgency that Portugal would fight and that other Western nations had faced in their overseas possessions, and he would attempt to identify these in the Portuguese context.

First, there were generally insufficient means available locally to counter problems when they began. This situation was certainly true in Angola, and the author was prescient in so writing some six months before the March 1961 attacks, as the navy was attempting to bolster its security in the *ultramar*.

Second, military units were generally poorly structured and inadequately armed to conduct the operations unique to an insurgency. Normally units were structured for the conventional war, force-on-force scenario and not for the patient work of tracking insurgents over difficult terrain and separating them from the source of their strength, the population. This premise likewise held for naval forces that were oriented toward blue water operations and that needed to be reoriented toward the rivers and inshore waters.

Third, the tactical employment of such forces tended to be conventionally oriented and thus could create more problems that it would solve. Such mismatched employment often played into the hands of the insurgents by alienating the population through an overreaction to a provocation or a misunderstanding of the political nature of an insurgency.

Fourth, personnel were often unprepared physically, morally, and militarily for the missions that they were to perform. Counterinsurgency required training just as specific as conventional war. Soldiers, sailors, and *Fuzileiros* needed to know the enemy and his environment, whether it was a Soviet submarine in the ocean depths or an insurgent patrol in the jungle depths.

Such teachings and lessons initially held only a passing interest with the military chiefs and their staffs, as they were far more fascinated with the large, multi-national exercises and operations in Europe and the North Atlantic.[70] The study of insurgency in the Portuguese military staff colleges had been treated more as a curiosity and simply a form of popular revolt that was sporadic and isolated but not in the mainstream of worthy topics. It began to receive more attention with the French military involvement in Algeria (1954–1962), beginning in 1959 with the Portuguese Army mission to the Centre d'Instruction de Pacification et Contre-Guerrilla (CIPCG) at Arzew in Oran province. This was a counterinsurgency school founded in 1956 that ran a series of arduous courses tailored for sector commanders (lieutenant colonels and colonels), district and sub-district commanders (lieutenants to majors), and junior officers and officer cadets and aimed at preparing them for their duties in Algeria and the waging of revolutionary war.[71] Also in February 1959, Roboredo initiated a request for an officer and three ratings to undergo Royal Marine training in what would become a first step in the reactivation of the Portuguese *Fuzileiros*.[72] As this awareness and interest increased within service circles, a naval strategy for counterinsurgency in Africa began to emerge.

In fighting a subversive war, a navy extends its traditional twin tasks of securing the open seas for friendly use and of denying their use to the enemy to encompass the narrow seas, lakes, and rivers of its threatened territories. Travel and traffic by water have always been cheaper and easier than by land, and thus in the rural, less developed areas, particularly in Africa, the contiguous waterways of a colony serve as vital arteries for commerce and war. Narrow seas, lakes, and rivers in particular hold great significance for military operations, as they present a natural obstacle to maneuver and provide ideal defensive terrain. They serve as natural boundaries to a battlefield. They are navigation aids and provide orientation. They are avenues of approach for combat and lines of communication for logistic operations. The enemy will likewise recognize their significance and value and seek to control the population, commerce, and combat along these waterways. In any insurgency the population is the actual battleground, and the contest is for the loyalty of the people. Thus, a navy in counterinsurgency must fight for the effect that it can secure ashore where people live. Because of this land orientation, its operations will almost always be a joint enterprise with ground and air elements.

The naval role in counterinsurgency differs little in the broad sense from that of the army in that insurgency is primarily a political problem affecting the population. The population will have grievances that must be addressed to counter the promises and claims of the insurgents. Once this is done, the slow and patient job of "reconquering the disaffected or neutral population and protecting and supporting those elements that remain faithful" must commence.[73] This task is the goal of a broad psychosocial offensive that will require close and regular contact with the population through medical visits to villages, public works projects, and physical protection from enemy intimidation.

All of these are jobs that the military can perform well and in doing so maintain valuable and positive contact with the population. The medical corps of the various services can improve the general health of the population and educate it in hygiene practices so that it can better care for itself. Military engineers can improve local commerce and health by expanding the traditional village infrastructure. Building schools and market places, drilling wells, and installing cattle watering troughs and community washhouses are all classic projects undertaken successfully during this type of war. This last job of physical security is one for the combat forces and generally requires organizing a local militia with a quick reaction regular force prepared to support it in time of crisis. With the rebuilding of trust in the population, confidence in the Portuguese government and its institutions would likewise be built, and the vital intelligence needed to fight the insurgent would flow. The vulnerable population will tend to side with the force it perceives to be the ultimate winner in this conflict, hence the psychological impact of every action must be considered. Not only must the military elements of the insurgency be destroyed, but more importantly its political organization dismembered and reduced, and these tasks are best accomplished through a broad advance on both military and civil fronts. In this context, the physical terrain, sophistication of infrastructure, strength and effectiveness of the enemy, and disposition and preparedness of the civilian population are among the foremost variables to be addressed. As the well-being of the population is the signal concern, and it lives ashore, the army will be the lead force with air and naval support. This latter support in Portuguese eyes was to be realized through a naval strategy embodied in half a dozen primary naval missions.[74]

First, as rivers, lakes, and the sea form most of the frontiers in Portuguese Africa, control of these fluvial and maritime borders was critical to limiting the flow of arms, infiltration of insurgents, and enemy logistic lines of communication, and was a primary naval mission. It required a full range of naval craft from small launches or vedette boats of modest size to more capable, larger craft for policing narrow seas or open ocean areas. Equipped with a solid communications suite and aviation support, such a fleet could present a formidable barrier to frontier penetration and complicate the insurgent's infiltration problem. In reality while this was conceptually sound, the resources required to seal any of the colonial borders were neither available nor affordable to any nation, even the wealthiest of the time. The river borders of Angola, for instance, consisted primarily of the River Zaire (66 nautical miles), the Cuango River (146 nautical miles), the Cassai River (253 nautical miles), Cuando River (121 nautical miles), Cunene River (152 nautical miles), the Cubango River (182 nautical miles), plus numerous smaller rivers totaling approximately 121 nautical miles. These river borders all together totaled approximately 1,040 nautical miles or 40 percent of the 2,643 nautical mile Angolan land border. Most of the river borders were located in remote and sparsely inhabited areas. Such a lengthy and isolated frontier was difficult to police even with a forceful naval presence. Indeed, naval forces could be organized and used more effectively in engaging the enemy in his known areas of operation or in supporting the population rather than in any series of static or locally mobile border patrols spread through the remote reaches of these rivers and consequentially absorbing large amounts of resources without commensurate gain. This reasoning was based on the fact that along these remote waterways enemy infiltration was very limited because of the difficult and isolated terrain. When borders were breached, insurgents faced many more days of travel through inaccessible and inhospitable country in a lengthy search for an opportunity to engage government troops, proselytize the population, or destroy infrastructure. As a consequence, naval forces were concentrated in the more accessible riverine areas where insurgent crossings were more likely because of the potentially lucrative targets of population and infrastructure.

Second, the transport and resupply of land forces in the waterway environment was a critical task. Portuguese Africa to a large extent and particularly in Guiné relied on rivers, lakes, and maritime coastline as its primary routes of communication for virtually every purpose. In Angola, there are 750 nautical miles of littoral and myriad rivers covering the vast colony, six of which were identified above. In Mozambique, the 1,400-nautical mile Indian Ocean littoral acted as the primary north-south artery, there being no competing parallel railroads or main highways. In addition to the ocean and many small waterways, there were also five important rivers in the Rovuma, Lúrio, Zambeze, Save, and Limpopo, which acted as primary east-west communication routes well into the interior of the colony and often beyond its western frontier into the neighboring countries. In Guiné, the lion's share of all traffic was water-borne on its rivers and narrow seas. These waterways were the key in many cases, and especially in Guiné, to the rapid redeployment of forces to counter enemy moves and to gain an advantage in out-maneuvering him.

Third, fire support of forces ashore has always been a key naval role, and counterinsurgency is no different. Artillery is a heavy weapon both in the weight of the gun itself and its ammunition. In the littoral and riverine environment such weapons are easily moved to the point of engagement and supported by naval vessels. Towed artillery cannot be moved easily in terrain broken by waterways and crossed by little more than trails or rutted tracks, nor can it be brought to bear on the enemy in a timely way and thus with any hope of success. River and coastal gunboats thus served an indispensable role in bringing relatively big guns to the fight rapidly.

The same can be said for aviation. Helicopters and light aircraft operating in conjunction with coastal or riverine craft could quickly deliver a blow to the enemy. Helicopters, configured either as gunships, or troop carriers, or a combination, could deliver heavy machine gun or cannon fire in support of disembarking ground forces and make these same forces far more potent than an insurgent unit. A naval-supplied base had the potential to refuel, rearm and return a helicopter to the fight quickly because of its proximity as opposed to that of a distant airfield. Aircraft tied to a far-off base potentially will be delayed in arriving and constrained in their time over the target because of extended transit times.

Fourth, just as the navy supported land forces, it also supported the police and other government law enforcement functions. These functions were critical in protecting the population and gathering intelligence across the entire threatened territory. Insurgency, because it was aimed at the population, deeply involved the police, customs, and immigration authorities, and to the extent that the littoral and river waterways required their presence, the navy facilitated their work.

Fifth, the maintenance of secure riverine and maritime communication routes was important not only in extending government authority throughout the territory but in maintaining the commercial and personal links within the population. While land routes were vulnerable to interruption, waterways were much less so, and if properly protected and policed, provided a valuable alternative. This was done with a small naval force regularly revisiting populated areas, patrolling selected routes, and becoming familiar with its local environment so that any change was readily noticeable and appropriate action could be taken. The maintenance of secure waterways included not only armed vessels underway, but equally as important, troops patrolling ashore where the population lived.

Sixth, as the land was where the population resided and the enemy operated for the most part, it was important to project power ashore. To do this with maximum effectiveness required the combined arms of air, naval, and land forces. In this context, naval forces planed and coordinated operations with army and air force units to bring maximum force to bear on the enemy to ensure his destruction. The most effective operations were those involving small, well-trained, and agile units. These relied on a heightened effectiveness achieved through surprise, mobility, and coordinated action that only smaller units could deliver. Large forces of any nature provided significant advance warning to the enemy, as they and their movements could not be concealed. Their operations took much time, talent, and manpower to organize and, when launched, were no secret. The insurgent could avoid contact or choose the battlefield. Results for government forces were thus generally disappointing. Conversely, if the insurgent massed large numbers, he too would present a high profile and would be vulnerable to conventional attack, playing into the hands of the stronger government forces. The constant pressure of small units in their low-key, low-cost approach was far more effective. Such units of well trained men who could penetrate rugged terrain to gather intelligence, kill insurgents, disrupt food collection and courier traffic, call down naval gunfire or air strikes where appropriate, and above all, maintain the all important contact with the population were most effective. Naval *Fuzileiros*, air force paratroops, and army commandos were just such specialized forces that operated effectively with naval and air support. This systematic and coordinated approach proved successful in keeping the initiative away from the insurgent.

Last, one of the most important factors in any successful insurgency was the availability of a sanctuary from which the insurgents could launch attacks on the government. Sanctuaries enable the insurgent to plan, train, arm, equip, and launch attacks, and when these have been completed, recover and rest from their operations in an area comparatively free from any threat by government forces. It served as a secure supply depot and headquarters for the insurgent leaders. Within the sanctuary, which was generally a sovereign country that shared a frontier, the insurgents were usually confined to one or more border bases by the host country. As controversial as it might be politically, cross-border operations were important to eliminate these bases and the consequent insurgent capabilities that they supported. Keeping the insurgent off-balance and on the defensive limited his ability to conduct effective operations against the government.

Between 1961 and 1974, the Portuguese Navy either performed or contributed to the performance of all of these missions. It extended active Portuguese presence from the coast inland along the river routes, and in the case of landlocked waters, transported vessels overland to be used on these bodies. From judicially situated depots and bases, it established and secured lines of communication in support of both near and remote populations and military operations. It brought with it important supporting firepower and in combined operations with its sister services multiplied their effect. It undertook effective crossborder attacks to neutralize insurgent presence in sanctuaries. The Portuguese Navy adapted well to the war that it had to fight and became an effective "brown water" navy. It learned well by doing and continually refined its approach, as is evident in its study of and adaptation to new doctrine and operational concepts. This evolution was made even more remarkable in that the Portuguese Navy not only learned to fight a new type war successfully but did so while shouldering additional NATO commitments occasioned by French withdrawal and new responsibilities. For a developing navy whose reach extended from its commitments in the North Atlantic to its widely spread operations in Africa, this was truly a remarkable achievement.

Notes

1 Francisco Comacho, "Baixa do Cassange," *Grande Reportagem* 137 (August 2002): 62–77. See also John P. Cann, "Baixa do Cassange: Catalyst for Righting a Wrong," *Revista Militar* 2508 (January 2011):17–32.

2 José Alberto Lopes Carvalheira, "Acção da Marinha em Águas Interiores (1961–1971)" [Naval Operations in Inland Waters (1961–1971)], in the unpublished collection *Participação da Armada na Defesa das Províncias Ultramarinas* [Participation of the Navy in the Defense of the Overseas Provinces], TMs [photocopy], 1972, 1.

3 Ibid., 2.

4 Peter Forbath, *The River Congo* (New York: Harper & Row, 1977), 384.

5 Adam Hochschild, *King Leopold's Ghost* (New York: Houghton Mifflin, 1998), 301.

6 Mike Hoar, *Congo Warriors* (London: Robert Hale, 1991), 10.

7 Forbath, 388.

8 Hoar, 11.

9 Ibid., 12.

10 Forbath, 390.

11 Hoar, 12.

12 Ibid., 13.

13 Ibid.

14 Forbath, 393.

15 Kaúlza de Arriaga, *Sinteses* [Synthesis] (Lisbon: Privately printed, 1992), 190.

16 Decreto-Lei Nº 41059, 8 April 1957, preamble.

17 Abílio Freire da Cruz Júnior, "Evolução das Infra-estructuras da Armada no Ultramar" [Evolution of Naval Infrastructure in the *Ultramar*], in the unpublished collection *Participação da Armada na Defesa das Províncias Ultramarinas* [Participation of the Navy in the Defense of the Overseas Provinces], TMs [photocopy], Lisbon: Ministério de Marinha, 1972, 1.

18 Telo, 530.

19 Cruz Júnior, 2; Portaria Nº 17 352 of 15 September 1959.

20 David do Nascimento Francosco, "Respigos da Guerra colonial em Angola" [Gleanings from the colonial war in Angola], *Revista Marinha* 5, No. 12 (January/February/March 2008), http://www.mga.gv.ao/revistamarinha/edicao12/memoria.htm (accessed 31 July 2011).

21 José Luís Leiria Pinto, "As Comuniçõess na Marinha: Dos primórdios a 1975" [Naval Communications: From the Beginning to 1975], Presentation in the Academia de Marinha, Lisbon, 1 June 2010, 8, http://

www.marinha.pt/PT/amarinha/actividade/areacultural/academiademarinha/Documents/textos_conferencias/1JUN10.pdf (accessed 31 July 2011).

22 Turíbio Abreu, "Infraestructuras Navais no Ultramar" [Naval Infrastructure in the *Ultramar*], *Anais do Clube Militar Naval* (April–June 1967): 427.

23 A. Alves Lopes, "Revista das Revistas" [Review of the Reviews], *Anais do Clube Militar Naval* (July–September 1962): 878.

24 António José Malheiro García, "Particiação da Armada na Defesa das Provincias Ultramarinas, Actividade Oceânica, Breve Retrospectiva da Actividade Naval na Década de 50" [Participation of the Navy in the Defense of the Overseas Provinces, Oceanic Role, Retrospective Brief of the Naval Role in the Decade of the 50s], in the unpublished collection *Participação da Armada na Defesa das Províncias Ultramarinas* [Participation of the Navy in the Defense of the Overseas Provinces], TMs [photocopy], Lisbon: Ministério de Marinha 1972, 1; and António José Telo, *História da Marinha Portuguesa: Doutrinas e Organização, 1924–1974* [History of the Portuguese Navy: Doctrine and Organization, 1924–1974] (Lisbon: Academia de Marinha, 1999), 336–346.

25 Ministério da Marinha, *A Marinha nos Últimos 40 Anos, 1926–1966* [The Navy in the Last 40 Years, 1926–1966] (Lisbon: Ministério da Marinha, 1966), chart facing 136.

26 García, 2.

27 Ibid., 2.

28 Cruz Júnior, 1.

29 García, 3.

30 Telo, 536.

31 Ibid., 536.

32 António Emílio Sacchetti, "A Armada nas Campanhas de África" [The Navy in the African Campaigns], *Revista da Armada* (May 1997): 6.

33 The four frigates would be the *Comandante João Belo* (F480) (class name), *Comandante Hermenegildo Capelo* (F481), *Comandante Roberto Ivens* (F482), and *Comandante Sacadura Cabral* (F483) built between 1967 and 1969 and displacing 2,230 tons gross. The four submarines would be the *Albacora* (S163) (class name), *Barracuda* (S164), *Cachalote* (S165), and *Delfim* (S166) built between 1967 and 1969 and displacing 868 tons surfaced.

34 The three frigates would be the *Almirante Pereira da Silva* (F472) (class name), *Almirante Gago Coutinho* (F473), and *Almirante Magalhães Correira* (F474) built between 1966 and 1968 and displacing 1,914 tons gross.

35 Telo, 561.

36 Ibid., 562.

37 Ibid., 522.

38 Ibid., 524.

39 Ibid., 525. Given the politics of the time, none of these bore German marks of origin in order to prevent attribution and consequent accusations by the insurgent organizations that Germany was taking sides.

40 Ibid., 526.

41 Ibid., 543.

42 Armando de Roboredo, "Marinha de Guerra Portuguesa na actual conjuntura" [The Portuguese Navy Meeting Current Challenges], *Anais do Clube Militar Naval* (July–September 1965): 480.

43 Ibid.

44 Estado-Maior do Exército (EME), *Resenha Histórico-Militar das Campanhas de África (1961–1974)* [Historical-Military Report on the African Campaigns (1961–1974)] (Lisbon: Estado-Maior do Exército, 1989), Vol. II, 19–20; and A. Teixeira da Mota, *Guiné Portuguesa* [Portuguese Guiné] (Lisbon: Agência

Geral do Ultramar, 1954), 128. Only the navigable river distances are used in the calculations, as coastal security was not a significant factor in either Angola (Atlantic Ocean) or Mozambique (Indian Ocean) because of the lack of insurgent seaborne capability and the distance of any fighting from these coasts. Insurgents could and did cross non-navigable sections, which in Angola, Guiné, and Mozambique were substantial, but it was not practicable to establish waterborne river patrols on these bodies because of shallow depths, narrow widths, or rapids.

45 *Jane's Fighting Ships 1946-47* (London, Sampson Low, Marston & Co., 1947), 252–258.

46 *Jane's Fighting Ships 1960-1961* (London: Jane's Fighting Ships Publishing Co., 1961), 251–256.

47 *Jane's Fighting Ships 1974-75* (London: Jane's Yearbooks, 1975), 267–274.

48 L.H. Gann, "Portugal, Africa, and the Future," *Journal of Modern African Studies* (March 1975): 2–3.

49 John P. Cann, *Counterinsurgency in Africa* (Westport, Conn.: Greenwood Publishing, 1997), 6–7.

50 Robert H. Clegg, ed., *Riverine Warfare* (Quantico: Marine Corps Command and Staff College, 1997), 3.

51 Victor Croizat, *The Brown Water Navy: The River and Coastal War in Indo-China and Vietnam, 1948–1972* (Poole: Blanford Press, 1984), 21.

52 Ibid., 36.

53 Ibid., 59.

54 John Forbes and Robert Williams, *Riverine Force* (New York: Bantam, 1987), 51.

55 Croizat, 150. The figure is for the U.S. riverine force, which was used only in the delta. The oceanic fleet was separate and used for coastal security duties. There was some overlap, but the poor seakeeping abilities of the riverine force restricted it to riverine duties.

56 Forbes and Williams, 27.

57 Sacchetti, 6.

58 Ibid.

59 Milan N. Vigo, *Naval Strategy and Operations in Narrow Seas* (London: Frank Cass, 1999), xvi.

60 Sacchetti, 6.

61 U.S. Marine Corps, *Campaigning* (Washington: U.S. Marine Corps, 1990), 3.

62 Estado-Maior do Exército (EME), *Subsídios para o Estudo da Doutrina Aplicada nas Campanhas de África (1961–1974)* [Aid to the Study of Doctrine Applied in the African Campaigns (1961–1974)] (Lisbon: Estado-Maior do Exército, 1990), 30.

63 Marcello Caetano, "Editorial," *O Mundo Português* [Portuguese World], 2 (1935): 218.

64 Hugh Kay, *Salazar and Modern Portugal* (London: Eyre and Spottswoode, 1970), 69 and 133. The author argues that even in England communism had become "the rallying cry of the revolutionary instincts of our age" and had done so "by power of words, by sheer bluff, perhaps by voluptuousness of contrast." It was largely the success of communist "evangelism" that made Salazar so suspicious of it.

65 Ibid., 238; and Edgar O'Balance, *Tracks of the Bear* (Novato, Calif.: Presidio Press, 1982), 103–112.

66 Jean Valluy, "Au Subjet du Manifeste des 81," *Revue Militaire Générale* (October 1961): 282.

67 Joaquim Moreira da Silva Cunha, *O Ultramar, a Nação e o "25 de Abril"* [The Overseas Provinces, the Nation and the "25th of April"] (Coimbra: Atlântida Editora, 1977), 31–32.

68 Armando de Roboredo, "Subsídios para Definir uma Política Naval Portuguesa" [Aids in Defining a Portuguese Naval Policy], *Anais de Marinha* (September–December 1956): 5–10.

69 Manuel Pereira Crespo, "As Missões das Forcas Navais na Guerra Revolucionária" [The Mission of Naval Forces in Revolutionary War], *Anais do Club Militar Naval* (June–September 1960): 537–550.

70 Ibid., 543.

71 Frédéric Guelton, "The French Army 'Center for Training and Pacification in Counter-Guerrilla Warfare' (CIPCG) at Arzew," trans. Martin S. Alexander, in *France and the Algerian War, 1954–62: Strategy, Operations and Diplomacy*, ed. Martin S. Alexander and J. F. V. Keiger (London: Frank Cass, 2002), 43–

44.

72 A. de Roboredo (*capitão de mar e guerra*), Estado-Maior da Armada, to Jaime Lopes (*capitão de fragata*), Naval Aide, Embassy of Portugal, London, 3 February 1959, memorandum "instrucão de 'comandos'", Coloredo Box 224/2082, Arquivo Central da Marinha, Antiga Fabrica Nacional de Cordoaria, Rua da Junqueira, Lisbon, 1.

73 Ministério da Marinha, *Manual do Fuzileiro – Operações Terrestres Especiais* [Marine Manual – Special Ground Operations] (Vale do Zebro: Escola de *Fuzileiros*, 1962), OT01-07.

74 Crespo, 543–550.

3

Breaking New Ground

The concerted push to assemble and employ the African or "brown water" navy, that is, one with a predominately littoral and riverine configuration, broke relatively new ground for the Portuguese. There was no established competence in building or operating a fleet of small boats and in projecting power throughout the river, lake, and littoral regions of the *ultramar* to the degree of intensity now required. Consequently, the construction of such boats and their management under combat conditions opened an entirely new horizon. The navy embarked on the acquisition of this fleet, the recruiting and training of the officers and men to man it, the re-establishment of the marines or *Fuzileiros* to project power ashore, and the construction of a strategic communications network, each a new venture. All of these were executed with careful and thoughtful moves within the financial and time constraints imposed by the impending African security situation to achieve a synergistic force of combined naval arms. As we shall see, the navy managed this change well and adapted to its new way of war with skill and enthusiasm, solving each problem with imagination and within its means.

The African Navy

Beginning in 1956, the navy departed from convention and energetically pursued the definition and acquisition of craft especially designed for the African mission, as there was a general acknowledgment that it did not have the necessary force capable of operating in the littoral and riverine environment there. In designing the force structure for the African navy, it studied several other forces and their experiences in similar situations and drew on their experience. The British model was useful, and indeed the initial thinking sought to extract certain applicable portions of the Royal Navy and Royal Marine experience, with the latter's commando brigades and special boat service detachments being of particular interest. The French experiences in Indochina and Algeria, however, appeared to be far more relevant. The French organization was smaller than the British one, was less conventionally oriented, and had been through a series of refinements over some nine years (1945–1954) in addressing the Viet-Minh threat in Indochina. Consequently, it provided a rich tapestry of unconventional war experience upon which to draw.

The French military had sought solutions to its power projection difficulties from the beginning of its campaign against the Viet-Minh in an effort to regain control of Indochina following World War II. Indochina represented the most difficult terrain and was characterized by an insidious combination of tropical climate, rugged mountains, impenetrable jungles, and extensive river systems. Tonkin, Annam, and Cochinchina, the three coastal provinces comprising the later entity of Vietnam, were largely roadless areas broken by numerous rivers and thus presented substantial difficulties in the overland movement of conventional forces. The climate is monsoonal, and the torrential rains have over the years chiseled razor-backed ridges and canyons from the bedrock of the jumbled mountain system. The gorges in this mountain range are often so steep that the contour lines on a map sit atop one another. In the central province of Annam there are massive limestone deposits that continue to dissolve in the tropical downpours to form needle-shaped pinnacles, sink holes, and culs-de-sac. Dark, gloomy, multi-canopied jungles with dense undergrowth mantle much of the country. These are festooned with corded vines in the lower levels. Another daunting feature is the huge breaks of bamboo with close-clumped and virtually impenetrable stalks half a foot thick.[1]

Overland troop mobility in this sort of terrain was historically very difficult and presented the French with severe problems. Initially airborne troops were used in an attempt to overcome these obstacles, and the parachutist strength had by 1954 reached the level of fourteen battalions. Unfortunately, because of the comparatively limited French resources, there was never enough lift capability available to move more than two battalions at any one time. It was quickly apparent that airborne operations were not the exclusive answer and that a different approach was needed. With so few roads, the primary lines of communication were naturally the coastal routes and river systems. In the northern province of Tonkin, the Red River and its delta provided the natural highway. In the southern province of Cochinchina, the Mekong provided similarly. The central province of Annam, however, was not so blessed and had many fragmented, shallow, and narrow waterways connected only by the open sea. Annam was thus relatively isolated. This isolation had retarded its economic development and also served the enemy. The French thus moved rapidly to exploit the river systems and to organize a fleet of riverine units to solve their transport, supply, escort and combat needs. The fleet of this brown water navy was composed largely of former U.S. and British landing craft, which were ideal for the Southeast Asian river environment because of their shallow draft. These craft were modified into various combat and transport vessels and supported army and naval operations throughout the nine-year conflict. Of these there are four types that are of interest to our story.

The primary troop, vehicle, and cargo mover for the French river transport force was the former British Landing Craft Tank, Mark 4, or LCT Mk.4, which was in constant use, primarily in Tonkin. There were four available in 1946, and this number had expanded to thirteen by 1954.[2] It was often called the "long LCT" to differentiate it from the U.S. Landing Craft Tank, Mark 6, or LCT (6), nicknamed the "short LCT." While the long LCT extended some 15 meters over its shorter brother, its carrying capacity was a dramatic 350 tons over 150 tons. The long LCT was well adapted to the conditions of Indochina, and this utility made it an attractive cargo vessel for local commercial shipping companies. As a consequence, the second-hand market for the craft was rapidly exhausted following World War II, and these vessels were inevitably in short supply. Those operating commercially in Indochina were often requisitioned by the French military for its major operations. The versatility and consequent popularity of the long LCT in Southeast Asia highlighted the craft to Portuguese naval planners, and a variant of it would become the *Lancha de Desembarque Grande* (Landing Craft Large), series 100 and 200, of the Portuguese African navy.

The true workhorse of the French Navy was the U.S. Landing Craft Medium (LCM), Mark 3, and its larger version, the Mark 6. It was used primarily for transport and patrol, although it performed many other missions as well. Living conditions on the LCMs were very difficult and were particularly so on long patrols. The French modified both the "short" Mark 3 and the "long" Mark 6 with armor and converted the versatile Mark 6 into a number of variants to meet local requirements. Many of these variants were also built from the keel by the Saigon Arsenal with its dry dock and extensive maintenance facilities located in the suburb of Phu My. There were also smaller yards for fleet service at Can Tho (Cantö) and My Tho (Mytho), the first about 120 miles southwest and the second about 60 miles west of Saigon. The French did not differentiate between the short and the long versions in their order of battle. Consequently, the count of 28 craft available in 1946 included both types, and this number had expanded to 91 by 1954, attesting to its utility.[3] The long and short LCMs were the basis for the *Lancha de Desembarque Média* (Landing Craft Medium), series 200 and 300, that would be purchased in the United States and modified in Lisbon. The long LCM likewise would serve as the model for the *Lancha de Desembarque Média,* series 100 and 400, to be built in Lisbon.

Initially twenty-six of the British Landing Craft Assault (LCA) were purchased by the French from Royal Navy stocks in Singapore, and at 9 tons displacement it was somewhat larger than the 7-ton U.S. Landing Craft Vehicle Personnel (LCVP). The LCA was displaced by the apparently more popular LCVP, popular perhaps because it was more readily available from U.S. stocks, and by 1952 the LCA had disappeared from the rivers. The LCVP became one of the most common craft despite the fact that it was comparatively slow, unwieldy, and too noisy for effective patrol work. Likewise, living conditions were particularly difficult in the cramped quarters of these small vessels. Despite the drawbacks, the usefulness of the LCVP prompted the French Navy in 1950 to build its own steel version at the Saigon Arsenal and designate it the *Engin d'Assaut* (EA). There were 32 LCVPs available in 1946, and the number of LCVPs and EAs together had expanded to 88 by 1954.[4] This French experience became for the Portuguese the genesis for the *Lanchas de Desembarque Pequenas* (Landing Craft Small) series built in Lisbon.

Lastly, the French made extensive use of the British Harbour Defense Motor Launch (HDML), a wooden-hulled craft of which over 480 were built during World War II. Originally armed with sonar, depth charges, and small weapons, it was designed to protect river estuaries and harbors against enemy submarines. The French modified it for the riverine environment of Indochina and renamed it the *Vedette de Port* (VP). Unlike the landing craft, the VP brought a strong combination of firepower, protection, communications, and habitability that made it an effective and popular riverine patrol craft. There were eight available in 1946, and this number had expanded to nineteen by 1954. This experience proved an invaluable guide for Portugal in the design of its *Antares*, *Bellatrix* and *Júpiter* classes of patrol boats.

A navy, however, fights only for the effect that it can secure ashore where people live. Sea power and land power are thus a joint enterprise, and to be decisive a naval power must have the capability of going ashore. The transition from naval conflict to land conflict is not an easy one and requires troops organized and trained for this purpose. In the French Navy this force was known as the *fusiliers marins* or sailor fusiliers. Originally formed by recruiting light infantry troops within the navy and training them accordingly through army schools, this organization has a long and proud history dating from the earliest French navies in which there were specialized formations of musketeers assigned to the larger ships. The first serious organization was the work of Cardinal Richelieu, who in 1627 created the *Régiment de la Marine*. Ships were now provided with troops who were capable of combat on both land and sea and who were led by officers attached to the ship. These troops were not simply passengers, for between their soldiering duties they served as an integral part of the ship's company and helped with the lower sails and other shipboard responsibilities.

The formations existed under various names over the centuries, and in December 1945 part of the force manned two river flotillas in Indochina known as the *Flottille Fluviale de Fusiliers Marins* (FFFM). The 1er FFFM was assigned to Tonkin with about thirty assorted craft, and the 2me FFFM to the Mekong with about sixty craft. On 1 January 1947, the two flotillas were reorganized as the *Force Amphibie de la Marine en Indochine* (FAMIC) under the admiral commanding French naval forces in the Far East. This command was split into two groups, the northern group or *Force Amphibie du Nord* (FAN) and the southern group or *Force Amphibie du Sud* (FAS). By the spring of 1947 a more formal division was made between army and naval riverine units, and the naval units became *Groupes de Combat Amphibies* in mid-June. In August these were again reorganized into naval assault divisions, nicknamed *dinassauts* after their formal name *Division Navale d'Assaut* (DNA), and in their constitution represented a natural evolutionary process in supporting land units along the many Indochinese rivers.

As the French experienced increasing frustration in moving both troops and heavy weapons through the road system of Indochina, the land formations of wheeled and tracked vehicles, so vulnerable to mines and ambush, were replaced on the water by DNAs. These DNAs were the nucleus of the French brown water navy. There were ten such units formed during the conflict, and all but one continued until the French withdrawal in 1954. Each DNA was composed of a number of different types of craft to address specific aspects of the threat environment: command and fire support, transport, and patrol and minesweeping, all based on the locally-modified U.S. surplus World War II landing craft medium (LCM). Depending on the task assigned, it would combine these various resources to meet the operational need. The force could be expanded or contracted, as required, and might be as many as two companies of *fusiliers marins* or army troops and a *commando* of 80 men to something smaller. The DNAs could range widely over the interconnected waterways of Cochinchina and Tonkin. The inland waters of Annam, however, were shallow and movement from one waterway to another required an exit to the sea. DNA craft were top-heavy with their armor and were unstable at sea. As a result, small boat units separate from the DNAs were employed in Annam. As Victor Croizat has observed, "This represented a highly flexible operational concept and explains why the *dinassauts* served with little change during the Indochina War, continued later as river assault groups in the Vietnamese Navy, and eventually became the river assault squadrons used by the Americans in Vietnam."[5] It is thus small wonder that this French experience held useful lessons for the Portuguese Navy in managing its forces in the riverine environment.

The primary mission of the French Navy in Algeria was that of foreclosing outside support for the uprising through a rigorous coastal blockade.[6] Consequently, the French naval experience there was less useful to the Portuguese in that the volume of coastal traffic in austral Africa was quite a bit different from that of the Mediterranean. A major shipping lane passed immediately along the 800-nautical mile coast of Algeria, and the task assigned to the French Navy required the monitoring of commercial shipping and fishing vessels in this lane, which had historically been a haven for illicit traffic. This rich smuggling environment afforded the convenient opportunity of potential outside support for the insurgent organization, the *Front de Libération Nationale* or FLN.

Like the Portuguese Navy, the French Navy was rebuilding from the effects of World War II, when the Algerian War began on 1 November 1954. Certainly it was with great relief that the war in Indochina had ended, where for nine years the French Navy had sustained a force of 10,000 men out of its 55,000 total, or about 18 percent. It was anticipating the reestablishment of its fleet and the participation in NATO operations, and not the conduct of coastal surveillance in Algeria.

During this first month, the French Navy in Algeria was strengthened, and the Algerian maritime surveillance or *Sumar* was organized and implemented using the well-founded and proven techniques developed in Indochina. *Sumar* was based on three principals: intelligence to guide the search, aerial reconnaissance to identify and track a suspect, and surface combatants to inspect and divert the target.

Intelligence on potential arms smugglers was gathered from a number of sources that required the close coordination and cooperation between the military and civilian intelligence services. The activities of suspicious vessels in FLN-sympathetic countries were tracked and reported, and when they took on war material, their names were added to either a "red list" or a "black list," depending on their origin and the degree of intelligence confidence. Arms came primarily from Czechoslovakia, Yugoslavia, Poland, and West Germany, sometimes directly but most often through transshipment. While the blockade was very effective, it came at a comparatively high cost in treasure and manpower, as in the end it required approximately 18,000 steaming days for the French ships and some 25,000 flight hours for its surveillance aircraft.[7]

This very effective yet expensive French control of the Mediterranean coastline in an area of voluminous merchant and fishing traffic was not required to the same degree in Portuguese Africa, where the shipping lanes were more removed and less intense. While substantial traffic passed between Guiné and the Cape Verde Islands, no comparable effort was made to smuggle arms directly from this thoroughfare. Likewise in Angola the primary shipping lane was far at sea, and any deviation of a ship from this route in aid of the insurgents would be quickly evident. Further, the fighting in Angola was distant from the coast, so it would be difficult to aid the insurgents from this direction. Even so from 1960 and particularly after March 1961, the Portuguese authorities in Angola considered every vessel transiting the coast a potential target for smuggling matériel or personnel ashore. Initially coastal security was a naval responsibility; however, the several vessels available at the time were two frigates and four patrol boats, and these were inadequate to police the coast of Angola. These vessels were not fast, and their maintenance and repair removed them from service too often to supply full coverage of the coast. By 1964 it was realized that collaboration with the air force in a system of aero-naval littoral reconnaissance would be the most effective use of resources, and this was pursued.[8] In Mozambique while the shipping lane passed next to the coast, the fighting was again inland and thus it would be difficult to aid the insurgents from the sea. The elaborate and expensive French solution was simply not needed, was unaffordable, and consequently held little appeal to the Portuguese authorities, who sought relatively low-key, inexpensive, and cost-effective solutions to security in Africa.

The Portuguese requirements were embodied in three types of vessels, patrol boats (*lanchas de fiscalização,* or simply, LF), landing craft (*lanchas de desembarque,* or simply, LD) of various class sizes, and rubber boats (*botes de borracha*), all a blend of the French and British experiences adapted to the conditions in Portuguese Africa. The LFs would be direct successors of the earlier coastal and river gunboats (*canhoneiras* and *launchas-canhoneiras,* respectively) that had ranged from 38 tons to 492 tons displacement. Their mission would be one of patrolling Portuguese territorial waters, inspecting vessels suspected of supporting the insurgent movements, and transporting small units of *Fuzileiros* to be inserted ashore in rubber boats. Once ashore, the *Fuzileiros* would gather intelligence, kill insurgents, disrupt food gathering and courier traffic, and make contact with the population. Because of the low-intensity nature of the conflict, it was not anticipated that these boats would face a conventional-type land force with its relatively heavy crew-served weapons, as the French had experienced in Indochina. Instead they would encounter small bands of insurgents armed with what each could carry. These would include recoilless rifles, machine guns, rocket-propelled grenades (RPGs), mortars, and mines, all dangerous enough in their own right but seemingly not requiring the heavy armor or extensive armament of their forbearers. With these constraints removed, the navy was free to abandon the wood and steel shipbuilding materials of earlier years and explore modern, lightweight fiberglass and plywood hulls for the new LF concept. In this era most boat-builders subscribed to the idea that "fiberglass was for bathtubs and not boats."[9] While a fiberglass boat was not novel at the time, such craft over six meters in length were rare. This did not inhibit the navy, however, from proceeding. The boats would not, like the riverine patrol boats of the U.S. Navy in the Mekong Delta, have to rely on high speed and heavy armament for defense, as they would be facing quite a different sort of enemy. Instead, the boats required range, ease of maintenance, shallow draft, maneuverability, and the capacity to carry small detachments of *Fuzileiros* and their equipment for insertion ashore.

The same can be said for armament. It was thought that heavy cannon and automatic weapons were not needed and merely complicated boat design, as they and their ammunition stores raised the center of gravity. Simpler, lighter and highly potent weapons were available and had been proven in Indochina. The new, lighter hulls and selectively installed armor would simplify maintenance, lessen draft, and add range, maneuverability, and increased speed to the new boats. Fiberglass is easily repaired, and such a hull offered a backhanded sort of protection in that the insurgents' main heavy ordinance was the rocket-propelled grenade (RPG) that would go clean through fiberglass without detonating its armor-piercing warhead. The hole that it left was easy to fix. Armor would likewise raise the center of gravity and complicate design. It was always a question of judgment about how many of the numerous vulnerabilities should be protected and to what degree: engines, fuel tanks, steering gear, and large-caliber ammunition stores. Further, the simplicity of design and reliability of well-tested and efficient diesel engines enabled long-range patrols in remote waters under harsh climatic conditions to be conducted with confidence.

With these notions in mind, the Portuguese Navy began to identify those boatyards capable of executing its concept on a trial basis, as it had not developed its own competence of working in fiberglass. It ultimately chose a British yard to produce a small series of prototypes that combined simplicity with its experience in Africa and ordered its first three in a class of four 18-ton patrol boats. The *Antares* (P 360) was the first and class name, and the initial three craft were built in the United Kingdom in 1959. Each had an innovative molded fiberglass hull 17 meters in length and was powered by two proven and reliable 250 horsepower Cummins geared diesel engines driving conventional screw propellers. Besides being lightweight, fiberglass also had the advantage of being immune to the teredo worm, a scourge of wooden boats in the tropics and particularly the Anglo-French VP.[10] With a top speed of 18 knots, *Antares* had a range of 600 miles at full power. The speed was also satisfactory on overcoming the maximum current of eight to nine knots in the Zaire River and in putting the entire Congo riverine frontier of 80 miles within an 8-hour patrol. It carried no armor, and armament remained relatively light with a single bow-mounted

20mm Oerlikon antiaircraft machine cannon. It was equipped with short-range surface search radar to aid navigation along the twisting waterways at night and to detect enemy craft. Crew accommodation was spartan in keeping with budget and weight limitations. It and its sister ships *Sirius* (P 361) and *Vega* (P 362) were initially deployed to Goa. *Antares* escaped to Mozambique, but the other two were lost with the invasion of India in 1961. The last of the class, *Régulus* (P 369), was completed in Portugal in January 1962 on a hull imported from the United Kingdom and initially assigned duties on the Zaire River in Angola. Later it was transferred to Lake Niassa, where it undertook important and delicate missions.

The success of fiberglass as a hull material coupled with the reliable diesel powerplant encouraged the pursuit of another more capable class of patrol boats. Accordingly, an additional eight vessels of the new and more robust 27.6-ton *Bellatrix* (P 363) class were ordered from Bayerische Schiffbaugesellshaft GmbH at Erlenbach am Main, West Germany, and delivered between 1961 and 1962.[11] This class would continue with the Cummins engine specifically modified for the harsh tropical environment. The first of three were assigned to Patrol Squadron Guiné and the remaining five to Patrol Squadron Zaïre. The *Bellatrix* design was likewise very successful with its augmented capabilities and improvements gained from experience with the *Antares*, and this positive development increased confidence to pursue further construction at home. In 1968, the remaining five vessels of the class were built in the Alfeite shipyard. From these the first three were deployed to Guiné and the remaining two to Porto Amélia, Mozambique. Additionally, those deployed to Guiné were fitted with 37mm rocket launchers.

Antares class patrol boat *Régulus* (**P 369**) at speed on the Zaire River. Photograph courtesy of archives of the Estado-Maior da Armada and *Revista da Armada*.

There were two one-of-a-kind designs during this period. The *Algol* (P 1138) was built and deployed to Angola in 1965, and the *Castor* (P 580) was constructed in the Estaleiros Navais do Mondêgo in Figueira da Foz and deployed to Lake Niassa in 1964. It was later transferred to the Malawian navy in 1968. Finally in 1974, the old paddle-wheeler *Chire,* owned by the Empresa Sena Sugar of Mozambique, was converted to a launch to operate on the Zambeze River and renamed *Sabre* (P 1138).[12] It was one of two such Zambeze River launch modernizations, the other being LFP *Tete* (P 137).

The remaining patrol boats used in Africa were made in Portugal of Portuguese design in either the Alfeite or Mondego shipyards. Specifically the *Alvor* (35.7 tons), *Júpiter* (43.5 tons), *Argos* (210 tons), and *Cacine* (310 tons) classes were a Portuguese concept based more on pragmatic interpretation of a number of factors, such as, operating environment, insurgent order of battle, the nature of counterinsurgency, and the lack of any time for lengthy studies or operating experience.[13] The concluding refinement in the small LF series came in 1973 with the construction of six *Albatroz* (48.6 tons) class vessels.[14]

Table 3.1a: Patrol Boats Small (*Lanchas de Fiscalização Pequenas*), 1961–1974

Class	Number of Ships	Displacement (maximum tons)	Dimensions (meters)	Speed (maximum)	Crew
Antares	3+1	18	17.0x4.6x1.2	18.0 kts	7
Bellatrix	8+5	27.6/35.7	20.7x5.1x1.2	15.1 kts	7
Castor	1	22	17.7x4.0x1.0	18.2 kts	7
Júpiter	6	43.5	21.0x5.0x1.4	20.3 kts	8
Alvor	3	35.7	20.7x5.1x1.6	12.3 kts	7
D. Aleixo	2	67.7	25.0x5.2x1.7	16.0 kts	10
Albatroz	6	48.6	21.9x5.3x1.9	14.0 kts	8

Table 3.1b: Patrol Boats Large (*Lanchas de Fiscalização Grandes*), 1961–1974

Class	Number of Ships	Displacement (maximum tons)	Dimensions (meters)	Speed (maximum)	Crew
Argos	10	210	41.7x6.7x2.1	17.3 kts	24
Cacine	10	310	48.1x7.6x2.1	20.4 kts	33

The large patrol boats (*Lanchas de Fiscalização Grandes*) played a prominent role in all of the theaters, but particularly in Guiné, where they were the most significant naval units. These were steel-hulled, armed with two Bofors 40mm cannon, two MG 42 7.62mm machineguns, and were often equipped with 37mm multiple rocket launchers loaded with 32 rockets. The LFGs brought more robust firepower and other capabilities to the fight along the rivers as well as a seagoing capability. Because of their size, they were less stealthy than the smaller launches and less able to operate in shallow water. Nevertheless, they were the queens of the rivers. Both the LFP and LFG vessels performed patrol and surveillance missions, performed escort duties for landing craft, and acted in a limited role as transports. There were other deployments and visits to the theaters by larger warships, particularly to Guiné, but they were occasional and less meaningful. A summary of the several classes is contained in Tables 3.1a and 3.1b.

This rush to build was not without its drawbacks. The two patrol boats of the *Dom Aleixo* (67.7 tons) class, for example, were originally designed to operate in Timor. Only after it was discovered that delivering them to the Pacific area would be fraught with nearly insurmountable practical problems were the two vessels in the class reassigned for use in the *metrópole* and Cape Verde.[15]

In addition to the need for patrol boats, there was a very practical need for landing craft of various sizes not only to move troops in the traditional way of amphibious warfare but also to move military cargo and maintain lines of communication with the population in an area that relied on rivers over a primitive road system. Unfortunately, the United Kingdom and the United States, the two countries that had done the most development work on landing craft, were advocates of decolonization and reluctant to sell these craft directly to Portugal to pursue a "colonial" war in Africa. Using an indirect process to partially solve the problem, Portugal employed a private commercial firm to contract with a similar U.S. firm in the early 1960s for the purchase of a number of old surplus World War II-era LCMs.[16] The craft acquired had all experienced a hard life, and many were in poor condition. They were shipped to Lisbon, where they were renovated and in some cases practically rebuilt in the shipyard at Santos. When delivered to the navy in 1963, they were designated *Lanchas de Desembarque Médias* (LDM). It is difficult to know today just how many of the U.S. LCM-type craft were acquired through this process, but it is probably safe to say that about one-third of the total number of LDs were U.S. in origin.[17] *Comandante* Beradino Cadete, one of the two officers in charge of the LD project, remembers the initial purchase of 25 landing craft from the United States being in two lots of 15 and 10 respectively.[18] He also noted that, despite their sad state of repair, their Gray Marine engines were quite serviceable, as they had been rebuilt in the United States through a contract with Fairbanks Morse prior to delivery.[19] There must have been some considerable attrition from the initial buy, as by December 1969 records indicate that 18 U.S.-built and 17 locally-built LDMs were in operation.[20]

The small and large landing craft, called *Lanchas de Desembarque Pequenas* (LDP) and *Grandes* (LDG) respectively, were adapted from a British concept, just as the LDM had been adapted from an American one. The plans for these craft originally came from the British Admiralty in 1962 and were modified from those of the World War II-era landing craft assault (LCA) and landing craft tank (LCT) designs.[21] The modifications made in Lisbon were designed to keep the craft versatile, yet simple and thus inexpensive. These vessels were built in Portugal in the Mondego shipyards over the intervening decade, and the last was delivered in August 1973.[22] In the case of the LDG, for example, one important change occurred in the design of the ramp. It was originally intended to disembark heavy armored vehicles, and as a consequence of the change in requirements for African operations, was lightened to accommodate only personnel and light vehicles.[23] Armored vehicles were of little use in a counterinsurgency and particularly in the terrain of Portuguese Africa. By the end of the conflict in 1974, a total of 89 vessels had been either built in Portugal or acquired from the United States: 26 LDPs, 6 LDGs, and 57 LDMs.[24] Seventy-three of them were employed in Africa: 51 in Guiné, 15 in Angola, and 7 in Mozambique. A summary of these

Bellatrix class patrol boat *Fomalhaut* (P 367) at speed on the Zaire River with its rubber boats alongside. Photograph courtesy of the private collection of José Augusto Pires de Lima.

launch classes is contained in Table 3.1c below.

Table 3.1c: Landing Craft (*Lanchas de Desembarque*), 1961–1974

Class	Number of Ships	Displacement (maximum tons)	Dimensions (meters)	Speed (maximum)	Crew
LDP 100	5	18	14.0x3.4x0.7	9.5 kts	4
LDP 200	17	18	14.0x3.4x0.7	9.0 kts	4
LDP 300	4	18	14.0x3.4x0.7	9.5 kts	6
LDM 100	19	65	17.8x5.0x1.6	9.5 kts	6
LDM 200	5	50	15.3x4.3x1.2	8.5 kts	6
LDM 300	13	56	17.1x4.3x1.2	8.5 kts	6
LDM 400	26	58	17.8x5.0x1.1	9.2 kts	4
LDG 100 (*Alfange*)	4	480	56.5x11.8x1.3	10.3 kts	20
LDG 200 (*Bombarda*)	2	652	56.2x11.8x1.9	9.5 kts	20

The operation of these vessels was different from that of other traditional ones in that, with their flat bottom, shallow draft, and anemic powerplant, they were difficult to maneuver and demanded skilled seamanship and substantial experience.[25] The missions of the LDs were extraordinarily important during the war not only for specific military operations but also in cooperation with the civil authorities in moving people, local market goods, and other assorted cargo. These were often conducted under the particularly difficult climatic and hydrographic conditions of severely restricted channels, narrow rivers, strong currents, heavy seas, and monsoon weather.[26] The LDPs and the LDMs were manned by petty officers and ratings who bore great responsibility in their operation and endured long assignments under spartan conditions. Accommodation was bare, and ventilation and air conditioning on the vessels non-existent. The crew was exposed to the brutal tropical sun above deck and to a furnace-like atmosphere below. Privacy was a casualty of combat, and the head was in many cases simply a steel or wooden box sheltering a seat hanging over the stern. The performance of the LD crews under some of the most difficult operating conditions imaginable remains one of the unsung naval contributions not only to military successes but also to humanitarian support.

Originally landing craft were only lightly armed and armored, if at all. They depended on fighter cover or the big guns of heavy cruisers and battleships for their defense, as they made their way from transport ships onto a hostile shore to insert troops and establish a beachhead. New uses for the craft in transporting personnel and cargo in areas where rivers were the primary avenues of communication left the heavy guns far away. In the restricted conditions of a river, where the banks could become so narrow that both sides of the craft were brushed with foliage and where the threat of ambush was high, there was a constant and deadly game of hide-and-seek between the riverine sailors and the insurgents. Even if the LDs were capable, speed was impossible with the often winding channels and a fear of running aground, particularly at low tide. While these slow craft might rely on air cover, specialized ceramic or grating armor, and relatively heavy traditional armament or other weapons tailored to the operating environment, the river often neutralized these measures with its confines. Inventiveness and imagination were key factors in the local situation, routinely forcing the riverine sailors to weigh tactical alternatives in a life and death setting.

LDM 307 underway in Guiné. Photograph courtesy Estado-Maior da Armada and *Revista da Armada*.

For instance, a key consideration was the progressive speed loss that came with an increase in the size of a load of ammunition, personnel or other cargo. The change in the physical factors of the river over the duration of operations was another. The cultural, political, and economic landscapes along the river represented yet a third. There were few documents and little corporate knowledge initially to guide these men. As a result, the margin of error could be fatally small.

There were a number of deficiencies that surfaced in the crucible of combat regarding the armament of the LFs and LDs. The Oerlikons and the 40mm Bofors on the larger vessels, for instance, were not equipped with munitions for use against land targets, and thus some adaptations had to be made with a consequent and substantial sacrifice in their rate of fire. This was an important point, as a high cyclic rate of fire was critical in delivering a destructive effect and suppressing the enemy. They were a World War II design, and by 1974 there were plans to replace them with more modern versions.[27] Because of this limitation, they were largely ineffectual against land targets, and their rate of fire was dangerously below that desired and needed to counter ambushes. A particularly grave problem was the lack of a lightweight, portable rocket-propelled grenade or rocket launcher-type weapon with varied munitions, and a heavy machinegun with a rapid rate of fire, such as the Browning .50-caliber heavy-barreled Mark 2, which was the mainstay of the PBRs in the Mekong Delta. There were also no side-mounted weapons. This deficiency was partially solved by mounting infantry mortars in the hole of the boat as well as using canisters of multiple rockets; however, the lack of directive and overwhelming firepower was increasingly a problem. Direct-fire mortars and light rapid-fire machineguns mounted along the gunnels, as on the PBR, would have been a more effective solution. These shortcomings were

LDG 102 *Ariete* discharging vehicles at low tide, August 1974, Guiné.
Photograph by Alexandre da Fonseca courtesy *Revista da Armada*.

particularly grave in Guiné, where by the mid-1960s onward the PAIGC was using more modern weapons than the Portuguese with their 122mm rocket launchers and the hand-held SA-7 *Strela* (NATO: *Grail*) anti-air missile, creating increasingly serious problems for the navy.

The RPG-7 rocket-propelled grenade (RPG) was a constant threat from an ambush along the river bank.[28] In Guiné, the Portuguese found that it was necessary to add steel armor plating on the LFs as a defense against the suddenness of an ambush, particularly with RPGs. Likewise the larger vessels that could accommodate the increased weight traded the Oerlikon 20mm for a Bofors 40mm cannon. As the PAIGC became more aggressive, *Comandante* Guilherme Almor de Alpoim Calvão, the imaginative commanding officer of Detachment of Special *Fuzileiros* Nº 8 (DFE 8), requested that a number of LDMs be converted to monitors, much as the French had done in Indochina and the Americans were doing in the Mekong Delta in defense of the omnipresent ambush.[29] The U.S. version of these vessels had grating and plate armor, heavy turreted 40mm cannon, multiple .50-caliber and 7.62mm machine guns, and side-mounted 81mm direct fire mortars, and were literally "battleships" of the rivers. While this request was denied, perhaps because of complexity and cost, adaptations and modifications continued, and mortar illumination and conventional rounds were always popular additions. The United States, for example, used flame thrower cannon mounted on LCMs to burn away riverbank foliage in the Mekong Delta to uncover and discourage ambushes. It also used water cannon adapted from fire boats and mounted on LCMs to wash out and collapse riverbank caves used for ambush. The fleeing Viet Cong or North Vietnamese would then be destroyed by heavy machine guns or mortars. Such heavy and persistent ambushes were not normally the case, however, in Portuguese Africa, and as a consequence, Portugal sought to keep the cost of the LDs low through their simple design and operation.[30] In sum, one had to be inventive with what was easily available to solve or lighten the problem of insurgent engagement.

LDP 108 disembarking *Fuzileiros* into their rubber boats. Photograph courtesy Estado-Maior da Armada and *Revista da Armada*.

The third leg of the African navy was the rubber boat, which could be launched from the *João Coutinho* class corvette or any of the LFs or LDs and facilitate *Fuzileiro* pursuit of insurgent elements along the riverbanks and littorals. The inflatable rubber boat, the 1934 brainchild of Pierre Debroutelle, an engineer with the French firm of Zodiac, remained in its design shops until after World War II, when military interest underwrote its more mature development. In 1952, Alain Bombard made an Atlantic Ocean crossing in a Zodiac Mark III from Las Palmas in the Canary Islands to Barbados and thereby established its true viability. Acquired in great numbers by the navy from Zodiac, this small three-meter-long raft could be easily carried on a LF or LP or larger vessel and launched with its crew to execute varied tasks. It was powered by either an outboard engine or paddles.[31] It was a sturdy and reliable craft with its multiple air compartments and served the navy well.

The uses of the boat, ultimately named the Zebro III, were many and varied. It was somewhat the jeep or helicopter of the waterways in that it served a host of missions from patrols to ambushes, to hydrographic work, to alongside maintenance, and to anything in between. Its uses were limited only by one's imagination. It proved extremely useful in patrolling the restricted canals and other shallow bodies of a river for which there was no other means of access. Its stability and ruggedness were nowhere more evident than on the Zaire River, where tree trunks and other dangerous debris were commonplace threats to a rupture in its air compartments, and where the large wakes of merchantmen threatened to capsize it.

Experience in the *ultramar* necessitated some modifications to the boats. Foremost was the attachment of a small metal guard around the propeller and its shaft to protect combat swimmers from being injured in their recovery. The guard also prevented damage to the engine from submerged obstacles without hindering the speed significantly. Daily maintenance of the boats and engines was critical despite their simplicity and rugged construction. Most important to our story, however, was its use in securing the river systems of the *ultramar*.

The primary mission of the navy in subversive war or insurgency was to prevent the enemy from using the navigable waterways for any of its purposes. This generally involved conducting coastal and littoral patrols to prevent insurgent use of the sea approaches to support subversive activities inland, and conducting the more complicated river patrols likewise to prevent their varied enemy use. In the coastal and littoral areas the sort of grueling and monotonous routine of identifying and inspecting small boat traffic was mind-numbing. The search for scarce targets and the repetition of negative results severely tested crews. If vigilance slackened, however, the enemy would be quick to notice.

In contrast to the littorals, operating on the rivers was very restive and posed additional problems with the channelization that limits military flexibility. Riverine operations thus carry a higher risk than do ground operations. Both defensive and offensive operations are required to control the river. Defensively, positions are occupied and security measures taken at key points along the waterway, particularly at crossings and constrictions. Offensively, sector patrols must be conducted continuously somewhere along the river, as active patrolling keeps the enemy reactive while government forces are proactive.

There were two general actions that were used to dissuade enemy activity and force a modification in his behavior. The first was simply the establishment of a presence on the rivers, their meanders, braided channels, canals, and oxbow lakes. The second was adding an element of surprise to this presence. Establishing presence was the most expensive of the

Zebro III boat underway with *Fuzileiros* on the River Cuito in the south of Angola. Photograph courtesy of Estado-Maior da Armada and *Revista da Armada*

two, as to be effective it required a large number of men, either on land along the riverbank or underway in boats, to provide a high revisit time and thereby the impression of a constant presence of government forces. Because it is impossible for troops to be everywhere, there are inevitable lapses in this presence through which the enemy can move. He will watch the movement of troops and note their pattern of behavior. From his analysis of these activities he will discern the holes in coverage and move to exploit these gaps. The alternative to tying down many numbers of troops in this sort of coverage is to introduce surprise. The routine will then have an unpredictable aspect, and the enemy will be thrown off balance. With this uncertainty, the insurgent will have to change his behavior. He will be dissuaded from using the now more dangerous river and will be forced to use other, more lengthy detours or hopefully to abandon his project altogether.

On the rivers of the *ultramar* one of the key tools of surprise was the imaginative use of the rubber boat. It represented a great economy of means in its flexibility and ability to carry a small force for clandestine insertion ashore to conduct an ambush or simply to perform a reconnaissance patrol. Rubber boats generally operated minimally in pairs for mutual support and carried three to four men each. They would sortie either from a fixed base on the riverbank or lakeside or from the moving base of a ship or patrol craft. The latter was less expensive and less vulnerable than a land base and offered the further advantage of operational flexibility. This flexibility translated into a varied and irregular pattern of patrols as to the time of day and to the mode of operation.

One of the most common methods of conducting any operation involving rubber boats was to tow them alongside a LF, as depicted in Photograph 3.2. This particular configuration allowed the *Fuzileiros* to board the boats and detach quickly either from a LF at speed or one slowing to investigate an unidentified contact. This posture also permitted substantial flexibility in operations. For instance, often at night a LF would pass along the targeted area of a river and launch its two boats with their *Fuzileiros* without slowing. The boats would then maneuver by silently drifting with the current and waiting for the enemy to expose himself, or by silently paddling to an appropriate site to set an ambush. This was particularly difficult, for the *Fuzileiros*, paddling quietly into the utter darkness of the river margins, could use no light and make no sound for fear of losing surprise and alerting the enemy. The riverbank at night with the inky blackness of its vegetal cover was a tricky operating environment.

Raids, reconnaissance patrols, or ambushes could likewise be set by inserting *Fuzileiros* ashore via rubber boat. This maneuver was generally performed at night, for it allowed the force to move in silence under cover of darkness from the water, overland, to spring its assault in the early morning hours before dawn, when the enemy slept his soundest and *Fuzileiro* presence was least expected. In approaching a target, *Fuzileiros* traveled cross-country and avoided roads because of mines, particularly in Guiné. The normal range of such a patrol was limited to about 30 kilometers due to the difficult terrain and particularly to the tidal action in Guiné, and could last as long as two days. Following the operation, the *Fuzileiros* would return to their point of embarkation and subsequently be recovered by rubber boats from a LP or LD. The aim of these operations was to keep the enemy off-balance and never to permit him any feeling of security.

If a LF were stopping to investigate a suspicious contact at night, it would launch its boats and direct them through the darkness by radio along compass bearings based on the radar return. This procedure was normally used only for short distances of less than four miles. Usually the *Fuzileiros* would carry a radar reflector in the boat to aid in course corrections to the target; however, if this were lost, then a steel helmet would be raised on a pole as a makeshift alternative.[32]

Boats would also be launched in daylight prior to reaching a target area and follow the LF after an appropriate interval. This tactic was pursued in the hope that the enemy would believe the area safe following the passage of the LF, expose himself in conducting his activity, and be caught by the second patrol of boats. Many times patrols of *Fuzileiros* would be only partially recovered from a target area as a decoy, leaving a force hidden in ambush. The variation in tactics was limited only to the imagination, but the rubber boat was invariably an integral and important part in adding flexibility to African naval operations and proved itself well in the conflict.

Fuzileiros

In designing the force structure for the African navy, Roboredo envisioned a series of ship classes ranging from the *João Coutinho* of 1,200 tons to the *Antares* of 18 tons to patrol the coastline and rivers of the *ultramar*. On each of these vessels there would be a detachment of *Fuzileiros,* for a part of controlling the narrow seas and rivers was the control of the coasts and riverbanks. This meant that the navy must have a force prepared to project power ashore from its vessels. Roboredo thus saw an immediate and potential need for a small nucleus of troops who were trained to operate in the littoral and whose numbers could be expanded rapidly in the event of any emergency.[33] This need would become increasingly apparent with the Portuguese expulsion from the anachronistic fort São João Batista de Ajudá in Dahomey (present-day Benin), the assault on the *Santa Maria*, and developments in the north of Angola, all occurring throughout 1960 and into the early months of 1961.

In 1959 he took the first steps to reestablish the *Corpo de Fuzileiros* or marine corps.

There were from the earliest times of the Portuguese Navy small forces of army troops on board the King's ships to fulfill a need for light infantry. It was not, however, until 1585 that specialization within the navy occurred with the introduction of specific instruction in the use of artillery and firearms for certain elements in the crews of ships bound for India. This instruction was aimed at providing a more robust protection for the ships themselves as well as the ports in this theater. More formally the *Corpo de Fuzileiros* can trace its origin to the creation of the *Terço da Armada da Coroa de Portugal* (Naval Regiment of the Portuguese Crown), which was formed in April of 1621 to supply naval troops for embarkation on these ships. It had the distinction of being the first permanently organized military unit in Portugal. This position has given it the singular privilege of always being to the right in any military ceremony and of breaking ranks ahead of all others in formation. The embarked infantrymen performed duties as sailors, as artillerymen, as boarding and landing parties, and as defenders against hostile boarding parties, depending on the requirements at hand. They distinguished themselves particularly in helping to reduce the pirate menace along the Portuguese trade routes.[34] These troops served aboard all vessels following the coast of Africa, across the Indian Ocean as far to the east as Japan, and across the Atlantic to South America. They became the personal guard of the Kings of Portugal and were integrated into the expeditionary forces in pacifying the African territories. They manned the numerous *fortalezas* or fortresses that protected the trading enclaves along the coasts of Portuguese exploration. Over the years the force underwent many diverse designations, such as, *Infantaria da Marinha* (Naval Infantry), *Brigada Real de Marinha* (Royal Naval Brigade), *Regimento da Armada* (Naval Regiment), *Batalhão Naval* (Naval Battalion), *Corpo de Marinheiros Militares* (Corps of Naval Soldiers), and *Brigada da Guarda Naval* (Brigade of Naval Guards).

The term *Fuzileiro*, however, first appeared in the navy in 1797 with the formation of the *Brigada Real de Marinha* and its division into three groups according to the primary specialties of its members. The first was composed of ten companies of *Artilheiros-Marinheiros* (Artillery Sailors), who were responsible for shipboard artillery, forts and gunpowder warehouses, as well as other tasks peculiar to artillery.[35] The second was composed of twelve companies of *Fuzileiros-Marinheiros* (Fusilier-Sailors), who were responsible for landing operations, shipboard defense against boarding parties, and the security of the Naval Arsenal.[36] The third was composed of ten companies of *Artífices e Lastradores-Marinheiros* (Artificers and Ballasters-Sailors), who plied their skills on board the King's ships and in his shipyards.[37] The full strength of the Brigade was 5,222 men.

A contingent of *Fuzileiros* accompanied King John IV and the Portuguese court when it fled to Brazil in November 1807 and arrived in March 1808 because of the French invasion. Later in 1822 when his oldest son, Pedro IV, declared himself Emperor Pedro I of the Kingdom of Brazil and broke with Portugal, this contingent formed the basis for the Brazilian *Fuzileiros Navais*.[38]

The Brigade was reorganized in 1807 and again in 1808 resulting in a reduction in its overall strength to 2,992 men. Again in 1823, the Brigade was reduced to two battalions of eight companies each or a total strength of 1,647 men. In October 1836 the Brigade was reformed as the *Regimento da Armada* with four battalions of four companies each or a total strength of 1,815 men.[39] In January 1837 the *Batalhão Naval* was created in yet another reorganization and consisted of eight companies for an overall strength of 681 men. The Battalion structure mirrored that of the Regiment with minor exceptions.[40] In 1840 the Battalion was augmented to 1,200 men. By 1851 the Battalion held only 835 men and was replaced with the *Corpo de Marinheiros Militares* with a strength of twenty-two companies. Historically the *Fuzileiros* had been light infantry, but with this change came a heavier, more robust force. Its troops were instructed in seamanship, infantry tactics, small arms skills, and landing party operations. Each embarked company had a squadron of artillerymen-cabin boys who were practiced in gunnery, gunlaying, and shipboard working parties. In 1875 the Corps was reorganized into three divisions, each with a section of *Fuzileiros* and artillerymen. These troops assumed the duties of sailors and general purpose troops. Another reorganization in 1884 created in the Corps six companies of *Fuzileiros* as well as companies of lookouts, artillerymen, firemen and stokers, and storekeepers. With so many reorganizations over a relatively short period, one might wonder if it were a force in search of a clearly defined mission. The Corps was consequently dissolved in 1890 under King Carlos I, and its duties assigned to other entities. It was briefly reactivated between 1924 and 1926 as the *Brigada da Guarda Naval* to furnish security for naval bases and ships, a forerunner of the *Companhas de Fuzileiros* (Companies of *Fuzileiros*), but again it was dissolved.

The need for another reactivation became evident well before the 1960 developments in the Belgian Congo. Roboredo anticipated that the coming conflict in Africa would be a protracted one and moved to make the necessary preparations. The notion of a ship-borne force able to project power ashore met with stiff resistance from numerous quarters. The arguments against the development of such a capability lay in the view that the navy was unprepared for a land war, that in the coming war there would be no need for amphibious forces, and that the building of this type of force would further dilute the already meager navy budget. Roboredo and Crespo did not accept these arguments and dispatched staff to the army center for special forces at Lamego, to Spain, to Algeria, and to the United Kingdom to examine the varied approaches in establishing such a proposed force.[41] While this research initially favored the British model with its force structure and use of rubber boats, the French model with its refinements through the Indochina experience held valuable lessons and would be used increasingly as the program matured.

Things were accelerated by an anticipation of developments in Angola and particularly by a plea from the Naval Command there on 11 April 1960 that voiced concern about the general security situation in the *ultramar* and in Angola in particular.[42] The naval commander in Angola recommended that a specialized landing force be established to operate from patrol boats and that it be instructed in infantry tactics and procedures. He also sought immediate permission to form a company of naval infantry within his own command and to train it. In response, Roboredo, now a *comodoro* or commodore, sought approval from the Chief of Staff of the Navy not only for the force in Angola but also for the formal establishment of a larger, permanent force for wider employment throughout the *ultramar*. He also suggested that foreign training be sought initially to establish a small cadre of officers and petty officers to serve as instructors in a school for training naval infantry.

Indeed, Roboredo had at first appealed to the French in early 1959 for a proposal to train a small contingent of Portuguese officers and petty officers at the École des Fusiliers at the Centre Siroco at Cap Matifou near Alger. This small group upon completion of training would help set the course for its own service by supplying the future instructors in Portugal.

The French were happy to oblige; however, the difficulty with their program was that basic officer training ran eight months with an additional two for specialized "commando" instruction. For enlisted personnel the periods were five and three months respectively.[43] The British responded with a more focused course of nine weeks in purely commando training in contrast to the French who had insisted on basic training prior to their commando course.[44] Although the French training had been Roboredo's first choice, it was far too lengthy in comparison to the British proposal, and the decision was subsequently made to use the more specialized and shorter Royal Marine instruction.[45] Accordingly, three lieutenants (junior grade) (*segundo tenentes*) and three petty officers were designated to attend the Royal Marine commando course in Lympstone, South Devon.[46] *Segundo tenente* Alberto Manuel Barreto Pascoal Rodrigues and three petty officers, Ludgero dos Santos Silva, João dos Santos Cândido Santinhos, and Mário José Baptista Claudino, actually completed the course on 30 September 1960 and returned to Lisbon shortly thereafter.

In February 1961, the first formal organizational steps were taken with the creation of a training program for prospective *Fuzileiro* sergeants and soldiers to prepare them for deployment in the *ultramar*.[47] Sergeants would later be recruited from *Fuzileiro* corporals who would be promoted on successful completion of the sergeant course. The initial course enrolled between 35 and 40 men recruited from within the navy and was designed to provide the training of troops capable of amphibious landings, of safeguarding naval installations, and of acting as a security force in coastal regions. It was conducted as part of the *Corpo de Marinheiros*, which was a dependency of Group Nº 2 of the Naval Schools in Alfeite. The training ground itself occupied land just south across the Tagus River from Lisbon and was borrowed from the Army. It was ideal in that it comprised the difficult thickets and forests of Alfeite and the Quinta do Antelmo, the swampy marshes immediately south of this area, and the dramatic mountains of the nearby Serra da Arrábida. Three subsequent and challenging courses were held in these areas before the specialized and formal school for the *Fuzileiros* was completed at nearby Vale de Zebro in June.[48] The value of having its own specialized school was that subsequent experience in the *ultramar* enabled the navy to modify the training to fit specific developments in each theater and the shifting methods of insurgent fighting. From this trained pool of graduates came the personnel to form the first detachment of special *Fuzileiros* [*Destacamento de Fuzileiros Especiais Nº 1,* or DFE 1] in October 1961, which deployed to Angola the following month.[49] This and subsequent deployments are detailed in Tables 3.2 to 3.5 below.

Table 3.2: Naval Disposition (Units of *Fuzileiros*), 1961–1974. DFE (*Destacamentos de Fuzileiros Especiais*) and CF (*Companhias de Fuzileiros*)

Source: Corpo de *Fuzileiros*, Unpublished history of the *Corpo de Fuzileiros, Part II: Fuzileiros Especiais* [Marine Corps, Part II: Special Marines], TMs [photocopy] (Lisbon: Ministério da Marinha, 1987), 17; and Luís Sanches de Baêna, *Fuzileiros: Factos e Feitos na Guerra de África 1961/1974*, Volume 1 [*Fuzileiros*: Facts and Feats in the African War 1961/1974, Volume 1 (Lisbon: Comissão Cultural da Marinha, 2006), 101–107.

Dates		Guiné		Angola		Mozambique		Total	
Year	Month	DFE	CF	DFE	CF	DFE	CF	DFE	CF
1961	November			1				1	
1962	May			1	1			1	1
	June	1		1	1			2	1
	August	1		2	1			3	1
	October	1		2	1		1	3	2
1963	February	1		3	1		1	4	2
	June	1	1	3	1		1	4	3
	September	1	1	4	1		1	5	3
	October	2	1	4	1		1	6	3
	November	3	1	4	1		1	7	3
1964	February	4	1	4	1		1	8	3
	November	4	1	4	2	1	1	9	4
1965	March	4	1	3	2	1	1	8	4
	June	4	1	3	2	2	1	9	4
	November	4	1	3	2	3	2	10	5
1966	August	4	2	3	3	3	2	9	7
	December	4	2	2	3	3	2	9	7
1967	February	4	2	2	3	4	2	10	7
1968	August	4	2	2	4	4	2	10	8
1969		4	2	2	4	4	2	10	8
1970	June	5	2	2	4	4	2	11	8
1971		5	2	2	4	4	2	11	8
1972		5	2	2	4	4	2	11	8
1973	April	5	2	2	4	3	3	10	9
1974	February	6	2	2	4	3	3	11	9
	April	5	2	2	4	3	3	10	9
	May	6	2	2	4	3	3	11	9

Table 3.3: Naval Disposition (Units of *Fuzileiros*), 1961–1974. Units of *Fuzileiros* Deployed in the Naval Command of Angola

Source: Corpo de *Fuzileiros*, Unpublished history of the *Corpo de Fuzileiros, Part II: Fuzileiros Especiais* [Marine Corps, Part II: Special Marines], TMs [photocopy] (Lisbon: Ministério da Marinha, 1987), 17; Luís Sanches de Baêna, *Fuzileiros: Factos e Feitos na Guerra de África 1961/1974*, Volume 1 [*Fuzileiros*: Facts and Feats in the African War 1961/1974, Volume 1 (Lisbon: Comissão Cultural da Marinha, 2006), 101–107.

Units		Dates		Comments
Type	Designation	Deployed	Redeployed	
Detachments (*destacamentos de Fuzileiros especiais*)	DFE 1	10 NOV 61	14 JUL 63	
	DFE 3	29 AUG 62	23 NOV 64	
	DFE 4	26 FEB 63	19 MAR 65	
	DFE 5	21 JUN 63	15 JUL 65	
	DFE 6	30 SEP 63	23 OCT 65	
	DFE 11	14 NOV 64	06 DEC 66	
	DFE 2	10 JUL 65	24 JUN 67	
	DFE 13	23 OCT 65	15 SEP 67	
	DFE 11	21 JUN 67	26 JUN 69	
	DFE 2	21 AUG 67	05 NOV 69	
	DFE 10	14 MAY 69	25 MAR 71	
	DFE 1	27 JUL 69	06 OCT 71	
	DFE 6	14 MAR 71	07 MAR 73	
	DFE 10	04 OCT 71	06 NOV 73	
	DFE 2	16 MAR 73	15 FEB 75	
	DFE 6	09 OCT 73	27 MAR 75	
	DFE 1	17 JUL 75	10 NOV 75	

Units		Dates		Comments
Companies (*companhias de Fuzileiros*)	CF 1	31 MAY 62	06 JUN 64	
	CF 4	01 JUN 64	09 JUN 66	
	CF 5	10 NOV 64	29 DEC 66	
	CF 10	08 JUN 66	05 AUG 68	
	CF 1	02 DEC 66	19 JAN 69	
	CF 11	17 DEC 66	24 JAN 69	
	CF 7	04 AUG 68	24 JUL 70	
	CF 5	05 AUG 68	06 SEP 70	
	CF 8	31 DEC 68	08 DEC 70	
	CF 9	17 JAN 69	08 FEB 71	
	CF 4	19 JUL 70	10 JUL 72	
	CF 6	31 AUG 70	06 AUG 72	
	CF 7	07 DEC 70	28 NOV 72	
	CF 5	30 JAN 71	23 JAN 73	
	CF 1	10 JUL 72	06 JUN 74	
	CF 3	06 AUG 72	13 SEP 74	
	CF 4	28 NOV 72	17 DEC 74	
	CF 6	09 JAN 73	21 JAN 75	
	CF 8	29 JUN 74	21 APR 75	
	CF 12	04 DEC 74	10 NOV 75	
	CF 5	21 JAN 75	10 NOV 75	
	CF 9	09 SEP 75	10 NOV 75	

Table 3.4: Disposition (Units of *Fuzileiros*), 1961–1974. Units of *Fuzileiros* Deployed in the Maritime Defense Command of Guiné

Source: Corpo de *Fuzileiros*, Unpublished history of the *Corpo de Fuzileiros, Part II: Fuzileiros Especiais* [Marine Corps, Part II: Special Marines], TMs [photocopy] (Lisbon: Ministério da Marinha, 1987), 17; Luís Sanches de Baêna, *Fuzileiros: Factos e Feitos na Guerra de África 1961/1974*, Volume 1 [*Fuzileiros*: Facts and Feats in the African War 1961/1974, Volume 1 (Lisbon: Comissão Cultural da Marinha, 2006), 101–107. *African detachments of special *Fuzileiros*.

Units		Dates		Comments
Type	Designation	Deployed	Redeployed	
	DFE 2	06 JUN 62	25 JUN 64	
Detachments (*destacamentos de Fuzileiros especiais*)	DFE 7	10 OCT 63	23 AUG 65	
	DFE 8	04 NOV 63	23 OCT 65	
	DFE 9	27 FEB 64	09 FEB 66	
	DFE 10	23 JUN 64	14 JUN 66	
	DFE 3	23 AUG 65	11 MAY 67	
	DFE 4	21 OCT 65	28 JUL 67	
	DFE 6	05 FEB 66	05 NOV 67	
	DFE 7	11 JUN 66	23 APR 68	
	DFE 10	10 MAY 67	09 MAR 69	
	DFE 3	25 JUL 67	19 APR 69	
	DFE 12	02 NOV 67	15 OCT 69	
	DFE 13	21 APR 68	25 JAN 70	
	DFE 7	20 FEB 69	16 SEP 70	
	DFE 8	19 APR 69	16 FEB 71	
	DFE 3	13 OCT 69	12 JUL 71	
	DFE 12	31 JAN 70	02 DEC 71	Relieved by DFE 22
	DFE 21*	21 APR 70		Deactivated 25 AUG 74
	DFE 4	14 SEP 70	24 JUN 72	
	DFE 13	22 JAN 71	20 OCT 72	
	DFE 8	09 JUL 71	12 APR 73	
	DFE 22*	16 NOV 71		Deactivated 25 AUG 74
	DFE 12	07 JUN 72	05 APR 74	
	DFE 1	06 OCT 72	28 JUL 74	
	DFE 4	07 APR 73	15 OCT 74	
	DFE 5	09 FEB 74	30 OCT 74	
	DFE 23*	01 JUL 74		Deactivated 25 AUG 74

Units		Dates		Comments
Type	Designation	Deployed	Redeployed	
Companies (*companhias de Fuzileiros*)	PF 1	09 APR 63	14 JUN 63	
	CF 3	14 JUN 63	12 JUL 65	PF 1 absorbed by CF 3
	CF 7	08 JUL 65	11 MAY 67	
	CF 9	02 AUG 66	09 MAY68	
	CF 3	10 MAY 67	21 FEB 69	
	CF 6	06 MAY 68	01 FEB 70	
	CF 10	20 FEB 69	12 JAN 71	
	CF 3	31 JAN 70	02 DEC 71	
	CF 11	09 JAN 71	06 OCT 72	
	CF 8	24 NOV 71	23 AUG 73	
	CF 2	06 OCT 72	11 JUL 74	
	CF 5	23 AUG 73	03 OCT 74	

Table 3.5: Disposition (Units of *Fuzileiros*), 1961–1974. Units of Fuzileiros Deployed in the Naval Command of Mozambique

Source: Corpo de *Fuzileiros*, Unpublished history of the *Corpo de Fuzileiros, Part II: Fuzileiros Especiais* [Marine Corps, Part II: Special Marines], TMs [photocopy] (Lisbon: Ministério da Marinha, 1987), 17; Luís Sanches de Baêna, *Fuzileiros: Factos e Feitos na Guerra de África 1961/1974*, Volume 1 [*Fuzileiros*: Facts and Feats in the African War 1961/1974, Volume 1 (Lisbon: Comissão Cultural da Marinha, 2006), 101–107.

Units		Dates		Comments
Type	Designation	Deployed	Redeployed	
Detachments (*destacamentos de Fuzileiros especiais*)	DFE 1	20 NOV 64	01 DEC 66	
	DFE 12	20 JUN 65	30 JUN 67	
	DFE 5	27 NOV 65	09 NOV 67	
	DFE 8	26 NOV 66	24 NOV 68	
	DFE 9	24 FEB 67	28 MAR 69	
	DFE 1	22 JUN 67	30 JUN 69	
	DFE 4	05 NOV 67	29 NOV 69	
	DFE 6	05 NOV 68	06 SEP 70	
	DFE 5	01 MAR 69	10 FEB 71	
	DFE 9	17 JUN 69	24 JUL 71	
	DFE 11	16 NOV 69	18 JAN 72	
	DFE 2	24 AUG 70	10 MAY 72	
	DFE 7	08 FEB 71	06 NOV 72	
	DFE 5	18 JUL 71	13 APR 73	
	DFE 9	22 DEC 71	03 DEC 73	
	DFE 3	03 MAY 72	20 MAY 74	
	DFE 11	01 NOV 72	01 NOV 74	
	DFE 8	03 DEC 73	03 DEC 74	
	DFE 10	13 MAY 74	24 JUN 75	
Companies (*companhias de Fuzileiros*)	CF 2	29 OCT 62	25 MAR 65	
	CF 6	19 MAR 65	18 MAY 67	
	CF 8	27 NOV 65	28 FEB 68	
	CF 2	02 MAY 67	15 JUN 69	
	CF 4	16 FEB 68	06 MAR 70	
	CF 1	13 JUN 69	01 JUN 71	
	CF 2	21 FEB 70	18 JAN 72	
	CF 10	01 JUN 71	07 MAY 73	
	CF 9	18 JAN 72	14 JAN 74	
	CF 11	06 APR 73	08 NOV 74	
	CF 7	07 MAY 73	22 NOV 74	
	CF 10	14 JAN 74	* 75	* Principally in JUN

To form additional units of *Fuzileiros*, the navy continued to recruit candidates from within its own ranks. Initially this process was seen as a "conversion" program for sailors and was thus termed a "conversion course." Because recruitment from within was quickly exhausted, it became necessary to implement a broader effort targeted at the civil population as a second source. Over the course of the war these two sources were able to fulfill the need of the School of *Fuzileiros* and its special *Fuzileiros* course by appealing to the desire of the applicants to be part of an elite force of growing fame in Africa, although as we shall see, this was not an easy or straightforward task. *Fuzileiro* officers on the other hand were recruited from among the graduates of the regular course at the Naval Academy (*Escola Naval*) and, later, those from the Naval Engineers (*Engenheiros Maquinistas Navais*) and Naval Supply (*Administração Naval*) classes. These numbers were complemented by cadets undergoing the Naval Reserve Officer course at the same institution.

The training course conducted at the *Escola de Fuzileiros* comprised two phases for the enlisted personnel. First, there was the basic recruit and technical training in military fundamentals and the aspects unique to the *Fuzileiros*. This phase was complemented by a second in which those graduates selected to be special *Fuzileiros* or *Fuzileiros especiais* (FZE) were integrated into detachments of special *Fuzileiros* (DFE), while the other candidates were assigned to companies of *Fuzileiros* (CF).[50]

The *Destacamentos de Fuzileiros Especiais* (DFE) were considered elite units and in fact were the special forces of the navy. They were composed of men with special abilities, inordinate self-confidence, and undaunted courage, and were proud to wear their distinguishing beret. They were also as a rule imaginatively led and noted for their unit flexibility and mobility. These characteristics gave them a unique advantage in finding and engaging insurgents effectively in the most adverse operating conditions, and in exploiting the slimy tropical environment that was habitually found bordering the lakes and rivers of the *ultramar*. The DFEs originally in 1962 comprised 75 men (2 officers, 7 sergeants, 8 corporals, 14 able seamen and 44 seamen), and later in 1967, this manning level was raised to 80 men (4 officers, 6 sergeants, 14 corporals, 32 able seamen, and 24 seamen).[51] The organization was also modified in each theater to address the operating environment, and in fact, each detachment developed an expertise in a particular geographic area and thus tended to be reassigned there to exploit this strength. Originally a DFE consisted of 4 sections of infantry and one support section, and these sections were variously called assault (*grupos de assault* or GA) or combat groups, depending on the theater. By 1968 the number of officers was increased to 4 to permit the commanding officer to have an officer lead each of the assault groups. The DFE could also be organized into 2 assault groups, each with two sharp-shooter sections armed with bazookas, MG-42 machine guns, mortars, rocket propelled grenades (RPGs), and logistical support, as needed.[52] Indeed, to increase unit flexibility, sections were further divided into sub-groups or teams of 4 or 5 men in Angola and Mozambique or a squad of 3 men in Guiné, each with a specific task of assault or support to add flexibility in exploiting the terrain and enemy deployment and in bringing surprise and overwhelming force on an unsuspecting foe. Subsequently there were DFEs with 3 officers and 75 men and even 2 officers and 70 men.[53]

Toward the end of the 1960s the navy began to recruit its *Fuzileiro* officers from within the *Fuzileiro* community, and there appeared the first of a long line of officers who had risen from the ranks to command a number of the DFEs and CFs.[54] In addition to its 4 officers, a DFE normally had six sergeants, including a storekeeper sergeant and a corpsman sergeant. The line sergeants were assigned to assault groups and charged with the maintenance of its rubber boats, engines, radios, and armament. The *Fuzileiros* in a DFE over the span of the war tended increasingly to be veterans who had elected to make the navy a career following either their initial six-year term of enlistment as a volunteer or four-year term as a drafted recruit.[55] This trend translated into a high level of experience and unit cohesiveness, as the veterans were skilled and motivated. These characteristics were particularly apparent when units experienced the stress of combat and were forced to perform effectively in the proverbial Clausewitzian "fog of war." During the war each DFE was deployed to the *ultramar* for a period of about two years (normally 23 months but a little less in Guiné), at the end of which it would return to the *metrópole* to refit and rest. Following a year-long period spent in replacing losses and undergoing refresher training, the unit would again deploy to the *ultramar*. The DFEs were designated from 1 to 13, and this number proved to be adequate to maintain the deployment cycle of 10 in the *ultramar* and 3 in the *metrópole*. Additionally, there were 3 African DFEs established in Guiné (DFE 21, 22, and 23) in the early 1970s and disbanded in August 1974. These were trained at the *Centro de Preparação de Fuzileiros Africans* or Center for Preparation of African *Fuzileiros* located at Boloma and led by officers and sergeants who had graduated from the *Escola de Fuzileiros* in the Vale de Zebro. The facility was established in February 1970 and deactivated in August 1974.

The *Companhias de Fuzileiros* (CF) were composed of 120 men and were trained for and charged with the security and immediate defense of naval installations and the security of the waterways of the *ultramar*. Additionally, they conducted inspections of maritime and riverine traffic, reconnaissance patrols, and ambushes in the contested zones of the rivers and lakes of the *ultramar*. Often they collaborated with army units in specific operations or furnished support for moving army troops by water. The CFs held designations numbering from 1 to 11 during the war, although there was a 12th at the end of the war, and this number proved adequate for a proper deployment cycle that maintained 9 CFs (2 CFs in Guiné, 4 in Angola, and 3 in Mozambique) in the *ultramar* and 2 in the *metrópole* on rest and refitting duties. These were on a similar rotation cycle as the DFEs. Further, as both surface and underwater mines were a threat in all theaters and particularly in Guiné, the navy established a small number of specially trained *Destacamentos de Mergulhadores-Sapadores* or detachments of sapper-divers. Members of these detachments were periodically assigned to the Naval Commands and Maritime Defense Commands, and operated with navy units along the rivers.

Officers of the Naval Reserve

Even as the conflict opened in early 1961, the navy was undermanned and had voiced this concern as early as 1958.[56] In an attempt to satisfy not only this current personnel deficit but also the need associated with the expansion of an unfolding war, the navy sought to create a cadre of capable but temporary junior officers who would ably meet the requirements to man and lead the African navy. While there had been a regular flow of permanent junior officers from the *Escola Naval* since its founding in 1845, this source had averaged only about 23 graduates per year between 1926 and 1957, and thus in its present state would not meet the accelerated wartime needs of the navy.[57] An additional program was required to augment this supply.

This problem was not new, for as early as May of 1944 there was discussion within the navy of forming a reserve officer program to augment the regular force, particularly in such specialties as mechanical, chemical, and electrical engineering.[58] Sometime later the concept gained ascendancy, particularly regarding the medical field, and in August 1957, a lengthy study was made of the structure and employment of reserve officers in the French Navy with a view to establishing a similar program.[59] The organization and use of the Royal Naval Volunteer Reserve in the United Kingdom was also examined as a possible model.[60] These thoughts were influential in advancing the concept of a naval reserve force within the Portuguese Navy, and on 26 November 1957 the Naval Reserve was established through Decree Law № 41 399. This law was comprehensive in its reorganization of the personnel and matériel reserves of the navy. By January of the next year the new fledgling reserve officer program had matured in its design stages and appeared ready to play a major part in an expansion of the junior officer ranks to meet navy personnel requirements. By May its special course for reserve officers was ready and intended to graduate and commission its first class of 20 officers later in the year. The army immediately raised objections to this program, asserting that recruitment of reserve officers would be at its expense and undermine a similar army program. The naval position, which prevailed, was that 20 officer graduates from a course held perhaps twice a year would hardly impair recruitment of the comparatively large numbers needed by the army.[61] Establishment of the Naval Reserve proved to be a wise and productive decision. As is evident in the following Table 3.6, the graduates from the permanent and reserve officer programs of the *Escola Naval* through 1965 grew, and reserve officer commissions exceeded permanent commissions from 1963 onwards. This trend held throughout the war.

Table 3.6: Permanent and Reserve Officer Graduates of the *Escola Naval* 1958–1965[62]

Year	Permanent Officers	Reserve Officers	Total
1958	77	20	97
1959	47	37	84
1960	57	36	93
1961	80	44	124
1962	57	46	103
1963	62	66	128
1964	50	64	114
1965	51	68	119

Within this program the navy initially sought to recruit to six specific categories of officer: line officers, naval construction engineers, naval surgeons and pharmacists, engineering officers, and administrative officers.[63] Candidates would be recruited from the national pool of college graduates in all of the sciences, in all of the engineering specialties, in the medical and pharmacology fields, and in the areas of finance and economics. Preference would be given to those who volunteered and particularly to those who already possessed documented seafaring skills within these sought-after disciplines. Once accepted, the officer candidates must complete two cycles of instruction. The first was essentially basic in that it combined a physical regimen with introductory courses on naval warfare. The second was more sophisticated, built on the first, and sought to develop and adapt the practical skills of the candidate in each naval specialty. The basic cycle was largely identical for all cadets, and the advanced one was tailored to the particular requirements of each category. On successful completion of two training cycles, each cadet would be promoted to officer candidate (*aspirante-a-official*) with a service obligation of not less than two years. Each had an option of renewing his contract for additional one-year periods to a maximum of five annual contracts. If posted to the *ultramar*, he would be promoted to the rank of *segundo tenente,* the equivalent of an ensign (U.S. Navy) or a sub-lieutenant (Royal Navy), on his departure from the *metrópole*. Promotion to *primeiro tenente,* the equivalent of lieutenant (junior-grade) (U.S. Navy) or a sub-lieutenant (Royal Navy) generally occurred after five annual contracts and commendable performance as a *segundo tenente*. As a Naval Reserve officer, this represented the maximum achievable rank.[64] The navy thus avoided with this limited program the pitfalls of disrupting the sacrosanct seniority of the permanent officer corps and was able to expand its junior officer ranks with much-needed talent. Most reserve officers viewed the experience as the initial phase of their mature lives and would remember their naval adventures with great fondness and loyalty when they left the service to pursue their familial and professional lives.[65]

On 11 August 1958, the first class of cadets began its 26-weeks of instruction at the *Escola Naval*. The experience was a success. In October 1959 the second class opened, and in October 1960, the third opened. In the midst of these initial classes, the navy expanded the Naval Reserve program to include additional recruiting sources and additional categories of officer, making the total now seven:

1. Line officer (*Marina* or M)
2. Naval construction engineers (*Construção Naval* or ECN)
3. Naval surgeons (*Médicos Navais* or MN)
4. Naval pharmacists (*Farmaceuticos Navais* or FN)
5. Naval engineers (*Engenheiros Maquinistas Navais* or EMQ)
6. Administrative officers (*Administração Naval* or AN)
7. *Fuzileiros* (*Fuzileiros Navais* or FZ).[66]

These moves were in response to adverse developments in Angola, Guiné, and Mozambique, and to the occupation of Portuguese India. With war on the horizon in the *ultramar*, clearly an expansion of both naval matériel and personnel would be required. Reflective of the expansion in categories, the fourth class, which began on 6 October 1961, graduated 44 cadets, 9 of which were the first Naval Reserve *Fuzileiros*. In May 1966, a new, eighth category of technicians and specialists (*Técnicos Especialistas* or TE) was created and included architects, lawyers, and civil and mechanical engineers. The ninth class began on 3 September 1966 with 69 cadets and graduated 8 of this new class. From 1967 onward the classes were accelerated to two per year and continued at this rate until the conclusion of the war. In 1973 the TE category was split into two, one of specialists and the other of technicians. Over the 25 courses conducted, 1,712 cadets were awarded commissions in the Naval Reserve. Many of these officers were selected to command naval vessels in all parts of the *ultramar*, and still others proved themselves in successfully leading *Fuzileiros* under the most adverse physical conditions against experienced and well-armed insurgents. These officers upheld the finest traditions of the navy and truly left a high water mark for their successors.

Despite an increased emphasis on recruiting and the inauguration of imaginative programs, such as the special courses for the Naval Reserve officers, there were substantial personnel concerns in late 1961 after less than a year into the war. An insurgency can swallow large numbers of troops in defensive operations, as the tempo of fighting lies with the insurgent. A small insurgent force can menace a large number of targets, even if it cannot hit them all. These targets must be protected for military or political reasons. Further, unless the population itself is protected, pacification cannot successfully occur. Consequently, the size of government forces will be determined by the vulnerable targets that must be guarded. In the *ultramar* there was a large population scattered over the vast areas of Angola and Mozambique and over the difficult terrain of Guiné. The nature of the insurgent and his way of war dictated under these circumstances that the navy would play an increased role in protecting infrastructure and the waterways, and in projecting power ashore.

A second demand on manpower stems from the fact that the war that you are fighting will only occasionally be the war that you expect to fight. This disparity between plans and reality is explained by the enemy's not doing what you expect. To adjust to these two unpredictable variables that Clausewitz called the "fog of war," troop levels must be increased substantially. No commander was ever condemned for winning a war with too many troops. Consequently, the navy worried extensively about having enough available personnel in the pipeline to address both anticipated and unexpected developments. This concern was aggravated by the fact that it required in its recruits a level of technical proficiency and commitment not normally found in draftees.

Table 3.7: Analysis of Naval Personnel Requirements[67]

	Officers	Petty Officers and Seamen
Authorized force level in 1961	976	8,869
Required force level in 1961	1,281	11,198
Projected force level in 1972	1,384	12,606
Actual force level in 1961	845	6,572
Deficit from authorized level	131	2,297
Deficit from required level	436	4,626
Deficit from projected level	539	6,034

The navy had entered the war understaffed despite its best efforts to anticipate personnel needs. The problem was largely one of resources, as not only was the navy short of personnel, but its ships suffered from a combination of deferred maintenance and advancing years.[68] Table 3.7 summarizes the personnel requirements as they were perceived late in 1961. The data in the table show that the navy was only 87 percent manned as authorized and only 66 percent manned in light of its commitments. It was also considered only 61 percent manned in light of its anticipated commitments a decade hence. As we know, the requirements anticipated in 1972 did not fully materialize, for the blue water ship deliveries were postponed or cancelled for various reasons and their crews were not needed until later or not at all. Nevertheless, the figures for 1961 ably describe the problem. The navy was in the process of manning the *Corpo de Fuzileiros* and the new ships of the African navy, and an immediate shortfall in the neighborhood of 436 officers and 4,626 petty officers and sailors was a realistic estimate and a substantial concern. In frustration, Roboredo noted that the requested numbers seemed modest and reasonable in light of other navies of equivalent capability that were able to sustain manning levels on the order of 15,000 men.[69]

Table 3.8: Officer Manning Deficiencies, 1961[70]

Rank	Required	Authorized	Deficiency
Vice Admiral (*vice almirante*)	1	1	
Rear Admiral (*contra almirante*)	7	6	1
Commodore (*comodoro*)	10	10	
Captain (*capitão de mar e guerra*)	41	35	6
Commander (*capitão de frigata*)	98	73	25
Lieutenant (*capitão tenente*)	172	139	33
Lieutenant (junior grade) (primeiro tenente)	428	295	133
Ensign (*segundo tenente*, and *guarda marinha* or *sub-tenente*)	524	417	107
Total	1,281	976	305

Roboredo wrote that to close this gap the navy would need over the next five years a net addition per year of 90 officers and 950 petty officers (*sargentos*) and seamen (*praças*) over and above present manning. Any more rapid closing of the gap would require aggressive measures.[71] To realize this goal the navy would need to graduate from its programs a minimum of 90 officer cadets and 1,680 enlisted recruits per year to meet both the increased manning levels and natural attrition.[72] The specific officer and enlisted deficiencies between the numbers authorized and those required are detailed in Tables 3.8 through 3.10. Roboredo added as a comment that although not detailed in this analysis, the number of seamen apprentices (*segundo grumetes*) must also expand to 1,878.[73] This important level, just above seamen recruit, was the traditional source of future seasoned and skilled hands who were traditionally needed to man ships and perform the vital yet basic shipboard tasks. The enlisted analysis is divided between crewmen and mess attendants and the total numbers reconcile with Table 3.7. It should be noted that of the 305-officer deficiency, 79 percent was in the junior officer ranks. This shortfall was the target of the Naval Reserve.

Table 3.9: Enlisted Manning Deficiencies (Crewmen)[74]

Rate	Required	Authorized	Deficiency
Chief Petty Officer (*sergeanto adjuante*)	73	69	4
Petty Officer 1st Class (*primeiro sargento*)	695	501	194
Petty Officer 2nd Class (*segundo sargento*)	936	853	83
Petty Officer 3rd Class (*cabo*)	1,422	1,154	268
Seaman (*marinheiro*)	4,300	3,290	1,010
Seaman Apprentice (*primeiro grumete*)	3,130	2,545	585
Total	10,556	8,412	2,144

Table 3.10: Enlisted Manning Deficiencies (Mess Attendants)[75]

Rate	Required	Authorized	Deficiency
Storekeeper First Class (*primeiro despenseiro*)	41	30	11
Storekeeper Second Class (*segundo despenseiro*)	40	40	
Cook First Class (*primeiro cozinhador*)	85	66	19
Cook Second Class (*segundo cozinhador*)	186	136	50
Steward First Class (*primeiro criado*)	130	76	54
Steward Second Class (*segundo criado*)	130	89	41
Baker (*padeiro*)	30	20	10
Total	642	457	185

As described in Table 3.6, the navy was meeting its officer goal of 90 cadets per year and indeed exceeding it primarily through the dramatic success of the Naval Reserve program and its consequent expansion of the junior officer ranks. By 1966 these goals had largely been met, as there were 1,235 officers and 13,145 enlisted in naval uniform.[76] The navy, however, was expanding differently than originally envisioned in the late 1950s in that it was launching a much larger African navy than anticipated and doing so at the expense of its blue water commitment. The delivery of the *João Coutinho* class corvettes would be delayed, and the primary naval effort would be directed toward the brown waters of Africa and the engagement of insurgents in a subversive war. The initial demands came suddenly in Angola in March of 1961 and found the navy making the best of its few resources on the scene, and as we shall see, it acquitted itself well.

Notes

1 John M. Collins, *Military Geography* (Washington: National Defense University Press, 1998), 371–372.

2 Nowfel Leulliot and Danny O'Hara, *The Boats: French Riverine Craft*, http://members.lycos.co.uk/Indochine/cefeo/boats.html (accessed 11 November 2011).

3 Ibid.

4 Ibid.

5 Victor Croizat, The Brown Water Navy (Poole: Blanford Press, 1984), 59.

6 Bernard Estival, "The French Navy and the Algerian War," trans. Paul Leahy, in *France and the Algerian War, 1954–62: Strategy, Operations and Diplomacy*, ed. Martin S. Alexander and J. F. V. Keiger (London: Frank Cass, 2002), 79.

7 Matthew Connelly, *A Diplomatic Revolution: Algeria's Fight for Independence and the Origins of the Post-Cold War Era* (New York: Oxford University Press, 2002), 144.

8 Mário Esteves Brinca (*capitão de fragata*), Estado Maior, Comando Naval de Angola, Estudo da "Directiva 1/64 – Para a Actividade Operacional das Forças Armadas em Angola" na Parte que Interessa ao Comando Naval de Angola [Study of "Directive 1/64 – For the Operational Function of the Armed Forces in Angola" Regarding the Part of Interest to the Naval Command of Angola], Luanda, 18 August 1964, Coloredo Box Angola/176, Arquivo Central da Marinha, Antiga Fabrica Nacional de Cordoaria, Rua da Junqueira, Lisbon.

9 Thomas J. Cutler, *Brown Water, Black Berets* (Annapolis: Naval Institute Press, 1988), 153.

10 The teredo or ship worm is a bivalve mollusk commonly known for the notorious damage it can cause in the timbers of wooden ships. It bores a long cylindrical hole in the wood that it inhabits, often in such great numbers that only a thin film of wood exists between holes. Some worms are said to grow in extreme cases to as much as two centimeters in diameter and a meter in length.

11 The first eight vessels in the class were: *Bellatrix* (P 363), *Canopus* (P 364), *Deneb* (P 365), *Espiga* (P 366), *Fomalhaut* (P 367), *Pollux* (P 368), *Altair* (P 377), and *Rigel* (P 378). The final five vessels were: *Arcturus* (P 1151), *Aldebaran* (P 1152), *Procion* (P 1153), *Sirus* (P 1154), and *Vega* (P 1155).

12 *Adelino Rodrigues da Costa, Dicionário de Navios & Relação de Efemérides (Lisbon: Edições Culturais de Marinha, 2006); and Setenta e Cinco Anos no Mar, 16th volume, (Lisbon: Comissão Cultural de Marinha, 2005).* http://reservanaval.blogspot.com/2009_03_01_archive.html (accessed 22 July 2011).

13 The three vessels of the *Alvor* class were *Alvor* (P 1156), *Albufeira* (P 1157), and *Aljezur* (P 1158). The six vessels of the *Júpiter* class were *Júpiter* (P 1132), *Venus* (P 1133), *Marte* (P 1134), *Mecúrio* (P 1135), *Saturno* (P 1136), and *Urano* (P 1137). The ten vessels of the *Argos* class were *Argos* (P 372), *Cassiopeia* (P 373), *Dragão* (P 374), *Escorpião* (P 375), *Hidra* (P 376), *Lira* (P 361), *Orion* (P 362), *Centauro* (P 1130), and *Sagitario* (P 1131). The ten vessels of the *Cacine* class were *Cacine* (P 1140), *Cunene* (P 1141), *Mandovi* (P 1142), *Rovuma* (P 1143), *Cuanza* (P 1144), *Geba* (P 1145), *Zaire* (P 1146), *Zambeze* (P 1147), *Limpopo* (P 1160), and *Save* (P 1161).

14 The six vessels of the *Albatroz* class were *Albatroz* (P 1162), *Açor* (P 1163), *Andorinha* (P 1164), *Águia* (P 1165), *Condor* (P 1166), and *Cisne* (P 1167).

15 António José Telo, *História da Marinha Portuguesa: Homens, Doutrinas e Organização, 1824–1974 (Tomo I)* [History of the Portuguese Navy: Men, Doctrine and Organization, 1824–1974 (Volume I)] (Lisbon: Academia de Marinha, 1999), 558.

16 Telo, 558. One commercial firm buying in the United States on behalf of the Portuguese Navy was Progresso, Lda.

17 Telo, 558.

18 *Comandante* is a title conferred on all Portuguese naval commanding officers, regardless of rank, and to all officers with the rank of lieutenant commander and above. There is no equivalent in English.

19 Telo, footnote 70, 559.

20 Estado-Maior da Armada, IV Divisão, *Características Principais das Novas Unidades Navais e do Material das Unidades de Fuzileiros* [Principal Characteristics of New Naval and Marine Units] (Lisbon: Estado-Maior da Armada, December 1969), 5–6.

21 A. de Roboredo (*almirante*), Chefe Estado-Maior da Armada, to Minister of the Navy, Lisbon, 14 December 1964, memorandum "Lanchas de Disembarque" [Landing Craft], Coloredo Box 224/601, Arquivo Central da Marinha, Antiga Fabrica Nacional de Cordoaria, Rua da Junqueira, Lisbon.

22 There were four of the LDG 100 series: *Alfange* (LDG 101), *Ariete* (LGD 102), *Cimitarra* (LDG 103), and *Montante* (LDG 104). There were two of the LDG 200 series: *Bombarda* (LDG 105), later redesignated LDG 201, and *Albarda* (LDG 202).

23 Telo, footnote 71, 559.

24 A. B. Rodrigues da Costa, "As Lanchas de Desembarque da Classe *Alfange* (1965–1975)" [*Alfange* Class Landing Craft (1965–1975)], *Revista da Armada* (November 1996): 10; João Falcão de Campos, "Armada Portuguesa: Lanchas e Navios" [Portuguese Navy: Boats and Ships] in *Guerra Colonial* [Colonial War], eds. Aniceto Afonso and Carlos de Matos Gomes (Lisbon: Editorial Notícias, 2000), 389.

25 Costa, 11.

26 Ibid., 13.

27 Telo, 566.

28 The RPG-7 is a recoilless, shoulder-fired, muzzle-loaded, reloadable, antitank grenade launcher. The initials RPG translate into both English Rocket-Propelled Grenade and Russian *Raketniy Protivotankoviy Granatomet*, "a rocket anti-tank grenade launcher." It fires a variety of 85-mm rocket-assisted grenades from a 40-mm smoothbore launcher tube and is light enough at 10.15 kg. to be carried and fired by one person; however, an assistant grenadier normally deploys to the left of the gunner to protect him from small arms fire. The RPG-7 requires a well-trained gunner to estimate ranges and lead distances for moving targets, for crosswinds as low as 7 miles per hour can complicate the gunner's estimate and reduce first-round hit probability to 50 percent at ranges beyond 180 meters. An RPG projectile screen of chain link fence will completely neutralize 50 percent of the rounds and degrade the penetrating capability of the remaining rounds. In addition to its anti-tank role, it can be used against personnel and for bunker-busting and as a side-attack mine system. Reloading and re-aiming the RPG-7 requires a minimum of 14 seconds, and firing leaves noticeable signatures in the form of flash, smoke, and noise. The unprotected gunner is extremely vulnerable to suppressive fires.

29 Telo, 560.

30 Roboredo to Minister of the Navy.

31 Turíbio Abreu, "O Bote de Borracha" [The Rubber Boat], *Anais do Clube Militar Naval* (July-September 1967): 603. While the boats could accommodate outboard engines greater than 35 horsepower, this limit was imposed to contain maintenance costs with acceptable sacrifice in speed.

32 Ibid.

33 A. de Roboredo (*capitão de mar e guerra*), Estado-Maior da Armada, 5 May 1959, point paper "*Fuzileiros*", Coloredo Box 224/2082, Arquivo Central da Marinha, Antiga Fabrica Nacional de Cordoaria, Rua da Junqueira, Lisbon.

34 Jorge Semedo de Matos, "O Terço da Armada da Coroa de Portugal" [The Naval Regiment of the Portuguese Crown], *Revista da Armada* (June 1999): 10–11.

35 A total of 1,770 men.

36 A total of 2,124 men. A company of *Fuzileiros* was composed of 1 captain (*capitão tenente*), 1 lieutenant (*primeiro tenente*), 1 second lieutenant (*segundo tenente*), 4 sergeants (*sargentos*), 1 storekeeper (*furrier*), 2 squad corporals (*cabos de esquadra*), 1 drummer (*tambor*), and 160 *Fuzileiros*.

37 A total of 1,328 men. There were nine companies of artificers with 132 men each and one company of ballasters with 148 men.

38 Carlos Lorch, ed., *Fuzileiros Navais, Brazil's Amphibious Warriors* (Rio de Janeiro: Action Editora, 1997), 34–36.

39 Each company was composed of 1 captain (*capitão*), 1 first lieutenant (*tenente*), 1 second lieutenant (*alferes*), 1 staff sergeant (*primeiro sargento*), 4 sergeants (*segundo sargentos*), 2 drummers (*tambores*), 8 corporals (*cabos*), and 92 privates (*soldados*).

40 Each company was composed of 1 captain (*capitão*), 1 first lieutenant (*tenente*), 1 second lieutenant (*alferes*), 1 staff sergeant (*primeiro sargento*), 1 storekeeper (*furrier*), 5 corporals (*cabos*), 5 lance corporals (*anspeçadas*), 64 privates (*soldados*), and 1 bugler (*corneta*).

41 Telo, 550.

42 Comando Naval de Angola to Estado-Maior da Armada, Luanda, 11 April 1960, Nota № 28 "Segurança das provincias ultramarinas", Coloredo Box Angola/176, Arquivo Central da Marinha, Antiga Fabrica Nacional de Cordoaria, Rua da Junqueira, Lisbon.

43 Jorge Alexandre da Fonseca (*tenente coronel*), Military and Aeronautical Attaché, Embassy of Portugal in Paris, to A. de Roboredo (*capitão de mar e guerra*), Estado-Maior da Armada, Paris, 3 February 1959, memorandum "Relaying approval for the training of 1 *lieutenant de vaisseau*, 1 *sous-officer* et 5 *marins* at the École des Fusiliers, Centre Siroco, Algeria", Coloredo Box 224/2082, Arquivo Central da Marinha, Antiga Fabrica Nacional de Cordoaria, Rua da Junqueira, Lisbon.

44 A. de Roboredo (*capitão de mar e guerra*), Estado-Maior da Armada, to Naval Attaché, Embassy of Portugal in London, 3 February 1959, memorandum "Request training for a group in principal", Coloredo Box 224/2082, Arquivo Central da Marinha, Antiga Fabrica Nacional de Cordoaria, Rua da Junqueira, Lisbon; and Jaime Lopes (*capitão de fragata*), Naval Attaché, Embassy of Portugal in London, to Estado-Maior da Armada, London, 3 April 1959, memorandum "Instruction of 'Commandos'", Coloredo Box 224/2082, Arquivo Central da Marinha, Antiga Fabrica Nacional de Cordoaria, Rua da Junqueira, Lisbon.

45 António Alves Leite (*contra almirante*), Sub-chefe do Estado-Maior da Armada, to Chefe do Estado-Maior da Armada, Lisbon, 1 May 1959, memorandum "Instrução de commandos", Coloredo Box 224/2082, Arquivo Central da Marinha, Antiga Fabrica Nacional de Cordoaria, Rua da Junqueira, Lisbon.

46 Luís Celestino da Silva (*contra almirante*), Superintendência dos Servios da Armada, to Estado-Maior da Armada, Lisbon, 6 June 1960, memorandum "Instrução de 'comandos'", Coloredo Box 224/601, Arquivo Central da Marinha, Antiga Fabrica Nacional de Cordoaria, Rua da Junqueira, Lisbon.

47 Decreto-Lei № 43515 of 24 February 1961.

48 *Escola de Fuzileiros*. Portaria № 18509 of 3 June 1961.

49 Portaria № 18774 of 13 October 1961.

50 Corpo de *Fuzileiros, Part II: Fuzileiros Especiais*, unpublished history (Lisbon: Ministério da Marinha, 1987), 14.

51 Luís Sanches de Baêna, *Fuzileiros: Factos e Feitos na Guerra de África 1961/1974*, Volume 1 [*Fuzileiros*: Facts and Feats in the African War 1961/1974, Volume 1 (Lisbon: Comissão Cultural da Marinha, 2006), 46.

52 Sanches de Baêna, 48.

53 *Capitão de fragata* Luís Jorge Matos, interview with the author, 10 February 2003, Bélem.

54 "*Fuzileiros*" draft article, TMs [photocopy], *Diário de Notícas*, 1995, 3.

55 Ibid.

56 Guerreiro de Brito (*vice almirante*), Chefe do Estado-Maior da Armada, to Minister of the Navy, Lisbon, 2 January 1960, memorandum "Programa de Preenchimento dos Novos Quadros" [Program for Acquiring New Personnel], Coloredo Box 224/2082, Arquivo Central da Marinha, Antiga Fabrica Nacional de Cordoaria, Rua da Junqueira, Lisbon.

57 Ministério da Marinha, *A Marinha nos Últimos 40 Anos 1926–1966* [The Navy in the Last 40 Years 1926–1966] (Lisbon: Ministério da Marinha, 1967), 194.

58 Manuel Ortins de Bettencourt (*captão tenente*), Minister of the Navy, Lisbon, 31 May 1944, handwritten point paper "*Reserva Naval*" [Naval Reserve], Coloredo Box 224/2082, Arquivo Central da Marinha, Antiga Fabrica Nacional de Cordoaria, Rua da Junqueira, Lisbon.

59 Roberto Ivens Ferraz de Carvalho (*captão tenente*), Paris, 31 August 1957, handwritten study "Preparation and utilization of reserves in the French Navy," Coloredo Box 224/2082, Arquivo Central da Marinha, Antiga Fabrica Nacional de Cordoaria, Rua da Junqueira, Lisbon.

60 J. Ramalho Rosa (*capitão de fragata*) to Estado-Maior da Armada, London, 7 December 1957, letter "Royal Naval Volunteer Reserves," Coloredo Box 224/2082, Arquivo Central da Marinha, Antiga Fabrica Nacional de Cordoaria, Rua da Junqueira, Lisbon.

61 António Alves Leite (*contra almirante*), Subchefe do Estado-Maior da Armada, to Superintendant of Naval Services, Lisbon, 5 May 1958, memorandum "Cursos Especiais de Oficiais da Reserva Naval" [Special Courses for Officers of the Naval Reserve], Coloredo Box 224/2082, Arquivo Central da Marinha, Antiga Fabrica Nacional de Cordoaria, Rua da Junqueira, Lisbon.

62 A. de Roboredo (*contra almirante*), Subchefe do Estado-Maior da Armada, to Fernando de Quintanilha (*contra almirante*), Minister of the Navy, Lisbon, 5 December 1961, memorandum "Reajustamento dos Quadros Permanentes do Pessoal da Armada" [Readjustment of the Permanent Manning Levels of the Navy], Coloredo Box 224/2082, Arquivo Central da Marinha, Antiga Fabrica Nacional de Cordoaria, Rua da Junqueira, Lisbon, 7.

63 A.B. Rodrigues da Costa and Manuel Pinto Machado, *O Anuário da Reserva Naval 1958–1975* [The Annual of the Naval Reserve 1958–1975] (Lisbon: Associação dos Oficiais da Reserva Naval, 1992), 135.

64 Portaria № 16 714 of 27 May 1958.

65 Rodrigues da Costa and Pinto Machado, 27.

66 Ibid., 23.

67 Ibid.

68 A. de Roboredo to Fernando de Quintanilha, 6.

69 Ibid., 7.

70 Ibid., 9.

71 Ibid., 8.

72 Ibid., 10.

73 Ibid.

74 Ibid., 10.

75 Ibid.

76 Ministério da Marinha, *A Marinha nos Últimos 40 Anos 1926–1966*, 146.

4

River that Swallows all Rivers

In 1482 King João II revived the earlier interest for a sea route around Africa to India, and the first of his newly commissioned and ambitious voyages was the expedition of Diogo Cão. Cão was an experienced naval captain who had made a name for himself fighting privateers along the coast of West Africa. He departed Lisbon, it is thought, in May or June of 1482 and followed the coast of West Africa as far as Fort São Jorge da Mina (Elmina) in present-day Ghana, formerly the Gold Coast. Here he reprovisioned and continued along the Central African coast through the Bights of Benin and Biafra and across the equator to Cape Santa Catarina, where he probably arrived in early August and anchored in the Bay of Loango. From this point onward Cão's seamanship was tested, as he was moving through uncharted waters further south than any European had ventured. The current and winds were against him, so he slowly tacked along the continental shelf taking advantage of the convection breezes. As August wore on, Cão came upon what appeared to be a bay or inlet with two spits of land 12 to 15 miles apart arcing into the Atlantic. The sea, however, had turned into a thick, muddy-red hue, and the water tasted sweet rather than salt, indicating its freshness. The waves breaking on the surrounding beaches were a brownish-yellow. As Cão sailed toward the apparent bay, he encountered an increasingly strong and powerful current reaching seven knots. As he got closer to shore, he saw floating islands moving with the current out to sea. Clearly he was entering the mouth of a silt-filled river. As a reflection of its great power, modern oceanographers have charted "a hundred-mile-long canyon, in places four thousand feet deep, that it has carved out of the sea floor."[1] Paulo Lowndes Marques, a *Fuzileiro* junior officer on the Zaire in 1966, remarked in a letter to a friend that from the air the mouth of the river appeared like a large brown clog in the stomach of the South Atlantic.[2] Likewise, Vice Admiral António Emílio Ferraz Sacchetti later remembered his experience on a midshipman cruise to South Africa, when suddenly the blue ocean turned brown as his vessel entered the discharge from the Zaire some 50 miles from shore.[3] Cão had indeed discovered a river larger and more dramatic than any European had seen to date.

Cão anchored about a mile upstream in a small cove on the left bank near the present-day town of Santo António do Zaire, where he went ashore and erected a stone pillar or *padroe* marking the discovery in the name of King João II.[4] Here he encountered and befriended the local Bakongo people and asked them the name of the mighty river. They called it *nzere* or *nzadi*, which in their language meant "the river that swallows all rivers."[5] Cão was apparently unable to pronounce the word as the natives did and said *zaire* instead, and that is the name by which it became known to Westerners. Almost five centuries later this important waterway that in part now separated the rich, beautiful, and most Portuguese Congo District of Angola from its Belgian counterpart became a deep security concern.[6] For the navy this 80-mile riverine border was the center of activity in Angola during the initial years of the conflict. While the navy began its action on the coast with a modest force, it soon moved into this grand river as rapidly as resources arrived and experience was gained in projecting power and securing the frontier from infiltration. As we shall see, it improvised to address the first contact, and after the initial shock, developed a measured and considered approach to joining its fellow services in securing the northern border of Angola.

An Amazing Land

Angola is a vast territory at 1,246,314 square kilometers, an area that is about fourteen times the size of Portugal or as large as the combined areas of Spain, France, and Italy. Its land frontier with its neighbors of the former Belgian Congo (Zaire), Northern Rhodesia (Zambia), and South-West Africa (Namibia) extends 4,837 kilometers and is so lengthy and remote that it is virtually impossible to control. The Zaire River, which comprises a relatively small part of the border in the northwest, remains full of thickly wooded islands that provided excellent cover for insurgents. Crossings could be and were made undetected at virtually any point. The terrain from the border southward remains likewise covered with dense tropical forest originating in the river banks of the Zaire, which gives way to thick elephant grass eight to ten feet tall, swamp, and mountain. This region shelters diverse fauna, such as crocodiles, elephants, deer, and *pacaças* or Angolan buffalos. The few roads through the area were beaten earth and were little better than tracks.

Angola is also a land of geographical contrasts. Topographically, it is bordered on the west by the Atlantic Ocean, where a coastal belt runs the length of the approximately 1,650-kilometer shoreline, rising to a central highland 50 to 200 kilometers inland that covers about 60 percent of the country. This highland varies in altitude between 1,000 meters and its highest point of 2,619 meters at Môca, a mount in the district of Huambo. Further inland, the land descends to an eastern plateau with an elevation as high as 1,600 meters.

The diversity of relief and the territorial extent of Angola produce a varied climate ranging from tropical wet in the Dembos region, to mild wet in the northern coastal plains, to tropical dry in the southern highlands, to semi-desert in the southeast. The rainy season occurs between November and May and is followed by a form of winter, known locally as the *cacimbo* or drizzle season, which extends to November.

Such vastness and diversity in terrain have always made communication difficult in Angola. This difficulty would extend to both the insurgents and government forces, and each would find its solution in very different ways. From external sanctuaries the insurgents would struggle over long and difficult passages to reach local populations that could be proselytized and tapped for food, shelter, recruits, and intelligence. On the other hand, the Portuguese would protect these populations by isolating the insurgents within the vastness of the country and destroying them with military force. In support of this strategy, the navy began its operations along the coast and moved into the rivers, as the fight matured. It began with a very small force and expanded it into a large and very effective riverine navy.

Angola Patrol

In Angola, the navy began with the small, three-vessel deployment consisting of the frigate *Pacheco Pereira* (F 327) and the patrol boats *Sal* (P 584) and *São Vicente* (P 586), all of which had been deployed to Angola at the beginning of 1960 in an attempt to prevent the internal unrest in the Belgian Congo from spilling into the north of the territory. Once the Belgian security forces had departed the Congo in mid-July, there arose a series of border incidents and a movement of refugees along and across the Zaire River. One such incident was firing aimed at the hydrographic vessel *Carvalho Araújo* (A 524) in the port of Noqui. The naval force monitored the movement of river traffic, which ranged from small canoes or *pirogas* to 20,000-ton merchant vessels bound for the Congolese port of Matadi, where there was a railhead for the line to Léopoldville. It also aided the movement of refugees and otherwise provided a reassuring presence along the water frontier.[7] All of this was fairly routine and done in accordance with the 10 September 1919 Convention of Saint Germain-en-Laye, which authorized the unrestricted freedom of fluvial navigation, except in the case of normal security and public order. This low-level tension continued throughout the year and into the early months of 1961, and as a consequence the patrol boat *São Tomé* (P 585) and the two additional frigates, *Nuno Tristão* (F 332) and *Diogo Gomes* (F 331), were added to the force.

On 4 March, opposite the Congolese city of Boma, some 45 to 50 miles upriver from Santo António do Zaire and just east of Pedra do Feitiço (Fetish Rock), the frigate *Nuno Tristão* received machinegun and heavy weapons fire.[8] The captain wisely did not return fire, as there was no wish to provoke incidents with an already volatile Congo. In retrospect, this activity was a part of UPA preparations for its infamous barbaric assault. This almost indescribably primordial attack occurred on 15 March across the northwest border of Angola and into the Dembos region, an area of rugged terrain and relatively isolated settlements and coffee farms. The concentrated assault of an estimated 5,000 UPA forces and the forced recruiting of perhaps another 25,000 overwhelmed local authorities and left the area paralyzed.[9] Several thousand whites, blacks, and *mestiços* were brutally and grotesquely murdered in unimaginable fashion over the next several weeks. Villages, towns, outposts, and farms were overrun, and the looting and destruction of property became a trademark of the mayhem. While the UPA quickly reached its culmination point, there remained thousands of attackers roaming about northern Angola searching for food and committing atrocities with precious few Portuguese resources available to round them up and restore order.

Total Portuguese Army forces in Angola at the time were the modest 8,000 described earlier. These were spread across Angola in various training roles, and were unprepared to repel any full-scale invasion. The modest infrastructure serving Angola likewise hindered efforts to bring help to the affected area. From the larger perspective the Portuguese military was equally unprepared, and following the 15 March attack, was unable to bring troops to the region in appreciable numbers until 1 May. It took until 13 June, some three months later, to reoccupy the first small administrative post of Lucunga.[10]

With this assault and the ensuing chaos, there was simply not enough manpower, skilled or not, to address the upheaval. A patchwork of civil-military defense was cobbled together to halt the UPA advance, kill or capture the perpetrators, and address the grave civil distress. The navy was drawn into this vacuum, and the importance of its small contribution of little more than 450 men proved to be disproportionate, despite the many non-traditional roles. This was due to its discipline, training, skilled leadership, and particularly its secure waterborne mobility that bypassed the rudimentary and vulnerable infrastructure.[11] While the deployment of detachments from each ship's company would reduce shipboard manning to between 25 and 30 percent of the normal complement, each vessel continued to execute its assignment and relied on the personal sacrifice of the remaining crewmen on board and the longer days and extra duties that it implied.[12] It

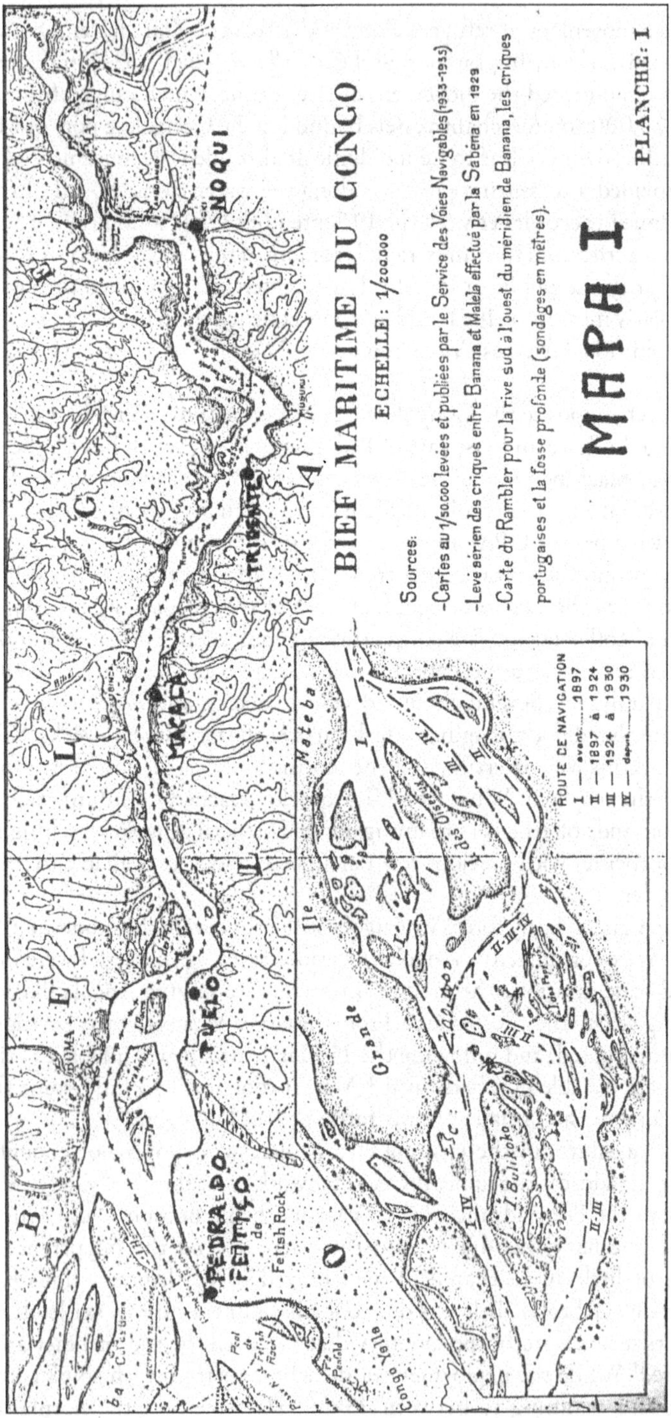

Zaire River border with the Belgian Congo (Chart in two sections). Copies of Belgian charts of the Zaire River used by the Portuguese Navy from March 1961 and annotated

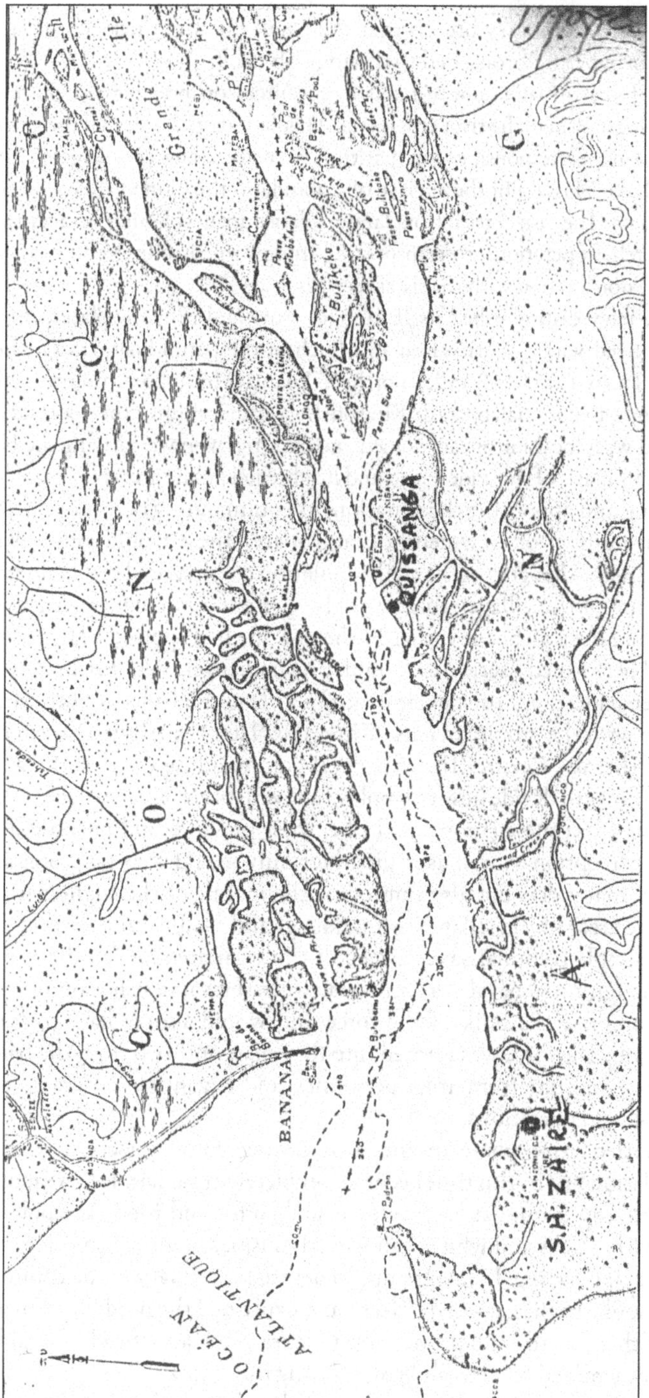

by the user to show the Naval Posts established during the initial years of the conflict.

was thus into this temporary breech that the small but stout-hearted naval presence was immediately thrown and proceeded to distinguish itself.

The naval force initially concentrated its resources on policing the 80-mile Zaire River frontier from Noqui, where the river crosses the Angola-Congo border, all the way to the Atlantic Ocean. It was further responsible for maritime security along the Angolan coastline in the Atlantic from Lake Massábi in the enclave of Cabinda to the Cunene River on the border with South-West Africa. The tasks varied from landing detachments of sailors to act in an infantry role, to performing relief operations, to transporting troops, to patrolling waterways as a reassuring presence, all in coordination with the sister services.

While the navy distinguished itself in many ways and in many places, the first and most significant occurred with the arrival on 18 March of the patrol boat *São Vicente* at Ambriz, a coastal village located some 60 miles north of Luanda. In approaching the village, the ship encountered a number of small boats drifting offshore at the whim of the tides and currents. These craft were filled with local European women and children who were fleeing the UPA and whose plight was symptomatic of the widespread and heightened public anxiety.

On landing and appraising the situation, its commanding officer decided to disembark the maximum number of crewmen he could spare. These would join a platoon of local troops and auxiliary elements of the civil population commanded by a lieutenant of artillery to secure defense of the village. There was also present a Portuguese Air Force lieutenant colonel, who had been airborne earlier in the day. He had spotted a large concentration of locals and had performed a series of intimidating maneuvers with his aircraft in a successful attempt to persuade them to stay clear of the village. He subsequently landed and now sought to help with the ground defense. Three days later the frigate *Pacheco Pereira* arrived in support of the *São Vicente*. The two naval commanding officers, the aviator, and the lieutenant now met to decide how to employ the available forces most effectively. As modest and inexperienced as these troops might be, their presence and purposeful activity were important in perception as well as reality. Not only would they be protecting the village from potential marauders but also improving the morale of the frightened citizens. After fortifying some areas of the village with sandbags and establishing a redoubt with sentries, they began a simple reconnaissance sweep of the local area for familiarization as well as security. Although most naval personnel had only the vaguest notion of land operations, they would comprise the bulk of the force and would simply have to learn these new duties on the job. The force was formed into four platoons, two from the frigate, one from the patrol boat, and one from army personnel, and began its accelerated acclimation in anticipation of land operations.

The unsettled atmosphere in the surrounding countryside was troublesome. The civilian population had by this time become completely armed. Indeed weapons had become as much a table-top feature at local cafés as had coffee and food. The polarization of the population, with blacks and whites being overly suspicious of one another, was dangerous in its vigilante-like setting. In an attempt to defuse this situation, the commanding officer of the frigate spoke to the gathered citizens and explained the need for cooperation and the uselessness of their hostile and provocative posture. Such an attitude, he said, would cause additional unwarranted friction and risk injuring innocents.[13]

Reflective of the tension was an incident that occurred one night just before dawn. There was suddenly a great piercing shriek and roar from within the redoubt, as if someone were being drawn and quartered. Everyone awoke in panic, grabbed his weapon, and raced

Pacheco Pereira disembarking *Fuzileiros*. Photograph courtesy Estado-Maior da Armada and Revista da Armada

to his post expecting to face an enemy onslaught. It was assumed in the confusion and darkness that the defensive perimeter had been breached and that one or more men had met an unfortunate end at the hands of the insurgents. Happily with the first light, it was found that nothing of the sort had happened. The alarm had apparently been caused by one of the men having had a severe nightmare and yelling in his sleep. The overreaction was reflective of the enormous stress on everyone.[14]

On 24 March following six days of very basic infantry training, an army and a naval platoon quietly conducted a sweep of the area around the village and discovered several strangers who were detained for further identification. As it turned out, most were recognized and released without further concern. Those few who were actual interlopers and potential threats were held under guard. That same day the *Pacheco Pereira* departed for Ambrizete to the north, leaving two sections of sailors commanded by an officer and equipped with a radio to maintain communication with the frigate. The next day the remaining prisoners were taken to Luanda on the patrol boat *São Tomé,* and the two sections recovered. For the moment, the army platoon and some militia represented the sole Ambriz defense.

As the severity of the overall situation in the north of Angola became clearer to the authorities, it was apparent that a more robust force was needed in Ambriz. Because of the paucity of resources, the obvious answer was to continue the naval presence in coordination with the army platoon already there. Consequently, two sections from the frigate *Nuno Tristão,* one commanded by a junior officer (*secundo tenente*) and the other by a naval reserve midshipman on his pre-commissioning cruise, were put ashore two days later on 26 March. Headquarters for the small force was established at the local movie house, for it provided a central and commanding position over the village. The personnel from the frigate, while they had been well trained in naval matters, were again not familiar with ground maneuvers. This weakness would be overcome in the subsequent weeks by learning from the experience of the army platoon and adapting itself as a land force. In addition to acquiring the skills of patrolling, many sailors had never driven a vehicle in their lives and thus were treated to the thrilling experience of learning to operate a jeep over bad roads. This indeed was an important skill, as the jeep provided the necessary mobility on extended patrols. With the progression of the training, the force gained confidence and was able to perfect a system of active reconnaissance and security patrols that would provide ample warning and protection against possible attack. Indeed, the two services learned to operate well together, a positive omen for things to come.

In conducting these activities, the force found contact with the local population to be mixed. This was quite natural, as everyone was extremely anxious about the alarming news from the interior. When the sailors first arrived, part of the local population had fled inland out of fear of the military in the unfamiliar and confused situation. Little by little individuals began to return to the village, as confidence in the friendliness of the newly arrived force built and its ability to protect them became apparent. Medical personnel within the force likewise offered treatment and care. Even so, it was difficult to build but so much trust within the local population, black or white, as a permanent garrison on constant alert spoke volumes about the gravity of the circumstances. In short, the village was an armed camp, and this situation in and of itself created enormous anxiety.

Conditions of insecurity persisted throughout the north of Angola and created the need for a permanent state of elevated military readiness. The general population continued to be vulnerable to the UPA, and this threat required additional manpower. Accordingly, once the situation at Ambriz was stabilized, the frigate *Nuno Tristão* recovered one of its two sections and moved to Ambrizete further north along the coast. The soldiers and sailors who stayed behind continued their patrols for the next month without incident. Because the village seemed relatively safe, arrangements were made to move the sailors, and on 21 April the frigate *Diogo Gomes* embarked the remaining naval force.

While events were unfolding at Ambriz, an additional drama was occurring at Ambrizete, a small port about 100 miles north of Luanda and the gateway to an area cut off by UPA forces. It represented one of the few avenues through which help could be brought to an isolated and terrified local population. On 22 March the patrol boat *São Tomé* arrived, and its commanding officer took the initiative in organizing defense of the town. Two days later the frigate *Pacheco Pereira* arrived and added an armed detachment from its ship's company. Later on 7 April, the frigate *Nuno Tristão* contributed two reinforced sections, each commanded by a junior officer, a *primeiro tenente* and *secundo tenente*.[15] In contrast to the news elsewhere that all was falling apart, the atmosphere in Ambrizete was disciplined and purposeful, and the people appeared determined to beat back the UPA rabble. They were organized and prepared for any enemy offensive and indeed had transformed the town center into a sandbagged fortress. As refugees arrived over the following days, the line of fortifications was expanded. This influx also generated the typical health problems caused by crowding in the small fort. On 14 April toward 2200 hours, one of the naval platoons sighted a suspicious group of men and fired on it. A second naval platoon supported the first with several bursts from a machinegun. There appeared to be casualties, as some of the men in the searchlight beam were seen to fall. Because assessment was difficult in the dark, all awaited dawn.[16]

At daybreak the troops found little trace of the assailants. Nevertheless, it proved that their system of patrols and defenses had worked and gave a boost in confidence. As the incident was assumed to have been a UPA probing action preceding a major attack, the town was put in a high state of alert and maintained this posture for several days and nights. During this period of "siege," those with engineering and construction skills passed the time improving the capabilities of the small port. In the "record" time of five days, a working party built a 25-meter pier from the beach into the sea that would accommodate vessels of up to two meters in draft.[17] This new infrastructure would facilitate support from the sea through the direct embarkation of personnel and supplies rather than their transfer by launches onto the beach.

Three weeks passed until the arrival of the frigate *Diogo Gomes* with its relief force for the *Nuno Tristão* detachment. For another two months the routine of guarding the town continued. On 12 June the *Nuno Tristão* made its final appearance. The next relief would be a contingent from Infantry Battalion 109 (*Batalhão de Caçadores 109*), which would make its way overland from Santo António do Zaire.

While waiting for the army to arrive, the governor of the District of Zaire asked the naval force to check on two villages, Tombôco and Quinzau, as their fate was unknown. It had not been possible to organize their defense with the shortage of manpower and the lack of communications, but now with an army battalion on its way down the coast road, the force at Ambrizete felt confident in embarking on an extended patrol. At dawn on 13 June, a mixed force of naval and civilian personnel left Ambrizete for Tombôco in seven vehicles, some in very bad shape. The track inland had become overgrown after several months of disuse, and it required seven hours to travel the 100 kilometers. The trip was without major incident, and the force found the Portuguese flag still flying, the village intact, and a group of about a hundred women weeding the airstrip.[18]

Again at dawn the next day, a second column left Ambrizete for Quinzau, a small village some 57 kilometers north along the coast. After having traveled only 10 kilometers, it encountered the relief, Company 114 of the battalion. On 19 June the naval force departed on the *São Vicente*, ending three months of naval presence.

The navy performed a number of similar support operations on the Chiloango River in the enclave of Cabinda, and particularly along the Zaire. From a naval standpoint Cabinda was hardly threatened. The paranoia from the attacks, however, ran high, and there was even a directive to look for submarines in Lake Massábi, which is only 2.5 meters deep and often isolated when the water recedes at low tide.[19] In truth, the navy acted more like a ferry service around the lake with its small launch, and this presence along with the regular coastal patrol by larger vessels from Luanda had a calming effect on the local residents.

The Zaire was quite different, however. From the first days of March there was a naval presence in Noqui. The frigate *Pacheco Pereira* arrived on 26 March to support the defense of the town and to evacuate its citizens, if needed. Despite the fact that Noqui was home to a company of 180 indigenous troops commanded by a captain, it was in a particularly difficult situation, as something in the neighborhood of 10,000 UPA terrorists were thought to have been receiving training in camps near the Congo village of Soio and were supposed to attack Noqui between 25 March and 3 April.[20] While the danger proved to be overblown; nevertheless, the threat was taken seriously.

Fetish Rock was yet another small and vulnerable village on the bank of the Zaire that from early March had been visited weekly by a warship. Its citizens refused to abandon it. Santo António do Zaire at the mouth of the river had an almost constant naval presence. Its nearby villages of Porto Rico and Sumba had been the subject of UPA attacks during this period and had received naval protection and support. A more permanent force of *Fuzileiros* would arrive in January 1962, of which we will hear more later. Patrols at sea extended as far south as the Cunene River, and naval detachments in the role of light infantry platoons served in and around Sá da Bandeira and Luanda, guarding various installations and playing an active role in their defense. In all cases naval personnel acquitted themselves well. Their high degree of effectiveness had as its basis the intense training that they had received aboard ship under operational conditions. This disciplined teamwork lent itself readily to other tasks, such as the temporary infantry duties that were so well performed.

Mopping-up operations became more robust from June onward, as army troops were mobilized in the *metrópole* and began arriving by ship in Luanda. The navy redirected its resources toward the towns of Noqui, Santo António do Zaire, and Landana in the enclave of Cabinda, as the authorities realized that restoring order in the northwest of Angola was always going to be a manpower-intensive land operation. The navy would play its traditionally supportive role in the undertaking and accordingly identified ways to apply leverage in favor of ground operations.

First, its primary mission was to prevent the enemy from using any of the waterways for its purposes. It would have to deny the sea approaches and rivers to the enemy and prevent his support of inland activity through these avenues. This would be done through both defensive and offensive operations. Defensively, the navy would establish static posts at key points along the rivers and the maritime shoreline from which it could project power. Offensively, it would conduct patrols continuously along these riverine and oceanic frontiers. This obvious requirement for a substantially increased and dynamic waterborne presence would require the creation of an extensive system of bases and their associated infrastructure as well as a tailored fleet of patrol boats with specially trained crews.

Second, the navy would supply the necessary waterborne transportation to give the army the needed agility to maneuver successfully against the enemy. This would entail the transport of troops and their perquisite logistic support. The navy would accomplish this through the operation of its newly acquired fleet of landing craft.

Third, the navy would supply waterborne artillery to provide land forces with firepower on remote, river-accessible battlefields, where the alternative of moving cannon across difficult terrain devoid of all but the most elementary infrastructure would likely be impossible or very difficult at best. The 4-inch and 40-mm naval guns of the *Alvares Cabral* class, and later the smaller purpose-designed *Cacine*, *Azevia*, and *Argos* classes with their 40-mm guns, were the most powerful that could be brought into the river confines of Africa for this task.

Fourth, the navy would support the police and customs service through its ability to project power throughout the river systems. In counterinsurgency the police are the force most attached and closest to the population for whose loyalty the battle is being fought.

The Second Phase

Alongside the army, naval resources continued to arrive in Angola. Principally these were the newly constructed *Belatrix* LFP class patrol boats *Espiga* (P 366), *Fomalhaut* (P 367), and *Pollux* (P 368), which were welcomed on 23 September 1961 by the Naval Command of Angola in a formal arming ceremony. These vessels had a maximum displacement of 27.6 tons and because of this were nicknamed "30 tonners." They were assigned to the Patrol

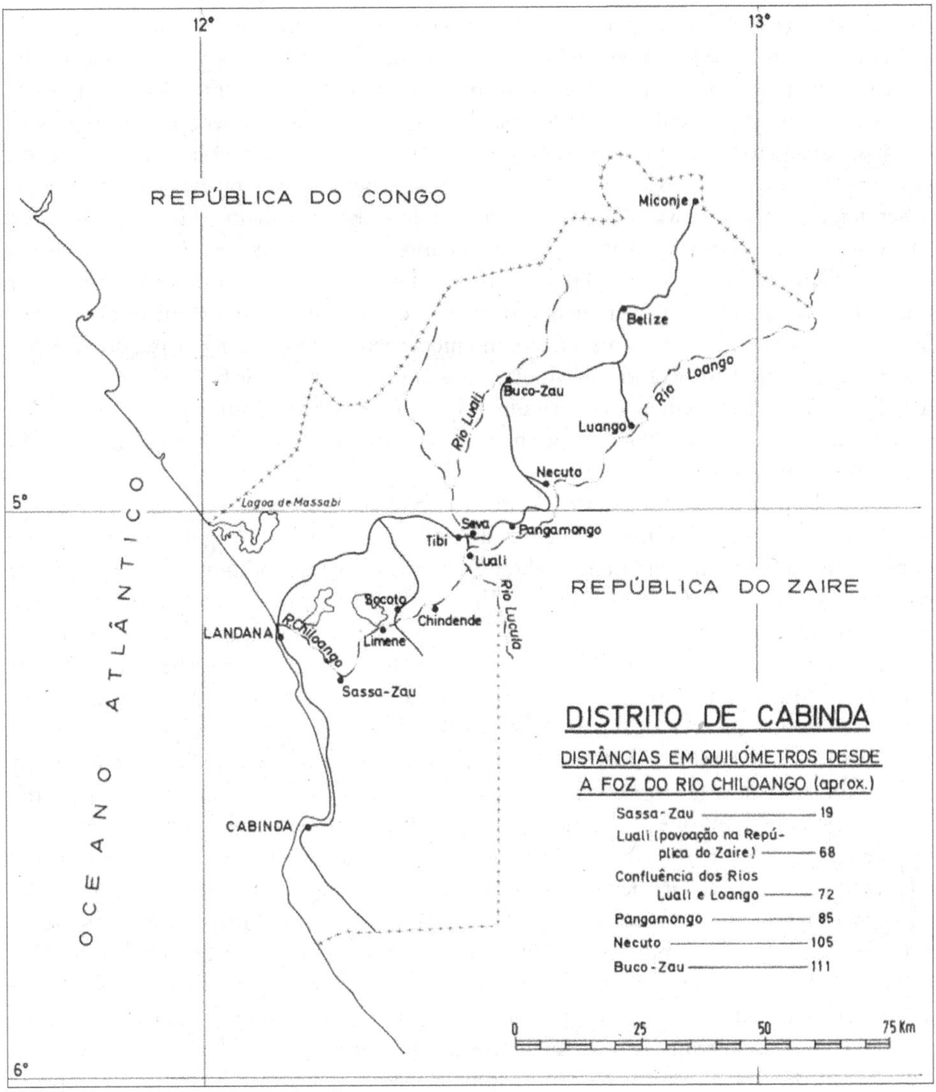

Enclave of Cabinda. Source: *Nem a Pátria Sabe, A Marinha na Guerra em Angola 1961–1963* by José Mexia Salema.

Squadron Zaire (*A Esquadrilha de Lanchas de Fiscalizaão do Zaire*) and were generally commanded by young junior officers of the Naval Reserve. Each had a crew consisting of a sergeant and a varying mixture of five corporals and sailors.[21]

Patrol Squadron Zaire was created in July 1961 and began operations with the delivery of the LFs later that year. It was part of the Maritime Defense Command of Santo António do Zaire, a sub-command of the overall Naval Command of Angola. The squadron commander was a lieutenant and was responsible for the operational and administrative functions of its launches and most particularly for their battle readiness. He largely occupied himself with the myriad tasks to this end and worried about the functions of navigation, communications, gunnery, boarding parties, amphibious landings, demolition, ambushes, and the many other details in training warship crews to fight effectively. In planning missions he studied the strategic and tactical situation, the available intelligence, the motivations of the enemy, and his likely courses of action. He then planned accordingly, developing a sense of the mission at hand and the requirements for its success. His most important responsibility, however, was the well-being of his officers and men, their understanding of and preparation for the squadron mission, and their motivation and excitement for fulfilling it as a team. All of these tasks represented an enormous responsibility for the young lieutenant and his squadron, but then such pivotal duties have always been held by able young commanders throughout the history of naval warfare.

As to the patrol boats, the navy sought to employ this new capability constructively as soon as possible and to assume an increased role in the defense of Angola. An immediate opportunity lay just south of Luanda, where there was a large area of sprawling and relatively remote sugar cane and cotton plantations. This rich cultivated area extended from the coast inland to the rugged mountainous rise to the high plateau. There was a sizable population living here that depended on the preservation of the plantations and their crops for its livelihood. Much of the area was naturally isolated, as the villages and settlements were connected to one another and to the main road to Luanda by primitive and narrow trails. The Cuanza River ran through the middle of this rich area and served as a natural waterway that would provide a far easier access to check on the population than an overland trek. The river itself remains one of the major Angolan watercourses with a length of about 900 kilometers and together with its tributaries forms the largest hydrographic basin in the country. Unfortunately, its navigability is marginal at best, as its depth is very irregular and generally shallow, and its length is broken regularly with fall lines. During the rainy season between January and July and with calm weather and a high tide, small ships with a draft of 2.5 to 3.0 meters can cautiously enter the river and navigate inland for some 214 kilometers to Dondo. This village is just downstream from the Cambambe Dam, where the river ends its descent from the plateau and begins its journey across the coastal belt to the Atlantic. In the dry season the depths in some places do not exceed half a meter, and the river is navigable only by the local *pirogas,* a graceful dugout canoe.[22]

The population in this region had been threatened by the approaching UPA attacks, and indeed some of the mayhem had penetrated parts of the area. As a consequence, the population was generally unsettled, and many had fled to Luanda in search of safety. At the end of August, the *Carvalho Araújo* with its 4.5-meter draft had attempted the transit upriver to check on the well-being of the citizenry and offer support, but it was simply not possible because of the low river conditions.

When the "30-tonners" became available for missions in late September, the *Pollux* and

Fomalhaut reported to Santo António do Zaire, and the *Espiga* drew the task of patrolling the Cuanza. It entered the river on 26 September and with its 1.2 meter draft had better luck. It reached the village of Bom Jesus some 85 kilometers upstream and established a base there. Later on 13 November it moved to the historic settlement of Muxima some 139 kilometers from the mouth, where there was the ancient *fortaleza* and the Chapel of Nossa Senora da Conceição, both more than 300 years old. On 14 December it finally reached the village of Dondo. As it passed through this area of poor infrastructure on its way upstream, it coordinated closely with the army and was able to help significantly with troop mobility and area security. On 22 December it was recalled to help with security in Luanda, and local naval presence fell to the *Mussulo,* a small craft under the command of a sergeant. By this time the area was considered to be relatively safe, and a stronger naval presence became an occasional thing. As a sort of departure ceremony on 29 March 1962, the *Espiga,* which had by then been joined by the *Fomalhaut* and *Pollux*, gave a "seapower demonstration" at Muxima, in which the three new launches and the local fishermen in their elegant *pirogas* held a "naval review." The *Mussulo* from its base in Bom Jesus continued to patrol between Barra do Cuanza at the mouth and Muxima. From time to time LFs would enter the river with their sections of *Fuzileiros*, but it was not until 12 November 1968, when LDP 108 was assigned to Bom Jesus, that there was a more robust and permanent presence. During the season when the river was low, the *Fuzileiros* would extend the patrol range with their rubber boats, and this presence was welcomed by the local population.[23]

The Cuanza River, which is located a little south of the east-west axis of the Luanda-Malange railroad, was much more than a route for possible movement of enemy agents or insurgents. It could be considered as a large trench that divides Angola in half and separates the north from the south. Together with the vastness of Angola, its poor roads, and the few river crossings, the Cuanza serves as a barrier to communications. There was a highway bridge some miles east of the Cambambe Dam on a primary paved road and another south of Malange on a poor dirt road leading to barren wasteland. There were also raft crossings on several bad roads that were unusable in the rainy season. Following the enormous destruction of infrastructure in the north, where portions of the area were cutoff with the loss of bridges, it was important that this sort of thing not be repeated in the south. The national highway system radiated from Luanda, and its infrastructure needed to be protected to maintain the critical lines of communication within the country. The few bridges across the Cuanza represented vital strategic links in this system, a fact that both the enemy and the Portuguese authorities understood well. The integrity of the road system would be key in waging war for both sides, and yet the insurgents never exploited this vulnerability early nor did the authorities see the need to guard it. As Rear Admiral José Mexima Salema observed, "The enemy had insufficient explosives, and we had excessive confidence."[24]

Arrival of the *Fuzileiros*

In addition to the arrival of the "30-tonners," the Naval Command of Angola had been expecting its first detachment of special *Fuzileiros* or *Fuzileiros especiais* during the second half of October 1961 to help alleviate the burden on the crews of its ships in acting as infantry ashore.[25] According to Mexia Salema, it would also potentially replace the army personnel at Ambriz (154), Ambrizete (481), Santo António do Zaire (562), and Noqui (228), a total of 1,425 personnel.[26] Certainly the 75 men of the incoming detachment

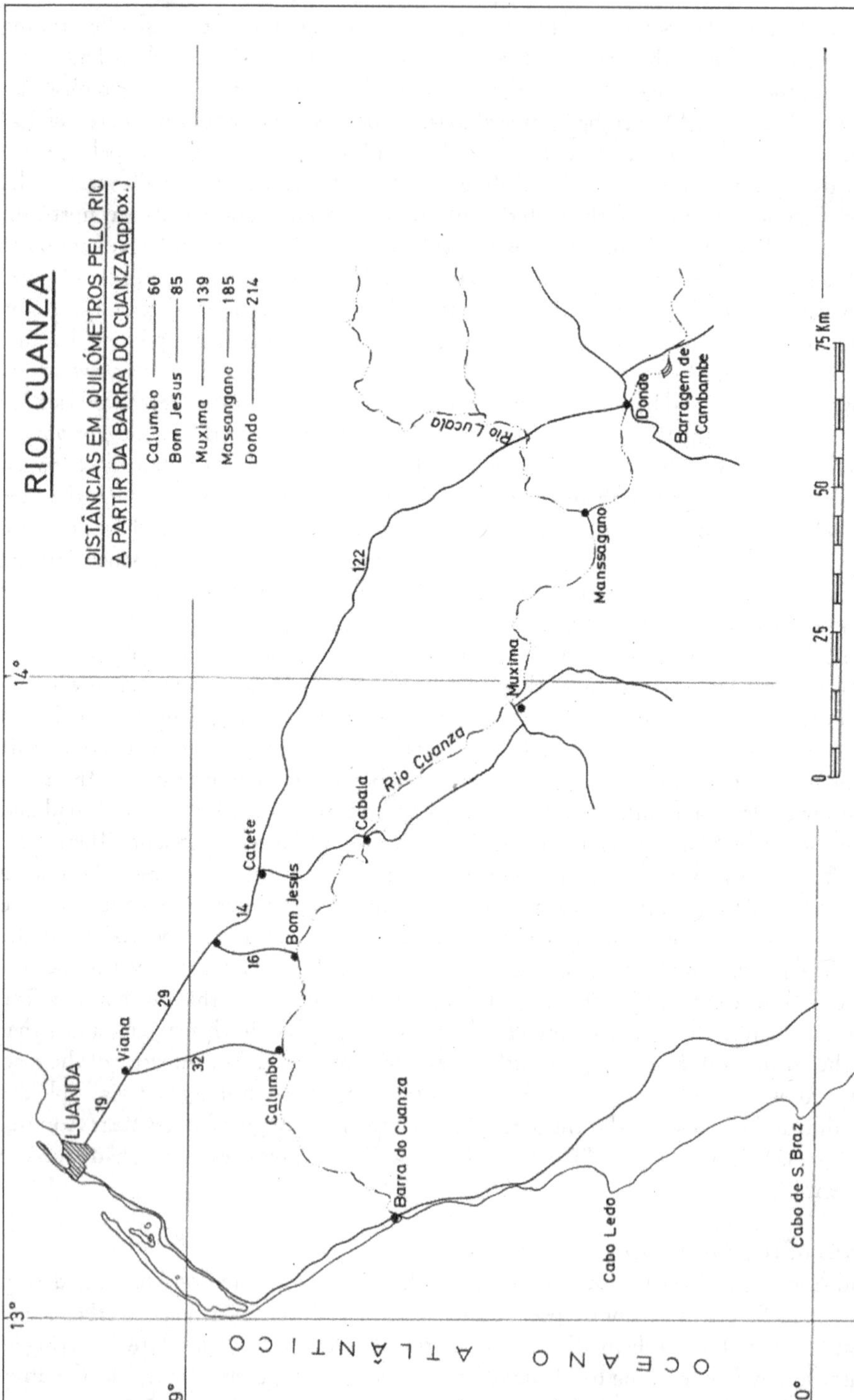

Cuanza River from Barra do Cuanza to Cambambe Dam. Source: *Nem a Pátria Sabe, A Marinha na Guerra em Angola 1961–1963* by José Mexia Salema.

were supremely capable, but to believe that one *Fuzileiro* was the equivalent of 20 Army personnel was unrealistic. Further the *Fuzileiros* were light infantry and required support. The more sanguine view was that they would complement land forces in a less static and more mobile riverine offensive.

The initial thought was that the expected detachment would establish itself at a base near its anticipated area of operations, so that it could become familiar with its operating environment. The unit, after all, would be arriving fresh from its training in the *metrópole*. While its *Fuzileiros* would be skilled in the traditional techniques, tactics, and procedures of their tradecraft, they would not have acquired a familiarity with the local terrain and operating conditions that would give them an advantage over or at least an equal footing with the enemy in the Zairian surroundings. This period of adaptation to Africa was an important part of the *Fuzileiro* acclimation process. Accordingly, it was thought that their use on the Cuanza River between Bom Jesus and Muxima in a relatively benign setting would serve this process well and provide the needed operational experience in working alongside the army before they moved to the Zaire and its higher operational tempo.[27] Things did not quite go this way.

Detachment of *Fuzileiros Especiais* Nº 1 (DFE 1) finally arrived by air on 10 and 15 November and the following week boarded the frigates *Diogo Gomes* and *Pero Escobar* to exercise in the south along the littoral and far from the area where they were needed most. Prior to boarding the ships, the lieutenant commanding the detachment gave a patriotic and rousing address to his troops, and as they marched up the gangway to the tune *Angola is Ours*, there was not a dry eye in the crowd of spectators.

During the early days of December the *Fuzileiros* made landings in Moçâmedes, Bengula, and Novo Redondo, which were as much a display of the new naval force as an exercise to retain proficiency. In a publicity move rivaling that of the U.S. Marine Corps, local newspapers were invited to witness the activity. Such events as an "attack" on the Morena Beach and the "occupation" of the Bengula Railway Station were reported with sober praise and portfolios of photographs.[28] While this excursion may have seemed almost frivolous in light of conditions that continued to exist in the north and did delay the force from becoming immediately engaged there, the effect on civilian morale was uplifting and important in a time of enormous concern. It reinforced the fact that the government was taking charge of the situation and discharging its duty to protect the population.

At the conclusion of the several weeks of demonstrations, the detachment was moved to São Salvador for a period of two months, where it participated in operations with other land forces in the neighboring region of Buela and in the area demarcated by São Salvador, Tombôco, and the M'Pozo River, which ran between the two towns. It was subsequently used to inspect traffic and patrol along the coast north of Luanda, along the lines of infiltration across the Zaire River, and along the margins of the Chiloango River and Lake Massábi within the Cabinda enclave. The detachment also operated from time to time with army elements supporting various sector commanders as reserve forces or laying ambushes and executing surprise attacks as a part of various coordinated plans. These occurred largely along the Ambriz-Ambrizete axis and around the small settlements or *sanzalas* of Caluca and Avé Maria near the Mebridege River (variously M'Bridge or Mebridge) south of São Salvador in the difficult terrain of the Dembos region. These locations are depicted on the nearby map. Following the arrival of Company of *Fuzileiros* Nº 1 (CF 1) in May and Detachment of *Fuzileiros Especiais* Nº 3 (DFE 3) in August 1962, the *Fuzileiros* would undertake more ambitious actions. Before these could occur, however, there needed to be a broader plan for security on the Zaire.

Posts Along the Zaire

As the second year of the war opened, it became obvious that while the political situation in the Congo was unsettled and fluid, the enemy had made good use of his sanctuary and now was better armed, more aggressive, and increasingly well organized. He was reappearing in force in areas that were thought to be pacified and making a concerted effort to expand his presence not only in the border areas but also in the interior of the country. His main lines of infiltration from the naval perspective were across the Zaire River first at Ponta Puelo approximately opposite the Congolese city of Boma and later in May near the more isolated Bulicoco Island and its islets further downstream.[29] Both of these areas were characterized by a myriad of small islands and thick undergrowth that provided excellent cover for insurgents seeking to cross undetected. During the events of March 1961, it was estimated that 200,000 Angolans had fled north for the sanctuary of the Congo to escape the combination of UPA terrorism and Portuguese vengeance.[30] This migration had left the northeast largely depopulated, and as relative peace returned, the displaced too began to return in a steady trickle. These returnees had in many cases been recruited by the UPA and often accompanied the insurgents to help them find their way and to give them credibility with the local population. The fact remained, however, that there was little population in the north to provide them with the all important support that they required, and thus these efforts made little immediate impact. Nevertheless, as the situation became increasingly stable and more attractive to refugees in the Congo, and as these citizens began to return in significant numbers, there would be an increasing security problem.

From the beginning of the new year, DFE 1 had operated almost constantly in cooperation first with paratroops around the devastated village of Nova Caipemba, about 150 kilometers south of São Salvador on the Loge River, and then with army units on the Plaines de Congo Yella south and west of Fetish Rock on the Zaire.[31] Later the DFE began regular patrolling along the Zaire in areas with the obscure names of Bulicoco Island, Quissanga, Lucala, Quibembe, Chichianga, Ponta Puela, and the Zaire tributary of Lué Pequeno next to Noqui, coordinating with "30-tonner" operations. It soon became clear that the small force in place, no matter how excellent, could not control the riverine border adequately to prevent enemy infiltration nearly at will.

Additional resources began to arrive early in the new year and were projected to continue to do so throughout 1962. Three new "30-tonners," *Altair*, *Rigel*, and *Régulus*, were welcomed on 20 February. CF 1 was projected to arrive in May. DFE 3 was to augment DFE 1 in August. Consequently, by late spring there was a sense of urgency within the navy to develop a strategic plan for effective security on the Zaire to complement the land frontiers and to deploy its expanding forces to achieve this end.

The original concept called for increased vigilance along the river supported by a series of small forts or *fortins* located at judicious intervals to establish a strong barrier to insurgent infiltration. By mid-month the plan *Dispositivo Detentor* (Deterrent Force) had been proposed for the eastern fluvial boundary with the Congo, the area of greatest riverine infiltration, and called for fixed posts to be established at dominant points between Noqui and Fetish Rock. The logic in choosing these initial locations was that they would divide this stretch of river into approximately four equal parts with an average of 7.5 miles

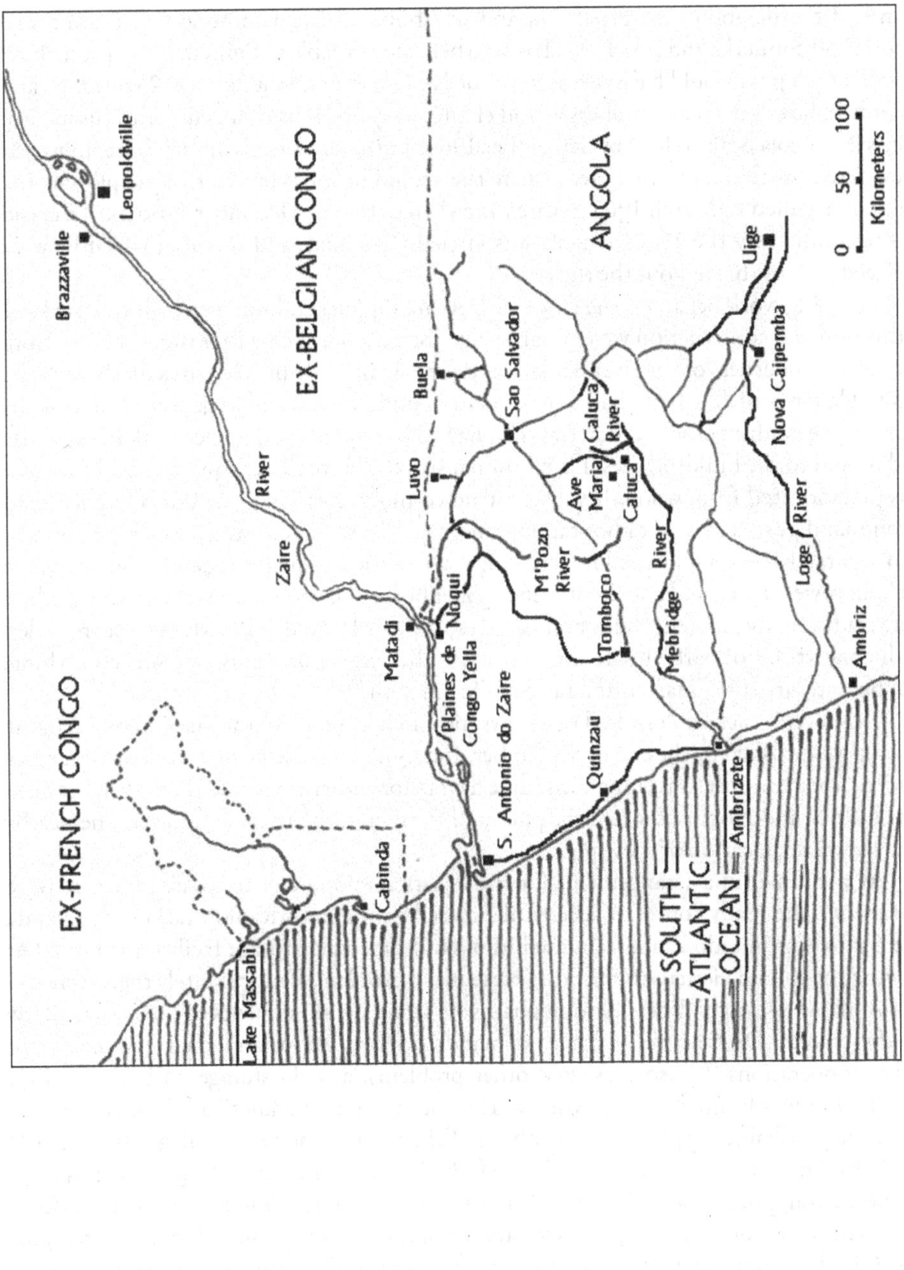

Northern Angola Operating Areas. Drawn by the author

between them. This division would facilitate the formation of patrol zones around each post and would equally apportion the potential surveillance workload. Later, a fourth post would be proposed and established on the Island of Quissanga, from which *Fuzileiros* were already operating in their rubber boats and being billeted in an abandoned sawmill that was flooded by the river from time to time. The posts were designed as the static logistic skeleton on which would rest the dynamic muscle of the *Fuzileiros* and "30-tonners." The plan had the flexibility for expansion and was built on the assumption that additional troops, "30-tonners", and larger vessels would become available to tighten frontier security.[32] Initially each post would have two sections of *Fuzileiros*, or about 24 men, 2 sergeants, and an officer; however, these numbers would change as conditions changed.[33] The numbers of DFEs in Angola built to four by September 1963, and as conditions on the Zaire improved, they were transferred to other areas where they could be more productively deployed. The number declined in March 1965 to three and then to two in December 1966 until the end of the conflict. By the 1970s Angola was virtually pacified, and the original DFEs were replaced by CFs throughout the theater.

Planning work began on the bases with Army support in June, and by July actual site excavation and construction were progressing. The task of carving four support bases from the virgin wilderness of the river banks was daunting in its difficulty, particularly with the limited labor available. Land had to be cleared of underbrush, and large stones removed by hand in the grading process. Material then had to be landed on the river bank in each case and moved to the building sites. Each post consisted of a small headquarters building that was prefabricated from wood. It was constructed in the form of a pavilion and contained a command post, a mess, a radio station, officer quarters, and enlisted barracks. There was also separately on each post a kitchen, sanitary facilities, a small magazine and armory, a lookout tower, a pier, and a shelter for the rubber boats and their motors. Vegetable gardens were traditionally planted, and sources of potable water located. All of this was surrounded with concertinas of barbed wire for security.[34] The *Fuzileiro* in this case was everything: combatant, carpenter, mason, and farmer. He did it all.[35]

This feverish activity resulted in the first post being completed at Puelo in mid-August. Macala was finished by the end of September, and Quissanga by the first week of December. Trident, the final post, was completed three days before Christmas, and the system between Fetish Rock and Noqui now had the potential to tighten the riverine frontier. The nearby map shows the location of these posts.

At the same time arrangements for the logistical support of this base structure were underway. The ready source of electrical power at the Naval Radio Stations of Luanda and Santo António do Zaire translated into handsome cold storage facilities at both, but moving the chilled victuals to the posts presented a problem. Unfortunately there were too few available resources. This situation put severe strain on all naval vessels, but particularly on the scarce LDs that were in high demand to move troops and their equipment for military operations. It also presented other problems, as cold storage on both the LDs and the LFs was limited or non-existent. This meant that schedules had to be adjusted to move the perishable supplies in the coolness of the night to prevent spoilage. The first LD (LDP 105) did not arrive until March 1963. Prior to that time the LFs struggled to carry the needed supplies in addition to their normal loads of *Fuzileiros*, rubber boats, sacks of mail, outboard motors, fuel, spare parts, and all of the other necessities for an isolated post. This initial but temporary solution was very impractical.[36] As time passed, conditions on the posts improved from their rudimentary nature to a more civilized and agreeable one. Native cooking was introduced, and this development was welcomed by both the post personnel and the launch crews.[37]

In October 1962, during the midst of the post construction when manpower was at a premium, military operation's increased. Elements from the expanded force of *Fuzileiros* combined with elements of Cavalry Battalion 345 and Parachute Battalion 21 to perform the first helicopter assaults of the war with Operation *Parafuso Grande* (Large Screw). Sixteen parachutists were airlifted in four *Alouette II* helicopters in a successful hammer and anvil operation culminating in the destruction of the UPA base at Caluca, which was in the midst of the area affected by the UPA attacks.[38]

Later in December of the same year, Operation *Ferrolho* (Rifle Bolt) began in which the *Fuzileiros* supported by the "30-tonners" ranged along the Zaire, sweeping the river between the strategic points of Quissanga, Fetish Rock, Puelo, Macala, and Tridente, all the way to Noqui.[39] This capability had not come easily or quickly and had been established only through an enormous effort on the part of naval personnel. In addition to the obstacles in establishing the Naval Posts, the *Fuzileiros* in their fragile rubber boats and the crews of the "30-tonners" had to overcome an adverse operating environment and address not only a human enemy but also a natural one. The Zaire itself was full of whirlpools, particularly opposite the post of Trident, giant tree trunks and branches, floating islands of grass and mud, and sharp rocks. Because of the flow and consequent change in the river, charts were rarely accurate. Nights on the river were opaquely black, and unannounced and

Naval Post at Quissanga with lookout tower visible in the center. Photograph courtesy Estado-Maior da Armada and *Revista da Armada*.

violent rainstorms would drastically reduce the effectiveness of patrols.[40] Radar was a help, but vigilant lookouts were more useful in spotting floating obstacles and guiding vessels during shoreline operations. Further, the river contained a vast region of canals along an eleven-mile stretch between Bulicoco Island just east of Quissanga and Fetish Rock, the most dangerous part of its length. The canals, which were estimated to total some 800 miles of waterway, ran between the numerous islands and small tributaries and proved to be ready enemy hiding places that were difficult to police.[41] The other islands with their interesting animal names of hippopotamus, egret, duck, fish hawk, turtle, hummingbird, iguana, tsetse, and so on also concealed the enemy in their thick brush. Nevertheless, these difficulties were overcome, and this operation and the procedures that it developed established the course for riverine security throughout the conflict and served as a model for future theaters.

Typical of operations during late 1962 was the October clearing of the many small islands and canals that compose the Bulicoco archipelago. This complex covers an area of approximately 6,000 square meters, not particularly large but one of the most complicated of any on the Zaire.[42] Quite naturally it attracted the enemy, as it provided excellent concealment and served as an ideal nighttime launching site for his canoes to cross into Angola. Its interior was a labyrinth of narrow canals, whose twists, turns, forks, and sandy shoals could easily lose troops. It was so complicated that even with a chart it was easy to be lost. Its canals were also so shallow and narrow that only the rubber boats of the *Fuzileiros* could penetrate them and negotiate the dense undergrowth along their banks, the foliage overhanging the water, and the vines drooping from the verdant canopy. Even in daylight these canals could be dark and often had the appearance of a tunnel or the interior of a ruined cathedral with the high jungle cover.

Preparations for the operation were extensive, and for the first time air reconnaissance was integrated into the plan to help guide the surface force through the waterway maze. This took the form of an Auster D-5/160 from the 2nd Air Region. The seasoned DFE 1 and the newly arrived DFE 3 were the designated ground forces. The contrast between the worn and stained uniforms of the veteran unit and the neat and clean ones of the fresh arrivals was obvious but belied the capabilities of the newcomers. These troops were transported to the area from Santo António do Zaire by the LFs during the early hours of the morning and launched in their rubber boats opposite Bulicoco in the predawn at the extreme low tide. The *Fuzileiros* began to explore the canal system inch by inch guided by the spotter aircraft. A number of empty encampments were discovered, searched, and then destroyed. One boat of *Fuzileiros* abruptly encountered two insurgents in a canoe at the close range of 30 meters, and both opened fire. The *Fuzileiros* immediately departed the boat according to procedure to avoid casualties and returned fire, destroying the canoe and killing an insurgent. The operation continued for three days. During that time 10 encampments and three *pirogas* were destroyed, but no more insurgents were found.[43] While such clear and hold operations are an important part of insurgent destruction, the preparation for them does not go unnoticed, and warning spreads. Consequently, the insurgents generally have adequate time to move, and few of any consequence are captured or killed. Nevertheless, the Bulicoco archipelago became unsafe to insurgents after October 1962 and remained so until the *Fuzileiros* and "30-tonners" departed a decade later.

Despite the feverish activity of building the posts and perfecting the naval presence on the Zaire, it took until March 1963 to make the river border effectively secure, virtually a year following the decision to do so. There were a number of factors leading to this delay. First, the dense growth along the riverbank and the numerous canals and their even smaller branches provided the perfect cover for insurgents seeking to infiltrate into Angola.[44] It also took time to learn the river and the likely patterns of effective insurgent evasion. This necessitated the exhausting and inglorious night patrolling of the canal and river system, the gathering of intelligence, and the collective accumulation of knowledge on and experience with the Zairian environment and its people.

Second, the LFs and the *Fuzileiros* took time to develop the tactics that worked and to perfect their skill in operating as a team. For instance, such refinements as air reconnaissance were only introduced with the operation in the Bulicoco archipelago. This resource was indispensable in learning the intricacies of the river and identifying potential enemy trails and encampments.[45]

Third, it took time to gain the confidence of the local population in the wake of the enormous civil disruption and consequent migration. Relations were gradually strengthened, and trust established, but it was slow and patient work. This positive relationship helped with the flow of critical intelligence, as there were few other sources. In 1961 the navy had only one intelligence officer, a commander (*capitão de fragata*), and he was located in Luanda. He was responsible for naval intelligence, its collection, organization, interpretation, evaluation, and dissemination. This arrangement proved woefully inadequate as events unfolded. The result was an ineffectual and unsatisfactory flow of usable intelligence both to the forces in the field and to the commanders. The navy was organized to respond to

Canoe being inspected on the Zaire River, September 1961. Photograph courtesy Estado-Maior da Armada and *Revista da Armada*.

Fuzileiros conducting an operation from Quissanga, April 1967. Photograph courtesy Estado-Maior da Armada and *Revista da Armada.*

movements of ocean traffic and associated developments. These were low key and fairly benign in nature, with a few fishing violations, perhaps casual smuggling, and the transit of Soviet-bloc surface vessels. Its connection with the Portuguese national police and intelligence service or PIDE (*Polícia Internacional de Defesa do Estado*), the *chefs de posto*, and the other interior elements in the web of intelligence would be second-hand, and thus direct and immediate information on non-maritime developments would be dependent on sources outside of its control. Most of this intelligence officer's information on Angola came either from the army or from PIDE. His primary circulated products *Informações Operacionais Quinzenais Angola* (series) [Biweekly Operational Intelligence Angola (series)] and *Informaçaõ Operacional Mensal Angola* (series) [Monthly Operational Intelligence Angola (series)] were little more than statistical reports of terrorist activity and provided no anticipatory analyses or dynamic reporting.[46] Tactical intelligence and its development thus became the *de facto* duty of the local forces.

Fourth, it took time to establish the logistic support required to maintain the posts and the vessels and men operating from them. The decision to build the posts and their actual construction ran well ahead of the needed support in transport and infrastructure development. It was a patchwork system that improved over time as resources became available in Angola, but in the early stages forced the troops to live and work under harsh and spare conditions and thus limited their initial capability.

By the spring of 1963 the network was complete and the complementary force of launches and *Fuzileiros* had learned the river system and its land approaches well. Each

Fuzileiros conducting an operation from Quissanga, April 1967. Photograph courtesy Estado-Maior da Armada and *Revista da Armada.*

launch operated on the average 22 days per month, and missions lasted between three and five days each. This operational tempo produced a constant presence. Once this power projection was perfected, Portuguese dominance along the Zaire forced the insurgents to move 1,000 kilometers to the east. This was necessary to skirt the naval presence and army patrols in order to reach the Dembos, the difficult terrain in which they were hiding and from which they operated. Neither the posts nor the forces that operated from them were ever challenged in a serious way. Yes, there were the occasional infiltrators moving across the riverine border, but the constant Portuguese naval presence eventually made the land route the preferred one. Mexia Salema quotes a crewmember of the Norwegian cargo vessel *Irma*, which had recently transited the river, as observing that no ship could unload matériel anywhere without being detected by the constant patrols or by the lookout posts.[47] Such security not only safeguarded the fluvial border but also made the waterway free from insurgent attacks on commercial shipping and military transport.

Experience gained during Operation *Ferrolho* prompted new thinking on Zairian security. Maintaining seven bases along the 80-mile length was relatively expensive in that it absorbed an inordinate portion of the scarce naval resources available in Angola. Additionally, the enemy could observe a post and note the timing of its patrols. He could then potentially avoid detection and contact. With the introduction of the LDPs into the equation beginning in March 1963, a new concept was born. While the LDPs were designed for moving cargo and personnel, they proved to be enormously versatile in other ways. Beginning with Operation *Ferrolho*, the navy began using the vessels as mobile bases to launch and recover *Fuzileiros* in their rubber boats. The standard LDP was modified to permit 12 to 15 men to live on board for short periods by sheltering the hold and outfitting it with bunks, installing refrigerated chests for rations, adding a communications suite, and mounting an Oerlikon 20mm machinegun for defense.

Also from 1965 onward, the LFs were re-gunned by substituting the more modern German-origin MG-42 for the outdated World War II vintage von Dreyse light machine gun. For the crew, the newer Heckler and Koch G-3 series assault rifle replaced the older Fábrica de Braço de Prata (FBP) m/947 9mm machine pistol. While the Oerlikon machineguns remained open mounts, an armor plate shield was added for protection of the gunner.[48] The crews became skilled marksmen with these new weapons, as each launch "adopted" a small, deserted island and put its name on it in the form of a large sign. The signs were perhaps 60 x 60 centimeters and were routinely destroyed by launch gunners from 600 meters range while traveling at full speed.[49] The friendly competition between the crews became a boost to morale and engendered great pride within the LF community on the Zaire, which self-styled itself humorously with the motto "Steel men in plastic boats."[50] This was, of course, a parody of the traditional phrase "Iron men in wooden ships" used to describe strong men withstanding the rigors of tempestuous seas and the other hardships and perils of naval service in the Age of Sail. Such romanticism abounded in the imagination of the youthful crews. Marques, for instance, initially saw his assignment to the post of Fetish Rock as one of continuing the epic of Diogo Cão's discovery and pacification of the Zaire, however illogical. He later learned to his astonishment that the great Fetish Rock

Fuzileiros conducting an operation from Quissanga, April 1967. Photograph courtesy Estado-Maior da Armada and *Revista da Armada*.

was only decisively occupied by the Portuguese in August 1915, and the entire left bank to Noqui in January 1916.[51]

This new waterborne capability not only added flexibility, mobility, and surprise to river operations but also proved far less expensive to sustain than the system of naval posts. Attacking the problem of river security with an increased intensity and applying the lessons and experiences gathered to date, the team of LDPs, LFs, and *Fuzileiros* ranged the length of the Zaire River border, successfully penetrating the canal system and denying it to the enemy. As a consequence, plans were made to consolidate the fixed presence on the Zaire and to deactivate several of the posts following Operation *Ferrolho*.

By 1966 the enemy had moved eastward, and the river had become relatively quiet. Marques observed that the patrols were routine. There were occasional incidents with clandestine fishermen, but nothing more. The crocodiles were far more dangerous, but they were more afraid of us than we of them.[52]

Operation *Mastro do Traquete* (Foremast) followed, and during this period the posts of Trident, Puelo, and Macala were deactivated in March 1967, May 1967, and December 1969 respectively. Operations at Macala, the post midway between Fetish Rock and Noqui, were actually wound down from May 1967 onward, and it acted increasingly as an intermediate support facility upstream of Fetish Rock until its full deactivation thirty-one months later. Operation *Mastro de Traquete* was replaced by *Mastro de Mezena* (Mizen Mast) in 1968. By the beginning of 1970 only Quissanga and Fetish Rock effectively remained between Santo António do Zaire and Noqui. These were important facilities, as they marked the boundaries of the most difficult section of the river frontier. Because of their position, they were upgraded to replace the retired post capability and to support LDP mobile base operations. A summary of these operations is shown in Table 4.1.

Life on the spartan posts passed with the rhythm of a micro-society created by the practical autonomy of semi-isolation. Post routines were ordered by the scheduled launching and recovery of the boats that each supported. The monotony of the missions, the sleepless nights on constant alert, the isolation, the meager living conditions on board both the launches and the posts, and the harshness of the climate tried everyone. Despite all of the vicissitudes and difficulties, the sailors exhibited an enormous courage and patriotism in the execution of their dangerous duties. Indeed, in virtually every case this shared experience of officers, petty officers, and sailors bound them in a fraternity of those who had served on the Zaire.

Leisure time was plentiful, and the men found many constructive pursuits. They read a great deal. Marques notes that he finally read *War and Peace* cover to cover.[53] Fishing was a popular sport, as excellent fish swam in the river, and their catch provided a welcomed enrichment to the normal fare of field rations. Hunting expeditions were also a great favorite, and game was often added to the menu. The occasional hippopotamus and elephant were also found. Overall life on the river despite its isolation and danger was not an extreme hardship. The men fell into a comfortable work routine governed by the social closeness that a small post of this nature brings. The rhythm was broken only by the monthly relief with the new personnel that it brought and contact with the enemy.

The special detachments of *Fuzileiros* were employed both on the river and in the littoral, often in coordination with the army forces at Santo António do Zaire and Noqui to effect the complementary navy mission of controlling the river approaches. Because of the effective river presence, it meant that the insurgents preferred to cross the land frontier into Angola, an area that was infinitely more difficult to police. They found it easy to cross quietly in places and at times that were free of Portuguese troops. The terrain along the border area was hilly with high grass, thick groves of trees, and hardly a settlement or person, almost all having fled in 1961. In such a vast and apparently empty countryside it was easy to be complacent.

The *Fuzileiros* often visited the frontier town of Noqui from their posts downriver to drink beer with their compatriots in the army company deployed there. It was a profoundly depressing place sandwiched between a barren clay hill on one side and the river on the other. The aspect of the town was squalid, and few buildings attained the dignity of two stories. In the words of Vasco Quevedo Pessanha, a *Fuzileiro* junior officer there in 1965, who recounted this incident, there was only heat, heat, and more heat.[54] The patrols and games of cards in the army camp were interrupted only by the arrival of the mail plane twice a week. While much has been written about the horror of insurgent war, there has been little on its sheer boredom, particularly when troops had free time with few amusements. Noqui was just such a place. It was completely safe more because the troops and the insurgents took great care to avoid each other, and there was no incentive to do otherwise. Under these circumstances it was difficult to maintain military discipline, and the attitude and morale grew deeply negative. Noqui was like a colony of forced vacationers, and the enemy would exploit this weakness.

In the beginning the army patrol that was sent the 10 kilometers to the fortified airstrip to meet the plane consisted of a GMC 2½-ton truck, 2 Mercedes Benz *Unimogs*, and 2 or 3 Willis jeeps. The personnel were dressed for combat and armed with a Bazooka, a MG-42, and G-3 rifles. As time passed, discipline and combat readiness became a shambles with the routine patrols, endless card games, and much beer. The insurgents noticed. They studied the twice-weekly trips to the airfield for mail and saw that now the men went barefoot and wore only T-shirts and pants. No longer was there a convoy of 40 armed soldiers, for now only the jeeps and a *Unimog* carrying a dozen men armed with the odd G-3 made the trip. Over the months the insurgents planned an ambush to take advantage of this nearly complete lack of security, and one day on a return trip the troops encountered the well-laid trap. Of the 12 men in the party, 11 were killed, and the twelfth was able to hide in the grass until the insurgents left the scene. Many hours later the survivor made his way to Noqui to deliver the sad news. In a somnolent setting, such as Noqui, it is easy to become complacent, and complacency kills.

Pessanha describes another incident with the insurgents reflective of the psychological dimensions of the river war. This was revealed when he traveled the short distance from his base of Trident to Noqui, again to drink beer and visit with his army counterparts in the hope of civilized entertainment. Normally the army surgeon assigned to the company joined the visitors for the social event; however, on this day he did not, as he was asleep. This was most peculiar at 1600, and on inquiry it was discovered that he had only just returned that morning from a dreadful adventure and was still recovering. It had all begun several days earlier in the wee hours of the night when two civilian vehicles filled with blacks, some of whom were armed, presented themselves at the frontier post and urgently sought the PIDE agent. A disaster had apparently occurred, and only the PIDE agent could resolve it.

Because Noqui was the last port on the Portuguese side of the Zaire before the river turned north into the Congo, it had not only a military presence but also offices of the normal frontier authorities of customs, immigration, and PIDE. PIDE energetically pursued the development of intelligence on the enemy, and in this African environment

Fuzileiros hunting on the Zaire River. Photograph from personal collection of José Augusto Pires Lima

assumed a more appropriate and subtle posture than in the *metrópole*. Its inspectors abandoned their standard intimidating dress and assumed a local wardrobe. As a result PIDE agents in their everyday clothes could be mistaken for peaceful civilians, such as local merchants or tavern keepers, and thus moved easily among the population with this non-threatening posture. They often crossed the border into the Congo to develop sources of intelligence on enemy capabilities, intentions, and activities, as gathering intelligence on the enemy was not simply chatting with informers or buying information from travelers. It was necessary to move in enemy circles, if one expected to gain anything more serious and substantial in value than casual gossip. The PIDE agents were thus well known in the Congo and among the insurgents, and it was for this reason that the nocturnal visitors had sought the PIDE official.

Apparently, earlier in the day on which the vehicles had arrived from the Congo a group of FNLA insurgents had fallen into an ambush mounted by Portuguese troops from a base some distance to the east of Noqui. It was bad enough that several insurgents had been lost, but the worst was that the deputy commander of the insurgent base of Kinkusu had been with the group and was gravely wounded. This base was one of the most important FNLA military camps, if not the most important one, for it served as the principal training site and logistical support facility for all FNLA insurgent forces operating in the north of Angola. Obviously such a base had the approval and support of the Congo government. It was thus logical to assume that the deputy commander, who was wounded by the Portuguese, would be rushed to a hospital in Léopoldville, now changed in name to Kinshasa, where he would receive the best attention of the FNLA and Congolese doctors. Amazingly the man would only permit himself to be treated by a Portuguese doctor. His colleagues knew of the doctor in Noqui and had thus come to seek his help through the only contact whom they knew, the PIDE agent. They had arrived at the Noqui frontier after having traveled many hours over narrow wilderness trails to beg this agent to order the doctor to return with them to save their comrade. After many supplications and much conversation, the PIDE agent spoke with the company commander, who after considering the situation decided to approach the doctor about the problem. Would he be willing to travel to the secret enemy base in the Congo to treat an FNLA principal who had been wounded by the Portuguese? Conditions were more than precarious, as there were no guarantees of a safe return, and his personal security would be non-existent. On the other hand, if the man were saved, then everyone in the region would know about the good will of the Portuguese. Was it worth the risk?

In the end the doctor accepted the challenge, packed a bundle of his clothes, prepared his instruments and medicines, and went alone with the insurgents for the return trip to Kinkusu. After some hours of bouncing and jarring over bad roads, he arrived at a large base reasonably organized and garrisoned, only to find that the wounded deputy commander had simply been laid in the grass. Overcoming all of the difficulties that it is possible to imagine, he succeeded in extracting the bullet and for some days and nights cared for the wounded man, until he was out of danger. He had finally returned to Noqui from his vigil both physically and emotionally exhausted.[55]

Table 4.1: Schedule of Yearly Operations on the Zaire and Forces Assigned

Year	Operations	Squadron Units Assigned				Comments
		LF	LDM 400	LDP 100	LDP 200	
1961		2/3 Variable				2 assigned 30 Sep 1 assigned 22 Dec
1962	Rifle Bolt (Ferrolho) and Rifle Bolt Alfa (Ferrohlo Alfa)	2/3/4 Variable				1 assigned 6 Mar
1963	Rifle Bolt Bravo (Ferrolho Bravo)	2/3/4 Variable		1 (a)		(a) LDP 105 assigned 27 Mar
1964	Rifle Bolt Bravo (Ferrolho Bravo)	2/3/4 Variable	2 (b)	2 (c)		(b) LDM 401 & 402 assigned 28 Sep (c) LDP 108 assigned 24 Mar
1965	Rifle Bolt Charlie (Ferrolho Charlie)	2/3/4 Variable	2	2	2 (d)	(d) LDP 201 & 202 assigned 11 May
1966	Rifle Bolt Charlie (Ferrolho Charlie)	4	2	2	4 (e)	(e) LDP 207 & 208 assigned 3 Jun LDP 208 reassigned Oct

Year	Operations	Squadron Units Assigned				Comments
		LF	LDM 400	LDP 100	LDP 200	
1967	Foremast (Mastro do Traquete)	2/3/4 Variable	2	2	4 (f)	(f) LDP 209 assigned 28 Apr
1968	Mizen Mast (Mastro de Mezena)	3/4 Variable	4 (g)	2/0 (h)	5 (i)	(g) LDM 403 & 409 assigned 5 Mar and 25 Sep respectively (h) Reassigned 16 Jul and 13 Oct (i) LDP 213 assigned 17 Oct
1969	Mizen Mast (Mastro de Mezena)	2/3 Variable	4		4 (j)	(j) Casualty LDP 202
1970	Mizen Mast (Mastro de Mezena)	3	4		6 (l)	(l) LDP 214 & 215 assigned Mar
1971	Mizen Mast (Mastro de Mezena)	3	4		6	

After several days at Noqui, Pessanha's combat group of *Fuzileiros* returned to Trident. The incident had left them wondering just how it would affect future combat operations in the north of Angola. Certainly those intimately involved on both sides would be changed. There were many such unusual episodes of kindness to the enemy, and the *Fuzileiros* wondered if the horror of war bred an emotion that peace did not.

By the mid-1960s, neither the MPLA nor the FNLA had met with any substantial success in a classic subversion of the population in the north or in truly displacing the Portuguese position there. This lack of insurgent progress occurred for several reasons. While the army lacked both the manpower and mobility to seal the land border completely in an area of poor roads, dissention between the MPLA and the FNLA, Léopoldville's favoritism of the FNLA, and Holden Roberto's failure of leadership served to limit any insurgent offensive. Friction between the two movements had its origins in the external recognition and choice of which one was to be the representative government of any independent Angola. As the FNLA was comprised largely of Bakongo, a people prevalent in the north of Angola and that area of the Congo immediately north of the common border, it felt that it more accurately represented the population of Angola at large, and this view was backed by Léopoldville. The MPLA on the other hand was comprised largely of the *mestiço* elite and was perceived to have less in common with its host and the people of Angola. As a consequence, there was competition and open friction between the two, and this misdirected energy diluted the attention of both in prosecuting the insurgency.

Léopoldville's favoritism of the FNLA was unabashed, and it worked to give its chosen movement every advantage. As an example, Léopoldville because of its own security problems did not permit insurgents to bear arms within its borders. Both the MPLA and the FNLA insurgents would be transported by Congolese soldiers to the Angolan border, where they would be issued their weapons from depositories. On returning from operations, their weapons would be cantoned, and they would return to their training base with a Congolese escort.[56] Léopoldville employed this control measure to discriminate against the MPLA. In 1962 the MPLA was often impeded from reaching the border, and its arms confiscated, whereas the FNLA was accorded privileged and unimpeded access. Roberto, whose eyes seemed permanently masked behind dark glasses, was unable to lead effectively in either the political or the military dimension despite his advantages, and Léopoldville sponsorship was unable to reverse this trend.

From the beginning the MPLA had been unwelcome in Léopoldville, and following the June 1963 recognition of GRAE as the *de jure* government of Angola, it moved its headquarters to Brazzaville. Its ability to project itself militarily into Angola became almost completely circumscribed by November, and it looked more and more isolated. In January 1964 at its Conference of Cadres (*Conferência de Quadros*) in Brazzaville, it was decided to begin rebuilding the movement as a serious revolutionary force. Part of this plan involved opening a front in the east of Angola through Zambia. The MPLA had made overtures to Kenneth Kaunda, the first president of Zambia following its independence from Britain in 1964. It had also befriended Julius Nyerere, the first president of Tanzania, likewise following its independence from Britain in 1962. These relationships were to prove fortuitous. Beginning in 1965, Tanzania and Zambia permitted the transit of Chinese and Soviet weapons and MPLA cadres across their territories to the Angolan border. Because of this access, the MPLA was able to open a major offensive and to conduct an intensive insurgent campaign in the eastern Angolan districts of Moxico and Cuando Cubango. Preparations were begun accordingly, and by the opening months of 1966 proselytizing of the population in the east was evident. The first armed incursions occurred in April, and the war had now clearly moved to the east of Angola. Portuguese resources were redirected to the east and southeast of the territory in response to the new threat. Naval operations would become an important component of the eastern front, and as we shall see, this dramatic projection of a naval presence inland followed the pattern that was set on the Zaire and that was being set in Mozambique. Before moving eastward, however, we need to examine developments in Guiné and Mozambique.

Notes

1 Adam Hochschild, *King Leopold's Ghost* (New York: Houghton Mifflin, 1998), 8.

2 Paulo Lowndes Marques, "Cartas Trocadas" [Antidotal Letters], *AORN* (December 2000): 7.

3 António Emílio Ferraz Sacchetti, interview by the author, 18 May 2006, Lisbon.

4 Robert Davezies, *Les Angolais* (Paris: Éditions de Minuit, 1965), 83.

5 Peter Forbath, *The River Congo* (New York: Harper & Row, 1977), 74.

6 Hélio A. Esteves Felgas, *O Clima do Congo Português* [The Climate of Portuguese Congo] (Carmona: Imprensa Angolana, 1959), 5.

7 Camões Godinho, "Algumas Notas sobre uma Comissão em Angola nos Anos de 1960 e 1961" [Some Notes on an Assignment in Angola in 1960 and 1961], *Anais do Clube Militar Naval* (January–March 1966): 14–27.

8 José Alberto Lopes Carvalheira, "Acção da Marinha em Águas Interiores (1961–1971)" [Naval Operations in Inland Waters (1961–1971)], in the unpublished collection *Participação da Armada na*

Defesa das Províncias Ultramarinas [Participation of the Navy in the Defense of the Overseas Provinces], photocopied manuscript, 1972, 2.

9 Willem S. van der Waals, *Portugal's War in Angola 1961–1974* (Rivonia: Ashanti Publishing, 1993), 64.

10 Estado-Maior do Exército (EME), *Resenha Histórico-Militar das Companhas de África (1961–1974)* [Historical-Military Report of the African Campaigns (1961–1974)] (Lisbon: Estado-Maior do Exército, 1988), Vol.II, 27.

11 Leonel Alexandre Gomes Cardoso, "A Acção da Marinha em Angola (1961–64)" [Naval Operations in Angola (1961–64)], *Revista de Marinha* (30 September 1964): 13. See also Leonel Alexandre Gomes Cardoso, "A Marinha em Angola 1961–64" [The Navy in Angola 1961–64], *Anais do Clube Militar Naval* (April–June 1964): 265.

12 Lopes Carvalheira, 6.

13 Ibid., 4.

14 G. Conceição Silva, "Destacamentos em Terras de Angola" [Naval Detachments Ashore in Angola], *Anais do Clube Militar Naval* (October-December 1961): 646.

15 Conceição Silva, 648.

16 Ibid., 650.

17 Ibid., 652.

18 Lopes Carvalheira, 8.

19 Vasco Quevedo Pessanha, interview by the author, 5 February 2003, Lisbon.

20 Lopes Carvalheira, 14. See also Godinho, 14.

21 José Mexia Salema, *Nem a Pátria Sabe, A Marinha na Guerra em Angola 1961–1963* [Not Even the Fatherland Knows, The Navy in the War in Angola 1961–1963] (Lisbon: Edições Culturais da Marinha, 1985), 139.

22 Mexia Salema, 142.

23 Lopes Carvalheira, 36.

24 Mexia Salema, 145. "Talvez da parte inimiga, insuficiência de explosives, e da nossa, excesso de confiança."

25 Ibid., 145.

26 Ibid., 146–147.

27 Ibid., 148.

28 Ibid., 150–151.

29 Ibid., 160.

30 Willem van der Waals, *Portugal's War in Angola 1961–1974* (Rivonia: Ashanti Publishing, 1993), 64.

31 René Pelissier, "Militaires, politicos, e outras mágicos" [Military men, politicians and other magicians], *Análise Social* (December 2002): 3.

32 Mexia Salema, 166.

33 A. de Roboredo (*vice almirante*), "Unidades de *Fuzileiros* em Angola" [*Fuzileiro* Units in Angola], commentary (despacho), Lisbon, 16 December 1965, Coloredo Box 224/2093, Arquivo Central da Marinha, Antiga Fabrica Nacional de Cordoaria, Rua da Junqueira, Lisbon.

34 Turíbio Abreu, "Infraestruturas Navais no Ultramar" [Naval Infrastructure in the *Ultramar*], *Anais do Clube Militar Naval* (April–June 1967): 427–436.

35 A. Pimentel Saraiva, "Postais do Ultramar: Angola–Postal № 2" [Postcards from the *Ultramar*: Angola – Postcard № 2], *Anais do Clube Militar Naval* (April–June 1968): 310.

36 Lopes Carvalheira, 22.

37 João Carlos da F. Pereira Bastos, "Dois Anos de Comissão no Zaire" [Two Years of Command on the Zaire], *Anais do Clube Militar Naval* (January–March 1965): 56.

38 John P. Cann, *Contra-Subversão em África, 1961–1974: O Modo Português de Fazer a Guerra* [Counter-

Subversion in Africa, 1961–1974: The Portuguese Way of War], 2nd ed., rev. Major General Renato F. Marques Pinto (Lisbon: Prefácio, 2005), 149.

39 Corpo de *Fuzileiros, Part II: Fuzileiros Especiais*, unpublished history (Lisbon: Ministério da Marinha, 1987), 30.

40 Abílio Freire da Cruz Júnior, "Evolução das Infra-estructuras da Armada no Ultramar" [Evolution of Naval Infrastructure in the *Ultramar*], in the unpublished collection *Participação da Armada na Defesa das Províncias Ultramarinas* [Participation of the Navy in the Defense of the Overseas Provinces], photocopied manuscript, 1972, 13.

41 Pereira Bastos, 51.

42 Ibid., 68

43 Ibid., 71–72.

44 Mexia Salema, 167.

45 Pereira Bastos, 56.

46 Paulo Lownes Marques and Vasco Quevedo Pessanha, interview by the author, 5 February 2003, Lisbon. Second Lieutenants Pessanha and Marques were graduates of the 7th and 8th Naval Reserve courses (CEORN 7° and 8°) respectively and served in Angola between 1965 and 1967.

47 Mexia Salema, 168.

48 Lopes Carvalheira, 30.

49 Pereira Bastos, 56–57.

50 Ibid.

51 Paulo Lowndes Marques, "Meditações acerca da Pedra do Feitiço" [Thoughts Regarding Fetish Rock], *AORN* (April–June 1997): 8.

52 Marques, "Cartas Trocadas," 7.

53 Ibid.

54 Vasco Quevedo Pessanha, "Histórias do DFE 13, Angola 65/67 – III" [Stories of DFE 13, Angola 65/67 – III], *AORN* (January–March 1999): 17.

55 Vasco Quevedo Pessanha, "Histórias do DFE 13, Angola 65/67 – IV" [Stories of DFE 13, Angola 65/67 – IV], *AORN* (October 1999): 23.

56 John A. Marcum, *The Angolan Revolution, Volume II, Exile Politics and Insurgent Warfare (1962–1976)* (Cambridge, Mass.: MIT Press, 1978), 42.

5

A Grim, Torrid Stretch of Swamp and Jungle

Of the three theaters of operations, Guiné was the most complicated and most difficult. It was also the most important theater for the navy, for here its activities were vital not only on the tactical but also on the strategic level. The reason was quite simple. About 80 percent of all cargo and personnel within the theater moved on the water either by sea or through the river system. Only about 18 percent moved overland, and a mere 2 percent by air.[1] In the final years of the war when road travel became difficult, fully 85 percent was waterborne. Water transport was equally as important for the PAIGC, and for this reason the policing of river traffic by the navy was as important as its transport role. The force that would prevail in Guiné would be the one that could successfully use the waterways to support its land operations while preventing the other from doing the same.[2] As in Angola, the naval mission was to dominate the sea, coastal, and river lines of communication and deny their use to the enemy, support the army and the population with its waterborne transportation capability, and project power ashore.[3] These objectives would be accomplished with the potent combination of LFs, LDs, and *Fuzileiros* to reduce the PAIGC and cut its men and their supplies that flowed into the country. As we shall see, the navy rose to the challenge, but was in part frustrated by an unresolved difference in approach with the army. Without such a resolution and a fully coordinated approach, it is doubtful that in the Guinean environment any divided force could be completely successful in securing the colony from a determined external foe.

A Complicated Theater

Guiné was the rump of what had originally been an expansive and rich enterprise operated by the Portuguese in the fifteenth and sixteenth centuries. The Guiné of these years stretched from its northern boundary of the Rio do Ouro in what today is Western Sahara to its southern boundary of Cape Santa Catarina just north of the Zaire River. The trade that was conducted along this coast that primarily bordered the Gulf of Guiné was centered in pepper, ivory, gold, and slaves, and the size of the commerce in these commodities gave rise to names for specific parts of the continent. For centuries they would be called the Grain Coast, for Guiné pepper was known as the "grains of paradise," the Ivory Coast, the Gold Coast, and the Slave Coast. Over time competitors in the form of the Spanish, the Danish, the Dutch, the French, the British, the Belgians, and finally the Germans reduced Portuguese holdings so that by 1886 it was delimited to the Guiné of today.[4]

There is nothing simple about Guiné from the period of its discovery by the Portuguese to that of the conduct of their counterinsurgency campaign there between January 1963 and April 1974. In the case of the first, there is indeed nothing more mysterious and complex from the historical perspective than the discovery of Guiné, as there is little known about the specific achievements of these early voyages beyond the names of a few of their leaders. Because of the obscurity and controversy surrounding this topic, it has developed into a "national industry" for Portuguese historians and has been so for close to 150 years.[5] The "traditional" discoverer of Guiné is Nuno Tristão, and the year cited is 1446; however, Nuno Tristão had not gone any further south along the West African coast than The Gambia at best by that time. Dinis Dias had rounded Cape Verde, the western tip of Africa, in 1444 or 1445, having passed the barren desert coast on the Atlantic side of The Maghreb.[6] It is likely that in 1446 Álvaro Ferandes had sailed as far south as the northern border of the present-day Guiné coast at Capo Roxo between the Casamance and Cacheu Rivers. Regardless of whether Nuno Tristão did or did not discover Guiné in 1446, he is incontestably one of the discoverers of the larger Portuguese-dominated Guiné of the fifteenth and sixteenth centuries, and as such is cited as the discoverer of the reduced Guiné of today.[7] Historical fact may be otherwise, but no one can say for certain, a testimony that myth is more powerful than fact.

The African history of Guiné is one of being a refuge for the many people from neighboring states who were driven out of their homelands by multiple invasions over several centuries. This migration produced a population pushed into a coastal cul-de-sac defined by the swamps and sea. The result was a complicated ethnic mosaic, a true black Babel. When the Portuguese arrived, their natural contact was with the population on the coast. Consequently, in moving to establish dominion over Guiné with their limited resources, they initially sought only to exercise organized authority over the coastal chiefs and their subjects. There was little penetration into the interior of the country other than by white adventurers and *mestiço* traders. As a consequence the territory was named the *Rios da Guiné do Cabo Verde* or the Rivers of the Guiné of Cape Verde without reference to the interior. The government seat was offshore in the more hygienic Cape Verde Islands and the primary commercial activity became slaving. In 1630 the first mainland authority was installed in Cacheu in the form of a *capitania mor* or major captainship. In 1692 Bissau was established, and during the ensuing centuries the country held little economic promise beyond the slave trade, which persisted until the latter part of the nineteenth century. Portugal abolished slavery in 1869, the last of the European nations to do so, and only formally throughout its Empire in 1875.[8] By the turn of the century Guiné had returned to its status as a true economic backwater.

Guiné was elevated to district status within the Cape Verde dependencies in 1835, and two years later its most famous governor, Honório Pereira Barreto, was appointed. He was left pretty much to his own devices to preserve the colonial possession and in 1837 negotiated agreements with the local chiefs as part of this charge. Thereafter he spent most of his time struggling to repulse the ambitions of the French and British. On the darker side, he also ran a family slaving business with his mother, Rosa de Carvalho de Alvarenga, the powerful Rosa of Cacheu, and is accused of prolonging the trade in Guiné.

Complications began for the Portuguese when they sought to take control of the interior of the colony. Indeed, Guiné was a land of violence, for between 1841 and 1936 there were no less than 81 campaigns, expeditions, and operations on the part of the Portuguese. These employed a minimum of 8,444 regular troops and 42,555 auxiliaries against practically every ethnic group within the population, an unusually high number over slightly less than a century for such a small and valueless territory.[9] Relative peace came to the country only after World War I and remained in full flower until the launching of the PAIGC armed struggle in January 1963. René Pélissier observes that it is not hard to wonder if the PAIGC insurgents simply resumed the conflict of their fathers.[10]

As with the obscurity of its discovery and the difficulty of the subsequent pacification of its peoples, Guiné remains a complicated land in which to project force. It is thus not easy to secure it against threats from either within or abroad. First, its climate is unappealing and hostile. The country is tropical and was described by Al Venter in 1973 as a "grim, torrid stretch of swamp and jungle."[11] It is a wet and steaming land under a burning sun. The intense humidity and enervating heat make for an oppressive atmosphere. While there is a dry season that provides some relief from November to May, it is not without discomfort.

As the dry season ends, and the sun reaches its seasonal zenith over Guiné, tropical weather systems develop and are characterized by low pressure areas and strong ascending warm air currents. These updrafts are fed from the continental air mass over the Sahara and create what is termed locally as the "east wind." The population experiences it as a hot, dry air current that comes from the desert to the east, absorbs moisture from the soil and vegetation, and carries a fine dust that affects those with respiratory problems.

The rainy season runs from June to October and ensures a high humidity. It is characterized by frequent monsoons that develop from the disequilibrium between the oceanic and continental air masses. These storms are magnified by the shock of the "east wind," and are characterized by violent electrical activity with the attendant thunder and lightning, tornados, strong winds reaching 60 knots, and heavy rainfall. In the coastal region annual rainfall averages 3 meters, and in the interior, 1.25 meters.[12]

Aerial view of the Corubal River mouth at low tide. Photograph courtesy of Estado-Maior da Armada and *Revista da Armada*.

Because of this pervasive dampness and heat, the staying power of any force becomes difficult. Ammunition, uniforms, maps, rations, medical supplies, and all of the other military matériel and varied paraphernalia of modern war not protected from the dampness or not used immediately will rot or rust. Equipment maintenance problems multiply by several factors over normal wear and tear in a temperate zone, and all machinery requires constant attention if it is to be reliable. It was indeed a place that defeated machinery with careless ease.

It is also a land humming with mosquitoes and many other kinds of insect life. Debilitating tropical diseases abound, and are transmitted by these *petites bêtes*. Venomous snakes thrive in such a habitat. Rapid rates of decay denigrate the quality of front-line medical care. In short, the climate becomes a very important component of Clausewitz's friction of war.

The topography of Guiné is likewise difficult. It can be divided roughly into two distinct geographical areas, the west and the north and east. The most important is the western one, which on a tactical level is characterized by a forbidding and inhospitable stretch of mangrove and swamp forests covering the coastal inlets and deltas of half a dozen rivers. Tidal action floods twice daily, and as the water rises, it fills these estuaries and creates vast tracts of impenetrable swamp.[13] Currents in the rivers during flooding and ebbing can reach 7 knots, enough to overwhelm the small engines in the majority of river transport. This tidal action particularly affects navigation in certain areas, such as Gadamael on the upper reaches of the Cacine River, where it is only possible for larger vessels to operate on the four or five days of high tide during a full moon.[14] At low tide vast expanses of dreary mud flats are exposed and impede the projection of naval power through the river system. Vessels must carefully travel their courses in the center of the channels, for they could easily become grounded and mired in the mud during ebb tide. The low water level would then leave them completely stranded, isolated, and vulnerable to insurgent attack. This necessary caution and the added requisite planning for each trip or patrol was an important component of wartime friction.

Further, the thousands of miles of Guinean rivers and tributaries are obscured from the air by mangroves and thick foliage, making clandestine insurgent movement simple and its interdiction a difficult military problem. Cameras aloft rarely see the forest floor. These rivers are navigable by medium and small craft deep into the country and provide vital lines of communication that cannot be matched by the primitive road system. Indeed many of the roads during the rainy season become rivers themselves, making passage all but impossible. The coast also has many small islands, the most important of which form the Bijagós Islets. The land rises in the northern and eastern interior areas, where the coastal forests gradually disappear, as the terrain changes into the sub-Saharan savanna plain of grasslands and scattered, scrawny trees. Elevation never exceeds 300 meters.[15]

On the strategic level the Guinean geography also plays an important role. Officially Guiné has a land area of 36,125 square kilometers, but this twice daily inundation covers as much as 22 percent of the country, and reduces the surface area to an estimated 28,000 square kilometers. From this figure an additional 3,200 square kilometers can be deducted for the area periodically flooded by rainwater.[16] Under these considerations, the habitable land mass is about 24,800 square kilometers, or about the size of Switzerland, or about one-quarter the size of the 95,440 square kilometers of the Congo District of Angola, the scene of action in the last chapter.[17] Its land frontier is about 680 kilometers, of which 300

LDP 304 stranded at low tide in Guiné. Photograph courtesy Estado-Maior da Armada and *Revista da Armada*.

comprise the northern border with Senegal, and 380 the eastern and southern borders with the Republic of Guinée.[18] Guiné is thus so small that the entire country became essentially a frontier and battle zone, making it extremely difficult to defend.

As if these impediments of climate, terrain, and geography were not enough of a challenge, the population represented another obstacle as much for the insurgents as for the Portuguese. In 1960 the population was 525,437, and was concentrated in the western coastal delta with about 100 people per square kilometer.[19] The arid eastern half was virtually empty with about one person per square kilometer, and it was here that insurgent infiltration occurred with the least opposition. Over 99 percent of the population was black and was fragmented into two primary groupings covering 28 ethno-linguistic groups, each exhibiting various degrees of loyalty to Portugal and the insurgents. Indicative of early exposure to the Portuguese, the coastal population is Christian or animist. The interior peoples are Muslim, reflecting their contact with the ancient interior trade routes from the Gulf of Guiné through Timbuktu to The Maghreb. There were less than 3,000 whites in Guiné.[20] As it was devoid of any reasonable economic potential beyond slavery, it was never a country of white colonization.

Guiné and the difficult Portuguese campaign to subdue the PAIGC there would look increasingly like a Pyrrhic victory, if indeed victory could be achieved by any definition. The greater mystery is why Portugal felt compelled to tie its national strategy to a colony of little economic value. The reason given by the government in Lisbon for clinging to Guiné at all costs was the political notion that its loss would set a dangerous precedent for the struggles in Angola and Mozambique and put at risk the enormous investments and developing economic potential in these two colonies. In 1972 this flawed concept would be challenged unsuccessfully by the ever-practical António de Spínola, Commander-in-Chief and Governor General of the territory, and thereafter it would become a moot point.[21]

Different Visions

From the very first there was a debate over the proper military strategy to be employed in Guiné, as there were significant differences between army and navy thinking. The navy favored a theater strategy of strangling the enemy by exploiting the unique Guinean topography and of exercising control over the various waterways from a central point. This control would give Portuguese forces the needed mobility and logistic lines of communication to defeat the enemy, but more importantly it would disrupt PAIGC power projection.[22] It would, if executed patiently, persistently, and tightly enough, make the waterways a successful barrier to infiltration by preventing the enemy from moving freely between regions of the territory and from penetrating it from his sanctuaries abroad. Likewise, dominance of the waterways would reduce insurgent ability to conduct operations in all but the unpopulated peripheral areas of Guiné.

The army on the other hand tended to favor the more traditional theater strategy of dividing the country into zones and sectors and assigning these to land force commanders. These would be supported with quick reaction or intervention forces held in a mobile reserve to help local forces overwhelm the enemy when it attacked. This *quadrillage* system was adapted from the French army strategy of pacification in Algeria and relied on the use of special elite troops to hunt and destroy the enemy within the defensive network. Naval forces, and the *Fuzileiros* in particular, were simply seen as the naval contribution to army strategy. The army tended to see the numerous waterways as obstacles that favored the insurgent, while the navy saw them as an opportunity and resource to be exploited to defeat the enemy. The debate was never resolved, and except for one or two areas, army strategy prevailed, as the overall theater commander was an army officer and saw things in terms of his service and its orientation. Nevertheless, there were situations in which army commanders were subordinate to naval commanders, and in these cases naval strategy did dominate.

Curiously, the PAIGC was similarly blind to the naval dimension, far more so than the Portuguese. Its leadership never grasped the notion of just how dependent the Portuguese were on their river lines of communication. It also never apparently realized the degree to which the war effort would be crippled by a serious mining offensive or any other activity that severed or blockaded the waterways. Certainly there were examples of how effective such means could be, particularly in the French Indochinese experience. A similar campaign, rather than the occasional mine, would have seriously and dangerously reduced Portuguese capability, particularly in the closing days of the war when the PAIGC controlled most of the land areas of Guiné. Plans were apparently considered but never given much importance or pursued earnestly, as the insurgents were oriented toward a land battle and subversion of the population, which lived ashore.[23] This orientation persisted, even though PAIGC leadership was fully aware of the large fleet of vessels supplying Portuguese outposts throughout Guiné on a continuous basis and the absolute Portuguese dependence on the system. As António Telo has observed, the naval effort was the principal military activity from the first to the last day of the campaign, and everything in Guiné depended on its successful execution.[24] Quite obviously the PAIGC missed an opportunity to conclude the war far earlier than occurred.

Naval Commitment

Clearly trouble was brewing in Africa with events in the Belgian Congo, throughout the north of Angola, and on the Pidjiguiti Dock in Guiné itself, and a naval presence was prudent. As a consequence, the frigate *Pero Escobar* (F 335) and the patrol vessel *Boavista* (P 592) were deployed to Guiné following the Pidjiguiti Dock incident in August 1959. These vessels were hardly more than a show of force, for they could do precious little to address the problem of overall river security. In the early years of the war approximately 60 percent of river transport was performed by a commercial fleet of about 60 vessels. It was vital that this supply line be protected.[25] As in Angola, the normal naval presence was the duty hydrographic vessel, in the Guinean case the *Pedro Nunes* (A 528), so the arrival of these two vessels was a start. Also in 1959 the Maritime Defense Command of Guiné (*Comando de Defesa Marítima da Guiné* or CDMG) was established and integrated into the Naval Command of Cape Verde and Guiné. Its commander was a lieutenant (*capitão tenente*) who also served as Captain of the Ports of Guiné and Chief of Naval Services.

The navy more effectively entered the Guinean picture on 19 May 1961 with the arrival in Bissau of two LFPs, the *Canópus* (P 364) and the *Bellatrix* (P 363), and two small landing craft, LDP 101 and 102, which would later be modified and redesignated as LDP 301 and 302 respectively. On 6 June the LFP *Deneb* (P 365) was added to this modest fleet. These vessels and their crews comprised the Patrol Launch Squadron Guiné (*A Esquadrilha de Lanchas de Fiscalização de Guiné* or ELFG), which was commanded by a junior lieutenant (*primeiro tenente*) and was the first permanent naval presence in the territory. The squadron commander reported to the Commander, CDMG, and likewise served as his chief of staff. The first deployment of this new force was to Farim at the head of the Cacheu River and then to Bolama, Buba, and Bubaque in the south. In each case, a small naval installation was established to support future operations.[26]

When the first incidents occurred on 17 July at the villages of São Domingos, Suzana, and Varela along the northwest border with Senegal, a LFP and a LDP were sent to the Cacheu River as a "permanent" force to establish a presence and police the river traffic for the ninety miles between its mouth and Farim. It was difficult to maintain much of a presence over this stretch, as there were only two vessels, and they were often needed for operations elsewhere. The LDPs were largely held in reserve in Bissau on the Geba River to assure the mobility of the only available intervention force in the country, a squadron of metropolitan cavalry. The two LFPs were alternatively used in the remaining rivers to show the flag and operated from Bolama, Bubaque, Catió, and Cacine in the south.[27]

The LFs were initially commanded by quartermaster sergeants (*sargentos de manobra*); however, during operations in the south in October, there were a succession of groundings. Some of these were quite grave, particularly those in the approaches to the Cacine and on Caió Island at the entrance to the Geba River. It thus became necessary to replace the sergeants with junior line officers or Naval Reserve officers who understood navigation and could more consistently guarantee the safety of the vessels and the execution of their missions.[28] The waters of Guiné were so difficult that the CDMG began accumulating detailed information on each river, port, and island, and compiling it in a volume that was eventually published in 1970 as the *Navigation Guide*. Thereafter it served as the bible for naval operations in Guiné.[29]

This was not the only advance in navigation. It was discovered that the land and water mediums were so intertwined in Guiné that it was necessary to combine the traditional

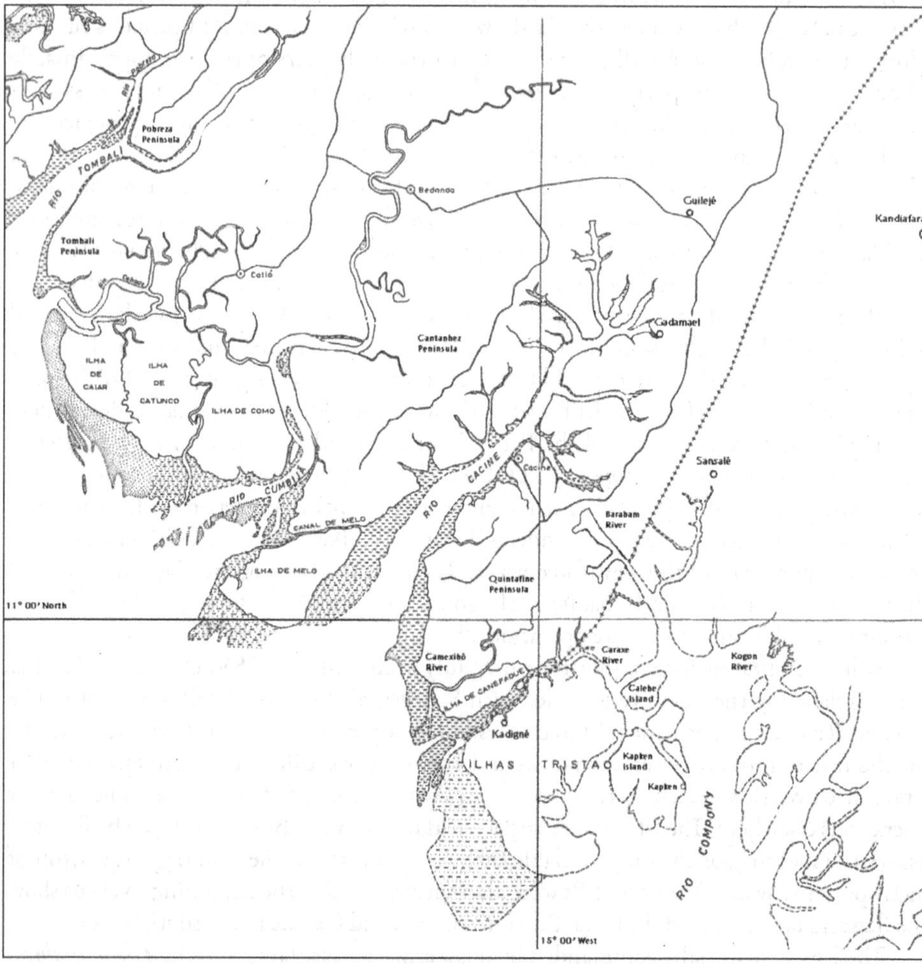

Southern border of Portuguese Guiné. Adapted from Instituto Hidrográfico Chart № 220 (1965).

navigational chart with the detailed terrain features of a topographical map in order to operate effectively in that environment. As the necessary hydrographic data was gathered, it was skillfully integrated with the land surveys into a series of detailed charts that even today represent a model of such work. By June of 1965 these charts had been completed and were proving indispensable in joint as well as single service operations.

In June 1962 the Detachment of Special *Fuzileiros* №2 (DFE 2) arrived in Bissau on two military aircraft. Its initial assignment was to guard the naval installations in Bissau and to act as a reserve force, and to this end it began nightly patrols of the harbor in rubber boats that would continue until the conclusion of the conflict. The following month a combat group or platoon was sent to guard the political prisoners on Galinhas Island and remained there until the spring of 1963. The remaining *Fuzileiros* in Bissau continued to perform sentry duty and to act as a security force on support vessels journeying to such destinations as the small village of Enxudé across the river from Bissau, and to the more distant towns of Buba, Bolama, and Cacine. This defensive and static posture of garrison duty was clearly not in keeping with the modern *Fuzileiro* concept envisioned by Roboredo. These men should have been operating along the rivers, making contact with the population, and seeking out the enemy.

During the fall of 1962, the situation in Guiné progressively deteriorated, as the enemy went over to the offensive and expanded its intense subversive activity in an attempt to isolate the region in the south. This was a coordinated offensive in that the PAIGC simultaneously increased contact over a wide and dispersed area along the northern border with Senegal in order to present an unattractive dilemma to the Portuguese authorities. The PAIGC hoped to divide and weaken the already thin government forces by forcing Portugal to protect all fronts at once.

Finally on 5 December the military command reacted, and a section of the DFE together with two army companies, one from Bissau and the other from Tite, began a reconnaissance mission in the Cachil swamp forest on the island of Caiar at the southern entrance of the Cobade River just west of Catió. There had been reports of armed enemy in the area hard at work subverting the population. In the waterways that encircled Caiar, three LFPs and two LDPs established a patrol to prevent any flight and on the morning of 6 December disembarked the forces at various points on the island in a cordon and search operation. After advancing about 8 kilometers inland, a section encountered two women, and this contact resulted in an exchange of fire with nearby insurgents.[30] The operation progressed over difficult terrain and was inconclusive in the final analysis, the insurgents having melted away. It did, however, offer the first experience in joint operations with the army and navy in Guiné.

Until 1968 the control and use of units of *Fuzileiros* were under the direction of the CDMG. His policy was to maintain a reserve in Bissau and to use these *Fuzileiros* only in specific operations that were always undertaken in coordination with and support of other naval units. This worked well, as these troops were specially trained to conduct patrols, police the rivers, and interdict the enemy in the littorals. These operations can be divided into two types, independent ones that involved patrolling and establishing a presence, and those conducted in force to strike at the enemy. When operating independently, the LFGs would patrol an assigned river for about 12 days, moving mostly at night and anchoring during the day. The intelligence that drove the missions came from the PIDE/DGS, various *chefs de posto*, and the army intelligence apparatus, and was coordinated through the naval staff.[31]

Patrol of *Fuzileiros* from DFE 1 in Guiné, 1965. Photograph courtesy private collection of *Capitão de Fragata* Abel Melo e Sousa.

Direct and frequent interaction with the population and with PIDE/DGS was something that the navy lacked. On the other hand strike operations would generally be assigned to a *Fuzileiro* detachment with its rubber boats and would involve a launch putting them ashore for a specific mission. Aircraft were used regularly, particularly in the Cumbijã River, to help coordinate such operations and to protect the launches from ambush. Unfortunately the radios were not reliable, and this hampered force coordination and effectiveness. Air operations were also used in the Cacine River, especially to protect a convoy.[32]

Table 5.1: Naval Forces in Guiné at year-end 1964

Unit	Arrival Date
LFP *Canópus* (P 364) and *Bellatrix* (P 363)	19 May 1961
LDP 101 and 102	19 May 1961
LFP *Deneb* (P 365)	6 June 1961
LDP 103	13 January 1963
Nuno Tristão (F 332) relieves *Vouga* ("V")	19 February 1963
Platoon of *Fuzileiros* Nº1 Absorbed by Company of *Fuzileiros* Nº3 on its later arrival	9 April 1963
Company of *Fuzileiros* Nº3	14 June 1963
LFG *Argos* (P 372)	30 July 1963

Unit	Arrival Date
LDP 104	9 August 1963
LP1, LP2, LP3, LP4 Patrol launches based on armed Algarve-type fishing vessels Quickly retired with arrival of LDMs	9 August 1963
LFG *Dragão* (P 374)	19 August 1963
Detachment of Special *Fuzileiros* Nº7	11 October 1963
Detachment of Special *Fuzileiros* Nº8	4 November 1963
LFG *Escorpião* (P 375)	December 1963
Ferry boat *Bor* (Naval Services)	Non-combatant
Motorized transports BM1 and BM2 (Naval Services)	Non-combatant
LDM 204 and 205 (ex-LDM 101 and 102 respectively)	13 January 1964
LDM 201 and 203	21 January 1964
LDM 306 and 307	30 January 1964
LDM 202, 301, 302, 303	23 February 1964
Detachment of Special *Fuzileiros* Nº9	29 February 1964
LDM 304	3 April 1964
Detachment of Special *Fuzileiros* Nº10 relieves Nº2	25 June 1964
LDM 305	3 August 1964
LFGs *Hidra* (P 376) and *Cassiopeia* (P 373) replace LFGs *Argos* (P 372) and *Dragão* (P 374), which are transferred to Angola.	19 September 1964
LFG *Lira* (P 361), replaces LFG *Escorpião* (P 375), which is transferred to Angola.	15 October 1964
LFG *Orion* (P 362)	13 December 1964
LDM 308 and 309 (ex-LDM 501 and 502 respectively)	6 December 1964
LDM 312 and 313 (ex-LDM 505 and 506 respectively)	15 December 1964
LDM 310 and 311 (ex-LDM 503 and 504 respectively)	16 December 1964

The *Fuzileiro* routine was to patrol the river daily in rubber boats with the support of an LDM. About every fortnight there would be a large operation that was invariably conducted at night in order to position for an attack at sunrise. *Comandante* Carlos Gomes noted that in the 13 months of his deployment between 1964 and 1966, he conducted 28 or 29 operations as the executive officer of DFE 10.[33] Only rarely were these done in conjunction with other DFEs.

Fuzileiro river patrols would be varied to keep the enemy off balance, and the favorite tactic was to spend the night hours floating and silently paddling in areas of likely enemy contact. Often the force would divide, some staying with the boats and others going ashore to establish an ambush. If the enemy were present, he would attack as the *Fuzileiros* were landing and most vulnerable. When traveling on a LF, the *Fuzileiros* felt exposed, as the launch could be heard a good 10 minutes before its arrival. Also, the rivers were often only 100 meters wide, and the launch was extremely susceptible to RPG fire. Gomes remembers that as commanding officer of LFG *Lira* (P 361) between 1971 and 1973, he was attacked 8 times by enemy RPGs, and only one hit his vessel.[34] Fortunately the insurgents had very bad aim, even at 50 meters.

Once ashore, the *Fuzileiros* were more adaptive, and walking quietly, could surprise an unsuspecting enemy. They traveled light and carried only 5 pouches of ammunition clips, a little food, and drinkable water. Mobility was the most important factor. They were armed with lightweight aviation rockets (37mm) launched from an adapted tube, three MG-42 machine guns, and sometimes a mortar. Gomes remembers slipping past sentries who were smoking and into a village to capture weapons and a potato sack of hand grenades.[35] The enemy would melt away when confronted by the *Fuzileiros* except in the south of Guiné, where regular PAIGC troops had infiltrated. There were few army positions there, and the navy likewise had less presence in the area. The PAIGC thus was able to develop a strong position in the southern border area and maintain its staying power in the face of weak challenges.

By 1965 this naval-only mission was under some pressure, and its oversight by the CDMG was viewed by the overall theater commander as out of step with what the army saw as the role of special forces. The army little understood the naval dimension of the conflict and the use of the *Fuzileiros* in seemingly routine, unspectacular, but vitally important operations against the waterborne logistics network of the enemy.[36] There was a tendency by the army to see *Fuzileiros* as simply another source of specially trained manpower to undertake operations in the army vision alongside its own special forces. The CDMG was forced to bow to army wishes. In February 1967, a directive returned the *Fuzileiros* to CDMG control for naval operations in the Cachu, Cacine, and Cumbijã river systems. The launches patrolling these rivers were then able to extend their reach with consequent effectiveness. Control and use changed again with the arrival of Spínola in 1968 and the implementation of his perceived solutions to immediate security problems. From the strategic view this change was shortsighted, as it broke-up an effective launch-*Fuzileiro* team that was denying the use of the rivers to the enemy. In any event, during the final years of the war, squads of *Fuzileiros* were routinely deployed on launches to counter the aggressiveness of the enemy and its ambushes. While this move helped the crews of the launches as a defensive measure, it impeded the *Fuzileiros* in their original mission of continuing the patient and methodical offensive against the enemy logistical system.

At the beginning of 1963 the fleet available to the navy in Guiné to meet its mission was composed only of a small and irregular assortment of craft. In addition to the three LFPs, the two LDPs, and the duty hydrographic ship described earlier, there was the aged torpedo destroyer *Vouga* ("V"), which patrolled the coast. There were also five vessels belonging to the Chief of Naval Services, which consisted of three small open cargo launches, the *Formosa*, *Corubal*, and *Pecixe*, the dredge *Geba*, and the old tugboat *Atro*. Altogether these were inadequate to address river security in light of the increasing PAIGC activity. Accordingly, during 1963 and 1964 the force was augmented by the arrival of a series of new units, providing an entirely new face. Table 5.1 describes the build-up over the two-year period. With the total number of vessels in the theater reaching 29 by the end of 1964 and those in the squadron numbering 23, it was appropriate to change the name of the squadron to reflect the new composition weighted toward transport craft. Accordingly, it was renamed Launch Squadron Guiné (*Esquadrilha de Lanchas da Guiné* or ELG). Of particular importance was the addition to the fleet of the three LFGs *Argos* (P 372), *Dragão* (P 374), and *Escorpião* (P 375). These vessels with their relatively large displacement, high speed of 16 knots, heavy armament in two 40mm Bofors, and access to most parts of the country served by the river system were theoretically ideal for moving to engage the enemy and guaranteeing the fluvial lines of communication. They were to prove themselves time and time again in the great "Battle of the Rivers."

Their deployment, however, was interrupted by an incident on 26 December 1963 in which *Dragão* while on patrol was violently attacked by the enemy in an ambush near the village of Tancroal on the left bank of the Cacheu River about 10 miles downstream of Farim. Post attack analysis revealed 22 hits on the hull and superstructure from light machinegun fire. One of the projectiles had penetrated the hull and ruptured the compressed air bottle that was part of the remote engine control system. *Dragão* had been temporarily immobilized until the bottle could be replaced.[37] The situation could have been far worse except for a measure of good luck. This class of vessels was clearly not designed to survive this sort of attack and proved to have many vulnerabilities, not the least of which was the magazine located in the stern above the waterline. It was consequently decided to harden the vessels with defensive protection around the magazine, the engines, and the auxiliaries, as a simple rifle shot had been able to immobilize a vessel of 200 tons. New construction would incorporate this protection.

The LFGs already in Guiné were replaced toward the end of 1964 with four newer vessels of the same class that incorporated the advanced armor. As in Angola, the LFs were re-gunned, with the MG-42 replacing the Dreyse, and the Heckler and Koch G-3 series replacing the FBP m/947 9mm machine pistol. Other revisions in armament were

LFG *Hidra* (P 376) in Guiné with its new armor modifications. Photograph courtesy Estado-Maior da Armada and *Revista da Armada*.

detailed in Chapter 3; however, the vulnerability of the vessels spawned a number of ideas that were reduced to two serious proposals. The first, advanced by *Comandante* Alpoim Calvão, the commanding officer of DFE 8, was that of a heavily armored monitor-type vessel built especially for the waters of Guiné. It would be fast, silent and heavily armed.[38] Unfortunately each of these capabilities involved compromises. A heavily armored and armed vessel could be neither very fast nor shallow enough in draft to operate effectively in the Guinean riverine environment. As also mentioned in Chapter 3, this project was abandoned as being too costly and perhaps unachievable with the technology of the time.

The second was that of a light, fast, quiet, and small LFP that would have both a shallow-draft and light armament in the vein of the PBR that was being used so effectively by the U.S. Navy in Vietnam. Its principal mission would be to carry a squad of *Fuzileiros* and insert them covertly. Its speed and silence would provide the mobility and surprise needed to counter the enemy, and its shallow draft would give it free range throughout the Guinean river system. The LFPs and LDMs were not particularly effective for this type of operation, as they were relatively noisy and slow and always gave the enemy ample warning. A prototype of this new LFP was introduced in 1971 as the *Corsair* and used experimentally until the end of the war, although it was never officially entered into navy inventory. The project never bore full fruit, as it was plagued with maintenance and equipment problems. Following the war, the *Corsair* was returned to Portugal.[39] As in most wars, the forces had to use what was available in the short run and make the most of it, and this the navy did well.

As a postscript to the 1963–1964 build-up, the LDG *Alfange* arrived in Guiné on 3 October 1965 and was the first of its class to be deployed. It had the capacity to transport 270 tons of cargo or a battalion of 450 men for a short voyage. This addition brought a substantial capacity to reach most parts of Guiné with troops and their logistic tail and to support the population. Because of its light armament, it was often escorted by a LFG or LFP to add firepower should an attack materialize. The next year its sister ship, the LDG *Montante*, arrived, and in July 1969 LDG *Bombarda* brought the total to three.

Maintaining the Fleet

In 1959, when the Commander of the CDMG also held the position Chief of Naval Services, the first priority had been the building of infrastructure, particularly the radio station in Bissau, which was completed in May 1961. Not the least among these was the expansion of the shipyard to accommodate the arrival of the "brown water" fleet and its maintenance and repair. This daunting task proved too much for the commander alone, and the command was augmented with an additional officer to assume these responsibilities. The young officer assigned was Lieutenant (*primeiro tenente*) (Engineer) Luiz Casimiro Mesquita Dias, who arrived in Guiné in November 1963 to oversee the running and expansion of the small shipyard. It consisted then of two old and decrepit slipways and a 900-square meter building. The slipways were in poor condition and badly in need of repair. Power to operate the railway cradle came from a manual block and tackle with the occasional assistance of a jeep. By the time Mesquita Dias had left in December 1965, the shipyard had 4,000 square meters under roof, and the workforce had expanded from five Europeans and perhaps 20 elderly local workers to a substantial operation supporting the entire "small boat" fleet. Expansion of the labor force drew on the local technical schools for shipwright apprentices, and the veteran employees taught them such basic skills as welding, engine and

LDG *Alfange* pier-side in Teixeira Pinto, Guiné, 1971. Photograph courtesy Estado-Maior da Armada and *Revista da Armada.*

boiler repair, woodworking, electrical systems, and electronics. The two slipways proved inadequate to handle the needed volume of repairs, so vessels would be beached and tidal action used to tilt the hull from one side to the other to perform maintenance. The larger, more complicated repairs would be done in the Cape Verde Islands, but this was to be avoided, as any vessel sent there would be out of service for three months.[40] By 1969, the yard had built its capability and capacity to service and maintain the LFGs *Lira* (P 361), *Orion* (P 362), *Cassiopeia* (P 373), *Dragão* (P 374), *Hidra* (P 376), which had been sent previously to Cape Verde.

In the beginning there was no maintenance plan, and repairs were made as required. This approach created a burdensomely fluctuating workload that was highly disruptive to the small yard with its very finite resources. In one of the worse environments of Africa, in which the shallow and muddy water with its suspended particulate rapidly wore all machinery, regular attention was critical. By the end of 1964 there was a six-month schedule of maintenance of all vessels assigned to the theater with man-hours allocated for emergency repairs. Spare parts were always in short supply, as Lisbon never sent enough of them. When the navy undertook a large operation, such as Operation *Tridente*, it would put an enormous burden on the yard facilities, its people, and inventories. Most of the time the yard worked 24 hours a day for 7 days a week to maintain the fleet.[41]

Indeed, the yard during this fleet expansion was under pressure to accommodate the maintenance of the *Argos* class LFGs arriving in Guiné and to add crew living spaces to the new LDM series 201 and 301. This addition of crew quarters would convert the LDMs into long-range transports with the potential to be used as mobile bases similar in capability to those that had experienced such success on the Zaire River. The 201 series vessels were fitted with eight berths and a galley that gave them the capability to act as a patrol craft as well as a transport and of carrying and launching *Fuzileiros* in their rubber boats to project power along the riverbanks. The holds of these launches were covered completely, while those of LDMs 308 to 313 were covered only partially, as they would be used exclusively for cargo. This conversion work extended to mid-1965.[42]

The yard also addressed the marginal living conditions on board the launches, as improving them was a constant concern of every ELFG/ELG commander throughout the conflict. Launch habitability was always an important consideration in an environment such as Guiné, for the crewmen were expected initially to live aboard for the better part of their two-year assignment. The spaces were small and constricted, poorly ventilated, and open to insects. There was little room to store anything beyond a few simple personal necessities. Further, the food afloat was more than likely prepared by someone who knew nothing about cooking, and it was consequently less that appetizing. In an effort to remove the crewmen from this stifling existence, the navy in 1966 built a barracks in Bissau to accommodate up to 60 men. This facility would allow the crewmen to move ashore when the launches were in the capital and to take a break from shipboard privations in more comfortable circumstances. Here, the food was prepared professionally, and there were storage facilities for personal belongings for which there was no room aboard the launches. As one might imagine, requests for these berths ashore generally exceeded availability, so a system of priorities was established to allocate them as fairly as possible. At the end of 1969, the barracks facility was replaced by another with an expanded capacity for 120 men. Two years later the Squadron moved into two new barracks facilities, each with a capacity of 80 men and a personal locker for each crewman.[43]

On board the launches, however, there was precious little that could be done to improve conditions, although many modifications were attempted. For instance, aboard the LDs side curtains and seals were added to the canvas awnings over the holds for use during the rainy season, and these did make conditions below significantly better. Typical of another helpful modification was the acquisition of fifteen 50-kilogram freezer chests at the end of 1968. These permitted crews to keep perishables fresh on long patrols, and with this improvement in diet came an improvement in health and morale. By mid-1970 every launch had a ventilating system and a freezer chest. Finally, from an operational perspective as the number of units available in Guiné increased over time, it became possible to reduce the length of patrols so that by 1971 none exceeded 30 days.[44] This spread the workload more evenly and made less arduous operational schedules for all.

The continual search to improve life on board the launches resulted in very tolerable working conditions in a forbidding environment. This proved to be perhaps the greatest strength in fighting the insurgents, as the crews remained healthy and able to perform effectively. In contrast, the enemy was forced to make a long and arduous journey across difficult terrain largely on foot and sometimes by canoe. He came from his sanctuary in Guinée or Senegal with little cover from the elements to reach the population or to make contact with Portuguese forces. He was weighted with his weapons, ammunition, rations, and perhaps some medical supplies. If he became ill or hurt, he had little prospect of useful medical help. Certainly there was little comparison between the endurance and sustainability of the two on an individual basis. In fact, the key to insurgent sustainability has always been an ample supply of recruits willing to suffer and die for the ideals of the movement. In the finest Maoist tradition, there were political officers present throughout the PAIGC military organization to make certain that there was no wavering from these ideals and to maintain morale in the face of a constant stream of casualties. Normally insurgent casualties run well ahead of government ones, and Guiné was no exception.

Medical Care

The tropical climatic conditions in Guiné and its complicated terrain combined to make the delivery of medical care to both the military and civil populations a difficult job. Yet, the CDMG Health Service (*Serviço de Saúde*) combined with the medical services of the other branches and the government to deliver effective support to the military, military dependents, and the population at large. The most important aspect of its operations was that of ensuring that habitable and sound sanitary conditions existed on the naval bases and facilities and aboard the LPs and LDs. This was most important, as historically armed forces have suffered more from poor hygiene and sickness than from enemy action.

In Guiné, such diseases as malaria, diarrhea, acute respiratory ailments, tuberculosis, internal parasites, onchocerciasis (river blindness), and other tropical diseases abounded. These represented a threat to both the military campaign and its strategy of caring for the population. Naval physicians were highly dedicated medical practitioners assigned to staff both the civilian hospital in Bissau and the Bissau Military Hospital (HM 214) with the aim of bringing superior medical care to the entire territory. For the military, helicopter evacuation of wounded from the battlefield to the Military Hospital for treatment and ultimately to the *metrópole*, if required, was the primary medical duty. As a secondary duty, the health and well being of the military, military dependents, and the population at large fell on the shoulders of the Health Service. Its reputation in this regard came to be substantial and played an important part in gaining the loyalty of the population.

Because a substantial part of the navy was African, treating these sailors required adjustments. For instance, the African *Fuzileiros*, who were married and polygamous and joined their families whenever safety permitted, required special medical accommodations, and in the case of DFE 21 in Cacheu, the CDMG assigned a doctor specifically to care for those African *Fuzileiros* and their families. In other cases, doctors would travel to units to respond to a specific need, such as the gastroenteritis epidemic at DFE 22 in Cacine, as later described by then Lieutenant Rui Abreu from his 1972–1973 tour of duty in Guiné.[45] The African *Fuzileiros* and their families were also flown to Bissau for needed attention when their ailments required more than what was available in the field.

The population at large was treated at medical clinics located strategically throughout the territory, and ultimately there were 51 such clinics established.[46] The reputation of Portuguese doctors spread well beyond the borders of Guiné, and this increasingly drew patients from far-flung locales to the clinics for treatment. Indeed, patients from Senegal, without documentation to cross the border, came to receive this care. Senegalese maternity patients were even given follow-up appointments.[47]

The traditional practice of a patient coming to the clinic was not always possible because of the long distances and difficult terrain over which many needed to travel. In order to reach these more remote people, it was necessary to establish mobile clinics. The goal of these was a monthly visit to every village that did not have regular contact with the more developed centers. Aside from the well understood government obligation to care for its population, it was hoped that this important facet of social operations and the confidence that it developed would prompt the all-important flow of intelligence and cooperation from the people.[48]

Preparing to Fight

Personnel arrived from the *metrópole* having gained only a basic understanding of the war in Guiné and required significant additional preparation in order to execute their mission effectively. Despite the development and publication of a series of manuals on the topic of subversive warfare and its study in the *metrópole*, the subtleties of how it was being fought in Guiné, with its diverse population and difficult physical terrain, was lost on most and required considerable time to acquire.[49] This acclimation occurred on a number of fronts and aimed to accelerate the situational awareness and tradecraft of all newly arrived personnel through a program of instruction in theory, practical skills, and operational procedures. All three of these had been refined through the inventory of experience previously accumulated on the rivers.

While personnel came from diverse ratings, such as, quartermaster, gunnersmate, machinistmate, radioman, and cook, there was a common theme and understanding of the war that all needed to acquire. Accordingly, the squadron implemented an operational training plan (*um plano de treino operacional* or PTO) to fill this need. The initial phase was conducted ashore and focused each rating on the requirements of his professional skill as would be needed in the theater. He was introduced to the various naval facilities and their function in support of the ELFG/ELG in its execution of theater naval strategy.

The second phase was conducted aboard each man's assigned vessel by his shipboard command. All were made familiar with their particular launch, its maintenance and daily routine, its organization, its safety procedures, and its arms and weapons. Associated topics were such things as tropical hygiene, combat readiness, and mission types and the profile of each. These two phases together lasted three weeks and by the end of this time each man was familiar with his launch, its potential and limitations, its care and maintenance, and the personal role that he played in making it an effective tool of war. Still, no one had yet been to sea.

During the following week the new crewmen entered their practical phase and spent time on the water learning to shoot accurately from a moving craft, to navigate the tricky waterways in day and night and at high and low tide, and to land troops. This portion of the training would be extended for several weeks in the case of a prospective captain or *comandante* of a launch until he was prepared to assume command.

The training was, of course, not without its surprises. Live fire exercises were initially conducted on the Geba River in an uninhabited area called Cãchiquinho, which was about a three hour drive by road and was located upstream from Bissau on the left bank. Here crewmen received arms instruction, familiarized themselves with their weapons, and practiced combat firing at established ranges. The insurgents noticed that the navy used this site regularly, and with their interest piqued, decided to have some target practice of their own. Accordingly they positioned themselves to surprise the next navy visit. As the trainees arrived and began their course of instruction, they were greeted by small arms fire from the insurgents. Fortunately no one was hurt from the bad marksmanship, but for many of the newcomers it was the proverbial baptism of fire. Later the enemy appeared with heavy weapons capable of delivering a large volume of lethal fire, and the situation became quite dangerous. This cycle of instruction was consequently moved to the small, uninhabited island of Coroa further downstream.[50]

The skills of the crew were honed over the ensuing weeks from the experience gained in daily operations on the rivers and along the coast. As operational tempo increased and additional launches arrived in the theater, there was a constant manning shortage. Certain key ratings, such as gunnersmates and machinistmates, were thus sent directly to their assigned launches and received their instruction there from the veteran crewmen in order to accelerate the training process.

Crewmen bonded together as a team and became adept at manning their launches, of which they were justifiably proud. Each vessel was not only the home but also the means of survival for the men, and as such, became a potent fighting machine with each man depending on and supporting his shipmates. Despite the oppressive heat and humidity and the ever-present enemy threat, morale was high, as the young sailors and their officers assumed important responsibilities with these small commands and were trusted with great latitude in executing missions.

The Progress of War

From the beginning of hostilities in 1963, the ELFG/ELG saw its primary responsibility as preserving the riverine communication routes and thus created a system of convoys to shepherd the supply vessels through the river system and protect them from insurgent attack. While the system was refined over the length of the conflict, and resources were allocated as required, it was composed of four primary routes radiating from Bissau:

- Bissau (or Cacheu) to Farim on the Cacheu River.
- Bissau to Bissum, a market village 30 miles upstream of Cacheu
- on the Armada River.
- Bissau (or Bolama) to Catió on the Cobade River.
- Bissau (or Bolama) to Bedanda on the Cumbijã River.

From these points the distribution system would be continued to the smaller ports, such as Gadamael near the frontier with Guinée. As the security situation was more acute on these extensions, it was necessary to escort the transports and often to augment the crews with a squad of *Fuzileiros* for protection against ambush along the narrow confines of the smaller interior waterways. Adjustments in routes were also necessary as the situation changed, such as with the route to Bedanda in which it became necessary to pass well away from Como Island after the army withdrew from it in 1967. Until that year the convoys had been the responsibility of the ELFG/ELG, but after then when the security situation worsened, they became the responsibility of the CDMG. Normally a convoy was organized in a column formation with a LDP or a LDM leading the way and a second following with the senior officer and convoy commander on board. Ambushes were frequent and indeed assured on certain routes, and the crews could expect to be attacked with bazookas, mortars, and rockets. Such attacks could immobilize a launch but never sink it, although many were damaged beyond repair. Some PAIGC experimentation with mines began in 1967, and this was countered by having *Fuzileiros* precede the convoy in their rubber boats to scout the river and its banks. Fortunately the PAIGC did not pursue this practice, for in the long run it would have caused the Portuguese some very serious problems. Varying the routes and times was done as much as possible; however, because of the predictable tides and mandated access to certain destinations this was not but so useful. Convoys were invariably supported by air cover on the most dangerous portions of their routes until 1973 and the appearance of the SA-7 *Strela* (NATO: *Grail*) shoulder-fired anti-aircraft missile. Thereafter, aircraft were no longer safe to fly below 2,000 meters altitude in missile-threat areas.[51]

With the 1963–1964 augmentation, the CDMG assigned five task units (TU) to operate along these four primary routes. These were initially:

- TU1 composed of three LFGs and one LP supported by a LFG,
- and operating in the Cacheu River as far upstream as Farim.
- TU2 composed of one LFG, three LFPs, and three LPs,
- and operating in the southern rivers of Cacine, Cobado, and Cumbijã.
- TU6 composed of two LDMs and a detachment of *Fuzileiros,*
- and operating in the Gebar and Bafatá Rivers.
- TU7 composed of two LDMs and a detachment of *Fuzileiros,*
- and operating in the area of Bolama.
- TU8 composed of two LDMs and *Fuzileiros* drawn from Bissau and operating in the Mansoa River.[52]

It is well to note that vessels were shifted from task unit to task unit as operations required, and such changes did not necessarily reflect any alteration in the primary concept of operations.

As the fleet expanded, the four LPs adapted from the Algarve fishing vessels as a stopgap measure proved too slow for operational employment and were struck from service. The two that were in relatively serviceable shape, LP2 and LP3, were ultimately used for local fishing in the Biljagós Islands. By the end of 1965 the squadron had 3 LFPs, 12 LDMs converted to patrol capability, 6 LDMs retained as transports, and 7 LDPs, a total of 28 units. These LDPs had likewise been given a somewhat permanent crew quarters by constructing a canvas shelter over six bunks and a galley.[53] Over the ensuing years the mix remained approximately the same, and the numbers grew with additions, substitutions, and strikes to a high of 39 vessels assigned to the squadron in the years 1969 and 1970. During the thirteen years of the war, 1967 was the year in which the squadron worked the hardest with its 29 vessels. It moved more cargo per vessel, traveled more miles, and suffered more casualties than in any other year. Table 5.2 graphically displays the operating statistics of the squadron from 1963 through 1971, the primary years of offensive operations. In the table it is evident that again naval presence on the waterways had a telling effect. The canoes destroyed and the attacks encountered show heavy contact with the enemy through 1968 and diminish thereafter. As in all cases, it is important to examine the actual naval activity behind these numbers and the story that these operations tell.

Table 5.2: Selected operating statistics for the ELFG/ELG, 1963–1971[54]

Year	Launches	Miles Steamed	Operations Supported	Troops Transported	Tons Cargo Transported	Canoes Destroyed	Ambushes	Deaths	Wounded
1963	11	10,500	42	6,213		99	9		1
1964	23	19,600	256	11,327	1,365	364	127		3
1965	28	88,958	271	31,992	3,275	374	102		8

Year	Launches	Miles Steamed	Operations Supported	Troops Transported	Tons Cargo Transported	Canoes Destroyed	Ambushes	Deaths	Wounded
1966	28	141,080	309	41,529	3,545	319	67		1
1967	29	166,865	278	35,945	3,575	195	56	4	7
1968	37	152,763	174	22,760	3,527	165	37	2	
1969	39	143,654	279	37,207	4,432	99	13		
1970	39	141,415	168	13,834	3,523	61	7		
1971	34	144,814	171	14,115	3,146	44	4		
Totals		1,009,649	1,948	214,922	26,388	1,720	422	6	20

Guinean Sanctuary

Conakry remains the capital of the former French colony of Guinée in French West Africa, which became the Republic of Guinée in 1958 in a ceremony that snubbed France and its president, Charles de Gaulle, personally. France had sought in its colonial process to give its overseas citizens a sense of belonging to the mother country through cultural, financial, commercial, and military links. These citizens came to France for their advanced education, and training in government, commercial, and military affairs. Each colony in effect became a microcosm of France, and in its independence was to continue to follow the French lead and accept support with a single exception, the Republic of Guinée. Sékou Touré, an avowed Marxist, had been elected as the prospective new leader in anticipation of France's granting independence to its colony. Anxious to distance himself from France, he had initiated an early, abrupt, and precipitous break with the *métropole* in the name of his socialist revolution. In so doing, he destroyed both his links with France and his country's economy. Sékou Touré proceeded to implement his socialist system, and the country became deeply beggared. The president of a neighboring Francophile country captured the essence of the Guinean distress in his comment that never again would Sékou Touré walk on the Avenue des Champs-Élysées.

Sékou Touré believed that he was in the vanguard of the march of society toward the inevitable goal of world socialism, as posited by Marxist historical determinism. According to this thinking, social countries were inherently peace-loving and only fought defensive wars. Such defensive war included anti-colonial wars and wars of national liberation, both of which were deemed just wars, for they advanced society toward the socialist utopia. Guinée's immediate northern neighbor, Portuguese Guiné, was viewed as part of the imperialist state of Portugal and its citizens as oppressed peoples striving to achieve independence. It was assumed that inside every Portuguese Guinean there was a true socialist just waiting to be released. Thus, it was only natural in 1962 that Sékou Touré should support Amílcar Cabral and his newly active PAIGC, whose goal was to displace Portuguese authority with a single-party socialist state. In a logical fraternal overture, Conakry was offered as a temporary home to the PAIGC to use as its headquarters and primary logistics base in its insurgency campaign to assume control of Portuguese Guiné. With Sékou Touré's unqualified support, the entire frontier between the two countries became a springboard for PAIGC assaults on

Portuguese territory. Portugal would tolerate some pain from this quarter, but there was a threshold at which it would react with crossborder operations to neutralize PAIGC activity, particularly in hot pursuit, a move that would also hazard Sékou Touré. In addition to broad international opposition to Portugal's African empire, Sékou Touré sought specific insurance against such an incursion and found it in part through the capture on 22 May 1963 of a downed aviator, the then Sergeant Pilot António Lobato. He was apprehended near the southwestern border in Portuguese Guiné by a group of PAIGC insurgents and brought across the frontier. Lobato was taken first to Conakry and then to the interior city of Kindia, where he was incarcerated as a "war criminal" in the prison *Maison de Force de Kindia* on 17 June. In 1969 he escaped from Kindia for a short period and on recapture was moved to *La Montaigne* in Conakry, from which he would later be rescued. The PAIGC and Sékou Touré now had a hostage whose life would potentially be the cost of Portuguese armed reprisal in the Guinean sanctuary.[55] In November 1963, six months after Lobato had been captured, Alpoim Calvão reported with DFE 8 to Guiné and during his assignment raised the question of contingency plans to retrieve captured prisoners of war. At that point there were none.[56] When Alpoim Calvão completed his tour in 1966, Lobato remained imprisoned, and there were still no plans to rescue him.

Because of the unusual delta topography of Guiné, the coastal waters and rivers had always been the primary transportation routes for both friend and foe, and the relatively unchallenged PAIGC used them heavily to infiltrate southern Guiné and to support its insurgents there. To this view it acquired four motorboats, the *Mirandela*, the *Arouca*, the *Bandim*, and the *Bissau*, for the specific purpose of logistically servicing its military operations. Indeed, things were going so well for the PAIGC that it had added the last two craft only as recently as May 1963. The PAIGC procedure was to depart Conakry on

Fuzileiros from DFE 1 Disembarking from an LD in Guiné, 1965. Photograph courtesy private collection of *Capitão de Fragata* Abel Melo e Sousa.

a periodic basis and navigate northward to the frontier, remaining within the protected coastal territorial waters of the Republic of Guinée and thus by international law theoretically immune from attack. Using this link, the PAIGC established and supplied four primary bases in the border area:

- Kadigné, a forward base on the marshland island of Tristão in the Îles Tristão about a mile across the Inxanche River from the Portuguese islands of Canefaque and Cambom. Tristão is dotted with settlements connected by footpaths.
- Boké, capital of the prefecture of the same name and an important military and logistical center in the Nunez River.
- Kandiafara, a forward interior base opposite the Portuguese village of Guilejé and colloquially known as the "corridor to Guilejé." The only means of communication in this area is either by water or by tracks impassable after rain. It is located on the right bank of the Kogon River about 45 miles from the sea. The river is little used, as it is difficult to navigate, and there is a rocky barrier at a bend some 20 miles from its mouth. Only small craft can successfully pass this obstacle.
- Sansalé, a forward base opposite Gadamael supporting operations around the Portuguese village of Cacine and the throughout the Quintafine Peninsula, also reachable only by tracks impassable after rain.

By the end of 1963 one and possibly two of these PAIGC vessels were further transporting arms and munitions into Portuguese territory and particularly into the adjoining islands of Como, Caiar, and Catunco, from the coastal depots of Kadigné and Boké to subvert the population. These operations took judicious advantage of the

Comandante Alpoim Calvão (right foreground) leading *Fuzileiros* on Operation *Chicuelina*, left bank of the Cacheu River, northern Guiné, 1963. Photograph courtesy Estado-Maior da Armada and *Revista da Armada*

Portuguese weaknesses in tactical communications and an inexact knowledge of the remote area. Indeed there were no hydrographic charts yet available for either the Cacine or the Cumbijã river basins, which were vital waterways to support military operations and the population in the south, or the Cobade, which circled around the northern portion of the island triumvirate. This vulnerability was known to the enemy and exploited in the sinking of a Portuguese motorboat at the confluence of the Cumbijã and Cobade Rivers on 8 July 1963 and an attack on the Portuguese ferry *Bor* on the Cobade River on 19 November, causing the loss of supplies and a casualty.[57] It was these attacks primarily that led to the 1963 and 1964 expansion of naval presence in Guiné to fulfill its mission of maintaining the waterborne lines of communication.

In order to carry the fight to the enemy, the Portuguese initiated the defensive measures of a proficiency training program, modified convoy procedures, and upgraded armor and armament on the LFs. Most important to our discussion, however, was the initiation of offensive search and destroy missions by the DFEs and LFs.

Operation *Tridente*

By early 1964 the border area with Guinée and the coastal areas around Catió and Cacine had become sufficiently infected with PAIGC insurgents that a serious Portuguese challenge was long overdue. The navy in particular worried that without such action its access to Catió would be closed.[58] Accordingly a joint operation styled Operation *Tridente* would combine army, navy, and air force resources to isolate and sanitize the familiar islands of Caiar, Como, and Catunco, which were bounded by the Atlantic Ocean and the Cumbijã, Caiar, and Cobade Rivers. Caiar had been the scene of the earlier December 1962 action, which had been purely a sweep through the island and had had no lasting effect. The expanded area of operations for *Tridente* now covered nominally some 210 square kilometers of land, only 170 of which were actually usable because of the tides.

The three islands were characterized by large tracts of rice patties with their intricate dike systems and alternatively by vast areas of very dense and impenetrable grasslands and swamp forests. These latter areas provided ideal hiding places for insurgents, as troops found passage through them very difficult going. Clearly the operation had its work cut out for it, and it was to be the first such full joint operation in any of the theaters.[59] It would last for more than two months and from the naval perspective would be supported by a substantial portion of its resources in Guiné. Over time the *Vouga*, the *Nuno Tristão*, three DFEs, one LFG, three LFPs, three LPs, six LDMs, and two LDPs were committed to the operation.[60]

Como and its adjacent islands were considered important both to the insurgents and to the Portuguese command for obvious reasons. From the point of view of the insurgents it was a perfect staging point, for it was remote, and this isolation brought with it security. It could be supplied by sea from the sanctuary of Guinée only about 25 miles distant or a few hours at most by boat, and it provided a springboard for PAIGC subversive operations further into Portuguese territory. From the Portuguese point of view it was perceived as a festering sore of insurgent activity and an unwelcome subversion of its population in a prime rice-growing and a very modest cattle-grazing region. The insurgents were diverting the rice crop and livestock to their own ends and establishing themselves as a relatively permanent fixture within the population. Portuguese intelligence estimated the PAIGC force on the three islands to be about 300, which number included about 15 military advisors from Guinée.[61]

Disembarking forces on the Island of Como, Operation *Tridente*, January 1964. Photograph courtesy *Estado-Maior da Armada* and *Revista da Armada*

The operation had five goals:

- To secure the Portuguese riverine lines of communication in the south.
- To protect the population from the PAIGC subversion and intimidation.
- To reinforce Portuguese administrative authority over the island.
- To improve the economic well-being of the population and the area.
- To inflict a grave loss of credibility and prestige to the enemy.[62]

The naval concept of operations in this effort was, first, to isolate the area by securing the surrounding waterways of the Caiar, Cobade, and Cumbijã Rivers, next, to disembark and support the land forces in their sweep for enemy troops, and last, to secure the maritime and riverine lines of communication so that a permanent presence could be maintained in the area. To this end the navy established three zones to control the inland waters around the target area. Zone 1 extended from the mouth of the Caiar to the point at which it joined the Cobade, and then along the Cobade until the shallow narrows of "Canbança do Brandão." Its commander was embarked in the *Deneb*. Zone 2 extended from the "Canbança do Brandão" along the Cobade to its confluence with the Cumbijã. Its commander was embarked in the *Bellatrix*. Zone 3 extended along the Cumbijã from its confluence with the Cobade downstream to its mouth, and its commander was embarked in the *Dragão*. These zones are identified on the nearby map. These three forces, with the aid of aerial reconnaissance in the form of an aged but capable P-2V5 *Neptune,* would prevent insurgent escape from the land forces sweeping the three islands by killing or capturing the fleeing insurgents and destroying their boats.

The operation was divided into three phases. The first began on 15 January 1964 with the landing of between 1,100 and 1,200 troops at various sites on the islands. The landings were given close air support by a single T-6 *Harvard* from the air force, and

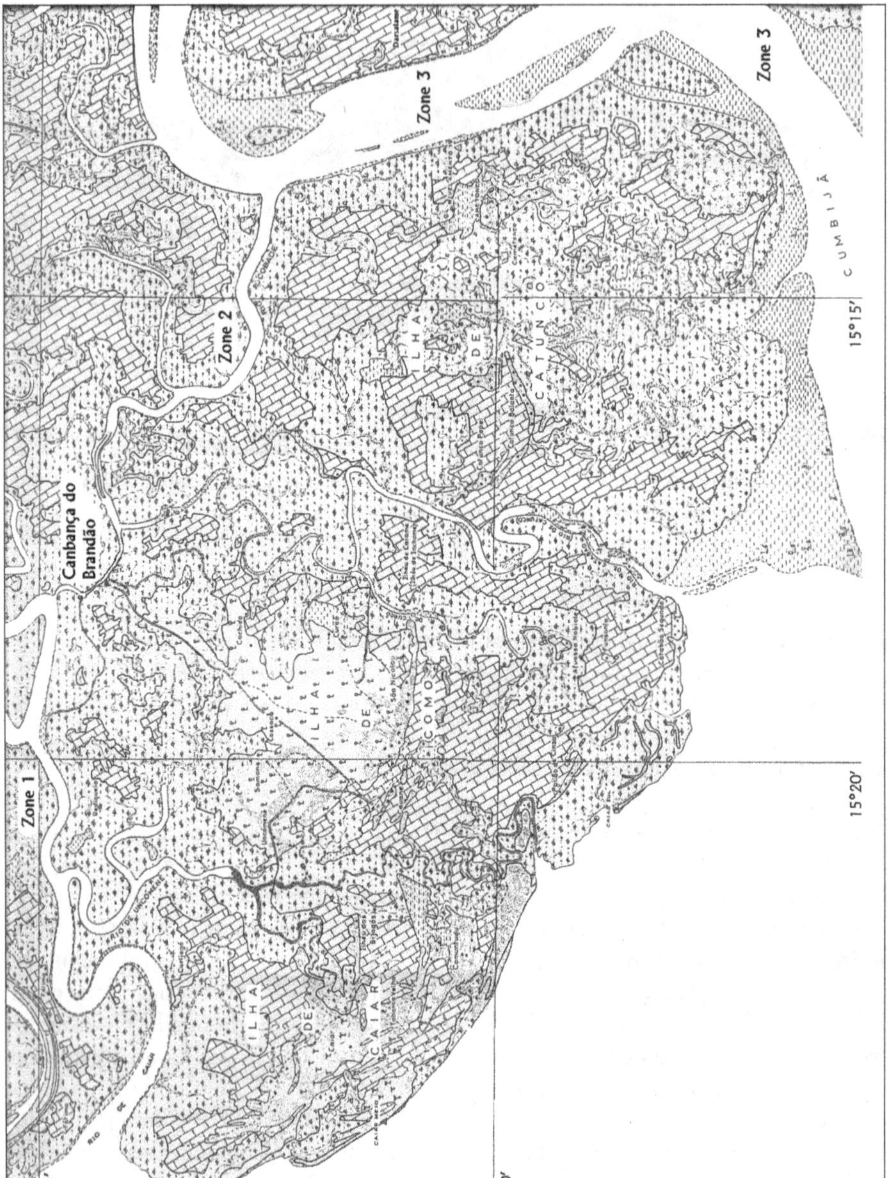

Operation *Tridente* Area. Adapted from Instituto Hidrográfico Chart Nº 220 (1965).

artillery provided fires from a support base in Catió some 5 to 10 miles distant, depending on where one was on the island group. As one might suspect, there was a challenge to the amphibious assault. There were a number of canoes identified by the patrolling *Neptune,* which vectored the surface craft to their locations for destruction. The *Deneb* took fire from the vicinity of "Cambaça do Brandão" later in the evening, as it patrolled about 500 meters offshore. *Bellatrix* came to its aid, and the two of them answered the enemy's machinegun fire. A radioman was wounded, and a rubber boat and a PRC-10 radio were destroyed on the *Deneb.* Armed natives appeared opposite the village of Darsalame on the left bank of the Cumbijã and were dispersed by fire from the *Dragão.* The *Neptune* later identified a substantial group of insurgents near the village of Cametonco on the Island of Catunco about 400 meters inland from the Cumbijã riverbank. This group fired at both the *Neptune* and later the *Dragão* before fleeing. And so it went over the several days of the first phase and into the second, with the landings encountering sporadic resistance from the insurgents and their local recruits while they tried to flee the islands in canoes or on foot or to hide in the swamp forests. The second phase occurred between 17 and 24 January and was centered in patrolling the three islands to establish a wide presence, to flush out insurgents, and to gather intelligence.

Following the landing and establishment phases, the third phase lasted from 24 January to 24 March and involved periods of intense fighting throughout the island of Como. The primary fighting occurred in the area of Uncomené near the river of the same name that separates the islands of Como and Caiar and in the Cachil swamp forest on Caiar. The insurgents suffered substantial losses in 76 killed, 15 wounded, and 9 taken prisoner, a casualty rate of around 30 percent.[63] These numbers do not, however, consider unknown casualties from artillery fire and close air support. Captured correspondence between PAIGC leaders confirmed their besieged and desperate state and the need for reinforcements.[64] The Portuguese forces suffered 9 killed and 47 wounded in the 71-day operation, but these numbers do not reflect the toll on troops from the climate and poor diet.[65] There were 193 personnel evacuated because of sickness. The troops in the field went for 23 days on combat rations, and while they were served hot meals the other 48 days, the drinking water was very bad and should have been used only to wash clothes or to bathe. A doctor observed that in one company of 151 men, he treated 132 for sickness of one form or another.[66]

In an insurgency, taking territory is rarely critical and usually irrelevant, for the struggle is over the loyalty of the population. Operation *Tridente* was a Pyrrhic victory in this sense; however, it did assert Portuguese sovereignty over an area where its presence had long ceased to be felt and disrupted enemy operations by denying the PAIGC a logistic base. While a contingent of army troops remained in Cachil as a caretaker force following the operation, it was eventually removed as not being worth the cost of policing the terrain. Indeed, it also tended to be an object of curiosity for the insurgents, as it was isolated from its support and seen as the proverbial "sitting duck."[67] Small numbers of insurgents consequently moved into the vacuum left by the departing Portuguese troops, and naval craft entering and leaving the Cumbijã River tended to give the islands a wide berth. In the end, none of the original goals of the operation were fully realized. General Arnoldo Schultz, the Commander-in-Chief of the Armed Forces in Guiné, was having limited results treating the insurgency with a conventional solution. As if to underscore the shortcomings of *Tridente*, Amílcar Cabral held his famous Cassacá Congress during February 1964 at his

Helicopter landing on a temporary platform on the *Nuno Tristão*, Operation *Tridente*. Photograph courtesy Estado-Maior da Armada and *Revista da Armada*

base near the settlement of that same name on the Quintafine Peninsula, which extends south of Cacine. Its purpose was to reorganize the PAIGC war effort and consolidate the independent commanders into a national army to be called the FARP (*Forças Armadas Revolucionárias de Povo* or Revolutionary Armed Forces of the People).

The numbers of both local inhabitants and insurgents remained small in the Como Island region, as it subsequently lost its importance to the latter as an area of local support and a refuge in their operations. Alpoim Calvão confirmed this when he returned to Como five years later in Operation *Torpedo* with DFE 7 and found only weak resistance.[68] The PAIGC moved progressively northward onto the peninsulas of Quintafine and Cantanhez adjacent to the Guinée border and proceeded to isolate the local market towns of Catió and Bedanda.[69] The ports of these besieged towns, however, remained the secure link to Bissau via the waterways. These moves positioned the PAIGC advantageously to subvert the interior of Guiné, as its lines of communication from its Guinean sanctuary through these two peninsulas became increasingly safe from Portuguese interdiction. For the Portuguese, this proved to be one of the grand operations that from time to time punctuated what might have been an otherwise sound and patient strategy of counterinsurgency in Africa. This type of large conventional maneuver seemed to hold a fatal attraction for local commanders, as it appeared to be a means to end the war quickly. In fact it was just the reverse. It inevitably fell short, for while many arms were generally found, insurgents captured or killed, and bases destroyed, the enemy tended to melt into the terrain or into the local population. The operation could not be concealed because of its large scale, and other areas of Guiné were denuded of troops to support it, a situation that left the population elsewhere vulnerable. It was not a sound counterinsurgency operation and invariably yielded disappointing results at great expense. The constant pressure of small patrols as part of a *tâche d'huile*-style strategy, for instance, was far more effective in its low-key, low-cost approach.[70]

End of Operation *Tridente* – Recovery of equipment. Photograph courtesy Estado-Maior da Armada and *Revista da Armada*

Operations on the Camexibó River

Exchanges with the enemy remained high in this region. Following Operation *Tridente*, the most significant encounters began when LDM 305 entered the mouth of the Camexibó River on 26 February 1964 during a full tide to conduct a five-day patrol. The timing could not have been more fortuitous for engaging the enemy, as it occurred during the final stages of the Cassacá Congress, which was being held nearby. Because of the dearth of hydrographic information, the mission was fortunately supported by the *Pedro Nunes*. This vessel was coincidently performing survey work in the mouth of the Cacine and provided important navigational guidance from its radar throughout the operation. The significance of this patrol is best understood by a quick look at the local geography. The Inxanche River separates the PAIGC sanctuary from Guiné by about a mile. The Portuguese islands of Canefaque and Cabom, which join at low tide to form one landmass, border on the river and are immediately opposite the PAIGC base of Kadigné. The islands are defined by the Atlantic Ocean to the west, and by the Camexibó and Nhafuane rivers to the north and east. Beyond these two islands lies the Quintafine Peninsula containing the PAIGC bases of Campeane and Cassacá. The Camexibó River penetrates deep into the interior of the peninsula, and its navigable portion ends just beyond Cassacá. Likewise the Barasam River has its mouth in Guinée and extends well into the top of the peninsula.

Insurgent logistics generally remain simple, manpower-intensive efforts, and the operation in this venue was no exception. Supplies and personnel were largely transported by the local dugout canoes or *pirogas*, which were relatively fragile affairs and not designed to negotiate the ocean. As a consequence, they tended to keep to the narrow and sheltered inland rivers that meandered extensively throughout the south of Guiné. Moving goods and men by canoe was far simpler than using porters, as a canoe manned by one or two men could transport a ton or so of cargo deep into the interior, while a porter could carry only perhaps 30 kilograms and consumed about a kilogram of food a day en route.[71] Further, clandestine overland travel was slow and arduous in the Guinean environment, particularly alongside a canoe that could blend into the normal waterway traffic and move with relative ease. It would be hard to know from a distance whether a canoe was taking legitimate produce to market or engaging in something illicit, such as smuggling arms. As a consequence, these islands and the waterways around them were ideal for insurgent penetration of Portuguese territory.

The crew of the LDM, reinforced with a small detachment of *Fuzileiros* from CF 3, proceeded upriver and flew no identifying colors. About mid-afternoon on 28 February, when the LDM stopped to anchor in the upper reaches of the river, the lookout noted the sudden appearance of a sizable group of armed men on the right bank. When they realized that they were being observed, they attempted to strike an innocent pose. An officer on board the LDM hailed the group and initiated a conversation in Portuguese, as the distance separating them was quite close. The apparent head of the group spoke excellent Portuguese, and while the conversation was proceeding, the crew armed its weapons. When it was judged opportune, the crewmembers opened fire on the enemy. Because of the surprise, there was only a half-hearted response from the insurgents, and they fled inland with undetermined loss.

The LDM continued upriver with the national ensign now hoisted. It intended to patrol the Camexibó to its confluence with the Nhafuane River and verify that it could link with the Inxanche and accommodate river traffic the size of the launch. The crew was now doubly alert in the expectation of enemy action on the return voyage. The next day, 29 February, as the launch approached the mouth of the Camexibó, the low tide revealed a line of rocks across the entrance that barred any exit. The LDM was forced to backtrack to safer water to await the incoming tide and sufficient depth to navigate the mouth of the river. Later that evening during the wait for the tidal change, the enemy attacked. At about 1920 hours the LDM received intense but inaccurate fire from both banks of the narrow river. The insurgents scored a few hits but injured no one. The crew answered fire with all available weapons and broke up the attack. Following this encounter, it was decided to continue patrolling the river in order to gain further experience and renewed confidence in the tactics developed during the firefights. As a result of this additional patrolling, four canoes were encountered and destroyed the next day, 1 March. On the following day the operation was terminated, and LDM 305 returned to Bissau.

The following conclusions were drawn from these encounters:

- The enemy was well armed in the area around Cassumba, a settlement at the foot of the Quintafine Peninsula, which divides the Cacine and Camexibó Rivers.
- The primary insurgent supply route sequentially followed the rivers Caraxe, Nhafuane, and Camexibó from the sanctuary in Guinée to the bases at Cassacá, Cassumba and Campeane on the Quintafine Peninsula without ever being exposed to the open ocean or to the broad and well-traveled Cacine River.
- The secondary insurgent supply route originated further south at Kadigné on the island of Tristão in Guinée and crossed the one-mile-wide Inxanche River, which marks the frontier, to the island of Canefaque, from which men and supplies could make their way via a more exposed coastal route or by the Camexibó to the aforementioned bases on the Quintafine Peninsula.[72]

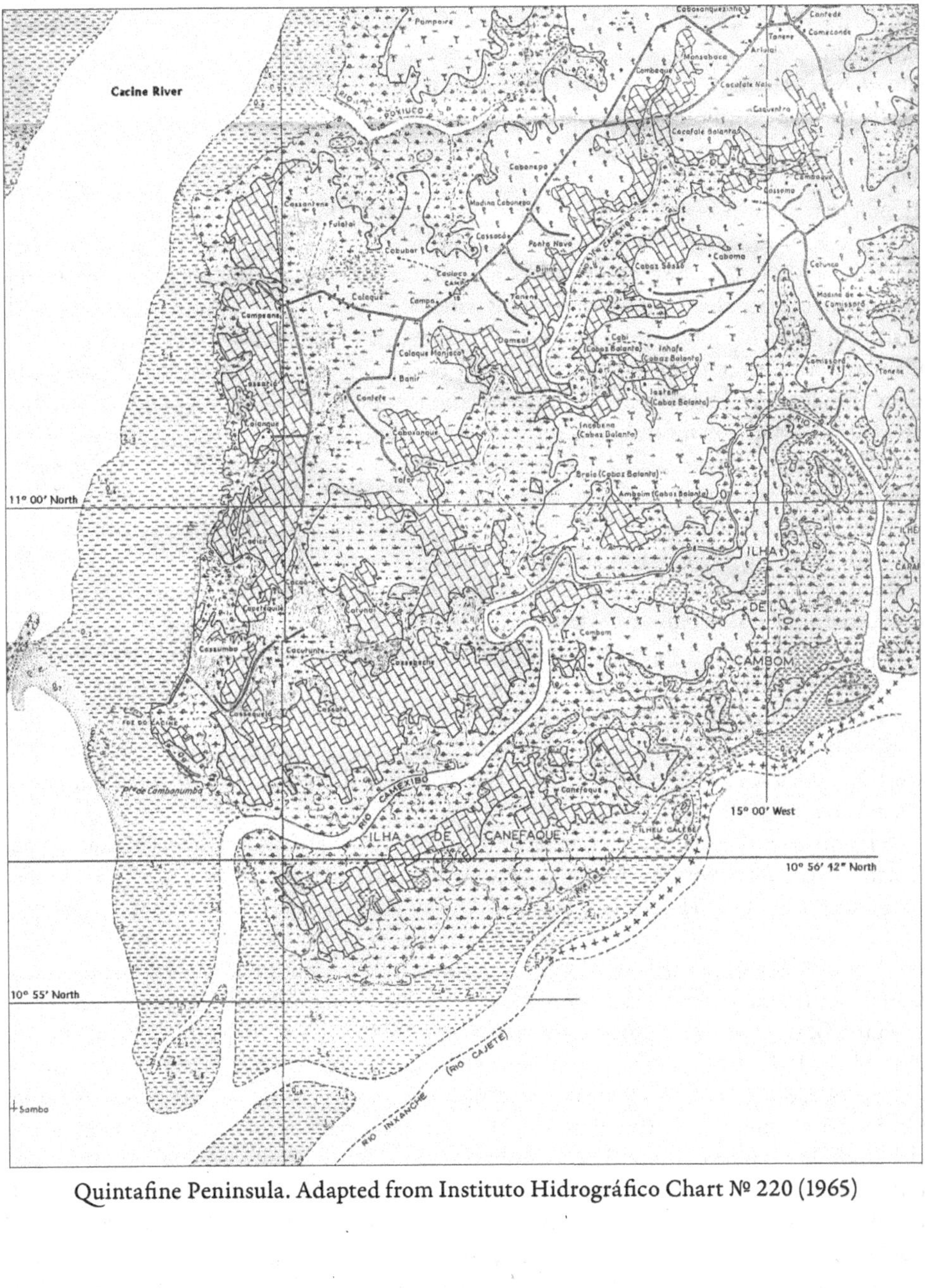

Quintafine Peninsula. Adapted from Instituto Hidrográfico Chart № 220 (1965)

From these experiences and observations it was decided to launch an operation based on two ambush sites. The first would be near the confluence of the Camexibó and the Nhafuane Rivers and designed to intercept traffic along the northern and more sheltered route. The second would occur in the Inxanche River next to Kadigné and be intended to interdict vessels on the southern and more direct route. The mission was assigned to DFE 8, would be led by Alpoim Calvão, and would be codenamed Operation *Hitler.*

Operation *Hitler*

It took two months from the earlier experience in the Camexibó River to prepare for this next operation. The initial February foray had begun as an exploratory sortie and resulted in a defensive reaction to the presence of a bold and confident enemy. This time the navy would attempt to control the tempo of operations with carefully laid plans. Preparation consisted mainly in gathering intelligence on the Quintafine Peninsula, the islands of Canefaque and Cambom, the water around them, and enemy operations on the Tristão Islands. This was done through aerial photography and observations from the duty hydrographic ship in the area. Other collection means apparently contributed little.

The plan was to use the LFG *Dragão,* commanded by the junior lieutenant (*primeiro tenente*) José Alberto Lopes Carvalheira, and the LDMs 304 and 306 to transport three sections of *Fuzileiros* from DFE 8 to the target area and to deploy the force in two ambush sites. The first site would be on an island in the Nhafuane River and designed to intercept traffic bound from Guinée for the Quintafine Peninsula. The other would be across the entrance to the protected waters leading to the port of Kadigné and would be designed to intercept Guiné-bound traffic as it departed the confines of the harbor inlet and before it was lost in the Inxanche River and its tributaries across the border. This ambush site would hopefully yield good results, as it was to occur in enemy territory and across a national border in an attempt to surprise the PAIGC. The insurgents would not be expecting a violation of national sovereignty. There was some risk in this plan, as we shall see, but it was deemed worth it.[73]

To observe the operation, Lieutenant (*capitão tenente*) Paulo Manuel Belmarço da Costa Santos, the deputy CDMG and a former naval aviator, was embarked on the *Dragão.* From the position of the *Dragão* at sea, the LDMs would proceed to an area near the mouth of the Cacine River, and from this position in darkness, one of them would tow two rubber boats and their complement of *Fuzileiros* to the Samba navigation buoy south and east of Canefaque Island. Here the *Fuzileiros* would man their boats and make their way across the several miles of water to the harbor inlet at Kadigné. The aim of the ambush was to board a sizable PAIGC vessel exiting the harbor, overcome the crew, and capture the war prize.[74]

The other LDM would transport the remaining *Fuzileiro* assault force into the Camexibó and proceed upriver into the Nhafuane to a previously identified island. Here the ambush would be established across the narrow confines of the small river. It was estimated that the site would be manned for several days, so in addition to the normal complement of combat gear, the *Fuzileiros* brought games of backgammon and checkers, books, and magazines for diversion during the long wait.[75]

The operation began as planned on 1 May with LDM 306 entering the Camexibó around 2200 hours on a rising tide. About an hour later near the confluence of the Camexibó and the Nhafuane there was a half-hearted ambush from the right bank that had little effect. Near midnight the LDM arrived with its *Fuzileiros* at the ambush site

Commanders Alpoim Calvão, Costa Santos, and Lopes Carvalheira, Operation *Hitler*. Photograph courtesy Estado-Maior da Armada and *Revista da Armada*

and disembarked the force. In departing, the LDM had extreme difficulty maneuvering because of the narrow confines and shallow depth of the river. On its return voyage it was again attacked at about 0200 hours of 2 May as it passed the site of the earlier attack. Clearly the enemy had been alerted because of the earlier contact and the fact that an LDM can be heard at least 10 minutes before it heaves into view.

The ambush site had not been well scouted in that there had not been adequate calculation on the height of the high tide. As the tide rose, it began to cover the island and submerged it entirely by a meter and a half. This development forced the *Fuzileiros* to climb the available trees, a situation that could have easily exposed them and revealed the ambush, if indeed the enemy was not already alerted. Certainly they were vulnerable, as the insurgents would guess that a LDM transiting these rivers at night was probably carrying an ambush party. By the timing of the transits the insurgents could easily approximate the site, a place to avoid. The *Fuzileiros* from their perches in the trees had an excellent view of the island and the river, but probably could likewise be observed by the enemy.[76]

The other half of the operation also met with its share of difficulties. During the evening of 2 May and the early hours of the following day, the rubber boats crossed from the Samba buoy and positioned themselves at the entrance to Kadigné under the command of Alpoim Calvão. Things were quiet until the morning of 5 May, when the *Fuzileiros* rescued a fisherman whose boat had overturned near the Samba buoy. His name turned out to be David. He was a native of Sierra Leone and lived for the moment in Katchek, which is located some kilometers south of Kadigné. In gratitude for his rescue and some glasses of wine, he was happy to give what information he had on the movements of the PAIGC in the area.[77]

Given the rising state of the sea that made it impossible to station the rubber boats off Kadigné and the difficulties that the *Fuzileiros* were experiencing on the island in the Nhafuane, it was decided to suspend the operation and await a better opportunity. By 15 May the weather and tides had improved, and the ambushes were reestablished. Unfortunately, the beginning of the rainy season again interfered with plans. The LFP *Canópus* had relieved the *Dragão* in support of the operation, and the smaller vessel began to suffer with the tropical storms and the rising seas. By 23 May, it was again decided to retrieve all personnel and await a weather change. LDM 306 consequently began its journey to the Nhafuane island a little after midnight and on the return trip was ambushed in force about 5 miles from the mouth of the Camexibó. Fire came from both banks for a length of two miles and was supported by mortars, heavy machineguns, and light arms. The LDM managed to cross the "zone of death," and later 58 holes of various calibers were counted throughout the hull and superstructure. One officer was seriously wounded in the head.[78]

Clearly the PAIGC was well aware of the operation from the moment its sentries noticed the launches. The initial light engagement was certainly evidence, and the heavier reception on the returns, a certain warning. Despite the cover of darkness, the noise of the LDM transiting to the Nhafuane gave much away. Likewise PAIGC observers on Tristão could easily see the patrol at the Samba buoy, clearly knew that something was happening, and avoided exposing their operations to unwanted attack. The insurgents had time on their side and were quite happy to wait for the Portuguese to tire in the face of the weather. There was also a message to the *Fuzileiros*: the insurgents own this part of Guiné. As if to reinforce this notion, Sekou Touré decreed two weeks later on 3 June that the territorial waters of Guinée would henceforth extend to 130 miles offshore and as far north as latitude 10° 56' 42" North, which parallel conveniently bisected Canefaque. Although most authorities would have laughed at such a declaration, Schultz bent to intimidation and suspended what promised to be needed and effective interventions along the Camexibó, Nhafuane, and Inxanche Rivers. This shortsighted and unwise decision allowed the PAIGC access to the interior of Guiné through these southern islands and peninsulas. Riverine operations in the area were not resumed until 1969, the year after Spínola relieved Schultz as Commander-in-Chief and Governor General of Guiné in an effort to bring new life to a failing campaign.

The period from this time until Spínola arrived in 1968 were some of the most difficult for the navy, as shown in Table 5.2. It struggled to stay ahead and came under increasing pressure from the frequent and well-armed ambushes on virtually all of its routes. It worked hard to maintain lines of communication to what became a series of besieged and isolated towns, such as Cacine, Catió, Bedanda, and Gadamael. The overall campaign in Guiné was clearly failing to address the insidious advance of the PAIGC. The navy continued to do its part with some imaginative operations alongside the more mundane ones.

Probably the most telling reflection of the fierceness of the conflict along the northern border is the experience of LDM 302. This was one of 51 such craft delivered to Guiné in the course of the war, and it arrived there in January 1964, having had an earlier career in the U.S. Navy. It was first attacked in April, as it landed *Fuzileiros* opposite Jabadá on the River Sindangolà, a tributary to the Geba. It was later assigned to the River Cacheu and was attacked several times there, before it finally came under such fire in December that two of the six crewmen were killed, and the vessel sank in the firefight. It was salvaged, repaired in Bissau, and returned to operation in January 1968. Six months later in June, it was again attacked in the same area as before, between Porto de Côco and Tancroal on the Cacheu, and burning fiercely, had to be run aground to prevent its sinking. It was again salvaged, repaired, and returned to service in November. Thereafter, it operated on the Geba and the

Fuzileiros on the Cacheu River. Photograph courtesy Estado-Maior da Armada and *Revista da Armada*

Rio Grande de Buba but was still not immune to attack. Finally, after over two decades of valiant service in two navies, it was struck from the navy list in July 1972.[79]

Spinola's Counter-Penetration Strategy

From May 1968 onward following the arrival of Spínola, there was a complete change in naval strategy. He abandoned the earlier one of securing the hydrographic basins and sought a counter-penetration strategy and a force to execute it.[80] At the tactical level, this came in the form of the Permanent Operational Commands (*Comando Operacional Permanente* or COP) and the Permanent Operational Group Commands (*Comando de Agrupamento Operacional Permanente* or CAOP) to which he assigned the detachments of special *Fuzileiros*. Spínola's concept was that even though the insurgents may swim among the population like the fish in the sea, they still needed to infiltrate all of the necessities of war, such as food, munitions, and new troops fresh from the training camps. He would seek to destroy the infiltration routes for these and starve the PAIGC within Guiné. He would do so by launching the ambitious and unspectacular Operations *Via Láctea* (Milky Way) and *Andrômeda*.[81] These operations were aimed at destroying four primary infiltration routes, all based on a river crossing or *cambança*: Sitatô, Jubembem, Sambuía, and Canja, two named for villages at the crossing and two others named for the small river crossed. These corridors were supported by bases located in Senegal: Sincha (Sitatô), Hernacono (Jubembem), and Cumbamory (Sambuía and Canja).

Operation *Via Láctea* stretched for many months and ran simultaneously with Operation *Andrômeda*. The aim of their initial operations was to locate and destroy the enemy logistic capability along a 12-kilometer front between the mouths of the Dunor and Quissir Rivers, two small tributaries of the Cacheu that straddle the Canja Corridor. This would deny the needed passages to PAIGC forces for moving their war materiel into

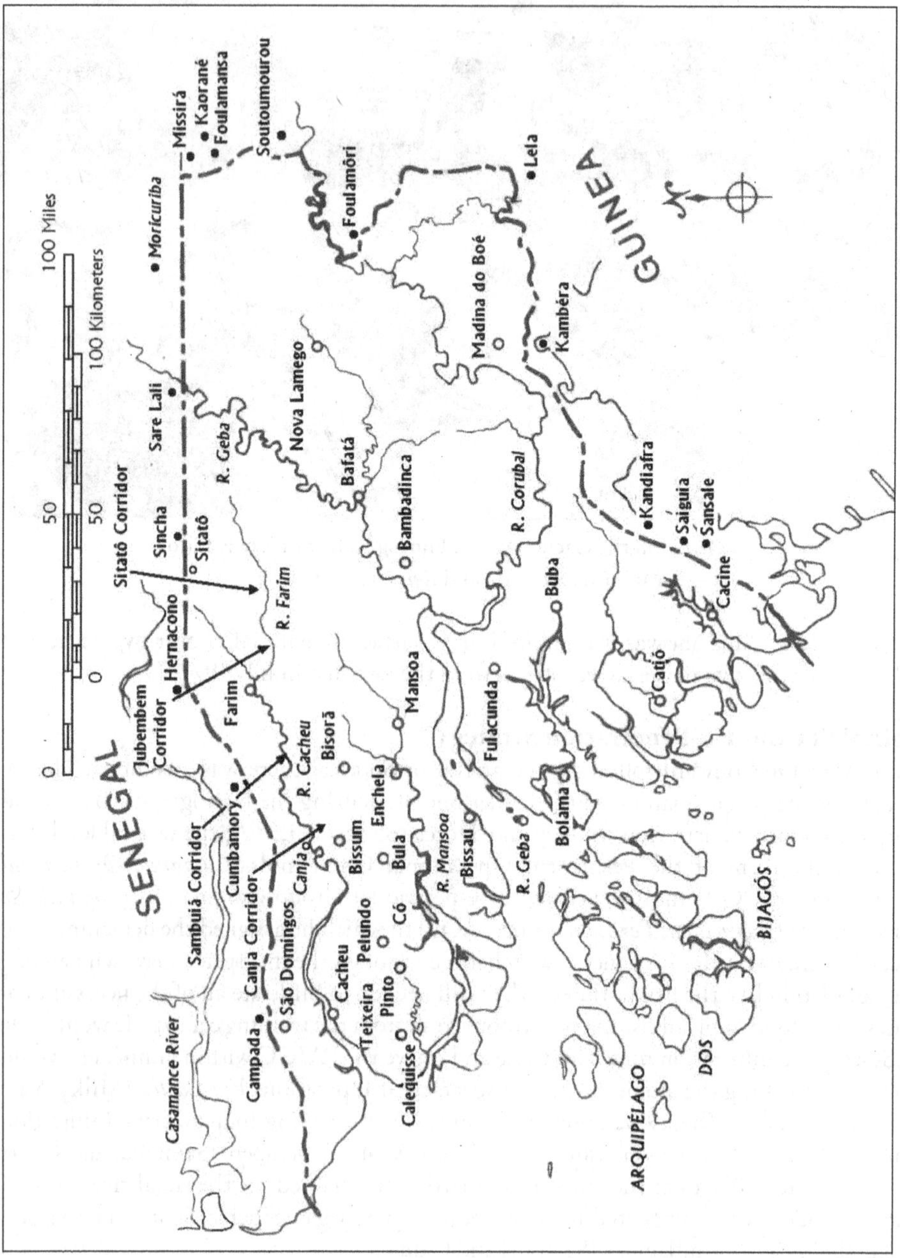

Map of Guiné Showing PAIGC Bases and Infiltration Routes in the North. Map drawn by the author.

Fuzileiros aboard LFG *Sagitario* (P 1131) in the Cacheu River. Photograph courtesy private collection of Admiral Nuno Vieira Matias.

the territory. The initial engagements in mid-1968 under *Via Láctea* were launched from mobile bases aboard LFGs and were a great success. As a result, the Canja Corridor was effectively blocked, and a frustrated enemy was forced to seek other routes or to see his operations wither.

This success encouraged Spínola to expand the operation, and he now sought to increase the blockade to 60 kilometers. This ambitious plan required an expanded support infrastructure to accommodate a significantly augmented force, and a needed naval base was established at Ganturé on the Cacheu just south of Bigene. It became the headquarters of Operational Command 3 (COP 3).[82] This Patrol Base Ganturé (*Base de Patrulhas de Ganturé* or Bapat Ganturé) was home to the two *Fuzileiro* detachments and two sections of CF 6, a part of TU 3, which provided logistical support.

In September 1968, the Sambuiá peninsula became an enemy sanctuary and a network of enemy dominated river crossings. This corridor stretched from the Senegalese frontier in the north to the Cacheu River in the south and was bounded by the rivers Talicó and Sambuiá, as depicted on the nearby map. It was serviced by the PAIGC base of Cumbamory in Senegal.

Terrain on the Sambuiá peninsula is flat, and the surrounding brackish waters are influenced by tidal action that causes the level to rise and fall several meters. The unproductive land between the high and low tides is without vegetation and is called the *bolanha*. It is filled with hydraulic works that enable the capture and retention of the rains in a vast dyke system for growing rice. It is also covered with fishing nets and dense mangrove swamps. Consequently, when the *Fuzileiros* disembarked from their boats and came ashore, they were faced with a difficult walk through a combination of soft muck, fishing nets, and wild mangrove swamp to reach dry land and the edge of the forest.

DFEs 12 and 13 in Operation *Dragão 68* (Dragon 68) had surprised the enemy in this area, defeated him, captured diverse war materiel, and taken into custody a number of civilians. In the course of the operation, the *Fuzileiros* had encountered large numbers of the population who were friendly and supportive of the Portuguese and who had told them of the many PAIGC arms caches on the peninsula. This intelligence laid the ground work for immediate future operations.

In Jamuary 1969 as a follow-up on this intelligence, Operation *Grande Colheita* (Great Harvest) was planned, and as it unfolded, the participating army troops discovered a number of the caches, recovered seven or eight arms and some munitions, and called the air force to destroy the remainder with napalm attacks. The on-scene army commander sent a message to Spínola apprising him of the discovery and intended destruction. Spínola immediately summoned a helicopter and shortly arrived on the Sambuiá peninsula. On appraising the situation, he concluded that paratroops should be brought from Bissau and inserted by helicopter to complete the search for additional caches. Lieutenant Nuno Vieira Matias, the commander of DFE 13, reminded Spínola that the *Fuzileiros* were trained and experienced in helicopter insertions and were immediately available. Spínola agreed and gave the order.

It was thus that 40 *Fuzileiros* from DFE 13 began the search, forgoing their packs and even drinking water so that the helicopters could carry the maximum weight in captured arms and munitions. Soon an enormous cache of matériel was discovered, as shown on the nearby map. Close air support was provided by Fiat G-91 and North American T-6 *Harvard* aircraft, as the site was near the frontier, and there was thus a strong threat of a counterattack from the PAIGC base of Cumbamory on the Senegalese border. The five

Fuzileiros of DFE13 in a typical landing on a Cacheu River *Bolanha*. Photograph courtesy private collection of Admiral Nuno Vieira Matias.

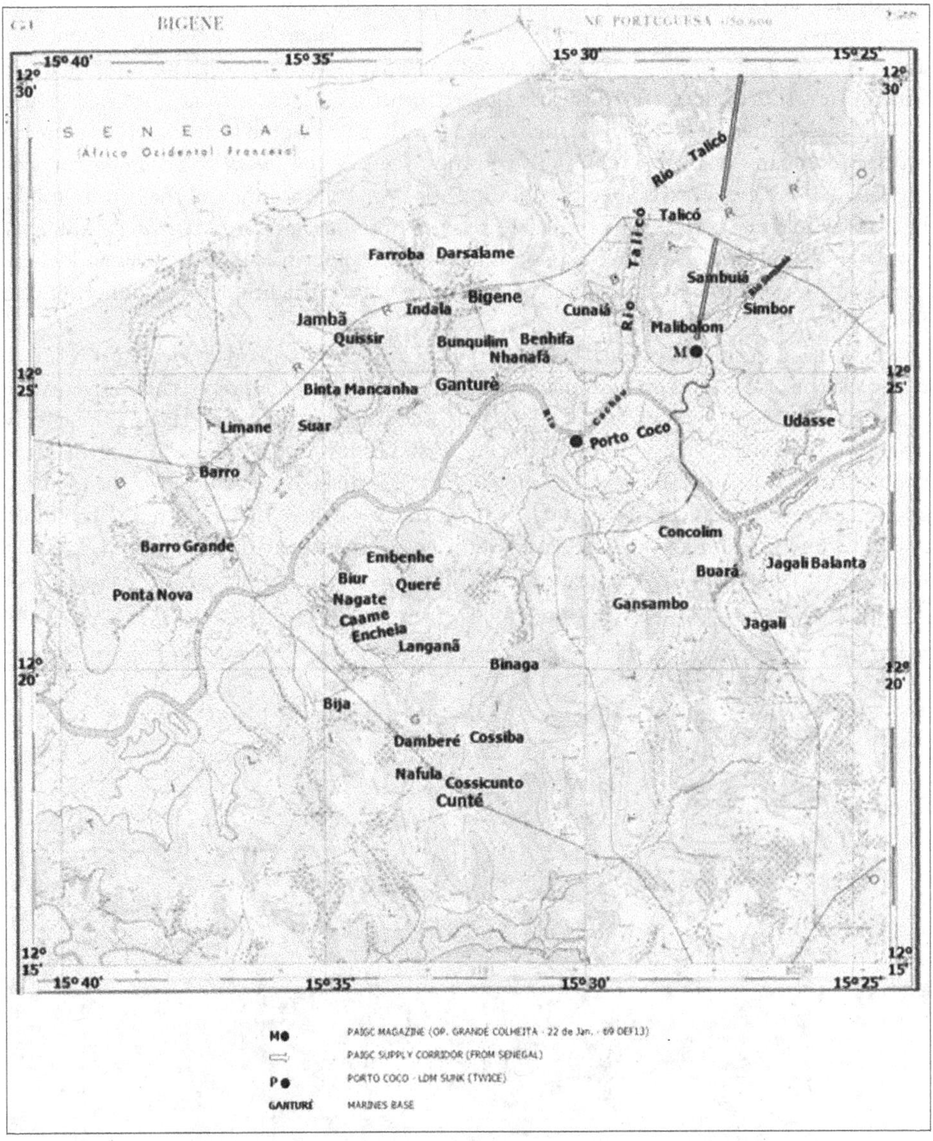

Sambuiá Peninsula and Operation *Grande Colheita*, January 1969. Map courtesy Admiral Nuno Vieira Matias.

helicopters began the evacuation of the arms and worked all day. The discovery included over 100,000 munitions, about 200 light and heavy weapons, uniforms, medicines, educational material, and moreover, perfume and Soviet pornographic magazines.[83]

By the end of the day, Spínola decided that the *Fuzileiros* would stay in the immediate area to be positioned for operations the following day. The *Fuzileiros,* however, had concerns about this decision, as they were being asked to remain overnight without food or water, within a few short kilometers of the Senegalese frontier, and under conditions that would be extremely dangerous during the night. Apparently, there would be fire support from an artillery company in Bigene within a two-mile radius of the *Fuzileiro* encampment. For the *Fuzileiros,* there was considerable question as to what the accuracy of the battery might be. Matias told the last helicopter pilot to relay to Spínola that the *Fuzileiros* would be at a place in the forest marked on the pilot's map where there would be large trees and where they would be able to protect themselves during the night, if detected by personnel coming from Senegal.[84]

At the end of the afternoon, the *Fuzileiros* began to be bombarded with mortar fire in their position at the arms cache and prayed for nightfall. In the darkness, they moved away under a well-practiced procedure of silently abandoning a position and leaving the enemy wondering where they had gone. It was fortunate they followed this plan, as during the night people came to the site. The next day, the *Fuzileiros* completed the removal of the matériel and fought an engagement to the north of the peninsula, where they captured eleven more machineguns, Czechoslovakian M-25s.[85] At the end of the second day and into the evening, the only available drinking water came from the pools of rainwater along the *bolanha,* not a particularly healthy option. With the conclusion of *Grande Colheita,* DFE 13 held the

LFP *Arcturus* (P 1151), LFG *Sagitario* (P 1131), and LFG *Cassiopeia* (P 373) moored at Patrol Base Ganturé, Right Bank, Cacheu River, Guiné, 1968. Photograph courtesy private collection of Admiral Nuno Vieira Matias.

record for the largest discovery of war materiel by a single unit in a single operation. This represented a heavy blow to the PAIGC and a welcomed decrease in pressure on Portuguese troops in the north of Guiné.[86]

Later in April 1970, the *Fuzileiros* of DFE 12, led by Lieutenant Mendes Fernandes, undertook Operation *Cocha* (Rope Strand), another successful yet risky engagement in the transborder frontier area of Cumbamory. Here the *Fuzileiros* fought off a fierce PAIGC reaction but, nevertheless, captured another large cache of war matériel, some ten tons of arms, munitions, mines, medicine, and educational material. It required seven hours to load the helicopters and remove the cache, and what was not removed was destroyed by air strikes.[87] This action represented another heavy blow to the PAIGC, and affected the morale of its troops and their ability to fight in the Guinean hinterland.

While these operations were aggressive and successful in disrupting PAIGC incursions, they were defensive in nature. The PAIGC threat remained alive in its sanctuaries of Senegal and Guinée, and Portuguese thoughts of offensive cross-border operations became a tempting consideration. While such operations were well within the Portuguese capabilities, they would entail a new dimension of political risk that could bring unforeseen difficulties.

Notes

1 António José Telo, *História da Marinha Portuguesa: Homens, Doutrinas e Organização, 1824–1974* (Tomo I) [History of the Portuguese Navy: Men, Doctrine and Organization, 1824–1974 (Volume I)] (Lisbon: Academia de Marinha, 1999), 575.

2 Ibid.

3 José Alberto Lopes Carvalheira, "Guiné: Esquadrilha de Lanchas e Outros Navios" [Guiné: Squadron of Patrol Boats and Other Ships], in the unpublished collection *Participação da Armada na Defesa das Províncias Ultramarinas* [Participation of the Navy in the Defense of the Overseas Provinces], TMs [photocopy] (Lisbon: Ministério de Marinha, 1972), 5.

4 Convention de Délimitation, 12 May 1886, Paris.

5 René Pélissier, *Naissance de la Guiné, Portugais et Africains en Sénégambie (1841–1936)* (Orgeval: Pélissier, 1989), 26n.

6 Avelino Teixeira da Mota, *Guiné Portuguesa*, II Volume [Portuguese Guiné, Volume II] (Lisbon: Agência Geral do Ultramar, 1954), 9.

7 Avelino Teixeira da Mota, *Mar, Além Mar, Estudos e Ensaios de História e Geografia* [The Sea, Beyond the Sea, Studies and Essays on History and Geography] (Lisbon: Junta de Investigações do Ultramar, 1972), 76–77.

8 Hugh Thomas, *The Slave Trade* (New York: Simon & Schuster, 1997), 787.

9 Pélissier, 14.

10 Ibid., 399.

11 Al J. Venter, *Portugal's Insurgent War, The Campaign for Africa* (Cape Town: John Malherbe, 1973), 13.

12 Estado-Maior do Exército, *Resenha Histórico-Militar das Campanhas de África, Vol. III, Dispositivo das Nossas Forças Guiné* [Historical Military Report of the African Campaigns, Vol. III, Disposition of Our Forces in Guiné] (Lisbon: Estado-Maior do Exército, 1989), 20–21.

13 John P. Cann, *Contra-Subversão em África: Como os Portugueses Fizeram a Guerra, 1961–1974* [Counter-Subversion in Africa: The Portuguese Way of War, 1961–1974:], 2nd ed., rev. Major General Renato F. Marques Pinto (Lisbon: Prefácio, 2005), 25.

14 Telo, 576.

15 Cann, 25.

16 Pélissier, 18.

17 Hélio A. Esteves Felgas, *O Clima do Congo Português* [The Climate of Portuguese Congo] (Carmona: Imprensa Angolana, 1959), 9.

18 Estado-Maior do Exército, 17.

19 Ibid., 27.

20 René Pélissier, *Le Naufrage des Caravelles, Etudes sur la Fin de l'Empire Portugais (1961–1975)* (Orgeval: Editions Pélissier, 1979), 208.

21 Marcello Caetano, *Depoimento* [Deposition] (Rio de Janeiro: Distribuidora Record, 1974), 191–192.

22 Telo, 577.

23 Ferdnando Oliveira Simões (second lieutenant), commanding officer, Secção № 2 de Mergulhadores Sapadores, to Comando da Defesa Marítima da Guiné, Bissau, 7 January 1969, memorandum "Mina Marítima" [Maritime Mine], Coloredo Box 236A/338, Arquivo Central da Marinha, Antiga Fabrica Nacional de Cordoaria, Rua da Junqueira, Lisbon. The first reported case of mining occurred on 6 April 1967 in the Armada River, a tributary of the Cacheu River, and caused only minor damage to a group of LDMs. On 29 December 1968 the Navy recovered an underwater explosive device from the Ungariuol River, which is a tributary of the Cumbijã River and is used as an approach to the village of Incala and to the interior port of Bedanda. Bedanda itself is about 15 miles from the frontier village of Guilejé and about 18 miles from the border in an area that was heavily infested with the PAIGC. Indeed the only reliable Portuguese line of communication to the village of Bedanda was by the waterway in which this mine was discovered while it was visible at low tide. The mine appeared to be homemade and manufactured from two large #10 tin cans. It contained about 5 kilograms of explosive and had an electrical detonator that could be activated either by the target vessel contacting a nylon line strung across the river or by an observer manually activating the mine. On the other hand, the Cobade River had a major strategic significance in that it was by this route and a tributary, the Cagopere River, that Catió was supplied. It was the primary support base for operations in the south of Guiné. There was a particularly narrow section of the river called the Cobade Strait (*Cobade estreito*). It was here that there were two additional mine encounters on 2 March and 27 May 1969. In the first instance, the device failed, and LDM 102 destroyed it by gunfire. In the second, the *Guadiana* lighter contacted a mine close to the Cambança do Brandão, killing five and wounding eight passengers. The lighter suffered an explosion, its cargo of petrol drums caught fire, and subsequently it had to be run aground. Ultimately, it sunk during a salvage attempt, as it was catastrophically damaged. From then on, naval convoys were preceded by a rubber boat advance patrol.

24 Telo, 577.

25 Ibid., 575.

26 José Alberto Lopes Carvalheira, "Acção da Marinha em Águas Interiors, 1961–1971" [Naval Operations in Inland Waters], in the unpublished collection *Participação da Armada na Defesa das Províncias Ultramarinas* [Participation of the Navy in the Defense of the Overseas Provinces], TMs [photocopy] (Lisbon: Ministério de Marinha, 1972), 1–2.

27 Ibid., 2.

28 Ibid., 3.

29 Comando da Esquadrilha de Lanchas da Guiné, *Guia de Navegação para LDMs* [Navigation Guide for LDMs] (Bissau: Ministério da Marinha, 1970).

30 Lopes Carvalheira, "Guiné: Esquadrilha de Lanchas e Outros Navios," 4.

31 Eurico Nelson de Campos Marques Pinto, *capitão de mar e guerra*, interview by the author, 6 February 2003, Lisbon.

32 Carlos Encaração Gomes, *capitão de fragata (Fuzileiro)*, interview by the author, 5 February 2003, Lisbon.
33 Ibid.
34 Ibid.
35 Ibid.
36 Telo, 580.
37 Lopes Carvalheira, "Guiné: Esquadrilha de Lanchas e Outros Navios," 30-31.
38 Telo, 582–583.
39 Ibid., 583.
40 Luiz C. Mesquita Dias, admiral, interview by the author, 10 February 2003, Lisbon.
41 Ibid.
42 Lopes Carvalheira, "Guiné: Esquadrilha de Lanchas e Outros Navios," 9-10.
43 Ibid., 27-28.
44 Ibid.
45 Rui Manuel Rodrigues de Abreu, deposition from Oral History Project on his service as a medical officer in Guiné 1972–1973. Rear Admiral Abreu was a lieutenant at the time.
46 Luís Nuno Rodrigues, "*For a Better Guinea!* Winning hearts and minds in Portuguese Guinea," Presentation at the Seminar "Legacies of Conflict, Decolonization and the Cold War," Lisbon, May 2010, 8, http://www2.lse.ac.uk/IDEAS/programmes/africaProgramme/events/conferences/africaCWMay2829/papers_pdfs/rodrigues.pdf (accessed 30 September 2011).
47 Colonel Luís Alberto Santiago Inocentes, correspondence with the author, 15 July 1995, London. Colonel Inocentes was Chief of Staff, Brigade Headquarters, Bissau, Guiné, 1970–1972.
48 Colonel Luís Alberto Santiago Inocentes, interview with the author, 14 April 1994, London.
49 Escola de *Fuzileiros*, *Manual do Fuzileiro* [*Fuzileiro* Manual] (series) (Vale do Zebro: Escola de *Fuzileiros*, 1962).
50 Lopes Carvalheira, "Guiné: Esquadrilha de Lanchas e Outros Navios," 16–17.
51 The SA-7 *Strela* (NATO: *Grail*) is a man-portable, shoulder-fired, low-altitude SAM system equipped with a high explosive warhead and passive infrared homing guidance. The SA-7 was the first generation of Soviet man portable surface-to-air missiles. Although classed as "fire and forget" types, the missiles were easily overcome by solar heat and, when used in hilly terrain, by heat from the ground. The SA-7a was introduced for service in 1968, but was soon replaced by the SA-7b, which became the most common production model. The SA-7b differs from the SA-7a primarily in its using a boosted propellant charge to increase range and speed. The SA-7a had a slant range of 3.6 kilometers and a kill zone between 15 and 1500 meters in altitude, with a speed of about 430 meters per second (Mach 1.4). The SA-7b has a slant range of about 4.2 kilometers, a ceiling of about 2300 meters, and a speed of about 500 meters per second (Mach 1.75). Both the SA-7a and SA-7b are tail-chase missile systems, and effectiveness depends on their ability to lock onto the heat source of low flying fixed and rotary wing aircraft.
52 Telo, 584.
53 Lopes Carvalheira, "Guiné: Esquadrilha de Lanchas e Outros Navios," 9-10.
54 Ibid., 14.
55 António Lobato, *Liberdade ou Evasão* [Freedom or Evasion] (Amadora: Erasmos Editora, 1996), 95–99.
56 Gomes interview. This was a point of substantial and continuing debate. Several days after the news of Lobato's capture arrived, Carlos Gomes, the officer in charge of a detachment of DFE 10, described a conversation over lunch involving himself, *Primero tenente* Metelo Napoles, and *Segundo tenentes* Castanho Paes, Malhão Pereira, Oliveira Monteiro, Couceiro, and Simões on the possibility of a rescue mission. The senior leadership was not yet in place to venture such a risky operation.
57 Guilherme Almor de Alpoim Calvão, *De Conakry ao M.D.L.P.* [From Conakry to the M.D.L.P.] (Lisbon:

Editorial Intervenção, 1976), 52

58 Guilherme Almor de Alpoim Calvão, correspondence with the author, 9 May 2005, Cascais.

59 Aniceto Afonso and Carlos de Matos Gomes, *Guerra Colonial* [Colonial War] (Lisbon: Notícias, 2000), 79.

60 José Alberto Lopes Carvalheira, "Acção da Marinha em Águas Interiors (Guiné)," 7; Telo, 585.

61 Ibid.

62 Ibid., 6.

63 Afonso and Matos Gomes, 81.

64 João Bernardo "Nino" Vieira, correspondence with Rui Demba Djassi and Domingos Ramos, 3 March 1964, undisclosed PAIGC base in southern Guiné, typewritten transcript furnished by Guilherme Almor de Alpoim Calvão in correspondence with the author, 9 May 2005, Cascais.

65 Afonso and Matos Gomes, 81.

66 Ibid., 80.

67 Guilherme Almor de Alpoim Calvão, correspondence with the author, 22 June 2005, Cascais.

68 Guilherme Almor de Alpoim Calvão, correspondence with the author, 9 May 2005, Cascais

69 Afonso and Matos Gomes, 81.

70 The *tache d'huile* technique was perfected by Louis-Hubert Lyautey during his Moroccan campaigns of the early Twentieth Century in which he progressively reoccupied hostile territory by offering Arab tribes French protection and access to commerce and social help. His expansion on a broad social-military front with the notion of building an Arab nation succeeded where his predecessors had relied on subjugation by the military column.

71 John P. Cann, "Moçambique, África Oriental Alemã e a Grande Guerra" [Mozambique, German East Africa and the Great War], *Revista Militar*, 54 (May 2002): 389.

72 Guilherme Almor de Alpoim Calvão, "Introducão as Operações na Guiné" [Introduction to Operations in Guiné], in the unpublished collection *Participação da Armada na Defesa das Províncias Ultramarinas* [Participation of the Navy in the Defense of the Overseas Provinces], TMs [photocopy] (Lisbon: Ministério de Marinha, 1972), 3–4.

73 Ibid., 4.

74 Ibid.

75 Ibid.

76 Ibid., 5.

77 Ibid.

78 Ibid., 5–6.

79 Malheiro de Vale and Baptista Mendes, "Heróis dos rios da Guiné" [Heroes of the rivers of Guiné], *Revista da Armada* 8 (May 1972), 16–17, http://www.marinha.pt/Conteudos_Externos/RevistaArmada/_FlipVersion/1972/index.html?pagenumber=147 (accessed 7 October 2011); Afonso M.F. Sousa, "Navegaçáo do Rio Cacheu na época da Guerra Colonial" [Navigation of the River Cacheu during the period of the Colonial War], http://ultramar.terraweb.biz/Imagens/Noticia/AfonsoMFSousa/Rio_Cacheu_Guine.pdf (accessed 7 October 2011); and "Guiné – LDM 302 atacada e afundada" [Guiné – LDM 302 attacked and sunk] RESERVANAVAL (15 November 2008), http://reservanaval.blogspot.com/2008_11_01_archive.html (accessed 7 October 2011).

80 Luís Sanches de Baêna, *Fuzileiros: Factos e Feitos na Guerra de África, 1961/1974* [Marines: Deeds and Feats in the African War, 1961/1974], vol. 3, *Crónica dos Feitos da Guiné* [Chronicle of the Feats of Guiné] (Lisbon: Comissão Cultural da Marinha–INAPA, 2006), 100.

81 Telo, 587.

82 Baêna, 107.

83 Admiral Nuno Vieira Matias, deposition from Oral History Project, July 1999, as quoted in Baêna, 114–115.

84 Ibid.

85 Ibid.

86 Ibid.

87 Ibid, 141–142.

6

Beneath the Burning Tungue Sun

Geographic conditions in Mozambique along its northern border with Tanzania appeared to destine the navy for a special role in this theater.[1] The border with Tanzania runs the length of the Rovuma River some 708 kilometers from its mouth on the Indian Ocean to its confluence with the Messinge River and then along a parallel of latitude an additional 48 kilometers west to the shore of Lake Niassa, a total of 756 kilometers. The entire riverine frontier runs through some of the most inaccessible, remote, and rugged tropical bush country in Africa and represented a porous border and easy opportunity for insurgent infiltration. Here, according to the naval historian António Telo, this riverine frontier appeared to offer the navy a unique opportunity to secure the Rovuma and its flanks of Lake Niassa and the Indian Ocean in a classic interior line of defense.[2] While the Rovuma would pose navigation problems for traditional craft, as it is shallow and fordable in many places during the dry season, the ubiquitous rubber boat teamed with air boats and observation aircraft could have been mobilized to establish an effective barrier. Unfortunately, this too would have required more resources than were immediately available, particularly the acquisition of new, specialized equipment and the requisite skills for using it to patrol a difficult riverine environment.

Consequently, the army was given responsibility for the security of the Rovuma River border and addressed the problem by establishing a series of fixed posts at intervals along the river, and land patrols from these posts attempted to police the frontier. This seems not to have worked at all, as once the insurgents were across the lightly policed river, they were able to elude army patrols easily in the difficult countryside. It would have been far more effective to interrupt the insurgent infiltration when the enemy was exposed and vulnerable as he crossed the river. Army ineffectiveness was well documented in both FRELIMO reports and the growing *de facto* presence of insurgents in the Cabo Delgado and Niassa districts from 1964 onward.[3]

Initially the navy was assigned coastal patrol responsibility in the Indian Ocean over an area that extended from the mouth of the Rovuma southward, across the Bay of Tungue, and as far as Ibo Island, a distance of approximately 120 miles. Unfortunately, the navy did not have the resources to patrol this area but so effectively at the time. As a result, the navy sought to concentrate its efforts on policing Lake Niassa, something that it could achieve with a more modest expansion. Its other prime objective from 1966 onward was to expand the coastal patrols, this time between the mouth of the Rovuma and the naval base at Porto Amélia, a distance of about 160 miles, and to prevent insurgent infiltration by sea.[4] The strategy in pursuing this two-fold plan was to prevent the insurgents from outflanking the army and extending the conflict beyond the two northern frontier districts and into Téte and Zambézia. In Niassa, the navy bent to this task with a will using the potent and tested combination of LFPs, LDMs, LDPs, and *Fuzileiros*. In the Indian Ocean, there was a more varied array of vessels in the frigates, corvettes, LFGs, LFPs, a single LDG, and *Fuzileiros* to secure the eastern flank. As we shall see, both were remarkably successful, despite the limited resources.

The Insurgent Problem

Of the three theaters of operations, Mozambique was the final one and probably would not have developed as such but for the granting of independence to Tanzania in 1961. It was the emergence of Julius Nyerere, first as its premier and later in 1962 as its president, that was the most telling development, as he was an ardent nationalist who was passionately committed to supporting and providing a home for African liberation movements. These included the African National Congress (ANC) and the Pan African Congress (PAC) of South Africa, Zimbabwe African National Union (ZANU) and Robert Mugabe in their struggle to unseat the white regime in Southern Rhodesia (now Zimbabwe), and most importantly to our story, FRELIMO.

Nyerere proved to be a skilled negotiator and peacemaker among his revolutionary guests, and as an avowed Marxist and advocate of the single-party state, encouraged a similar policy with these fellow travelers. He was considered a model leader among those in the fraternity of emerging African states, although the average Tanzanian would have had difficulty understanding this view. During the early years of his tenure, he managed to destroy the fragile Tanzanian economy primarily through the arbitrary nationalization of hundreds of white-owned farms. This conversion from a functioning rural commercial economy to a dysfunctional collectivized Marxist one was an economic disaster. In a similarly ill-conceived ideological decision, he replaced English with Swahili as the national language with all of the commercial and cultural isolation that it implied. He personally presided over an increasingly militant, xenophobic, and beggared state and held divisiveness in line through the liberal use of his Preventive Detention Act and East German-trained security police to imprison opponents. As with most paranoid strongmen, Nyerere was constantly blaming his self-induced problems on mythical exterior forces and alluded frequently to a "white imperialist plot."[5] His apparent commitment to human rights on the world stage was clearly at odds with his actions at home. The future FRELIMO government in 1975 would embrace similar policies and in so doing spawn its own insurgency.

Eduardo Mondlane, who with Nyerere's help had consolidated most of the disparate Mozambican nationalist movements into FRELIMO, was personally endorsed by him as its leader in a September 1962 inaugural national conference at Dar es Salaam.[6] Mondlane was an intellectual educated in South Africa, Portugal, and the United States, and it is believed that Nyerere selected him to lead FRELIMO while he was teaching anthropology at Syracuse University. Soon after this inauguration and in anticipation of the struggle, FRELIMO sent its first 250 young volunteers to the newly independent Algeria for military training.[7] Later the United Arab Republic provided similar support until the 1970s. As training matured, recruits were flown to more efficient, purpose-designed centers in the Ukraine aboard Aeroflot aircraft and given their initial instruction by seasoned insurgent professionals. This process was able to produce better trained personnel in volume not only to replace losses but also to expand the FRELIMO army. The graduates were then returned to the Tanzanian camp at Chingoe under Chinese supervision.[8] FRELIMO began with a disorganized force of uncertain strength and by the early 1970s had an active force of about 7,200 regulars and 2,400 popular militia.[9]

Mondlane and Nyerere also established a network of bases on the Tanzanian side of the border. The primary one was Nachinghea, and depots were built at Songea, Tunduru, and Lindi. There were also five bases next to the border for staging incursions: Mbamba Bay, Chamba, Lukwila, Newala, and Mtwara. It was from these that Mondlane maintained his insurgent campaign into Mozambique.[10] As one would expect, Nyerere controlled the flow of arms from China, the Soviet Union, and Eastern Europe on behalf of FRELIMO.

Initial FRELIMO strength was derived from the overt support of the Makonde people, who lived in the north of the Cabo Delgado district and immediately across the Rovuma on that portion of the Makonde Plateau in Tanzania. They formed a bellicose and itinerant nation that had been in place at least a thousand years.[11] René Pélissier describes the Makonde as a tribe of "intransigent warriors" who are "allergic to all forms of authority and outside influence."[12] Over the years they successfully rejected Islam, Christianity, and German and Portuguese attempts to administer them. They tended to remain animist and to worship their ancestors. By the early 1960s the Makonde in Tanzania had became thoroughly infiltrated by FRELIMO cadres and thus were the major source of insurgent recruits.[13]

This sudden welcoming of outsiders was due to the granting of independence to a black-ruled Tanzania and its subsequent hostility towards white-ruled Mozambique. Prior to 1961, the Makonde people had been divided by a border with no fence or strict frontier enforcement. This nominal division did not affect their tribal unity, as they were free to move back and forth across the international border unhindered. The national polarization initiated by independence brought almost complete restriction to intratribal communication, and the Makonde in Tanzania became concerned with fighting the Portuguese to reestablish their freedom of movement within their tribal region. Prior to this time the border had had little meaning to them. Now, however, insurgent activity had drawn Portuguese forces into the Makonde ancestral grounds of northern Mozambique in defense of the national border, which was being threatened by a hostile Tanzania and its FRELIMO surrogate.

FRELIMO leadership was Bantu in origin and held in contempt by the Makonde; however, the Makonde in Tanzania were willing to align themselves with FRELIMO to expel the Portuguese and reestablish the link with their people in Mozambique. This was a short-range goal, for over the long run linking with FRELIMO would put Bantus in charge of Mozambique and make the Makonde subservient to them. For FRELIMO, its alignment with the Makonde meant limited success, for the Makonde were interested only in regaining their own ground and links to their people and not in having the Bantu or anyone else transit their area. In turn, the Makonde held no interest in pushing further south outside of the Maconde Plateau, so FRELIMO was quickly stalemated in the north as much from intertribal rivalry as from Portuguese martial activity.[14]

FRELIMO initiated hostilities on the evening of 24 September 1964 with an assault on the residence and secretariat of the small administrative post or *posto* of Cobué in the Niassa district. The following day the launch LFP *Castor* (P 580) was fired upon while on patrol in Lake Niassa, and the *posto* in Chai, on the southern edge of the Makonde plateau in the Cabo Delgado district, was assaulted. Later in December, the *posto* in Olivença, just north and east of Cobué, was attacked. A FRELIMO prisoner taken there revealed that FRELIMO was using N'Gombe, a remote settlement in northwestern Niassa, as a base. Accordingly, the navy sent *Castor* and a section of *Fuzileiros* to conduct an amphibious operation against it on 5 January, and the operation managed to consume three days, as the insurgents fought to prevent the small security force from landing.[15] The *Fuzileiros* were able to come ashore only four at a time in a small aluminum boat, and thus the ability to concentrate force and maneuver against the enemy was limited. *Castor* had to return to Metangula for reinforcements in the midst of the operation and lacked either an Oerlikon or a Dreyse automatic deck-mounted weapon to support the force ashore. The available airpower, a Lockheed PV-2 *Harpoon* and two North American T-6 *Harvards* at Vila Cabral, remained grounded and unable to help because of the weather, as it was the rainy season. Eventually the Portuguese prevailed, and Radio Tanzania at Dar-es-Salaam confirmed two days after the operation that FRELIMO had suffered 8 killed and many gravely wounded and that the insurgents had been trained in Algeria. Clearly the Portuguese needed a more substantial and coordinated force to address the threat on Lake Niassa.

FRELIMO had commenced operations with only a handful of trained combatants, and its first moves were tentative in that its leadership was divided over the nature of its campaign.[16] The internal divisions were in part generated by military failure, and dissention grew so great that disaffected elements assassinated Mondlane on 3 February 1969. Indicative of this dissention was the breakaway group of COREMO (*Comité Revolucionário de Moçambique* or Revolutionary Committee for Mozambique), which was formed by Paulo Gumane. It was Maoist oriented and received support from China. Unwelcomed in Tanzania, it established a base at Macheke in Zambia in 1964 and with a force of about 400 made incursions into Téte district to lay the odd mine and intimidate the local population.[17] From the time that it kidnapped eleven Mozambican agricultural technicians in March 1971 and was forced by the Zambian government to free them, it suffered a credibility problem and never matured either as a political movement or military force.

FRELIMO had begun with a planned program of infiltration, subversion of the population, and raids. There was the hope of mass insurrection against the Portuguese authorities, again in the vein of Holden Roberto's logic, but the population was too dispersed and divided for this course to be a realistic expectation. The Makonde in Mozambique, for instance, did not necessarily share the revolutionary fervor of their kin across the border. Some Makonde were persuaded to join FRELIMO; however, true to their traditions, most rejected this intrusion and were subjected to the standard tools of terror, such as, murder, torture, and selective kidnapping, when they did not provide active help. In 1973 Neil Bruce made the observation that, according to defectors, more than 450 Makonde had been murdered by FRELIMO, 1,000 wounded, and 6,500 captured since 1964.[18] The accuracy of these figures is less important than the fact that atrocities were being committed on quite a large scale by African against African. In a country of 9 million people, the population was composed of 19 tribes and 17 different language groups. For FRELIMO, it was important to create a broad popular base across these myriad factions, and yet its practices destroyed any genuine hope of doing this.

Niassa, the northern border district immediately west of Cabo Delgado, was thinly populated because of its rough terrain and yet attractive because of its fertility and ease of cultivation. It was the home of the Nianja, who were treated in the same rough fashion that FRELIMO had earlier treated the Makonde, the Makua, and others. Even by the end of the war in 1974, FRELIMO had created support only among a small minority of the population in the north, and so few further south, that it was exceedingly difficult for it to govern Mozambique for decades afterward. When this failure became evident in the late 1960s, FRELIMO would be forced to seek a new strategy and open a second front in the

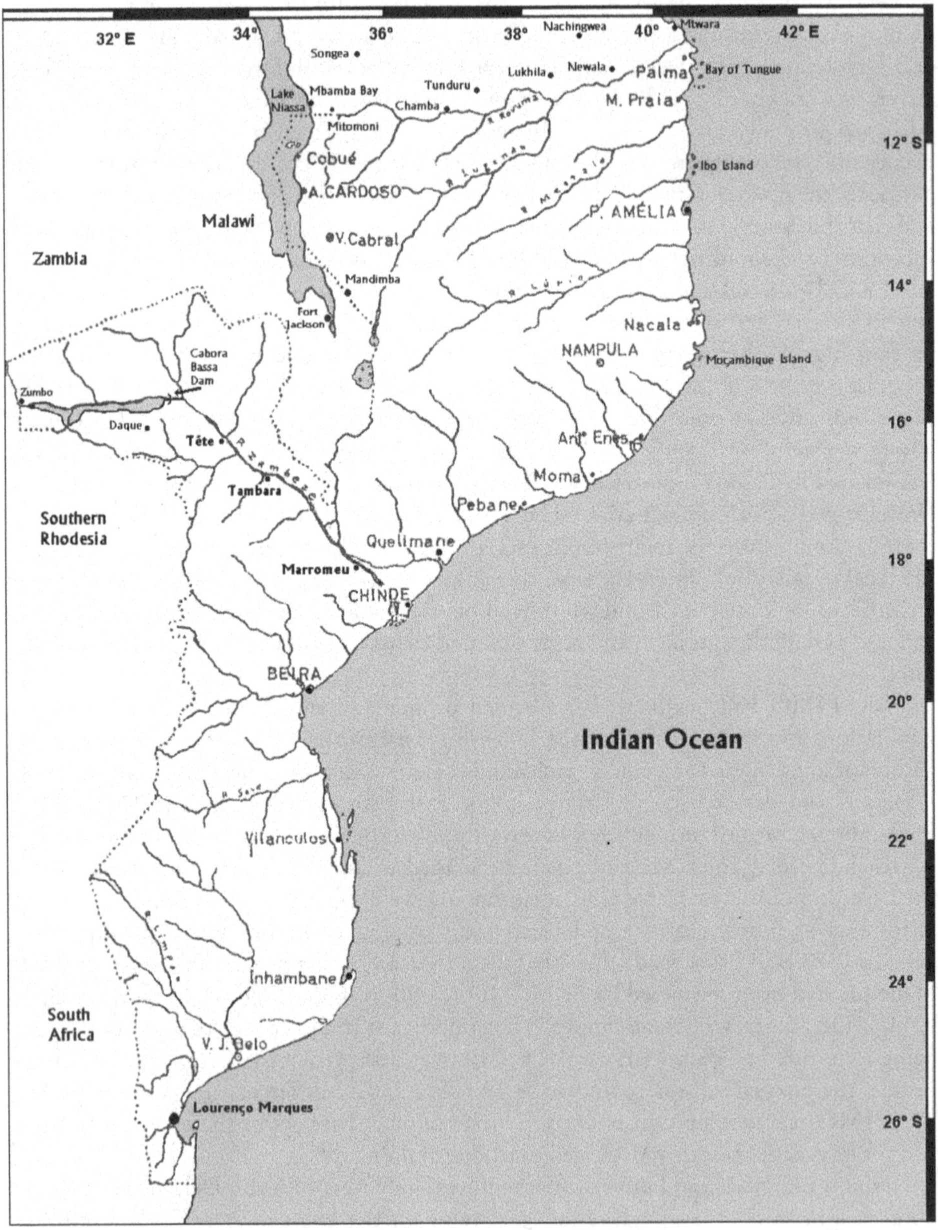

Mozambique, Showing FRELIMO Bases. Modified by the author from a CNM briefing map.

Téte District. In looking at a map of the area, one can readily see that it would have been far easier to use Malawi for that front; however, its president would not permit it for fear both that his communication through Mozambique to the sea would be severed and that such activity would attract unwanted military into his country.

Naval Commitment

The Naval Command Mozambique (*Comando Naval de Moçambique* or CNM) was created in 1957 at the same time as that in Angola and was initially preoccupied with the construction of basic naval infrastructure. Early on it built the headquarters in Lourenço Marques, radio stations at Machava (Lourenço Marques) and later, between 1964 and 1965, in Beira, Nacala, Metangula on Lake Niassa, and Porto Amélia on the Indian Ocean, offices in Lourenço Marques and Beira, and port installations in Metangula and Porto Amélia. Because the navy had committed the bulk of its resources to Angola and Guiné, CNM was reduced to a handful of vessels and inevitably appeared to be a lower priority as the war progressed. Its immediate inventory comprised the lone frigate *Álvares Cabral* (F 336), the old *aviso Bartolomeu Dias* (F 471), the hydrographic ship *Almirante Lacerda* (A 525), the small patrol launch *Antares* (P 360), a survivor of the Indian invasion of Goa, and the old Zambezi River gunboat *Téte*, a true relic.[19] From October 1962, Company of *Fuzileiros* Nº 2 (CF 2) was deployed to Lourenço Marques to guard naval facilities, and because of a lack of DFEs, initiated training for counterinsurgency operations. Personnel so trained were formed into two platoons, one deployed to Cobué and the other to Metangula on Lake Niassa. In the spring of 1964, *Castor* arrived at the Indian Ocean port of Nacala and was transferred to Lake Niassa in the fall of that year, as hostilities threatened. This was the second such operation, after the hydrographic launch *Mina,* of moving a modest size craft from the Indian Ocean across the many physical obstacles to Lake Niassa. It was not without its problems and called for engineering work in repairing and strengthening the load-bearing capacity of the roads and bridges between the port of Nacala and the beach at Meponda on the lake. The experience gained from this venture set the tone for numerous, larger, and more challenging future efforts to reinforce the naval squadron on Lake Niassa. The next year significant forces began to arrive and be deployed, as FRELIMO activity began to intensify in the north.

The progressive subversion of the population in Niassa occurred steadily through all of 1965 and reached its full extent in October 1966. Of two primary infiltration routes, one was by water over Lake Niassa, and the other directly across the Rovuma River between the villages of Milepa and Chamba.[20] The insurgents who took the lake route came southward from ports in Tanzania and landed both directly on Portuguese territory and further south in Malawi to infiltrate along the Mozambique-Malawi border as far south as Lake Chiuta. The Portuguese persuaded Dr. Hastings Kamuzu Banda, the first president of Malawi, to deny sanctuary and passage through that country. Banda, however, did not at the time have adequate forces and was thus unable fully to control insurgent use of Malawian territory, particularly in some of the more remote areas that abutted Mozambique and its districts of Niassa and Zambézia. He also found it to his political advantage to accommodate both FRELIMO and the Portuguese as much as possible to avoid friction with either. As a counter to the incursions across the Rovuma, additional army troops were moved into Niassa and Cabo Delgado to strengthen security operations and begin pacification of these districts.[21] To disrupt the waterborne incursions naval forces sought to intercept

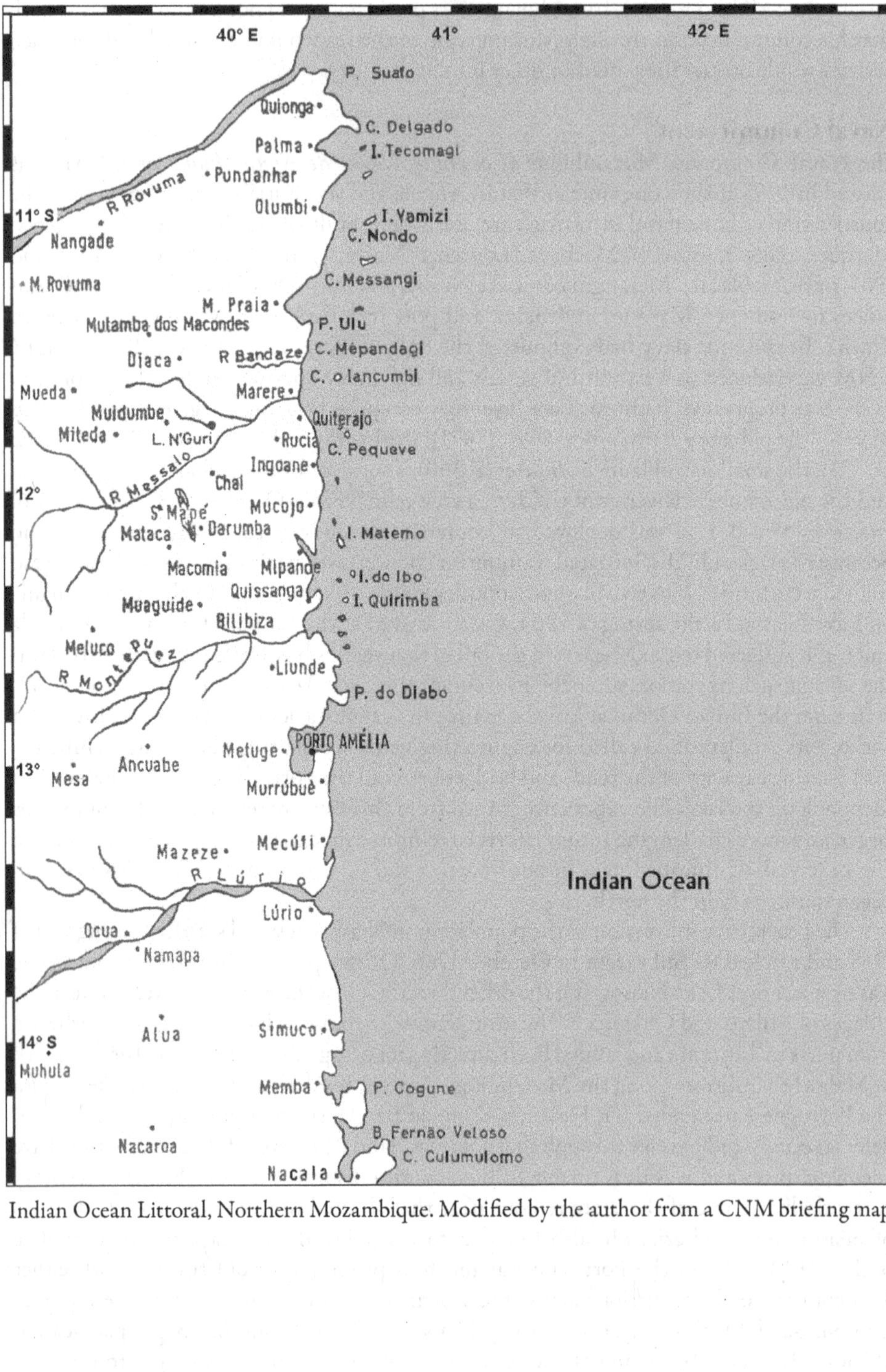

Indian Ocean Littoral, Northern Mozambique. Modified by the author from a CNM briefing map.

infiltrators while they were still at sea and vulnerable, for once ashore, they easily melted into an intimidated population or sought refuge in the difficult terrain and tended to become "invisible." Developing this interdiction capability required the establishment of a significant naval presence on Lake Niassa.

The value of an inland naval force cannot be understated in frustrating an enemy. History may have served as an accurate guide for the Portuguese Navy, for it was in the summer of 1915 that the Royal Navy purchased two Thornycroft 40-foot (12.2-meter) mahogany motor launches for the identical purpose. These craft had two 100-horsepower gasoline engines that powered twin screws and produced a top speed of 19 knots. They mounted a 3-pounder forward and a Maxim gun aft to address the anticipated German gunboats. The Royal Navy transported them some 6,100 miles from London to Cape Town and thence another 3,210 miles overland through a combination of railway and ox-wagon to Lake Tanganyika to challenge German domination there. The rail transport was rudimentary but effective, and employed such quaint practices as having ratings assigned to brush locomotive sparks from the boat canvases to avoid fire damage. The real challenge was crossing the Mitumba Mountains by way of the disused ox-wagon track. It had to be negotiated by steam traction engines, trek oxen, and native labor, all pulling the boats on their carts up unimaginable grades and across the most forbidding terrain. The trip was made successfully in four months, and once on the lake, the two craft dominated and controlled it in short order.[22]

Lake Niassa is a similar body and could likewise be described as an inland sea. Its water is quite pure, and it has no tides. It does have about a 5-meter seasonal change in level from its May-high to its December-low because of its various underground rivers and seasonal rainfall. Conditions on both of these freshwater lakes are like the ocean and can easily become untenable for small craft with high winds from the north, consequent heavy seas, and waves reaching three meters in height. The British were forced to cease operations and seek shelter when the weather became severe, and this would prove true for the Portuguese on Niassa. Such conditions, of course, affected the enemy too. The FRELIMO insurgents in their canoes or Tanzanian vessels, however, represented quite a different opponent from the German gunboats, as they were not seeking a naval engagement. In fact they hoped to avoid naval contact altogether in their transit to remote areas of infiltration. Here again, the potent and effective combination of LFs, LDs, and *Fuzileiros* would have to dominate the littorals to stem this infiltration and disrupt insurgent use of the lake. This disruption would force the insurgents to go by land across difficult terrain and daunting mountains and not by the easier water route. Thus, FRELIMO would lose the logistical battle in supplying its forces in Mozambique, and its strategic reach would be substantially limited.

Operação Atum

The Mozambican territorial waters on Lake Niassa were formally established by the November 1954 Anglo-Portuguese "Accord over the Frontiers of Mozambique and Nyassaland." These extended from the northern to the southern land frontier, a distance of some 115 miles, and westward to the midpoint of the lake, an average of between 14 and 21 miles. Excluded were the Malawian islands of Chizumulu and Likoma, which fell within these waters. Inside of the year, Portugal had established a hydrographic mission on the lake and initiated the charting of its territorial waters and coastline, an area equivalent to a quarter of the size of the Mozambican landmass. For this purpose the navy converted

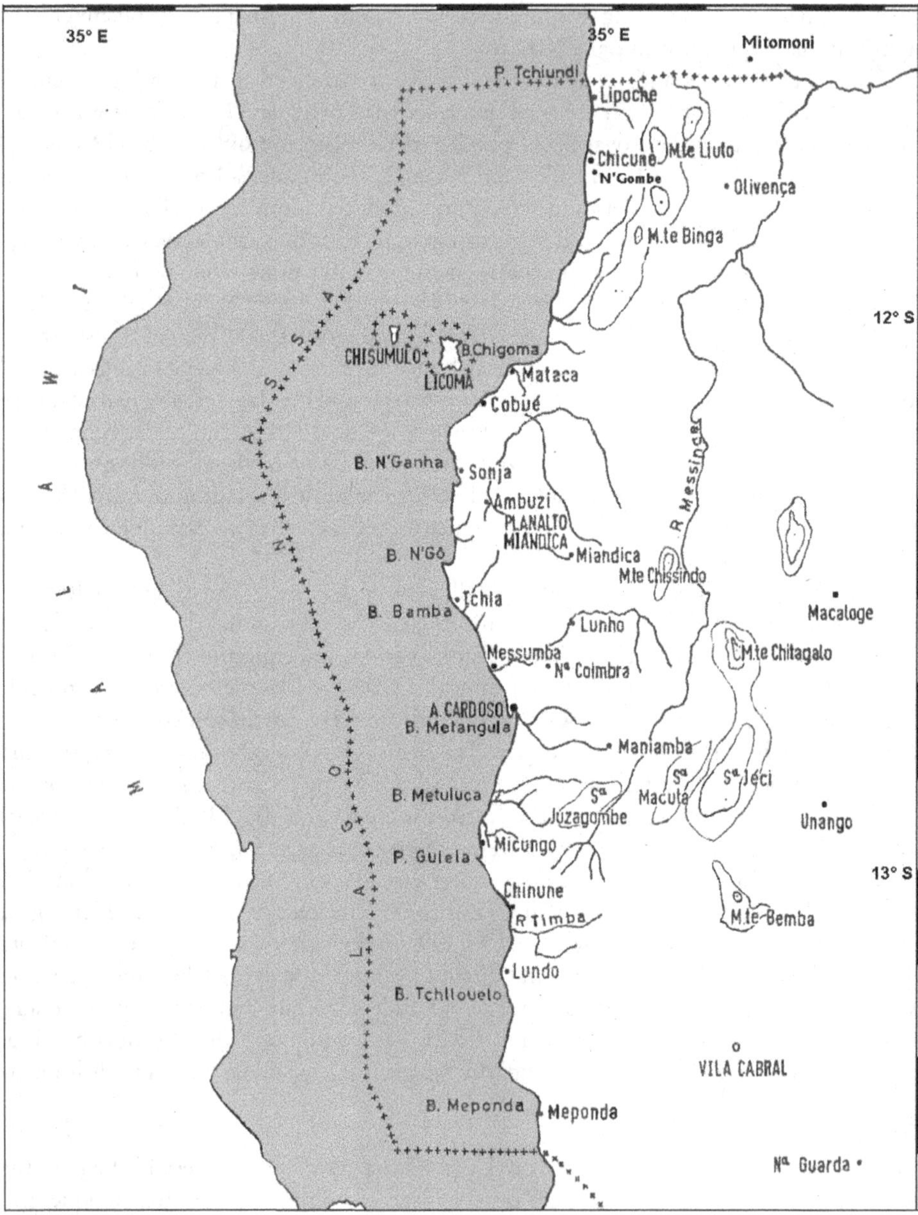

Lake Niassa and Western Niassa. Modified by the author from a CNM briefing map.

a river cruise boat into the hydrographic launch *Mina* and transported it there.[23] When the FRELIMO troubles began, the *Castor* and *Mina* were the only available vessels and hardly adequate for the task of policing the lake, although *Castor* had done a credible job from its base at Cobué in showing the flag and discouraging infiltration.[24] Indeed, it was originally thought that, as the situation stood in early August 1965, the *Antares* and LFP *Régulus* (P 369) might be sent as reinforcements, for they would be easier to transport with their manageable size and in the end would require less sophisticated logistic support than larger, more capable craft. *Régulus* was expected to be transferred to Mozambique from its duties on the Zaire in Angola. These two would be augmented by two locally manufactured launches, one from the village of Lipoche next to the Tanzanian border and the other from Cobué, designated LP 1 and LP 2. If these resources proved insufficient in both seakeeping ability and numbers, then the larger craft *Marte* (P 1134) and *Mercúrio* (P 1135) could be added to the Lake Niassa force.[25]

As the month of August passed, and infiltration increased, it became apparent that a more substantial presence definitely would be required. Further, because of insurgent presence, the land routes between Vila Cabral, Metangula, and Cobué were frequently mined. As a result, support of anticipated army and *Fuzileiro* units deploying in the vicinity of the lake would be more easily effected using the water link along the coast. This logistical strategy would further require the availability of LDs on the lake. Accordingly, in the fall of 1965 a major effort was planned under the name *Operação Atum* or Operation Tuna to move an additional four vessels, *Marte*, *Mercúrio*, *Régulus*, and LDM 404, from the Indian Ocean to Lake Niassa.

As in the Royal Navy experience of 1915, the execution of this assignment would not be easy, for the infrastructure was not designed to accommodate the heavy cargoes envisioned. The rail lines were built with the traditional clearances for standard sorts of shipments and not for oversized, bulky items, such as naval vessels. There was also limited rolling stock to accommodate such loads. Further, the normal highways were relatively rudimentary affairs and were best used in the dry season. While paved roads were easy routes, they tended to connect the principal towns and not the villages and the more remote sites. These routes required specialized vehicles, particularly for heavy loads, to negotiate the poor roads, tracks, and trails. In many cases these latter *pistas* could degenerate into rutted tracks through deep mud and sand. Vehicles could and did become stuck in these primitive roads and required hours to extricate. During the rainy season, which in Mozambique runs from November to April, unpaved roads became quagmires of soft mud and sand and were virtually impassable. Rivers rose and routinely jeopardized the modest bridges serving the routes. Heavy logistic operations after mid-November were thus increasingly difficult, and the risk of serious delays or accidents was high.

The *Castor* and the *Mina* were relatively small craft with weights of about 15 and 18 tons and lengths of about 17 and 12 meters respectively. Their transport to and launching on the lake had been well within the limitations of the road and rail infrastructure. After being loaded at Nacala, they had transited by rail westward to Vila Cabral and thence by road carrier to Meponda on Lake Niassa. Their weight and dimensions had enabled them to fit onto rail flatcars and pass unhindered through the system without special consideration. Three of the four vessels anticipated to be moved by Operation Tuna were more than twice as large in tonnage as *Castor* and *Mina* with a commensurate increase in physical dimensions. Consequently, the movement of these larger vessels required more homework.

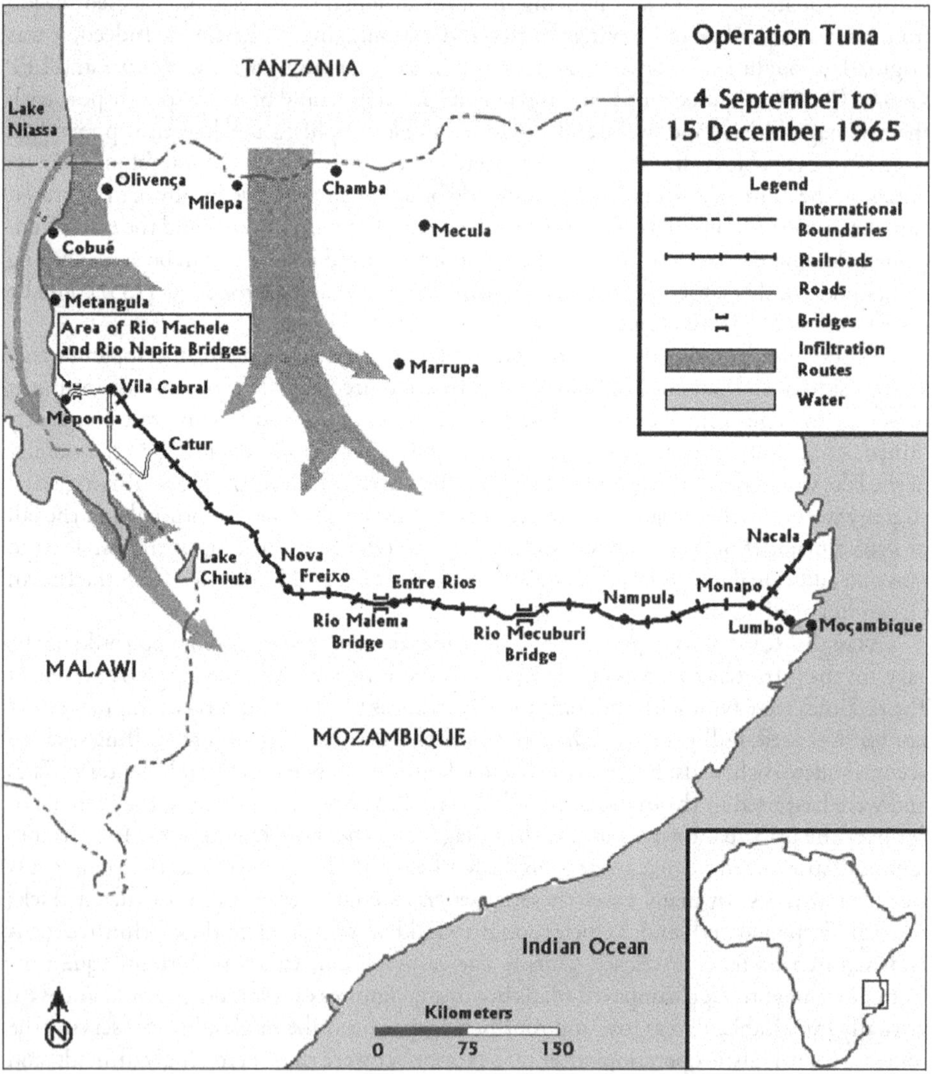

Operation Tuna . Map drawn by the author.

The first task was to examine the anticipated rail and highway routes to identify potential problems for the project, and this was begun in early September 1965. Initially it was thought that the vessels could be retrieved from the ocean at Nacala and transported to Nampula by rail; however, there was inadequate clearance beneath the overpass for the Lumbo-Monapo road at kilometer 66. The logical alternative was to use the Nacala-Monapo road, but this too presented difficulties. It would be necessary to reinforce five bridges and to regrade and level large portions of the undulating road to accommodate the heavy transporters. Nacala was thus abandoned as too costly an origin in time and treasure. Accordingly, the Lumbo-Monapo rail branch became the obvious answer, for at Lumbo there was potentially sufficient water depth to beach the vessels near the shoreline and move them onto rail transport. The spring tides would occur on 13 and 14 September, and thus conditions would be most propitious for a recovery on the high tides of these days. With so little time remaining until these dates, there was a rush to prepare and to complete seven key tasks:

- Construction of a 300-meter rail spur from the line that served the old pier at Lumbo across the beach to the low water mark.
- Transportation of the boat cradles from Nacala to Lumbo to receive the launches.
- Completion of railway work at the grade crossings at kilometers 38, 40, and 69 to permit the passage of the loaded railcars carrying the larger launches.
- Completion of a study on the use of the various rail and road alternatives available.
- Requisition of a 35-ton capacity heavy road carrier from Lourenço Marques to transport the launches over any road portion of the trip.
- Preparation of the rail extension and cradles in time for the tides on 13 and 14 September.
- Collaboration with the Directorate of the Mozambican Railroad in planning and executing Operation Tuna.[26]

Not all went as planned. The launches *Marte* and *Mercúrio* arrived as deck cargo on the freighter *Beira* and were floated in the bay of Moçambique Island on 9 September. The cradles weighing three tons each were then unloaded at Nacala and moved to Lumbo to receive the launches. On the night of 17 September one of the launches was loaded in its rail-mounted cradle and pulled ashore, but at this point progress halted. The rail authorities viewed the difficulties of continuing as so insurmountable and the project as so impracticable that they refused to proceed. The launch was consequently returned to the sea, and the impasse became a deep embarrassment. The search for a solution ended with the selection of Captain (*capitão de mar e guerra*) Pedro da Conceição Mouzinho, a distinguished naval engineer, to head the enterprise. He brought with him the skilled and talented naval carpenter Carlos Águas Trindade.[27] While Trindade held the title of carpenter, he was equally a rigger in that his expertise drew on both of these traditional naval trades to solve the problems of moving heavy objects.

As Mouzinho saw it, there were three distinct phases within the project. Phase one was the retrieval of the launches from the ocean and securing them to their cradles aboard the rail flatcars. Phase two was the movement of the railcars with their launches across northern Mozambique. The third and final phase was the transfer of the launches to road carriers, their transport over a primitive road to Meponda, and their launching on Lake

Rail Spur Across the Beach at Lumbo. Photograph courtesy Estado-Maior da Armada and *Revista da Armada*.

Niassa.

At this point it appeared that the next opportunity for a successful execution of phase one would be during the second fortnight of October.[28] In the meantime the frigate *Pacheco Pereira* (F 337) arrived at Moçambique Island towing LDM 404, which was also destined for the lake. Because the LDM had a flat bottom and thus required no cradle, it could be loaded directly onto a flatcar. It did not have to wait for the higher spring tides to float it the additional height of a cradle. This development meant that the operation could proceed immediately with the transfer of the LDM. Further, the LDM was the approximate dimensions and weight of the larger LFs and would thus provide a point of reference for their transport.

In the meantime careful preparations were made to load the LDM on the train and transit the rail infrastructure. Phase one lasted three days and was completed in Lumbo on 29 September. Phase two began with some complications at the Monapo bridge, but the LDM arrived at Nampula on 2 October and continued on to Vila Cabral. The procedure developed to negotiate the several bridges en route required, first, that the boat be raised through a system of jacking the vessel and building a log crib beneath it for support. When the LDM had been elevated the 2.4 meters needed to clear the bridge structure, the train crept forward until the vessel had crossed the bridge. The elevated boat was then lowered for the trip to the next bridge. On reaching Vila Cabral, the LDM was transferred to the road carrier for the final 60-kilometer trip to Meponda. Serious difficulties developed on this route, as the transport was mishandled, and consequently the LDM spilled into the road three times. As a result, the trip took an excessively long 30 days. Many of the problems were directly attributed to a lack of strong leadership and skilled direction at the scene.[29]

Mercúrio Raised for Bridge Passage. Photograph courtesy Estado-Maior da Armada and *Revista da Armada*.

While LDM 404 was making its tortured journey between Vila Cabral and Meponda, the merchant ship *Rovuma* arrived at Moçambique Island on 8 October with its deck cargo of *Régulus*. Five days later the sea was calm enough to load the launch on its railcar. This was to be a simple operation in light of the size and tonnage of *Régulus*; nevertheless, complications arose in the rail transport phase on the Catur-Vila Cabral section of the line. The train had proceeded through a crossing somewhat too rapidly for the circumstances, and the car carrying *Régulus* derailed. This incident dislocated the vessel in its cradle, but fortunately Trindade's skills were available, and the difficulties overcome. It did, however, raise the question as to whether the roadbed could successfully support the additional weight of *Marte* and *Mercúrio*.

While *Régulus* continued to Meponda, serious doubts were voiced about the transport of these two larger vessels in light of the experience in moving LDM 404 over the crude road between Vila Cabral and Meponda. Certainly substantial additional engineering and logistical support would be needed over and above that required by the earlier efforts, and a long list of supplies and equipment was submitted. The rainy season was fast approaching, so solutions to the problem assumed an increasing urgency.

All of the difficulties associated with the earlier moves were magnified because of the increased size of these two vessels. For instance, *Marte* and *Mercúrio* were 70 percent heavier than *Régulus*, a half meter wider, and four meters longer. These increased dimensions would severely test the transportation system. The rail line would be used only so far as Catur, because from the *Régulus* experience, it was thought that the section beyond could not accommodate the additional weight. This limitation dictated that the launches be transferred to heavy roadcarriers for the trip to Meponda via Vila Cabral. Even so, there was considerable doubt that the roadbed between Catur and Meponda would be capable of supporting the 70-ton aggregate weight of a carrier loaded with a launch and its cradle, as it was little more than a dirt track. Clearly difficulties were anticipated.

Wrecked Bridge over Rio Machele. Photograph courtesy Estado-Maior da Armada and *Revista da Armada*

The first problem was that of locating two heavy roadcarriers, as there were none in Mozambique. Negotiations were opened with South Africa to identify and obtain this equipment, and after some searching, its army made available two *Centurion* tank transporters.[30]

With the transporters on their way to Catur and a security force coming from Vila Cabral to support the operation, loading of the launches began at Lumbo on 19 November. Just after midnight on 28 November, the train with its launches departed Nampula and advanced slowly, reaching the Rio Mecuburi and clearing it by midmorning the next day. The *Mercúrio* was only a little over 200 kilometers into the trip, and at this point the project was already 26 precious hours behind schedule. This lost time was important in that the entire operation was a race against the approaching rains. Progress was agonizingly slow, as like LDM 404, the vessels protruded over the sides of the flatcars to the extent that the now tedious and time-consuming jacking procedure was regularly required. Everything was simple in concept but seemed to be difficult in execution with the heat and burning sun. On a bright note, some lost time was regained when the Rio Malema was crossed in an uneventful eight hours on the evening of 29 November.

The train arrived at Nova Freixo on 30 November, and after some small delay, reached Catur on 1 December to confront additional obstacles. Attempts had been made in advance to coordinate with the security force in Vila Cabral for a rendezvous at Catur. The infantry company, however, was skeptical of the scheduled progress based on its experience with LDM 404 and did not arrive until 2 December. The transporters were likewise late and arrived on the same day as the troops. During the evenings of 2 and 3 December, it rained torrentially, transforming the entire station area into a veritable lake. Despite this inconvenience, the boats were transferred to the carriers and traveled the 60 kilometers over saturated roads to Vila Cabral without incident, arriving in the evening of 5 December. This relatively uneventful trip was credited to the extraordinarily stout British Leyland tractors, which hauled the carriers through rutted, winding roads, negotiated 10 percent grades, and overcame a final six kilometers of mud.[31]

It was imperative to continue the last leg promptly, as additional rain would make the situation impossible. Accordingly, the convoy departed Vila Cabral after a day of rest and resupply. If there was any optimism that all would be easier over the next 65 kilometers to the lake, it was soon dashed. Going proved inordinately slow because of the progressive softening of a poorly constructed road, despite the fact that a 200-man working party had inspected the road for repairs and cleared the shoulders of brush just days before. Its load bearing capacity had deteriorated with the rain to the point that after about 25 kilometers the carrier with *Marte* seriously slipped, and restoring it took time. Various short but strong rainstorms further softened the road. By now the offending transporter began to slip constantly. In mid-afternoon on 7 December, the convoy arrived at the Rio Machele, the first of three primitive bridges to be crossed. Progress was encouraging, for only 12 kilometers remained to Meponda.

As the convoy approached the bridge, it encountered a long, steep, 700-meter grade. The Leyland trucks negotiated this obstacle well and prepared to cross a bridge that supposedly would support 100 tons. In retrospect, the surveys certifying this capacity were clearly out of touch with reality. When the first transporter pulled onto the bridge with *Marte*, all went well until the rig was completely supported by the bridge. The progressive increase in weight to the full load proved too much, as the beams cracked, and the transporter settled into the wrecked infrastructure. It required until the morning of 8 December to raise the bridge platform and reinforce the remaining beams so that the transporter could continue its crossing.[32] For the second vehicle carrying *Mercúrio,* a 100-meter ford or "drift" was constructed nearby, as it was pointless to risk using the bridge further. This second project used so many logs that two enormous trees were destroyed in the process. The crews of the two launches were present and lent a hand. Among them was the junior lieutenant (*segundo tenente*) José Deolindo Torres Sobral, commanding officer of *Mercúrio,* of whom we will hear more later.

The convoy proceeded a short four kilometers before reaching the bridge over the Rio Napita. This structure proved to be worse than the previous bridge, was totally rotten, and had to be rebuilt completely. Nevertheless, by the end of the day the transporters were across the river. It was a short two kilometers to the next bridge, and its roadway was repaired with steel plates brought from Meponda. As the convoy proceeded past this last bridge, the second vehicle followed in the tracks of the first over the naturally spongy terrain. For a seemingly unexplained reason the ground gave way beneath the second rig, and its cargo tilted 30 degrees to one side. By the time the transporter was recovered from the sinkhole, the tilt had increased to 40 degrees.[33] The convoy finally arrived in Meponda at sundown on 9 December. With little more than raw manpower, trees, and a few tools, the convoy had progressed through deteriorating road and weather conditions and had brought huge cargo loads over nearly impassable roads and bridges, a feat that would be difficult under normal conditions.

From the very first, the journey from Vila Cabral had proven most challenging with the naturally spongy roadway and the poor, rutted surface. The entire crew had struggled constantly to maintain orderly progress. With the rebuilding of two bridges and the recovery of one vehicle from a sinkhole, discouragement and extreme fatigue had become the worst enemies. The launching of the boats proved relatively anticlimactic. The transporters backed down a ramp into Lake Niassa, and as the boats floated in their cradles, LDM 404 and *Régulus* pulled them free. Damage to the vessels was noteworthy, and once it had been repaired, the patrol boats became operational.

The force on Lake Niassa was reinforced again during 1966 with LDM 408 and LDPs 107, 203, and 204. Finally with *Operação Roaz* or Operation Dolphin between 5 July and 23 August 1967, *Saturno* (P 1136), *Urano* (P 1137), and LDM 407 were likewise brought to the lake.[34] This force was formed into the Launch Squadron Lake Niassa (*Esquadrilha de Launchas do Lago Niassa* or ELLN), and by the end of 1969 there were 14 launches on the lake and two in Porto Amélia. According to the navy, three additional *Júpiter* class launches were needed to patrol Niassa effectively, an additional LFP and support base in Moçimboa da Praia to patrol the Indian Ocean from Porto Amélia, and an additional seven launches to patrol the Rovuma.[35] No additional forces were available, however, and the ELLN maintained its 1969 force level until the end of the war. Its principal missions were interdiction of the enemy on the lake, support of the *Fuzileiros*, and logistical support of the military and the population. This last responsibility had become a naval one, for the road system had deteriorated physically, was often mined, and was thus not a reliable communication link. During 1971, for example, the ELLN transported 17,993 personnel and 6,216 tons of cargo in performing this latter task.[36]

One of the very real problems facing the ELLN was its restriction to Portuguese territorial waters. This situation gave the insurgents a relatively free passage through the unpatrolled waters of Malawi, and they took full advantage of it to transit to sparsely populated parts of both Malawi and Mozambique and to extend their influence further into Portuguese territory. Consequently, in order to extend the reach of the ELLN and to foreclose this avenue, Malawi was courted as an ally.

Malawi was granted its independence in 1964 and inherited a battalion of 2,000 soldiers headquartered at Cobbe Barracks in Zomba in its south and commanded by Brigadier Timothy Lewis, a long-time confident of Banda, the first Malawian head of state. This was the extent of its armed force, as no navy had been needed until now. Banda was a populist leader who had spent the better part of his adult life as a successful family physician in both the United States and the United Kingdom before returning to his homeland in 1958 to lead the campaign for independence. He sought to preserve the farm economy and the traditional way of life for Malawians. In doing this, he strengthened the system of traditional chiefs, founded organizations for women and youth, and attempted to make peace with his neighbors. He established close ties with South Africa, which provided financing, military and police training, and tourists for the resorts on Lake Niassa. He established even closer relations with Portugal, as the primary external commercial links for his country were two railway lines that ran to the Mozambican ports of Nacala and Beira. He also cooperated fully with Portuguese security forces, an unpopular activity with other heads-of-state in the newly independent African nations.

Jorge Jardim, the powerful and charismatic Beira businessman and intelligence service operative, became involved in gaining Banda's help against FRELIMO. Jardim was a clever, dynamic man with a good sense of humor and represented an influential presence in Niassa-Malawi border area. He seemed to be involved in everything. Banda, for instance, asked

Transporter with *Mercúrio* Crossing the "Drift". Photograph courtesy Estado-Maior da Armada and *Revista da Armada.*

Jardim to capture one of his opposition leaders who had fled Malawi and was hiding in the Niassa district border town of Mandimba opposite Fort Jackson in Malawi. Jardim knew only that the man was a Malawian and a diabetic. Arranging to have coffee with a group of Malawian expatriates, he identified the man as the only one who refused sugar.[37] Jardim worked closely with one of Banda's paramilitary youth groups, The Young Pioneers.[38] This group was assigned to patrol the Malawian borders to halt FRELIMO use of Malawian territory and were trained, equipped, and supported by the Portuguese. This help was ultimately extended to a seaborne effort with the decision to lend *Castor,* now renamed the *John Chilembwe* (variously *Jobo Chilembwé*), to Malawi in August 1968 to form its navy. When the transfer occurred, the commanding officer of *Mercúrio* and two of his crewmembers were "loaned" to run the launch, as there was no Malawian naval heritage. These men were temporarily detached from the Portuguese Navy and worked for and were paid by Malawi. The balance of the crew was drawn from elements of The Young Pioneers, who then underwent seamanship training in Metangula.[39] Maintenance and repairs were likewise performed by the Portuguese in Metangula. Mutual support also extended to the Malawian provision of fuel for the ELLN, which was transported in Portuguese LDMs across the lake to Metangula. The relationship was further strengthened in March 1969 when *Régulus* followed *Castor* to Malawi and was renamed *Chibisa.* Close cooperation and mutual support in this vein continued throughout the war.

The strategy succeeded well initially through a combination of a mutually supportive

LDM 408 and an LDP Being Transported to Lake Niassa in May 1966.
Photograph courtesy Estado-Maior da Armada and *Revista da Armada*.

naval presence on Lake Niassa, the favorable political position of Malawi, and the paramilitary forces operating there. These forces with their identities sanitized collaborated with the navy from time to time in special cross-border operations against the insurgents, activities that today remain shrouded in secrecy. A substantial amount of useful intelligence was likewise gathered that led to successful ground operations. This tightened security on Lake Niassa would ultimately force the insurgents to seek a new strategy, but as we shall see, much occurred before then.

Niassa Operations

Naval operations on the lake centered on the primary naval base of Metangula and its satellite Cobué to the north. The installation at Metangula was alternatively called Vila Augusto Cardoso during Portuguese ownership and was named after the first naval commander to explore Mozambique. It was a well-ordered and immaculate facility sited on a secure peninsula together with a lighthouse and an airstrip. In a moment of enthusiastic hyperbole, it was even labeled "magnificent" and "majestic."[40] From August 1967, it supported four *Júpiter* class LFPs, four "400" class LDMs, one "100" class LDP, two "200" class LDPs, and a company of *Fuzileiros Navais*. There was likewise a radio station that served as a vital part of the world-wide naval communications system and an army infantry company encamped nearby in more reduced circumstances.

The army patrolled the local area, which was a difficult undertaking, as it was rugged terrain, and the few available roads were invariably mined. This poor road system resulted in slow and unresponsive logistics that relied on supplying the base by truck. There was consequently an annoying shortage of almost everything. The food was terrible, and there was no significant native game to augment the rations. Fishing proved a disappointment, as well. Insects abounded in the hot, tropical climate. The mined roads also reduced the army to foot patrols with their limited range and ability to police the vast tracts of northwest Niassa.

Table 6.1: Naval Augmentation of Mozambique, 1961–1971

Unit	Arrival Date	Operating Area
AH *Almirante Lacerda* (A 525) – hydrographic	Permanent	Indian Ocean
LC *Tête* – river gunboat	Permanent	Zambezi River
Mina – hydrographic mission	Permanent	Lake Niassa
LP 1	Early 1966	Lake Niassa
LP 2	Early 1966	Lake Niassa
LFP *Antares* (P 360)	Nov 1962	Indian Ocean
LFP *Castor* (P 580)	Nov 1964[1]	Lake Niassa
LDM 404	Nov 1965	Lake Niassa
LDM 405	May 1966	Lake Niassa
LFP *Marte* (P 1134)	Dec 1965	Lake Niassa
LFP *Mercúrio* (P 1135)	Dec 1965	Lake Niassa
LFP *Régulus* (P 369)	Nov 1965[2]	Lake Niassa
LDM 408	May 1966	Lake Niassa
LDP 107	May 1966	Lake Niassa
LDP 203 and 204	May 1966	Lake Niassa
LFG *Argos* – returned to Guiné in 1966	Feb 1965	Indian Ocean
LFG *Dragão* – returned to Guiné in 1966	Feb 1965	Indian Ocean
LDG 103 *Cimitara*	Aug 1966	Indian Ocean
LDM 407	Aug 1967	Lake Niassa
LFP *Urano* (P 1137)	Aug 1967	Lake Niassa
LFP *Saturno* (P 1136)	Aug 1967	Lake Niassa
LFP *Sirus* (P 1154)	1971	Indian Ocean
LFP *Vega* (P 1155)	1971	Indian Ocean

1. Transferred to the Malawian Navy in August 1968 as *John Chilembwe* (variously *Jobo Chilembwé*).

2. Transferred to the Malawian Navy in March 1969 as *Chibisa*.

Nevertheless, army troops engaged the population and supported it with various civic programs, including a small hospital. Ricardo Manuel Migães de Campos, a medical doctor who had received his commission through the Naval Reserve, described his duties at this facility during his assignment in 1968 and 1969 as being quite routine but important to both the military and civilian populations. He was the lone doctor in the area bordering Lake Niassa and cared for about 1,200 military and about 2,000 civilian personnel. Wounds from gunshots and mines and sickness from tropical diseases were the most common maladies, although he only encountered a single death and treated five wounded.[41]

Metangula had a 1,200 meter airstrip with a Dornier DO-27 and a Cessna at his disposal for airlift evacuation, and he flew about 100 hours in the course of a year performing this task. These two small aircraft could transport patients to the larger airfield in Vila Cabral in about 20 minutes, and from there it was only a 4-hour flight by C-47 to Beira, a primary airfield and hospital. Isolation and the consequent boredom were problems, and various activities were organized to counter them. A local radio station was established, and it broadcast music, jokes, stories, news, and interviews. These were all popular and helped to combat psychological problems among the troops. Personnel were also regularly rotated to Cobué for a change of scenery and, after six months on Lake Niassa, were again rotated to Ponta Delgata on the Indian Ocean. Relations with the local population seemed to be more positive than those of the army because of tighter naval discipline and the fact that each day in an overture of good will the sailors would walk among the local people without their arms.[42]

More importantly, the population inland was vulnerable to FRELIMO intimidation, and thus the decision was made to relocate it near the water where it could be more easily protected and supported. If FRELIMO did not have access to the population, then it could not extract the traditional support in the form of food, recruits, shelter, intelligence, and taxes. Thus, the entire native population within 10 miles of the water was moved to the lakeshore, and its former villages were put to the torch. As an important part of the support, the naval officers at Metangula founded a school for the local children, and their wives along with other available military personnel taught some 350 students for three days a week. An unforeseen dividend of this project was the close relationship established between the teachers and their students. As their parents were often FRELIMO fighters, the children knew where their parents had planted mines and would helpfully reveal this information to the teachers.[43]

Cobué, located some 50 miles to the north of Metangula and opposite the Malawian islands of Licoma and Chisumulo, was the site of an old mission with its imposing but rather plain church. It had been founded and was still run by Italian priests, although the conflict severely reduced its operation. The village itself was a planned development associated with the mission, but its population had abandoned it almost totally with the advent of war. The vacant buildings accordingly were converted to accommodate a detachment of *Fuzileiros Especiais,* one of *Fuzileiros Navais,* and an advanced naval command post.[44] Like Metangula, it was relatively spartan. In contrast, however, it was near the Tanzanian border and consequently in the midst of insurgent activity.

Patrols were conducted along the entire 115-mile coastline based, first, on the need to demonstrate a presence and, second, on intelligence ranging from the specific to the very general. Intelligence was gained from three sources: prisoner interrogation, reconnaissance flights, and normal operations. Sometimes it was provided by Jardim and was based on his contacts in Malawi, but his help was only incidental to naval operations.[45]

The normal patrol profile would entail the sortie of either a LF or a LD from either Metangula or Cobué with a platoon of *Fuzileiros* embarked and to remain at sea for 5 days. During this period, the *Fuzileiros* would be landed from time to time to conduct foot patrols, ambushes, and cordon and search operations, and to gather intelligence from the population. At the beginning of a patrol, the LF would assume station about 1,000 meters from shore with its radar operating for navigation and identification of local water traffic. If a suspicious contact was identified either through radar or by lookouts, it was investigated. The patrol would continue to an opportune landing site to disembark the *Fuzileiros* for their foot patrol. Once the site was identified, and this might be done based on intelligence, experience, or simply a suspicion of enemy activity, the *Fuzileiros* would be put ashore in their rubber boats or from a landing craft. When they were ashore, the launch would stand ready to support and assist. The patrol would adjust its tactics to be covert or overt, depending on whether or not it was thought the landing had been observed and was known to the population. The launches were noisy, so it was generally assumed that FRELIMO knew when operations were afoot, but there were also deception techniques similar to those on the Zaire to help conceal the exact nature of naval activity. The greatest threat for those ashore, however, was discovered to be mines and not FRELIMO insurgents, as the area was sparsely populated. At the conclusion of the 5-day cruise, the LF crew would recover its *Fuzileiro* contingent, and all would return to base for a 3-day rest.

At times these missions suffered from rushed and thus incomplete planning. This resulted oftentimes in having the *Fuzileiros* walk great distances and only occasionally surprising FRELIMO. FRELIMO bases were a distance from the lakeside and on high ground in the mountains to the east. This meant that unless the enemy ventured from his retreat, the *Fuzileiros* had to seek him out. If he were found and engaged, then subsequent missions would seek to exploit this experience. If prisoners were taken, then their interrogation would shape future mission planning and execution. Reconnaissance flights would be used to confirm and revise the intelligence picture.[46]

The specific experiences and observations of *Fuzileiro* junior lieutenant (*secundo tenente*) Raul Patrício Leitão add important amplification to the foregoing general pattern of operations. Leitão was deployed to Metangula in late December 1966 and began his acclimation with "learning" operations in January. He was assigned to the DFE there, which was divided into three platoons or combat groups of about 25 men each. Leitão commanded one of the groups, and in the field his *Fuzileiros* seemed to be regularly but intermittently in contact with FRELIMO elements. The *Fuzileiros* under Leitão's command were generally young men of about 18 or 19 years who had joined the navy at 16 and volunteered for this specialty. Indeed, they were an accurate reflection of the *Corpo de Fuzileiros* at large, as it was a young organization with approximately one-third of its members being combat veterans, a potent mix of youth and experience. Leitão's group operated initially in the area of Malawi south of Metangula, but soon he was transferred to Cobué in one of the many personnel rotations designed to provide a change of scenery. It was a time of opportunity, and he was soon face to face with FRELIMO. On 23 March 1967 in one of his initial operations, he and his group of 25 *Fuzileiros* were taken by Torres Sobral in his launch to a point a little over 15 miles north of Cobué and put ashore at about 0500 hours just prior to sunrise. There had been no specific indication of enemy activity between Cobué and the Tanzanian border; however, this perception may have been because the FRELIMO elements in the mountains could easily see and hear any approaching Portuguese force and avoid it. The mined roads forced all traffic to move by water, so it was not unusual to see or hear Portuguese launches underway. The Portuguese would take advantage of this activity to make noise or to be silent, depending on the deception scenario. In this case, it was hoped that the noisy launch had not been heard at the early hour and that the enemy remained unaware.

Leitão and his *Fuzileiros* moved over rough ground in the nether light and followed the standard practice of avoiding the tracks and trails, as the insurgents would not only mine them but would also mine their shoulders. The group walked for an hour and covered about three kilometers over difficult terrain with no particular objective other than simple reconnaissance. As daylight approached, Leitão sought an observation site on the top of a nearby hill. He was enjoying a smoke with his medic, radioman, and bodyguard, as the remainder of the group deployed nearby and in so doing surprised two 12-year-old boys. From their broken Portuguese, Leitão learned that they had left a FRELIMO base without authorization to fish at the lake. According to the youths, the base was about five miles east of the hill and was divided into two encampments, one containing warriors, and the other, camp followers. There was always a man with a bazooka guarding the base to warn of approaching danger, but then the boys had managed to avoid him in leaving. The boys also described a protective minefield surrounding the base and knew how to negotiate it. Leitão imagined from their description and his knowledge of the area that there might be a dozen or so men in the base and that his *Fuzileiros* could easily handle them. Had he thought that there were more, then he would have called for reinforcements before beginning his march to attack the base.

It took the *Fuzileiros* about two hours to negotiate the irregular terrain and reach the site. The party paused at the top of a hill about 300 meters from the base to take stock and develop a plan of attack. With only 27 men, it would have to be simple. The insurgents were visible through the trees and were unsuspectingly going about their daily routine in preparation for the noon meal. Leitão planned to leave the two boys, the medic, the radioman, the mortar bearer, and a *sepoy* outside the minefield, which the boys had identified, and proceed with the main body in a column through the mines.[47] He would then have his men shift to a line abreast to sweep through camp, using the perimeter minefield as the anvil in a hammer-and-anvil tactic. Because the terrain and undergrowth limited line-of-sight communication, Leitão briefed his *Fuzileiros* that he would allow five minutes for deployment of the force around the enemy camp. At the end of that time, all would move forward in execution of the attack. No one would fire until he heard Leitão fire. This timing and fire discipline was necessary to coordinate the attack with incomplete visual contact.

During the five-minute deployment, Leitão observed that the base was a village surrounded with a series of small fences, and the population appeared relaxed and unsuspecting. He thought this unusual, as he knew that Torres Sobral's launch had been quite noisy in landing his force. Suddenly about 30 meters from the village a tree fell unexpectedly. Still no one took notice, as apparently a tree falling in the bush is a routine event. As Leitão began his move forward and neared the village, he realized that his group was hopelessly outnumbered, but it was too late to worry, as the group was committed to attack.

When the assault began, the FRELIMO insurgents were completely surprised and either fled or fell in place during the five-minute fight. In the end, there were about 60 insurgents killed or wounded, and a single *Fuzileiro* wounded. On average the *Fuzileiros* fired about 60 rounds each from their weapons. In the excitement, some had fired their entire personal ammunition supply of 100 rounds, others only about 30 rounds. The *Fuzileiros* collected all of the weapons that they could find and lobbed a few mortar rounds into the camp before returning to the lake and the launch. By sunset, the entire party with its captured weapons had returned to Cobué.

There were a number of follow-up raids to the village site in which prisoners were captured and interrogated, and the one nice surprise to be revealed in the intelligence was that the two boys had not been punished. The prisoners were allowed to build a village at Cobué, and it was expanded to 200 people with the subsequent capture of fighters and the relocation of their families. The village became a partial source of local labor and modest crops and in turn was the recipient of military largess, particularly food and aspirin.

The success of operations was measured by the number of weapons captured rather than insurgents killed or FRELIMO activities disrupted. The aim of this policy was to avoid killing the enemy, who might actually be an unwilling local forced to fight by FRELIMO. Indeed, many Portuguese soldiers were wounded in effecting this policy and trying to maintain good relations with the population. Despite the war, the people trusted the Portuguese and regularly came to their bases to receive medical treatment.

This use of captured weapons as a measure of effectiveness seems to be a strange yardstick in that an almost endless supply was available in Tanzania, and for that matter Guinée, the Congo, and Zambia. The lost weapons were easily replaced, but the insurgents themselves required recruitment, training, combat experience, and loyalty to be useful. This process of personal development took far longer and was infinitely more complicated than delivering technologically dated weapons from obsolete and overflowing Communist bloc stockpiles. When surrounded or surprised by overwhelming force, insurgents would quickly abandon their weapons with their heavy weight to increase their mobility in fleeing the fight and to help in blending with the population. The weight of a Kalashnikov AK-47 assault rifle, for instance, is 4.8 kilograms, a clear impediment to rapid flight, and because the local population was unarmed, a man with a weapon would attract immediate suspicion. Perhaps a better measure of effectiveness would be the extent to which social programs, prosperity, and political freedoms were contributing to the well-being and satisfaction of the population over that offered by FRELIMO. The war was, after all, one of ideas, and while military security is one dimension, it is not the most important.

Indian Ocean Operations

The war began on the central plain in Cabo Delgado, the littoral of which was characterized by numerous bays and offshore islands that provided excellent entry points for FRELIMO insurgents infiltrating by sea from the north along the coast. The strategy of FRELIMO was to dominate the littoral of Cabo Delgado and hence control the riverine and littoral populations from whom its fighters hoped to obtain fish and other provisions.[48]

The Portuguese authorities had always maintained a naval presence in the small base at Porto Amélia, where the Maritime Defense Command of Porto Amélia (*Comando da Defesa Marítima de Porto Amélia* or CDMPA) was headquartered. Its mission was to protect Portuguese sovereign waters and their littorals in its zone, to conduct maritime inspections of transiting craft, to provide civil and military logistical support along the littoral, and to participate in joint military operations. Over the years, the CDMPA acquired six permanently assigned ships with which to execute its responsibilities, as shown in Table 6.2.

Table 6.2: LFs Permanently Assigned to Porto Amélia by Year

	61	62	63	64	65	66	67	68	69	70	71	72	73	74
LFP *Antares* (P360)			■	■	■	■	■	■	■	■	■	■	■	■
LFG *Argos* (P372)					■	■								
LFG *Dragão* (P374)					■	■	■	■						
LDG *Cimitarra* (103)						■	■	■	■	■	■	■	■	■
LFP *Veja* (P1155)											■	■	■	■
LFP *Sirius* (P1154)											■	■	■	■

Frigates and corvettes were assigned on a periodic rotation basis to augment the permanent force. Initially, the intent was to have two ships available, but the coverage began with a single ship, the frigate *Álvares Cabral,* in June 1960. The old *aviso Bartolomeu Dias* was added in December, and from then on there were two. This level was maintained until April 1966, when the British blockade of Beira as a part of the UN embargo against Rhodesia caused the number of ships to be increased to three. In this second phase, two of the ships were assigned to patrolling the waters off Beira and watching the British ships. The third ship was assigned to CDMPA and spent its time patrolling the Quirimbas Archipelago. In the third and final phase, the new corvettes of the *João Coutinho* class replaced the frigates. The deployments are shown in Table 6.3.

Table 6.3: FFs and FCs Assigned to Mozambique by Year

	61	62	63	64	65	66	67	68	69	70	71	72	73	74
FF *Bartolomeu Dias* (F471)		■	■	■	■	■								
FF *Diogo Gomes* (F331)						■	■							
FF Álvares *Cabral* (F336)	■					■	■	■		■	■			
FF *Pacheco Pereira* (F337)				■	■	■		■	■					
FF *Vasco da Gama* (F478)				■			■	■						
FF *D. Francisco d'Almeida* (F479)		■	■			■	■	■	■	■				
FF *Comandante João Belo* (F480)									■	■				
FF *Comandante H. Capelo* (481)										■	■			
FC *João Coutinho* (F475)										■	■	■	■	■

	61	62	63	64	65	66	67	68	69	70	71	72	73	74
FC *Jacinto Cândido* (F476)														
FC *General Pereira d'Eca* (F477)														

The frigates assigned to the CDMPA were kept busy with normal surveillance and amphibious operations. While there was the occasional transport of commandos and paratroops from their bases in Nacala and Lumbo to the front in Mocímboa da Praia and return following their operations, the ships would also land *Fuzileiros* in nighttime covert operations. These would be along the coast and generally around the mouth of the Messalo River, which is surrounded by the islands of the Quirimba Archipelago, which are restricted inner waters or narrow seas. For the frigates, navigation through this labyrinthine island chain in darkness presented certain dangers, as the charts were inexact, and the currents freakish and unpredictable. The islands were surrounded by coral reefs, and if the radar failed, it was very difficult. Even with perfect radar, it was invariably a tense passage for the ship's crew.[49] Once through the islands, the ship would lay about two miles off the beach because of shelving and launch the *Fuzileiros* in their rubber boats in the predawn twilight. Each frigate held 12 of the *Zebro III* boats and was capable of launching an entire DFE toward the shore. The boats were operated by members of the ship's landing party, who had been specially trained for the task at the *Escola de Fuzileiros*. The lead boat carried a radar reflector and would be guided by shipboard radar, with course corrections being relayed by radio. The landing was designed to put the *Fuzileiros* ashore at daybreak, whereupon the rubber boats would return to the ship. Four or five days later, the landing party would collect the *Fuzileiros* and any prisoners and return to Porto Amélia.[50]

Nó Górdio

Despite the successes on Lake Niassa and the Indian Ocean, insecurity of the Rovuma River remained a problem. FRELIMO infiltration continued at a high pace to the extent that General Kaúlza de Arriaga, the Commander-in-Chief Armed Forces Mozambique, decided to conduct a large hammer-and-anvil operation in the area east of Mueda during the first weeks of July 1970. In the three months prior to July, FRELIMO had been responsible for 1,079 incidents, 841 or 78 percent of which were in the Cabo Delgado district. This activity had resulted in 39 Portuguese dead and 269 gravely wounded.[51] In short, FRELIMO was making an unacceptable challenge to Portuguese authority. Within this area there were believed to be the majority of a 2,500-man enemy force interspersed with the local population.[52] Arriaga planned to bring together a task force of some 8,000 men from the army, air force, and navy to destroy the insurgents in an operation he styled *Nó Górdio* or Gordian Knot. Its aim was to isolate the center of the Maconde Plateau, where FRELIMO had its important bases of Gungunhana, Moçambique, and Nampula, and to destroy its force. This would be done through siege, heavy strike, and a sweep by ground forces.[53]

The operation went as planned and lasted some 36 days, but was flawed in several respects. It was the largest such operation undertaken in the *ultramar* during the war and made a major hole in the budget. Lisbon complained, and no similar operation was ever again initiated. While many insurgent bases were destroyed and weapons captured, the enemy by and large melted into the 20,000-strong local population fleeing the area to avoid the fight. FRELIMO moved eastward and largely escaped. The operation could not be concealed because of its size, and thus gave FRELIMO ample warning. Also other areas of Mozambique were stripped of troops to support it, and thus the population was left vulnerable elsewhere. In the end, the operation yielded disappointing results at great expense. FRELIMO avoided contact for the most part and lived to fight another day. Like most insurgent movements, it would choose its own battlefield. Within three months the level of FRELIMO activity had returned to nearly pre-operation intensity. Even so, the FRELIMO campaign remained confined to the border area along the Rovuma because of logistic limitations and an unreceptive population. After six years of fighting and taking casualties, FRELIMO had little to show for its efforts. It was time for a reappraisal.

The north of Mozambique was in itself a formidable barrier, as FRELIMO insurgents had to travel by long distances over relatively barren land to find targets of opportunity. So even if the Rovuma River border was porous, and insurgents could wander almost at will through Niassa and Cabo Delgado, it was not a target-rich environment. The Portuguese held periodic offensives, the largest of which was *Nó Górdio*, to discourage FRELIMO, but the heart of Mozambique was south of the Zambezi River, some 1,000 kilometers away. To even the most enthusiastic FRELIMO fighter, the prospect of crossing such a vast expanse of hostile territory and relying on support from an indifferent population was daunting, if not impossible. With no victory in sight, a new strategy was needed to reach the Portuguese center of gravity in the south.

In 1968, Zambia had given permission for FRELIMO to establish bases there.[54] Following *Nó Górdio,* FRELIMO began to move its troops to Zambia and develop a series of bases along the Zambian border north of the Zambezi River and the Téte district of Mozambique. These forces transited Malawi, with Banda turning a blind eye much to Portuguese distress.[55] Indeed, Al Venter notes that FRELIMO insurgents were traveling openly by the busload from Tanzania and were guarded by the Malawi police, who were making certain that they did not linger on the Malawi side of the border.[56] This development forced Arriaga to shift his attention to the northeast.

Téte was, like Niassa and Cabo Delgado, a sparsely populated area. Within the district, however, Portugal in 1969 had embarked on an ambitious project at Cabora Bassa (variously Cahora Bassa) to dam the upper reaches of the Zambezi River as a source of electrical power. The dam was also designed to create an enormous reservoir 280 kilometers in length and 38 kilometers at its widest point.[57] This source would irrigate here-to-fore dry but fertile lands in an effort to bring prosperity to Téte and ultimately Mozambique and to harness this income for the *metrópole*. The navy was assigned the responsibility of defending the river while the dam was under construction, and once the lake was formed, of defending it too. This project and its lake were seen potentially as an effective block to FRELIMO infiltration through Téte and into Rhodesia and southern Mozambique. As it was, by 1971 FRELIMO was active in the area south of the Zambezi in Téte near the village of Daque and at the several neighboring villages of Deveteve, Nura, and Serra do Comboio.[58] These FRELIMO bases also hosted Zimbabwean insurgents, a source of great concern to Southern Rhodesia, which began conducting "hot pursuit" operations into Téte.

In 1972, the CNM had a modest force of one DFE at the town of Téte downriver from the dam site and another at the neglected settlement of Zumbo at the far western end of the projected reservoir. David Livingston, the missionary explorer who had visited the village in the latter half of the nineteenth century, described it as a "sleepy hollow where horrible black-snouted pigs wallowed in fetid mud pools."[59] Little had changed in the intervening century, and Portuguese presence on the upper Zambezi remained limited, a situation that left Téte insecure and the Rhodesians frustrated.

At this time it was decided to create a Maritime Defense Command (*Comando de Defesa Maritima* or CDM) of the Zambezi Ports, and the new command was charged with developing a plan to secure the waterway from enemy infiltration and to use it to supply the already large numbers to troops moving to the district. Such a plan would aim to bypass the dangerous and problematical road link that was increasingly vulnerable to mines and ambushes. The great problem with policing and using the Zambezi, however, was its strong current. This translated into a need for powerful launches to navigate upstream. The navy was consequently forced to look at new technology for this mission and identified hovercraft as the vessel of choice for the job.[60] By the time the defense plan for these waters had been completed, the inventory of required equipment had expanded to 6 hovercraft, 36 assault boats, a principal support base at Sena/Mutara, and four secondary bases at Téte, Tambara, Marromeu, and Chinde, all complemented by amphibious helicopters and floating bases for the *Fuzileiros*. After *Nó Górdio*, the enormous expense of establishing a large force with sophisticated equipment in the remote reaches of Téte district went against policy at the ministerial level, particularly regarding naval forces in Africa.[61] The importance of Cabora Bassa, however, overrode this policy and an exception was made. Unfortunately, development of the plan had taken considerable time, and it was not completed and presented until March 1974, too late for implementation in the course of the war. The timing was most unfortunate, as like the missed opportunity on the Rovuma, naval policing of the Zambezi could have had the same success as that of the Zaire. The development of the Cabora Bassa reservoir would have formed a nearly impenetrable barrier and thereby have created security on the upper Zambezi and conditions for substantial economic expansion in the area.

Naval power is a valuable adjunct to land power, but army commanders have to understand how to use it for it to be an effective ingredient in the force mix arrayed against an enemy. This certainly was the case for Mozambique, for in the end it can be said the navy played an important strategic role on Lake Niassa and in the Indian Ocean that belied its small numbers. Timely and properly employed on the Rovuma and the Zambezi Rivers, additional small forces might have had an even greater impact in protecting Mozambique, containing FRELIMO, and helping neighboring Rhodesia to secure its borders.

Notes

1 António José Telo, *História da Marinha Portuguesa: Homens, Doutrinas e Organização, 1824–1974* (Tomo I) [History of the Portuguese Navy: Men, Doctrine and Organization, 1824–1974 (Volume I)] (Lisbon: Academia de Marinha, 1999), 609.

2 Ibid.

3 Ibid., 613.

4 Ibid., 612.

5 Al J. Venter, *The Zambesi Salient: Conflict in Southern Africa* (Cape Town: Howard Timmins, 1974), 193.

6 John Marcum, *The Angolan Revolution: The Anatomy of an Explosion (1950–1962)*, Volume 1 (Cambridge: M.I.T. Press, 1969), 284.

7 Ian F. W. Beckett, "The Portuguese Army: The Campaign in Mozambique, 1964–1974," in *Armed Forces*

and Modern Counterinsurgency by I. F. W. Beckett and J. Pimlott, eds. (London: Croom Helm, 1985), 140.

8 Venter, 81.

9 Neil Bruce, "Portugal's African Wars," *Conflict Studies*, № 34 (March 1973): 22.

10 Venter, 48; Bruce, 8.

11 José Verdasca dos Santos, *Memórias de um Captão* [Memories of a Captain] (Lisbon: Universitária Editoria, 2004), 143.

12 René Pélissier, *Naissance du Mozambique: Résistance et Révoltes Anticoloniales (1854–1918)* (Orgeval: Pélissier, 1984), 19.

13 Venter, 48.

14 Peter J. H. Petter-Bowyer, *Winds of Destruction* (Victoria: Trafford, 2003), 229–230.

15 Abel Barroso Hipólito, *A Pacificação do Niassa: Um Caso Concreto de Contraguerrilha* [The Pacification of Niassa: A Concrete Case of Counterguerrilla War] (Lisbon: privately published, 1970), 38.

16 Malyn Newett, *A History of Mozambique* (London: Hurst & Company, 1995), 523.

17 Bruce, 8 and 20.

18 Ibid.

19 Telo, 609.

20 Hipólito, 33–45.

21 Ibid.

22 Peter Shankland, *The Phantom Flotilla* (London: Collins, 1968).

23 Teixeira de Agullar, Reis Arenga, Silva Ribeiro, Santos Serafim, Albuquerque e Silva, and Melo e Sousa, *A Marinha na Investigação do Mar 1800–1999* [The Navy in the Investigation of the Sea 1800–1999] (Lisbon: Instituto Hidrográfico, 2001), 94 and 96.

24 Gomes Ramos, "Por Terras Nunca de Antes..." [Over Lands Never Before...], *Anais do Clube Militar Naval* (April–June 1966): 292.

25 Comandante-Chefe, Forças Armadas Moçambique, to Chefe do Estado-Maior General das Forças Armadas, Lourenço Marques, 27 September 1965, memorandum "Reforço de Meios Navais no Niassa" [Reinforcing Naval Means in Niassa], TMs [photocopy].

26 Captain (Engineer) Pedro da Conceição Mouzinho, Portuguese Navy, "Relatório sobre a Operação Atum" [Report on Operation Tuna], Naval Headquarters, Lourenço Marques, Mozambique, 14 January 1966, TMs [photocopy], 2–3.

27 João Soares Cabeçadas, "'Navegando' do Índico ao Lago Niassa" ['Navigating' from the Indian (Ocean) to Lake Niassa], *Revista da Armada* (May 1974): 9.

28 Mouzinho, 2–3.

28 Ibid., 5.

29 Ibid., 6.

30 Ibid., 10.

31 Ibid., 14.

32 Ibid., 17.

33 Ibid., 18.

34 Comando da Operação Roaz, Ordem de Serviço № 1 [Operation Dolphin Command, Service Order № 1], Catur, 22 August 1967, TMs [photocopy].

35 Telo, 612.

36 Ibid., 613.

37 Carlos Augusto Pereira da Costa Matos, interview with the author, 15 April 2000, Lisbon. Colonel Costa Matos was the governor of Niassa between 1962 and 1966.

38 José Freire Antunes, *Jorge Jardim Agente Secreto* [Jorge Jardim Secret Agent] (Venda Nova: Bertrand

Editora, 1996), 199–204.

39 Santana Lopes, "Agente Agreloso «nosso homem no Malawi»" [Agent Agrelos 'our man in Malawi'], *Diário de Notícias*, 22 April 2004, website: http://macua.blogs.com/25_de_abril_o_antes_e_o_a/2004/04/agente_agrelos_.html (accessed 15 October 2011); Francisco Manuel Lhano Preto, from Oral History Project, July 1999. Captain Lhano Preto is a special *Fuzileiro* and the last commanding officer of the *John Chilembwe* (variously *Jobo Chilembwé*), July 1973 to July 1974.

40 Ricardo Campos, "Missão Metangula – Parte II" [Mission Metangula – Part II], *AORN* (April 2000): 22.

41 Ibid.

42 Ricardo Manuel Migães de Campos, interview with the author, 30 January 2003, Lisbon.

43 José Deolindo Torres Sobral, interview with the author, 31 January 2000, Lisbon.

44 Delmar Barreiros, "Cobué: A zona mais pachola..." [Cobué: The prouder zone...], *Revista da Armada* (November 1984): 16–17.

45 Torres Sobral interview.

46 José Deolindo Torres Sobral and Raul Patrício Leitão, interview with the author, 10 April 2000, Lisbon.

47 *Sepoy* is a term originally applied to a native of India in the military service of a European nation, and in its most common application, was used in the British Indian Army to describe an infantry private. Leitão in this case used the term to identify an African private in the Portuguese Navy. *Sepoy* today remains a rank in the armies of India, Pakistan, and Bangladesh.

48 Adelino Rodrigues da Costa, *As Ilhas Quirimbas* [The Quirimbas Islands] (Lisbon: Edições Culturais da Marinha, 2003), 86.

49 Ibid., 92.

50 João Ferreira Barbosa, editing notes, 17 June 2011, Lisbon. Vice Admiral Ferreira Barbosa served as a junior officer on the FF *Vasco da Gama* (F478) patrolling the coast of Mozambique, 1967 to 1968.

51 Carlos de Matos Gomes, *Moçambique 1970, Operação Nó Górdio* [Mozambique 1970, Operation Gordian Knot] (Lisbon: Prefácio, 2002), 21.

52 Ibid., 10.

53 Luís Sanches de Baêna, *Fuzileiros: Factos e Feitos na Guerra de África, 1961/1974* [Marines: Deeds and Feats in the African War, 1961/1974], vol. 4, *Crónica dos Feitos da Moçambique* [Chronicle of the Feats of Mozambique] (Lisbon: Comissão Cultural da Marinha–INAPA, 2006), 140. DFE5, commanded by Lieutenant Vidigal Aragão, and DFE11, commanded by Lieutenant Fernandes Maia, participated in the operation.

54 Telo, 616.

55 Adelino Serras Pires and Fiona Claire Capstick, *The Winds of Havoc* (New York: St. Martin's Press, 2001), 83.

56 Venter, 47–48.

57 Telo, 616.

58 Henrik Ellert, *The Rhodesian Front War, Counter-insurgency and Guerrilla Warfare 1962–1980* (Gweru, Zimbabwe: Mambo Press, 1993), 88.

59 Ibid., 84.

60 Telo, 618.

61 Ibid.

7

Lands at the End of the Earth

Although geographic conditions in eastern Angola would dictate a campaign led by the army, the navy had proven itself on the Zaire and would again play a key role from 1965 onward in bringing similar security to the large internal river systems. There were four primary such systems in eastern Angola, and these were the Zambezi, Cuando, Cuito, and Cubango. All of these either provided a natural obstacle to maneuver or an avenue of approach in that the insurgents either had to cross them or follow their courses to penetrate into the interior where there were worthy targets. For the Portuguese they would serve as avenues of approach for combat and transport lines of communication for logistic operations. The navy would seek to control these systems and the commerce on them. It would also seek to engage the population on the littorals and be a positive influence on the economic and political landscape to counter insurgent proselytizing. As in Mozambique, the navy would have to project power by populating the distant and remote river systems with its launches and *Fuzileiros*.

The navy opened its eastern offensive on 22 April 1966 with the deployment of a combat group from DFE 13 and its six rubber boats to Lungué-Bungo.[1] This was a spartan base created in the bush some 200 kilometers southeast of Luso on the road between Lucusse and Luvuei next to the river of the same name, an important tributary of the Zambezi, as shown on the nearby map. The local terrain contained areas of dense vegetation, other areas so completely flooded that it was almost impossible to follow the course of the river, and still others that were totally deserted. This difficult terrain was periodically interrupted by the symmetry of a tilled field of crops, an ordinary cluster of huts, and perhaps a small enemy encampment.[2] As one *Fuzileiro* there wrote, this was a remote corner of Angola remarkable for its hot climate and the "boredom of guerrilla war," apparently ignoring the fact that first contact with the enemy occurred a mere three days after the *Fuzileiros* arrived.[3]

The source of the Lungué-Bungo, like that of the Cuito, lay in the elevated region just south of Munhango or about 150 kilometers southwest of Luso. The river meandered for upwards of two thousand kilometers before crossing the frontier with Zambia to join the Zambezi. It moved at a relentless seven knots through distant and isolated regions of extensive swamp forests and dense elephant grass. It teemed with life. Plentiful fish played in its rapids, and spectacularly colorful birds inhabited its sandy banks. Hippopotami wallowed happily in the mud, and like giant floating boulders, blissfully violated the Zambian frontier. It was also a river of *Fuzileiros* and alligators.[4]

When the *Fuzileiros* first arrived, they discovered that "disputes" between the MPLA and the thousand or so local people had shown the enemy's weakness. In fact, the insurgents were making such poor progress with the locals that they had stretched their credibility in claiming that they would drink the river dry, and then the *Fuzileiros* would not be able to come.[5] The *Fuzileiros*, however, were quick to establish a nearly constant riverine presence with the mobility of their rubber boats and to engage and befriend the local people to gain their confidence. At the time, this part of Angola was about as remote from the influences of

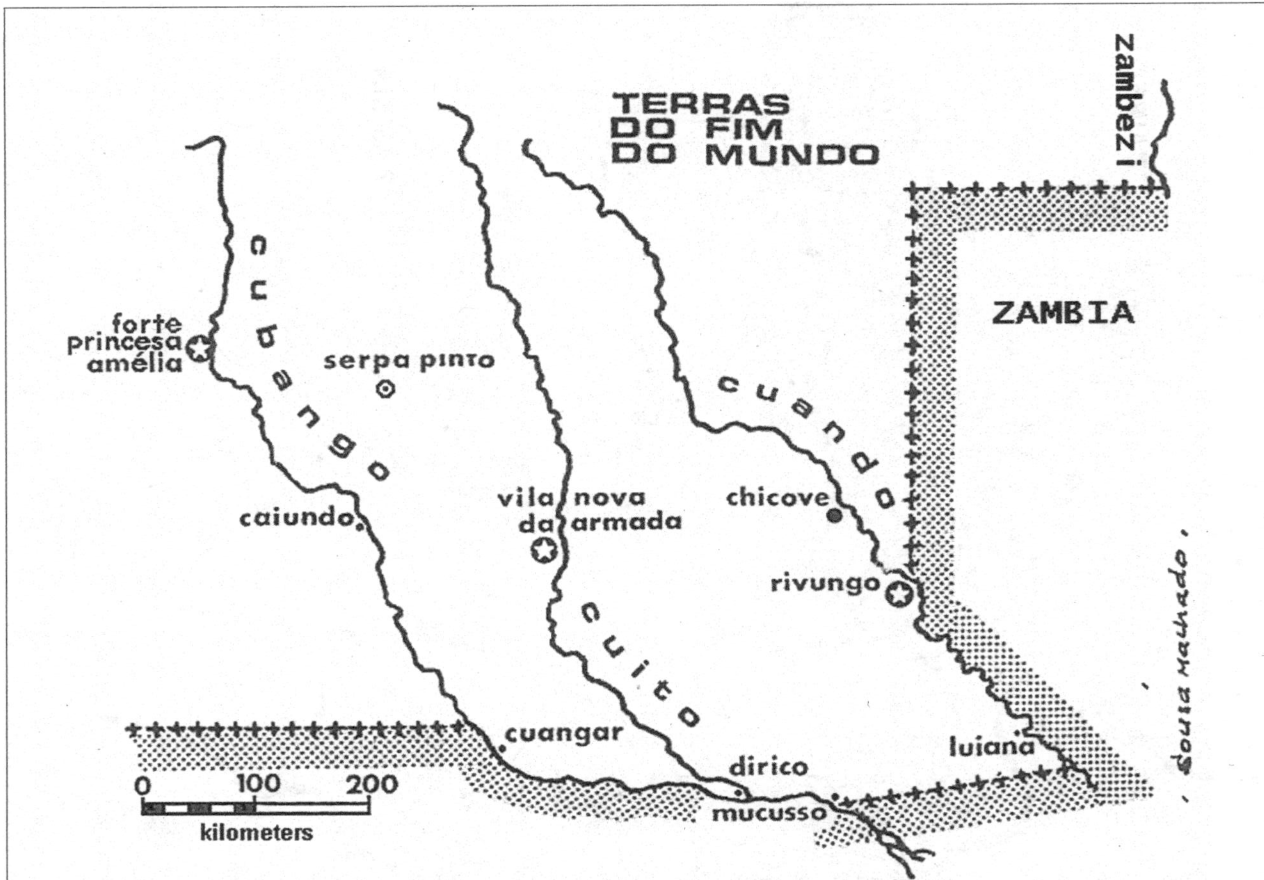

Cuito Cuando District, Angola, Lands at the End of the Earth (*Terras do Fim do Mundo*). Map drawn by Souia Machado for *Revista da Armada* and used courtesy Estado-Maior da Armada and *Revista da Armada*.

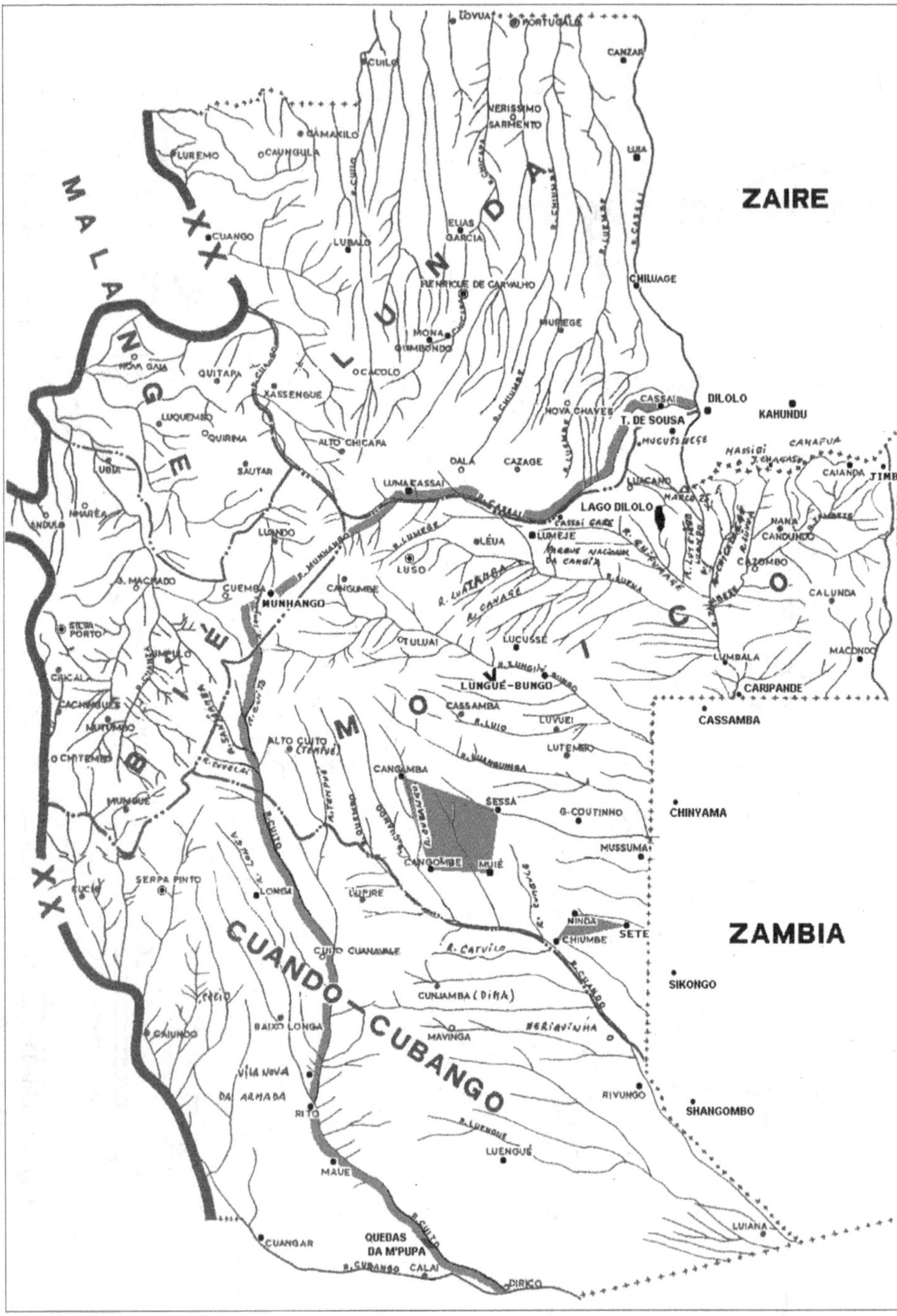

Zone of Operations, Eastern Angola, 1968. Courtesy António Pires Nunes, *Angola 1966-1974, Vitória Militar no Leste* (Lisbon: Prefácio, 2002), back cover.

modern civilization as one could imagine, and in the first year of *Fuzileiro* deployment, the war seemed very distant.[6] Soon afterwards though it became a hotbed of insurgent activity, and as we shall see, the navy expanded its presence in this remoteness and established a successful offensive in support of the army campaign against the enemy penetration from Zambia.

The Insurgent Problem

Northern Rhodesia was granted its independence and became the Republic of Zambia on 24 October 1964, following Tanzania by some three years. Kenneth David Kaunda, a former schoolteacher turned politician, became its first president. He had become an ardent nationalist in the 1950s, had led the drive for Zambian independence, and like Julius Nyerere of Tanzania, was passionately committed to supporting and providing a home for African liberation movements. He and Nyerere thought alike, as both espoused the single party socialist state and clung to political power through this vehicle. The journalist Chanda Chisala correctly, if emotionally, describes Kaunda as a power-hungry, selfish, greedy dictator who has little respect for human rights and less tolerance for contrary opinions.[7] In 1972 he bulldozed his new constitution into effect and banned all political parties except his own. Citizens could be and were jailed for such trivialities as not displaying his portrait in their offices. While espousing Christian principles, he was happy to detain dissidents without trial and abuse them with beatings, starvation, torture, and solitary confinement.[8] He used the term "stupid idiots" to describe his opponents, who eventually became a majority of Zambians.

If Kaunda was a bad political leader, then he was an even worse economic one with his catastrophic record of mismanagement. He inherited the second-wealthiest nation in Africa, after South Africa, and proceeded to reduce it to the bottom of the ladder of world economies by any measure. He nationalized the private commercial sector both to direct the dispensing of jobs and to support his socialist concept. This included everything from copper mines to hairdressers and dry cleaning shops. It has been estimated that Kaunda controlled 40,000 patronage positions in the capital of Lusaka alone.[9] Zambian industry withered. Kaunda had assumed that the copper mines would be an inexhaustible source of revenue to fund his policies and hired thousands of unnecessary hands to buy political acquiescence. Unfortunately Zambian copper production peaked in 1969, the year before nationalization, and subsequently began its long and steady decline.[10] Kaunda, in the pithy words of journalist Melvin Durai, allowed the Zambian economy to slide halfway down Victoria Falls while he hypnotized his countrymen with the traditional waves of his white handkerchief.[11] His trademark was a white linen handkerchief woven tightly between the fingers of his left hand.

Zambia was blessed with fertile land, reliable rainfall, and enormous agricultural potential. It was self-sufficient in food supplies at independence, and yet Kaunda's misguided agricultural policy created debilitating food shortages. Kaunda had government officials telling farmers what to grow, purchasing their crops when harvested, and selling them at heavily subsidized prices.[12] Generous agricultural sector loans were granted with little attempt at collection, a not-too-subtle political bribe. Corruption in other sectors was equally as bad or worse with the predictable result of wide-spread and persistent economic decline. Zambians remember Kaunda's rule as a time when shops were so bare that even the relatively well-off had trouble buying soap.[13]

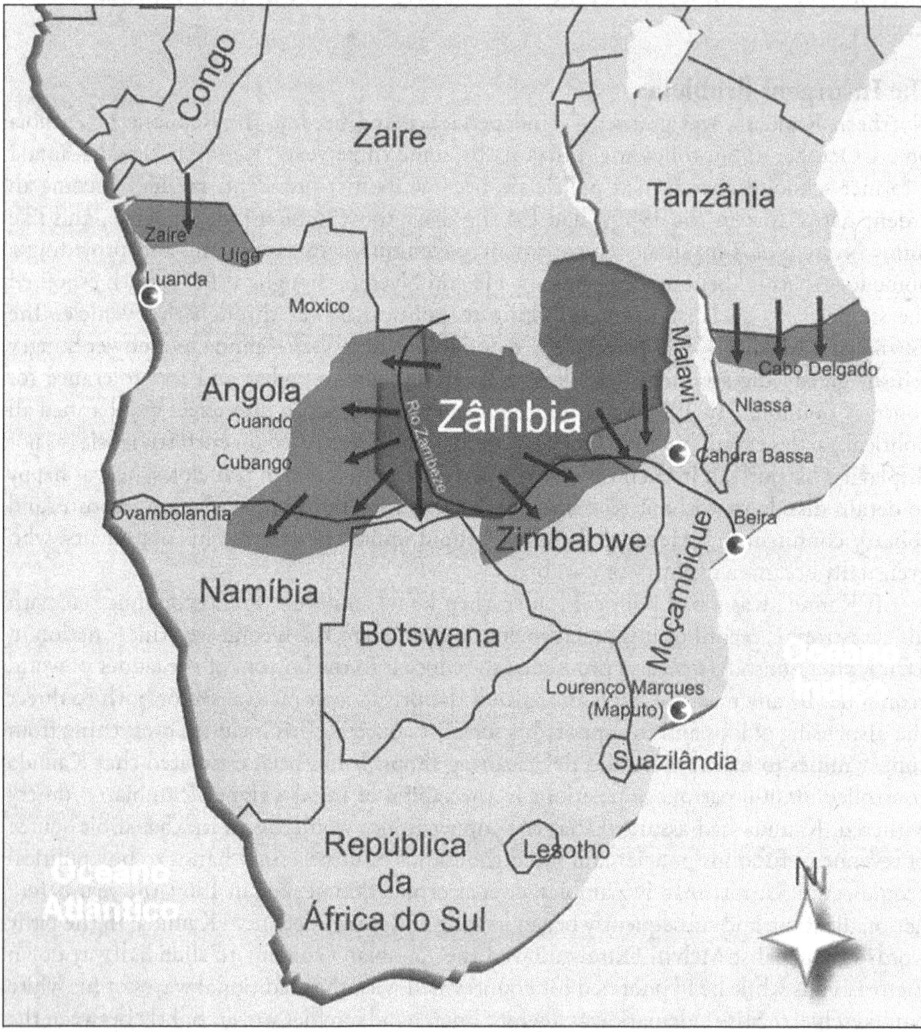

Southern Africa, showing the central location of Zambia and the direction and extent of insurgent thrusts into its neighboring countries in 1968. Courtesy António Pires Nunes, *Angola 1966-1974, Vitória Militar no Leste* (Lisbon: Prefácio, 2002), 11.

Kaunda implemented many other foolish and idealistic policies. His most bizarre was that of promoting a national "self-sufficiency" through the erection of tariff barriers and currency controls and of thereby isolating the Zambian economy from the rest of the world. This included an idealistically driven embargo on trade with apartheid South Africa. Such trade could have easily alleviated the food shortages that plagued his country, but Kaunda felt that it was more important for Zambians to suffer rather than to break with his ideal. Of course the State House pantry never suffered.

As long as Kaunda was able to exploit the colonial dowry, he could pursue his misguided economic and African nationalist policies. Once it was exhausted, however, his political future became tenuous. While the tide was with him though, he made Zambia the home for numerous nationalist movements. Indeed he hardly met one that he did not like. His landlocked country shared a frontier with no less than six countries, three of which were fighting active insurgencies, Angola, Southern Rhodesia, and Mozambique. This gave him ample opportunity to make trouble for his neighbors. Within two years of coming to power, Kaunda offered sanctuary to the MPLA and UNITA, among others, to pursue their campaigns against the Portuguese in eastern Angola.

Frustrated with Léopoldville's restrictive position on operations in northern Angola, the MPLA resolved at its January 1964 Conference of Cadres in Brazzaville to begin a calculated move to Zambia. From there it could reestablish its offensive. While Agostinho Neto elected initially to remain in Brazzaville, he would put his trusted associate Daniel Chipenda in charge of the eastern front, and from this point, things developed rapidly for the MPLA.

The supply chain in support of this offensive began with Julius Nyerere in Dar-es-Salam, through which arms flowed from such supplier-states as the Soviet Union, Communist China, Czechoslovakia, Bulgaria, and Cuba. Dar-es-Salam was not only a port of entry but also the center for training the armed elements of the African National Congress (ANC), South West Africa Peoples Organization (SWAPO), Zimbabwe African People's Union (ZAPU), Zimbabwe African National Union (ZANU), MPLA and FRELIMO.[14] From this center of mischief, arms supplies and trained insurgents flowed to eastern Angola over a lengthy trail that wound through Tanzania and Zambia for nearly 1,000 kilometers to Lusaca. From here there was a northern route of another 400 kilometers that served forces entering the Cazumbo Salient and a southern one of about 300 kilometers that supplied thrusts both across the Cuando River and along the Zambesi into Angola, as shown on the nearby map.

In April 1966, following an intense effort to proselytize the population in the east, first in the district of Moxico and later in Cuando-Cubango, the MPLA infiltrated a large group of combatants into the Cazombo Salient.[15] This is the large, approximately square geographical protrusion that is bounded by Zaire and Zambia on three sides and measures about 240 kilometers per side. It is crossed diagonally by the Zambezi, which ultimately flows through Zambia, over Victoria Falls, and through Mozambique to the Indian Ocean. Because of its shape, exposed borders, and remoteness, it was quite vulnerable to incursions. These infiltrated MPLA combatants showed a remarkable improvement over earlier Portuguese experience in subverting the population and employing selective terror when it did not cooperate. Subversion of the population in the east was estimated to be a modest 6 percent in 1965 and had grown to about 42 percent by 1968, the year that the MPLA offensive attained its height.[16]

In October 1966 following the penetration of the Cazombo Salient, there was a surge of activity to the south in the triangle bounded by the settlements of Ninda, Sete, and Chiume. These were located next to the Zambian border and about 375 kilometers southeast of Luso in an area called *Terras do Fim do Mundo* or "Lands at the End of the Earth." This area is more than 1,000 kilometers from the Atlantic Ocean, and the settlement of Luiana in the extreme southeast is equidistant from Luanda on the Atlantic and Beira on the Indian Ocean. It was this remoteness and the fact that the temperate savannah climate of central Angola, as it spreads south into this area with its lower altitude, becomes so harsh and desiccated that it prompted early explorers to give it this apt name. Such an operating environment favored the insurgent in that he was easily able to detect Portuguese forces at considerable distance and did so generally before they were aware of him. This insurgent advantage made it difficult for Portuguese forces to find and destroy the enemy, and as we shall see, substantially influenced the crafting of a campaign plan.

In November and December 1966, some MPLA insurgents penetrated the northeast corner of the Salient near the border settlements of Jimbe and Caianda. Portugal protested, and a fortnight later in reaction to this pressure Chipenda was ordered by the Zambian government to remove all of his forces from Zambia, leaving him with the only option of invading Angola. This somewhat successful pressure had its roots in Zambian dependence on the Bengula Railway (CFB) to export its copper ore across Angola. The railway always represented a tempting target for insurgents, and thus Zambia found itself caught between the practical need for foreign sales and the ideological desire to support nationalist movements. Several temporary closures in December 1966 and again in the spring of 1967 for attacks or acts of sabotage on the CFB carried a strong message to both Zambia and Zaire. As a consequence, during early 1967 the MPLA was ostensibly pushed out of Zambia and infiltrated the east in two primary areas, Lake Dilolo on the western edge of the salient, and a larger area located about 265 kilometers due south of Luso and bounded by the settlements of Sessa, Muié, Cangombe, and Cangamba. By 1968 this surge had penetrated as far west as Bié district, and as a result of such overextension, various MPLA columns found themselves quite vulnerable. Considerable numbers were destroyed or captured, but by 1970 there were still 1,300 men in Zambian bases and an estimated 3,850 running loose in Angola creating mayhem.[17] There were clearly limits to diplomatic and economic pressure in the face of Kaunda's strong feelings about African nationalist movements.

The MPLA was not alone in exploiting the east. The UPA/FNLA and its military wing, the ELNA, likewise saw the east as an alternative opportunity to the stalemate in the north and felt that it was losing politico-military ground to its competitors through inaction. The organization had fielded three battalions by 1970 following a regrouping from the *jacquerie* of 1961. These were launched separately into Angola from the north, the northeast, and east in a general invasion. The northern group, which was fortuitously discovered in concentration, was destroyed with strong attacks by the Portuguese Air Force.[18] The northeastern group crossed in force near Santa Cruz, a settlement some 600 kilometers northeast of Luanda, and was destroyed by several companies of commandos in one of the more brilliant operations conducted in Angola, *Operação Golpe de Flanco* or Operation Flank Attack.[19] The eastern group crossed from its base at Kizamba through Teixeira de Sousa, a primary border town and station for the CFB, to reinforce one of its groups already near Luacano and soon clashed with MPLA forces. The MPLA had a strong presence in the area and after its earlier treatment by Léopoldville was not about to be

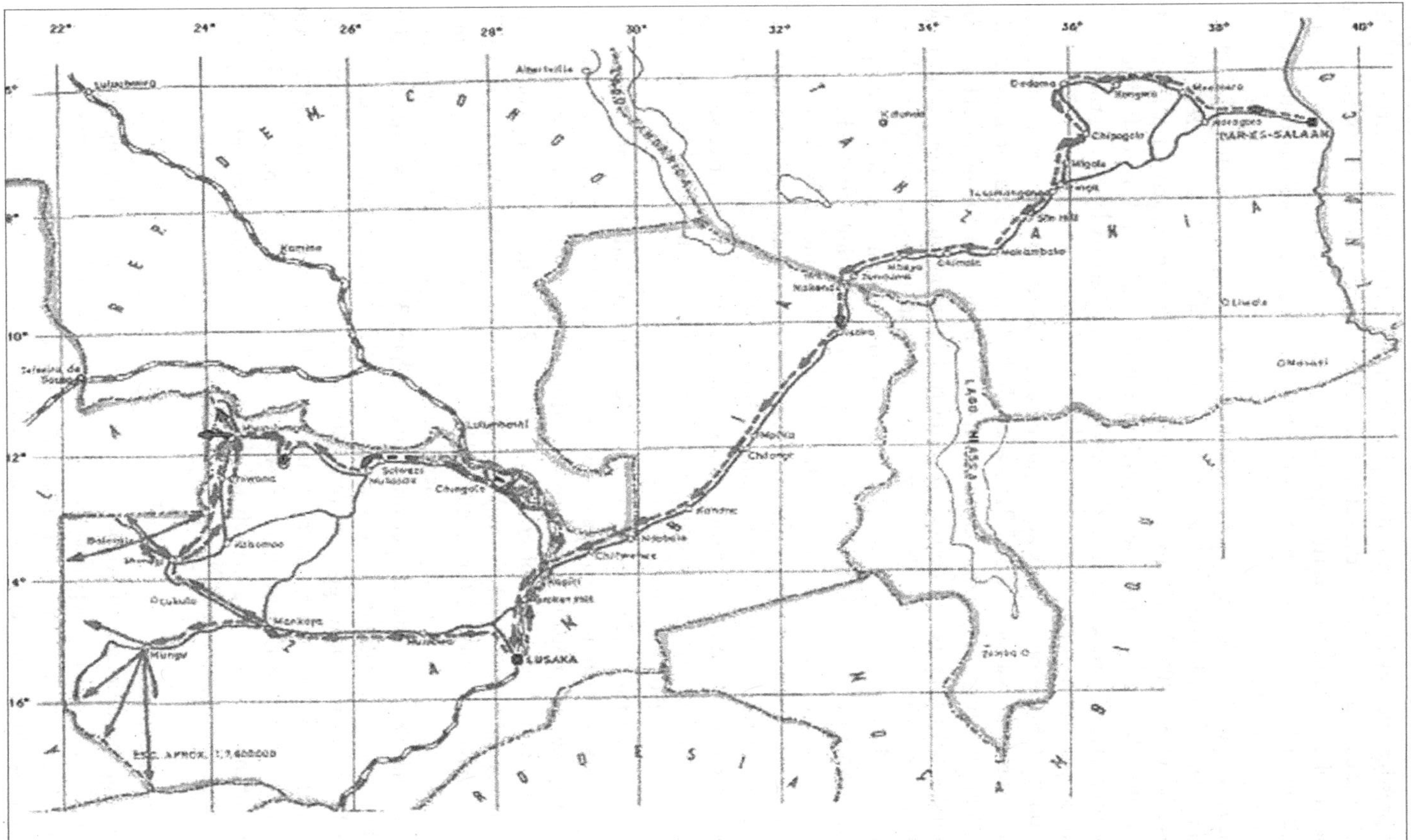

Insurgent infiltration route across Tanzania and Zambia, providing access to eastern Angola, Rhodesia, and the Téte District of Mozambique from 1968 onwards. PIDE archive map courtesy Dalila Cabrita Mateus, *A PIDE/DGS na Guerra Colonial 1961–1974* [The PIDE/DGS in the Colonial War 1961–1974] (Lisbon: Terramar, 2004).

displaced by its competition. As a consequence of its defeat, the UPA/FNLA lost enormous face and prestige and key international support from the Organization of African Unity (OAU). At the conclusion of 1970, the UPA/FNLA had approximately 6,000 men isolated in the north of Angola in the nearly impenetrable Dembos forest region, of whom only about 2,000 were armed.[20] The northeastern and eastern groups had ceased to exist as effective fighting forces.

UNITA also entered the fray, as previously described in Chapter 1. Savimbi's first attack occurred in December 1966 on the post of Cassamba. He made another two weeks later on Christmas Eve, when 500 UNITA insurgents attacked the Portuguese garrison of Teixeira de Sousa and suffered a disastrous defeat with 234 dead. UNITA was soon alienated from its vital Zambian support, as Portugal struck at the fragile Zambian treasury by closing the railway to Zairian copper exports for one week. Again in April 1967, there were two UNITA acts of sabotage on the CFB infrastructure, and again Portugal closed the railway and threatened lengthier closures unless attacks ceased. Thereafter UNITA was unwelcome in Zambia, and the MPLA likewise was put on notice not to interfere with the CFB. Savimbi was forced by circumstances into an improbable posture, claiming that a true nationalist movement should operate from bases within Angola. Perhaps this was a necessary policy, as in July 1967 he was finally and completely expelled from Zambia. Certainly the implementation of such a policy ensured his isolation. By 1969, UNITA was surrounded, and Savimbi counted fewer than 1,500 followers. In order to survive in defeat, he and his men came to an accommodation with the Portuguese, and between 1971 and 1973 UNITA activities were restricted to a prescribed zone at the headwaters of the Lungué-Bungo, and it agreed to cease operations against the Portuguese.[21] As part of this understanding, UNITA would receive arms and medical support and would be free to engage the MPLA.[22] By this time Savimbi had a force of about 500, of whom 250 were armed.[23]

In contrast, the army in the Eastern Military Zone in 1968 had 55 infantry companies, two companies of commandos, two squadrons of cavalry, an artillery battery of 88mm field guns, two engineering companies, and a construction company. There were also Auxiliary Forces consisting of three groups of *Fiéis* or "Faithful" (2,318 men), 71 groups of *Grupos Especiais* or Special Groups (2,279 men), one group of *Leais* or "Loyals" (128 men), 31 groups of *Flechas* or "Arrows" (1,665 men), and various armed militias (5,331 men), a total of 11,721 additional men over the approximately 7,500 regular forces.[24] Further there were approximately 1,200 air force personnel and perhaps 300 naval personnel, bringing the total number of Portuguese forces to about 20,700.[25] This number yields a ratio of 3.2 to 1 over the insurgent aggregate of 6,350 men. While comparable ratios of other counterinsurgencies were higher, such as, Malaya at 37.5 to 1, Cyprus at 25 to 1, Algeria at 16.7 to 1, Kenya at 4.6 to 1, Vietnam in 1964 at 4.1 to 1, and Vietnam in 1968 at 8.75 to 1, isolation of the insurgents in a sparsely inhabited and barren region belied the apparent weakness of this Portuguese ratio.[26]

Action-Counteraction

The strategy of the nationalist movements was to seek independence for Angola through armed conflict rather than negotiation, although the UNITA strategy was less clear. Accordingly the MPLA from its Zambian bases planned a two-pronged assault. The southern one would be mounted from Mungu, Shangombe, and Sikongo and known as the Route of the Cuando. It would follow this river valley westward with the plan of reaching the populated and wealthy district of Bié and the Central Plain of Huambo, the heart of Angola. From this point the insurgents hoped to control the entire country and to reach all the way to Malange through an axis of advance along the Cuanza River valley.[27]

The northern one was called the Route of the Luena, or the "Agostinho Neto Route" by the MPLA, and was to be launched from Chipango and Cassamba and aimed along this river directly at Luso and from there to the highland plain of Malange. The hope was to gain control of the Luanda-Malange railway, reach Luanda, and link with forces coming from the north.[28]

Campaign plans for the UPA/FNLA are much less distinct. Its plan can be imputed from the attempt in 1970 to infiltrate three battalions in the north with the goal of controlling the rich, coffee-growing region north of the Luanda-Malange railway and paralyzing the Angolan economy, an objective that failed in 1961. This offensive action would bring its forces to the gates of Luanda and precipitate a sudden conclusion to the conflict. The offensive was abandoned in September 1972, because it was isolated logistically deep in Portuguese territory, besieged by both the MPLA and the Portuguese, and thus stood little chance of success.

UNITA simply intended to establish a base deep in the interior of Angola, and using some notion of the *tâche d'huile* theory of expanding control, mobilize an ever increasing number of the population to gain the "total independence of Angola."

There were substantial weaknesses in the campaign design of all three in that their lines of communication would be long and vulnerable, or in the case of UNITA, non-existent. The goals of each would rely increasingly on the weak strategy of hope, as each moved further and further from its external support and progressively isolated itself deep in the hostile interior of Angola.

If these organizations were going to rely on classic proselytizing of the population for support, then it would not come willingly. The Angolan people were experiencing new political and economic freedoms and financial prosperity and would hardly welcome what would be tantamount to Napoleonic-type foraging by foreign armies. Then too, the basic premise of all three insurgencies had been removed with successful responses to the people's grievances. Nationalism for the sake of nationalism and the political goal of a single party state running a country for the benefit of its oligarchy or chief-of-state held little popular appeal. Lastly the greatest enemies of the insurgents were each other, as all three were in competition for the spoils to be mined from governing Angola. There was no thought of a coalition government for the greater good of the diverse population.

In countering this multi-axis assault, the Portuguese were quick to see that UNITA and the UPA/FNLA would be easily contained and that the MPLA represented the real threat. They thus developed a three-phase theater strategy of first checking the expansion of the insurgent penetration. This would mean defining the population battlefield and bringing security to those threatened. Next, the security forces would surround the insurgents and limit them to a geographic area bounded by the Cuito, Cuanza, Munhango, and Cassai Rivers. This was admittedly a substantial tract, but it was thinly populated by any standard and would provide little sustenance. The insurgents could thus do little damage in this isolation and would indeed slowly starve. Within it Portuguese security forces would relentlessly pursue the enemy, who would become increasingly harried and besieged. Finally in 1973 and 1974, as the cordon drew increasingly tight, the enemy would be completely destroyed.[29]

The need for this lengthy approach was prompted by a number of factors. First, Portugal had limited manpower to police the vast region of the east. This limitation dictated an approach that enlisted the sparse terrain, geographic remoteness, and harsh climate as allies in isolating the insurgents in an attritional war. Second, these three regional characteristics appeared to favor the insurgent in that he could easily hide or move largely unhindered by Portuguese forces. Consequently, with a containment strategy in which Portuguese forces would define and then gradually reduce the area of insurgent contamination, the enemy would be forced to fight from a progressively reduced and isolated position and be ultimately destroyed. The few local people living in the east and southeast could hardly subsist themselves, much less support the insurgents with food, recruits, intelligence, and shelter. In summary, Portuguese theater strategy was based on sound reasoning following a considered appraisal of opponent strengths, battlefield terrain, and resident population.

Conversely, the several insurgent organizations based their strategies on the hope that the population would welcome them or acquiesce and that Portuguese forces could be overcome. This approach required a leap of faith from a population experiencing unprecedented material gains, an unlikely event. While the insurgents were skilled fighters, they chose a battlefield in which Portuguese mobility could easily outflank and reduce their foot soldiers over time in what would become a universally hostile environment. Lastly, the Portuguese strategy was designed to wear the enemy both psychologically and physically and to reinforce the notion in his mind of the substantial cost in treasure, time, and lives without commensurate gain. Ultimately, at the national level it was aimed at convincing Portuguese adversaries that their political objective was neither attainable or nor worth the apparent cost.

Naval Force Projection

The Portuguese Navy enjoyed a rich heritage in the skills of exploration, mapmaking, population support, development, and combat in the east of Angola. Such household names as Hermenegildo de Brito Capelo, Roberto Ivens, Carlos Viegas Gago Coutinho, and numerous others led an illustrious parade of Portuguese naval activity in this area. In 1956 after an absence of some 40 years, the navy returned in the form of the Angola River Brigade (*Brigada dos Rios de Angola*) and began an hydrographic survey of the south and southeast of Angola. Over the next four years the Brigade produced some 38 hydrographic charts. This survey guided the construction of airfield and riverine infrastructure on the Cubango to support air operations and a river transport service of two tugboats, and four cargo and two passenger barges. The service was inaugurated on 24 October 1960 and proved a great boon to the local population that lived along the river.[30]

While the navy had earlier augmented its presence on the disparate waters of the Cuanza on the Atlantic, the Zaire in the north, and on the Chiloango and Lake Massábi in Cabinda, it was now called to support and help secure the population of the south, southeast, and east. To this end it established a presence at four sites on key rivers: Lungué-Bungo on the river of the same name, Chilombo and Lumbala on the Zambezi, Rivungo on the Cuando, and Vila Nova da Armada at the confluences of the Cuito, Longa and Cato Rivers. This naval augmentation of the east was facilitated by the closing of certain posts on the Zaire and the consequent consolidation, reduction, and transfer of forces.

As in Mozambique, the move inland by the navy was made through a combination of water, rail, and road transportation. The easiest vessels to move, and thus the easiest

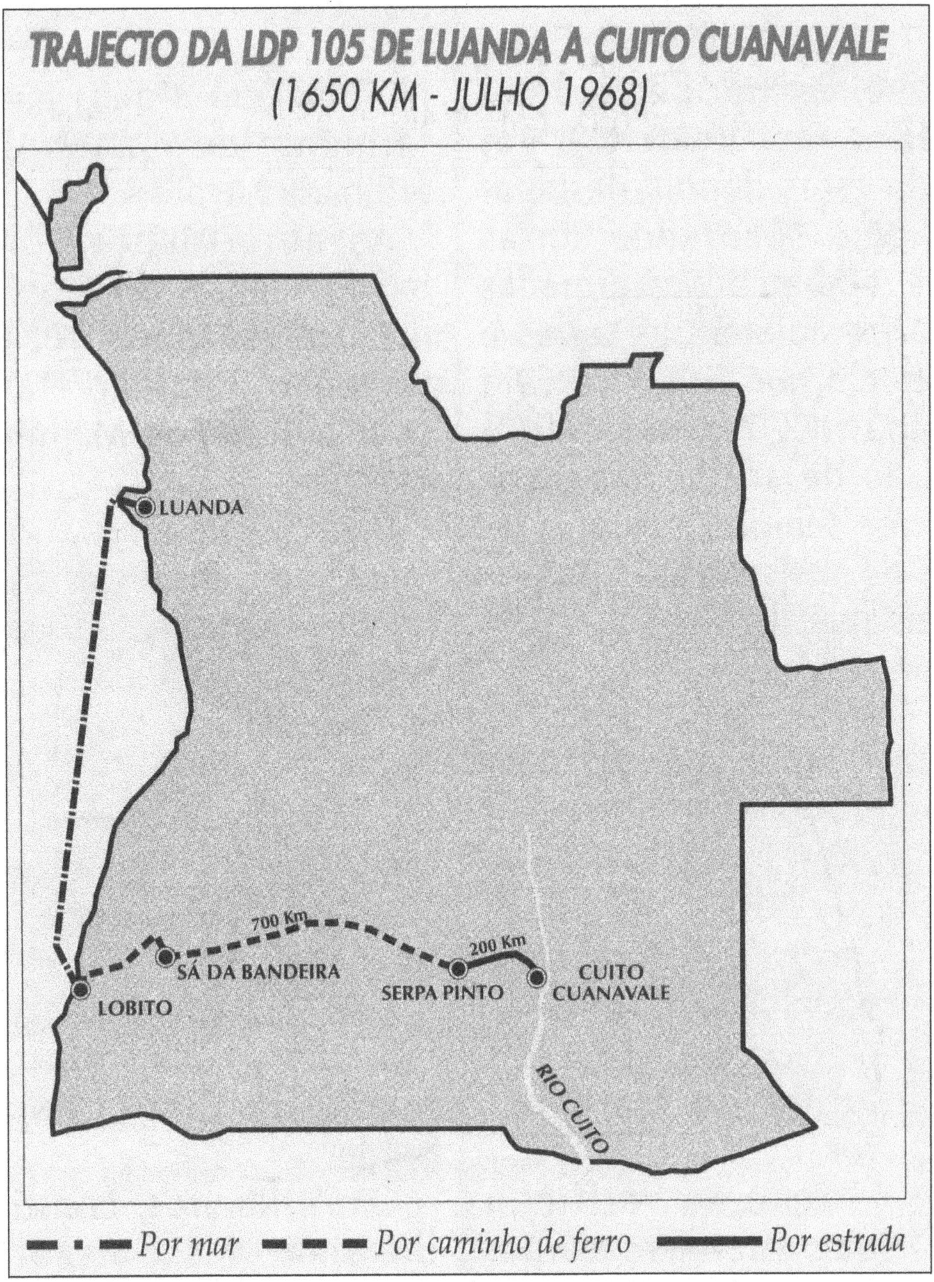

Routes of LDPs 105, 208, and 210. Maps courtesy of António Emílio Ferraz Sacchetti, "A Armada nas Campanhas de África" [The Navy in the African Campaigns], *Revista da Armada* (June 1997)

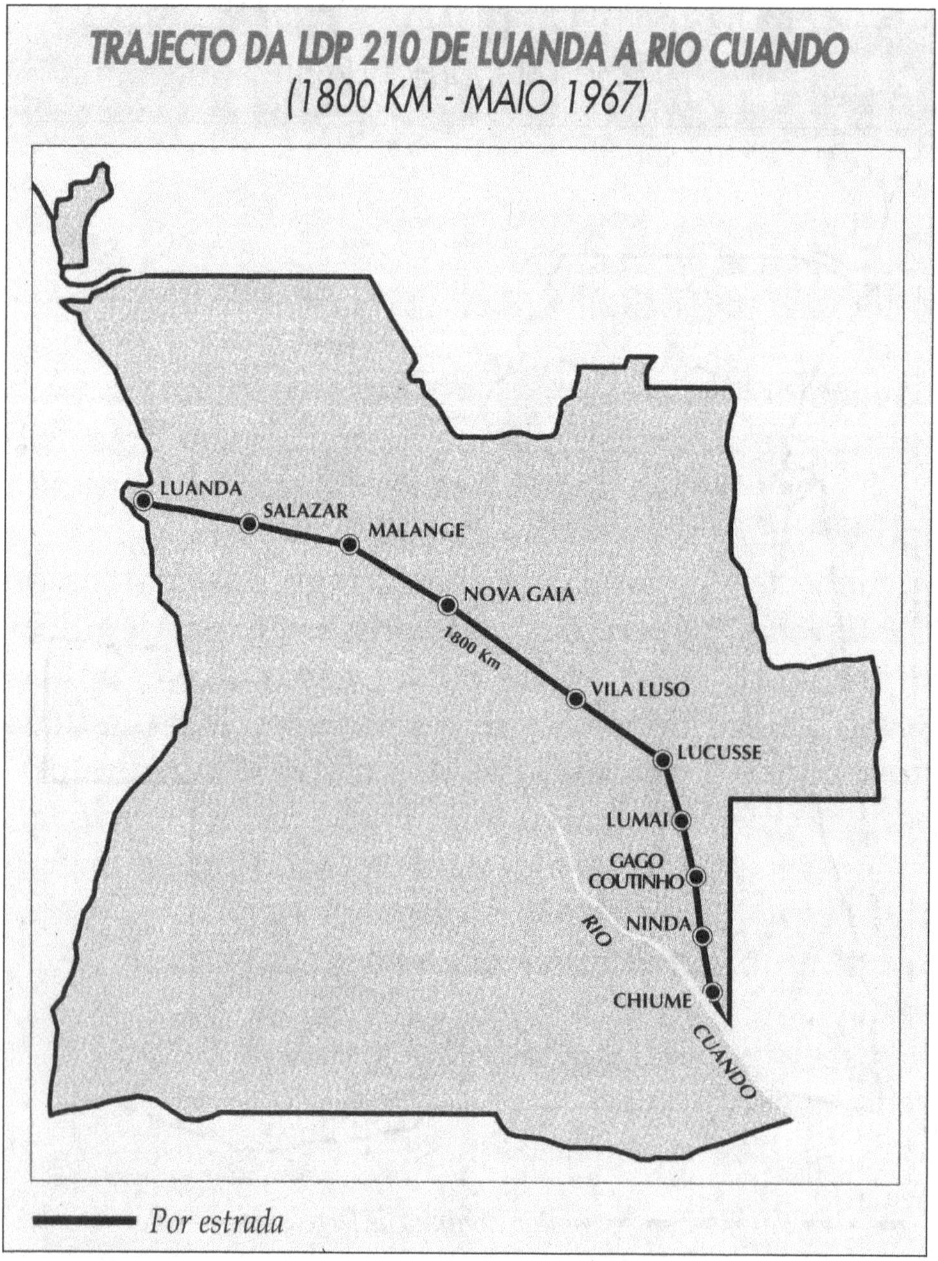

Maps courtesy of António Emílio Ferraz Sacchetti, "A Armada nas Campanhas de África" [The Navy in the African Campaigns], *Revista da Armada* (June 1997).

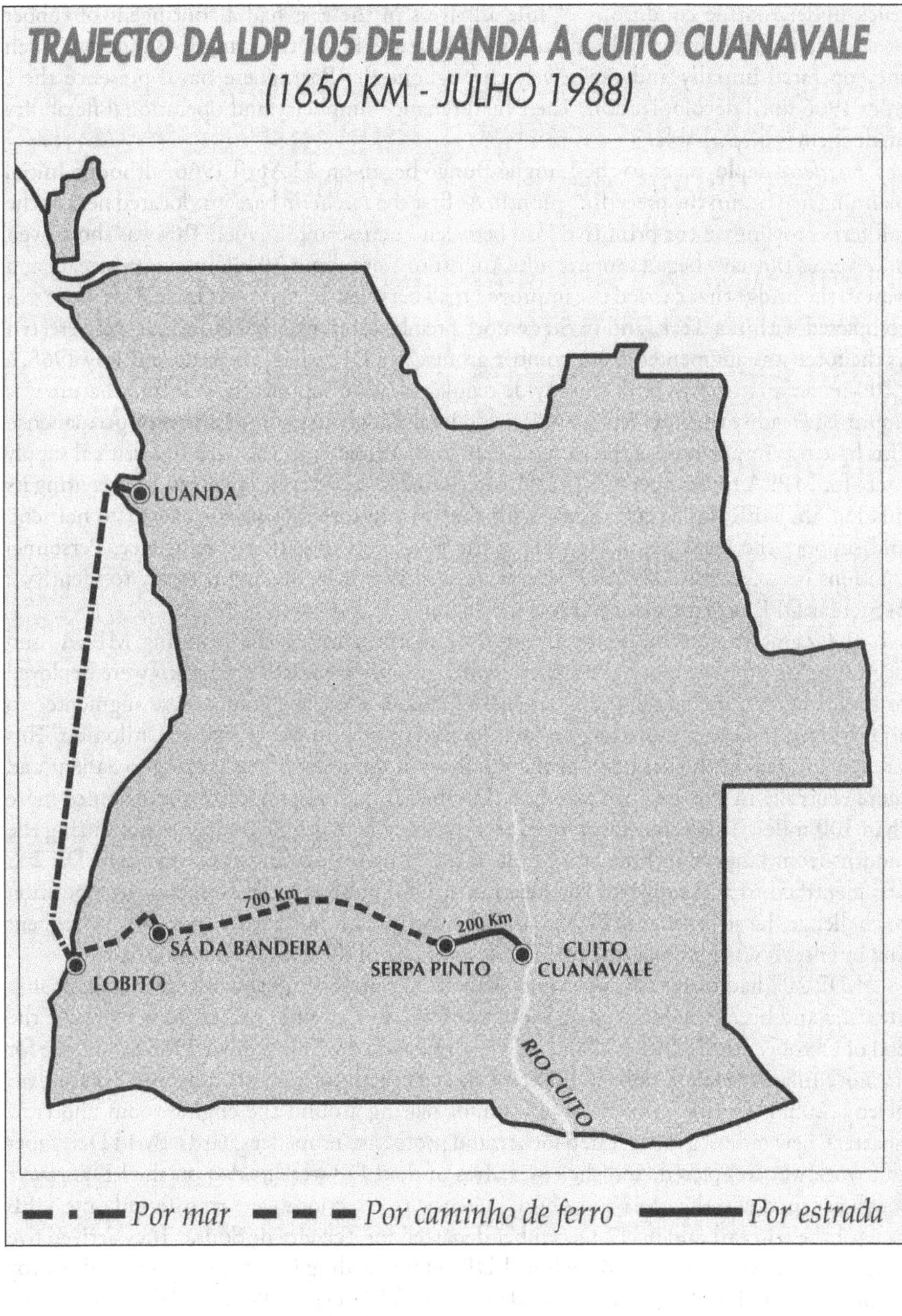
TRAJECTO DA LDP 105 DE LUANDA A CUITO CUANAVALE
(1650 KM - JULHO 1968)
LUANDA
LOBITO
SÁ DA BANDEIRA
700 Km
200 Km
SERPA PINTO
CUITO
CUANAVALE
RIO CUITO
Por mar
Por caminho de ferro
Por estrada

projection of presence and to some degree power, were the proven rubber boats. These could be airlifted together with their crews for an immediate response or transported by rail or truck under routine conditions. While all rivers in the east had a contingent of rubber boats because of their versatile and utilitarian nature, it was the Lungué-Bungo on which they operated initially and exclusively throughout the Portuguese naval presence there from 1966 until decolonization. Their maintenance simplicity and operational flexibility made them indispensable.

Fuzileiro deployment to the Lungué-Bungo began on 22 April 1966, although initial planning had begun the preceding month. At first the *Fuzileiro* base was located next to the raft ferry crossing on the primitive road between Lucusse and Luvuei. This was short-lived, however, as the navy began moving it in August to a site about 30 kilometers upstream and west to the bridge that carried the improved road between Lucusse and Luzi. This move was completed within a week, and in September prefabricated wooden buildings were erected, as the force was augmented from combat groups to a DFE. Later in June and July 1968, a 1,100-meter airstrip was built to provide regular aviation support. Base infrastructure was improved steadily through March 1971, and increasingly it assumed an air of permanence. This base was important, as the Lungué-Bungo was directly in the path of a critical supply route for MPLA forces operating in the interior near the river headwaters. In executing its mission, the DFE was to coordinate with the army in interdicting the enemy, to befriend and support the local population along the river, and to gather intelligence. Personnel rotations between this and other sites were such that it is not useful to try to identify a particular DFE as being deployed to a specific site.

The Zambezi was the easternmost river in the path of the invading MPLA, and beginning on 18 November 1966 two combat groups of *Fuzileiros especiais* were deployed to Lumbala with their rubber boats. On 14 October 1967, the groups were augmented to a DFE-sized force and moved again 30 kilometers north to the village of Chilombo. This site was located on the left bank of the Zambezi in the heart of the Cazombo Salient and more centrally in the area of Cazombo, Lumbala, and Caripande, an extension of more than 100 miles. This extension proved to be navigable by LDP-sized launches during the months from January to June as a result of the rainy season, and consequently LDP 208 was identified to add support. The location at Chilombo put the *Fuzileiros* in a position to challenge the advancing MPLA columns directly, and thus enemy contact was frequent and intense. It was here that the one *Fuzileiro* officer in the entire war was killed.

LDP 208 had originally arrived in Angola on 3 June 1966 aboard the merchant ship *Arraiolos* and been disembarked at Santo António do Zaire to operate from there. At the end of October, it was detached and arrived in Luanda on 7 November 1966 to prepare for its move inland to the Zambezi. First, it was cut in half for ease of transport. Next it was given a 20mm Oerlikon machinegun, armor plating around the engine room and crew quarters, new radios, a refrigerated locker, and protective propeller guards. By 14 December this work was completed, and the two halves of the LDP were loaded on the LDG *Aríete* for their trip down the coast to Lobito. Here the two sections were transferred onto CFB cars for the trip east and on 17 December departed for Teixeira de Sousa. They arrived five days later and were joined into a whole LDP before heading into the bush. A road convoy shepherded it to Lumbala, where it was launched on 1 January 1967. It had traveled with its crew some 2,454 kilometers, 352 under its own power on the first leg to Luanda, 430 on the *Aríete*, 1,331 on the CFB, and 341 by road convoy.[31]

It was during the time when the launch was being transferred from the rail cars to the flatbed trailers of the road convoy and its sections being rejoined that UNITA chose to attack Teixeira de Sousa. Two days after UNITA was repulsed, a combat group from DFE 2 moved from Lumbala to Cazumbo to intercept the convoy and escort it to the launching site and base in Lumbala. The group was ambushed by the enemy en route and two *Fuzileiros* were wounded gravely and nine lightly. Except for a broken axel on one of the vehicles near Chilombo, the convoy arrived at Lumbala without further incident.[32]

From 5 January LDP 208 was used to patrol the Zambezi River between Cazumbo and Caripande. Eight days after commencing patrol operations, the launch and its crew were attacked from the riverbank at the confluence of the Zambezi and Calupemba by seven enemy using automatic weapons. Of the thirteen *Fuzileiros* on the launch only one was lightly wounded. Five years would pass uneventfully before another incident, and in the meantime LDP 208 would perform its vital logistical support operations in an area bereft of roads.[33]

The cargo launch *Caripande* also operated along this section of the river performing parallel duties. It was a legacy of the defunct Angola River Brigade and had formerly operated on the Cuito. At the conclusion of Brigade duties, it was moved to Luanda in August 1967 and next loaded on the LDG *Ariete* for Lobito in October 1968. From there it traveled by rail and road to Chilombo and arrived on 3 November. This steel-hulled vessel was powered by twin engines and boasted an eight-meter cargo hold with a four-ton capacity. For unexplained reasons it did not enter service until 17 December 1969, but from that date it operated between Chilombo and Lumbala and normally resupplied troops at Caripande, when LDP 208 needed augmentation or was out of service.[34]

Additionally, the navy established a presence on the Cuando from 26 June 1967 with the arrival of LDP 210 in eastern Angola. It was based at the settlement of Rivungo on the right bank of the river, which defines the frontier with Zambia in that area, and was located in the vicinity of Neriquinha and Luiana in the extreme southeast. This small presence on the remote, complex, and lengthy river frontier proved difficult to support and presented a hardship on the small force of three sailors and five *Fuzileiros* who manned the launch. The force was designated as the River Cuando Naval Detachment (*Destacamento de Marinha do rio Cuando* or DESTACMAR-CUANDO).[35]

LDP 210 had arrived in Luanda on 30 January 1967 as deck cargo on the merchant vessel *Sofala*, and work began immediately to modify the launch for its inland mission. It was to be transported by road convoy the entire way and was thus loaded onto two tandem flatbed trailers so that it would straddle each. Half of its 16-ton weight would be supported by each trailer. The road convoy departed Luanda on 18 May and passed successfully through Salazar, Malange, Nova Gaia, Quitapa, Xassengue, Cacola, Luso, Luatama, and Lucusse. The convoy was forced to stop between Luvuci and Lumeci for 17 days to repair a broken vehicle; however, the procession continued to Gago Coutinho, Ninda, Chiume, and the River Cuando, where it arrived on 26 June having traveled some 1,800 kilometers. On 29 June, it was launched at Txicove, near Tchia, and about 9 kilometers southwest of Chiume, and began its patrolling duties within five hours.[36] Its presence was immediately challenged, as the following day it was attacked from the right bank near the island of Cambe with automatic weapons fire and hand grenades from an enemy patrol of eight men. The attack was without consequence.[37] Over the next 40 days the launch patrolled about 1,500 miles of river and made a complete reconnaissance of the Cuando from Chiume to Kongola. From this groundwork were developed the ideal profile of a patrol and the procedures to be followed to secure the river, its islands, and banks, and to achieve the most efficient logistic and military operations in the area.[38] In February and March 1969, a small supporting airstrip was constructed and later replaced with a more capable field in July 1970. The Rivungo base facilities were electrified in February and March 1970 and permanent lodging and offices were built by December. In March 1971 storehouses and a magazine were completed.[39]

There was little navigational information on the Cuando, and thus patrols were based largely on aerial reconnaissance photographs. There were no charts or reliable maps of the area, and indeed it was a largely unknown region. The river had never been navigated by anything other than a canoe, and apparently no white man had been much seen in the area since Serpa Pinto had conducted his expeditions to the Zambezi basin in 1869 and 1877. The river current was only 2 to 3 knots, but the river itself wound its way through many meanders and switchbacks with their myriad branches. This sinuous characteristic made patrolling a long and tedious process. The length of a patrol between the Caprivi Strip and the upper reaches of the Cuando was some 940 miles round trip because of the wandering nature of the river and took between 12 and 13 days depending on what was encountered. A patrol required about 135 hours of navigation, but it could only be done in the daylight, and air support in the form of a T-6 *Harvard* from Gago Coutinho was indispensable. Fuel and supplies were difficult to obtain in such remoteness, where there was a single army post and no other government presence. This meager logistic support was supplemented by hunting, as the area was full of game. The MPLA was supposed to be in the area, as this river was its Route of the Cuando, which was mounted from Shangombe and Sikongo just across the river frontier; however, the insurgents were not seen often. When they were encountered, the crew responded with heavy fire, and the insurgents vanished.[40]

On 23 July 1969, there was an incident in which the launch was attacked from the high grass opposite Mungulhi with machinegun fire, which was returned by fire from the Oerlikon and two MG-42s. The launch maneuvered for two hours to fix the enemy and hold him in place until air support could arrive. The intimidating effect of the heavy Oerlikon kept the enemy at bay, and while his casualties were unknown, the superior firepower of the launch over that of the insurgents was an effective deterrent. From the point of view of the insurgents, the river patrol was to be avoided as a needless impediment, for their primary target was the population further inland to the northwest. Small groups of insurgents traveling light would be little match for a heavily armed force and would be relying on the vastness of the *Terras do Fim do Mundo* to hide and avoid Portuguese land and naval patrols during their transit.

Vila Nova da Armada, the most important of the eastern river posts, was established on the Cuito River on 31 July 1968, when LDP 105 arrived. The Cuito was navigable from Cuito Cuanavale as far as Quedas da M'Pupa, the dramatic rapids some 400 miles downstream past Riabela, Vila Nova da Armada, Rito, and Maue or Mané.[41] The site of Vila Nova da Armada was in the district of Cuando-Cubango on the right bank of the river and between the confluences of the Cuito and the Longa to the north and the Cuito and the Cato to the south. Cuito-Cuanavale, Baixo-Longa, Longa, and the more distant Serpa Pinto were neighboring towns. By that December the base had a platoon of *Fuzileiros Especiais*, and by March 1969, a company of *Fuzileiros Navais* (CF 3). The construction of permanent buildings was begun in February 1969 and concluded in December 1970. Included in these improvements were electrification, a 2,200-meter airfield, supply warehouses, magazines, repair shops, messing facilities, and living quarters.[42]

Assembly of the necessary launches at the new base was fairly straightforward, despite its being considerably inland and remote. LDP 105 had an uncomplicated trip in that it had left Luanda on 17 July 1968 on board the LDG *Aríete* for Moçamedes, and once there, was transferred to the Moçamedes Railway for its trip to Serpa Pinto. Here it was loaded onto flatbed wagons, moved from Serpa Pinto to Cuito Cuanavale, and launched into the river on 31 July. Transfer was uneventful, and the launch together with its accompanying crew became the Naval Detachment Cuito (*Destacamento de Marinha do rio Cuito* or DESTACMARCUITO).[43] On 11 December 1968, LDP 105 was joined by the locally manufactured transport launch *Cuito* with an 18-ton capacity, and on 31 August 1970, by another such launch *Longa* with a 10-ton capacity. The former was made in the Sorefame Shipyards (*Estaleiros da Sorefame*) in Lobito and transferred in six pieces by a combination of rail and road to be assembled and launched at Cuito Cuanavale. The latter was formerly known as the *Expresso de Xicove*, as it had been used as a ferry on the Cuando between Xiungue and Chicove. The primary duty of LDP 105, the *Cuito*, and later the *Longa* was logistical transport to support the maneuver of land forces against the enemy, although as we shall see, they were successful in their other assignments too.

On 8 October 1970, His Excellency Professor Joaquim Moreira da Silva Cunha, Minister of the *Ultramar*, along with a number of other dignitaries, presided over the inauguration of Vila Nova da Armada. In a singularly solemn ceremony, military honors were rendered, the national flag was raised, speeches were delivered, and troops were reviewed in a parade.

CF 3, which was supported by the three launches, serves as an example of what could be accomplished in the *Terras do Fim do Mundo*. In 1973, CF 3 consisted of 6 officers, 15 sergeants, and 31 *Fuzileiros*, and these were divided into three platoons. The unit was responsible for an immense area of 37,000 square kilometers, which was greater than the Alentejo region of the *metrópole*. The normal *Fuzileiro* assignment was the routine patrol of the river and its tributaries in the ubiquitous rubber boats, but in 1973, the year that the campaign in the east was effectively concluded, there were some 19 actions and operations, or about one every 19 days.[44] During these 19 events the *Fuzileiros* accounted for 50 enemy dead and the destruction of four encampments.[45] In an operating area of this magnitude, finding four enemy camps was a noteworthy feat in itself. Probably the most important accomplishment of CF 3, however, was within its own backyard, where it established a school for the neighboring population, assisted in the improvement of local hygiene and sanitation practices, ran a transportation system along the river, and assisted in the construction of nearby houses and villages.[46]

By 1970 there were bases on five of the rivers in Angola, and this presence was maintained until decolonization, although by 1973 the several insurgent organizations had ceased to exist as effective fighting forces. While the disposition on the Zaire was judged the most important, the naval presence on the inland rivers was similarly critical, because it served not only to counter insurgent infiltration from the sanctuaries of Zaire and Zambia but moreover to support the population and policing of UNITA activity. These modern-day naval personnel were in their own way an extension of the luminaries who centuries earlier had gone into the unknown depths of Angola not only as explorers but also as agents in bringing improvements to the lives of those whom they met. This tradition of humaneness was without doubt the greatest legacy that the Portuguese Navy left in the east of Angola.

Notes

1 Abílio Freire da Cruz Júnior, "Evolução das Infra-estructuras da Armada no Ultramar" [Evolution of Naval Infrastructure in the *Ultramar*], in the unpublished collection *Participação da Armada na Defesa das Províncias Ultramarinas* [Participation of the Navy in the Defense of the Overseas Provinces], TMs [photocopy], 1972, 17.

2 A. Pimentel Saraiva, "Postais do Ultramar: Angola – Postal Nº 2, Luanda, Zaire, Cabinda e Leste de Angola" [Overseas Postcards: Angola – Postcard Nº 2, Luanda, Zaire, Cabinda and the East of Angola], *Anais do Clube Militar Naval* (April/June 1968), 312.

3 Manuel Pinto Machado, "Postais do Ultramar: Angola – Postal Nº 3, Lungué-Bungo fins do octobro 68" [Overseas Postcards: Angola – Postcard Nº 3, Lungué-Bungo End of October '68], *Anais do Clube Militar Naval* (October/December 1968), 695–696.

4 Ibid.

5 Ibid.

6 Ibid.

7 Chanda Chisala, http://www.zambia.co.zm/articles/kaunda.html, accessed 1 February 2007.

8 Martin Meredith, *The Fate of Africa* (New York: Public Affairs, 2005), 381.

9 Ibid., 380.

10 Annual Zambian copper production fell from a peak of 700,000 tons in 1969 to fewer than 300,000 in 1995. During the years of Kaunda oversight, cash was drained from mining to fund other discretionary programs to the point that routine equipment maintenance and replacement were almost entirely foregone. Today huge investments are needed to replace outdated machinery and import technology to regain competitiveness. It has been estimated, for instance, that the Nchanga open-pit mine, the country's most productive, needs $150 million in new equipment. At present, cash flow is so anemic that the Zambia Consolidated Copper Mines, the government mining entity, cannot buy a simple gravel crusher to harden the pit roads during the rainy season. On the other hand, a tour 3,000 feet down into the Konkola mine shows the huge potential, and huge potential costs, that investors face. It is a vast formation that has 3.8 percent copper ore, about three times as rich as many mines in the Americas and big enough to last 100 years. Countering this potential is the cost of digging, which has been estimated at $600 million. Despite these problems, mining giants, such as the South African Anglovaal and the American Phelps Dodge were showing interest in 1996 with the accelerating improvement in world copper demand and the consequent high prices. By 2003, however, credentialed investors, such as AngloAmerican, had abandoned their investments as unattractive because of unforeseen capital requirements to modernize the operation as well as other local problems. For instance, electricity and fuel costs were uneconomically high, and the needed work permits to import the required technical experience were not forthcoming. As the major, recognized companies with mining pedigrees withdrew or avoided further involvement in Zambia, they were replaced with relative unknowns with uncertain mining credentials. This development led to further reversals in Zambian mining. Lastly, while the government wishes to privatize its mines and add funds to its coffers, it still wishes to dictate beyond any reasonable level how private commercial firms will run their extraction businesses in Zambia.

11 Melvin Durai, http://www.melvindurai.com/kaunda.htm, accessed 1 February 2007.

12 Robert Guest, *The Shackled Continent: Power, Corruption, and African Lives* (Washington: Smithsonian Books, 2004), 152.

13 Ibid., 153.

14 Dalila Cabrita Mateus, *A PIDE/DGS na Guerra Colonial 1961–1974* [The PIDE/DGS in the Colonial

War 1961–1974] (Lisbon: Terramar, 2004), 283.

15 António Pires Nunes, *Angola 1966–1974, Vitória Militar no Leste* [Angola 1966–1974, Military Victory in the East] (Lisbon: Prefácio, 2002), 21.

16 Ibid., 6.

17 Ibid., 24.

18 Ibid., 25

19 Ibid.

20 Ibid., 25.

21 Adelino Gomes, "Exército e UNITA Colaboraram antes de 74" [Army and UNITA Collaborate before 74], *Público* (19 December 1995), 2-4.

22 Cabrita Mateus, 199–207.

23 António Pires Nunes, 19.

24 Ibid., inside front cover; and João Paulo Borges Coelho, "African Troops in the Portuguese Colonial Army, 1961–1974: Angola, Guinea-Bissau and Mozambique," *Portuguese Studies Review* (Spring-Summer 2002), 129–150.

25 Ibid., 67.

26 John P. Cann, *Contra-Subversão em África* [Counterinsurgency in Africa] (Lisbon: Prefácio, 2005), 30.

27 António Pires Nunes, 40.

28 Ibid.

29 Ibid., 42.

30 José da Cruz Moura da Fonseca, "A Marinha no Leste e no Sueste de Angola" [The Navy in the East and Southeast of Angola], *Anais do Clube Militar Naval* (October-December 1981), 619–629.

31 António Emílio Ferraz Sacchetti, "A Armada nas Campanhas de África" [The Navy in the African Campaigns], *Revista da Armada* (June 1997), 7.

32 José Alberto Lopes Carvalheira, "Acção da Marinha em Águas Interiores (1961–1971) " [Naval Operations in Inland Waters (1961–1971)], in the unpublished collection *Participação da Armada na Defesa das Províncias Ultramarinas* [Participation of the Navy in the Defense of the Overseas Provinces], TMs [photocopy], 1972, 32.

33 Ibid.

34 Ibid., 33.

35 Ibid.

36 António Luís Marinho de Castro, interview by the author, 30 January 2003, Lisbon. *Segundo tenente (Fuzileiro)* Marinho de Castro was graduated in April 1966 in the 8th CEORN.

37 Lopes Carvalheira, 33.

38 Ibid.

39 Cruz Júnior, 19.

40 Marinho de Castro interview.

41 Lopes Carvalheira, 34

42 Cruz Júnior, 19–20.

43 Lopes Carvalheira, 34.

44 António José Telo, *História da Marinha Portuguesa: Homens, Doutrinas e Organização, 1824–1974* (Tomo I) [History of the Portuguese Navy: Men, Doctrine and Organization, 1824–1974 (Volume I)] (Lisbon: Academia de Marinha, 1999), 605. The difference between an action and an operation was that an action used two or less combat groups, while an operation used more than two.

45 Ibid.

46 Ibid.

8

Operation *Mar Verde*, the Strike on Conakry

On 22 November 1970, the imprisoned Portuguese aviator António Lobato received his passport to freedom. In the early hours of the morning he became aware of sporadic gunfire nearing his prison, *La Montaigne* in Conakry, and thought initially that there was a coup d'état in progress against the autocratic president of the Republic of Guinée, Ahmed Sékou Touré. It soon became apparent that shots were being exchanged with the prison guards. After several resounding explosions and over the continued crackle of small arms fire, a voice suddenly shouted, "Lobato! It is us."[1] The door of the cell swung open minutes later, and Portuguese troops guided him to freedom. By 0430 hours that morning he was delivered on board the Portuguese patrol boat LFG *Dragão* (P 374) in Conakry harbor. He shifted to the task force flagship LFG *Orion* (P 362) shortly thereafter, and received a warm welcome from the operational commander, *Comandante* Alpoim Calvão. The task force got underway at 0900 on a northerly course and arrived the next afternoon at the island of Soga in the Bijagós Islets of Portuguese Guiné. Instead of sleeping that evening, Major Lobato partied all night in celebration of his first day of freedom in seven and a half years and his return to Portuguese soil.[2] For Lobato and his twenty-five fellow prisoners, the strike on Conakry was an unqualified success. Unfortunately, not everyone was to agree.

By late 1967 the campaign in Guiné was not going well, and in fact, as the junior lieutenant (*primeiro tenente*) Alexandre Carvalho Neto, the military assistant to Spínola, would write, "The situation was absolutely catastrophic, on the brink of collapse. Bissau had become practically surrounded."[3] The President of the Republic, Admiral Américo Tomás, who visited Bissau in February 1968, returned to Lisbon to report to Salazar that "the war was held by a thread."[4]

Major General (*brigadeiro*) António de Spínola confirmed this observation with an inspection visit of his own and described the situation as "desperate."[5] He criticized *Brigadeiro* Arnaldo Schultz, the Governor-General and Commander-in-Chief, for not having an offensive aimed equally at the socio-economic and military problems and further accused the local military commanders of disguising the true state of affairs.[6]

Spínola, who habitually wore the traditional monocle of a cavalry officer, had a broad portfolio of experience on which to base his observations. His résumé included leading a volunteer force in the Spanish Civil War in 1938 and acting as an observer on the German eastern front opposite Leningrad in November 1941. In 1955 he was made a member of the Administrative Council of the steel concern Siderurgia Nacional in addition to his normal military duties and thus became a beneficiary of Salazar's strategy for managing his military through such appointments.[7] Military pay was poor, and to advance in pay and promotion, ambitious officers were often either removed from the immediate military environment or had their position enhanced by assigning them to lucrative and prestigious special positions.

Normally these were at high levels of government or industry in both the *metrópole* and the *ultramar*, and it was these postings, promotions, and pay that Salazar controlled. Spínola thus had Salazar's ear and confidence.

At age 51 as a lieutenant colonel, he had assumed command of Cavalry Battalion 345, and later in November 1961, departed for Luanda as part of the army reinforcement following the outbreak of violence in the north of Angola. In this assignment, he further burnished his reputation and gained the respect and loyalty of his officers and men by leading from the front and enduring the dangers and hardships that they suffered. Likewise, he won the admiration and affection of the local population and its leaders through his pacification efforts. He traveled widely in Angola during his assignment and departed in 1964, when his tour of duty was completed, to return to Lisbon and to senior staff duty. It was while in this assignment that he undertook his survey of Guiné and on his making his report remembered Salazar saying, "It is urgent that you leave for Guiné."[8]

Spínola assumed command in May 1968 as a newly-promoted *brigadeiro* and saw his first task as one of drastically reducing PAIGC military capability and thus tilting the balance of war in favor of Portugal.[9] He proceeded to implement an aggressive and imaginative offensive against the PAIGC. He sought both a political and military victory, and as part of the political dimension initiated a plan to win the population through a carefully orchestrated program of social and economic measures that lifted its standard of living. Education, health, infrastructure, animal husbandry, and agricultural cultivation were improved markedly under his comprehensive blueprint, "A Better Guiné."[10] These improvements were publicized and supported in a well-designed psychological operation to explain the changes and secure the backing of the people. The military dimension of this plan was the protection of the population from insurgent intimidation and the defeat and destruction of PAIGC armed capability. To this purpose the armed forces assumed an aggressive posture in its new modified organization that emphasized the recruiting of Africans and in its increased tempo of operations.[11]

Spínola believed that the widespread and thorough PAIGC intimidation of the population would force him to move quickly in implementing "A Better Guiné," or he would irretrievably lose the battle for its loyalty.[12] The rivers, which served as primary logistical lines of communication in Guiné and which were so important to the general's programs, had for four years been progressively challenged by the PAIGC. In the south of Guiné particularly, the four PAIGC supply bases across the frontier had played a pivotal role in this encroachment. During this time, the PAIGC had acquired four Soviet P-6 class fast patrol boats. These were very capable 66-ton craft armed with two 25mm antiaircraft guns and two torpedo tubes and could reach speeds in excess of 40 knots. This was in addition to an assorted collection of locally manufactured motor launches consisting of the *Arouca*, *Bandim*, *Bissau* and *Mirandela*. Further, the Republic of Guinée had similarly received three 75-ton *Komar* class fast patrol boats capable of speeds exceeding 40 knots. These were armed with two surface-to-surface missiles and two 25mm antiaircraft guns.[13] This sophisticated capability on the part of both the PAIGC and its host enabled the PAIGC to project power from Conakry to the depot of Kadigné on the island of Tristão and then to the Portuguese islands of Canefaque and Cambon.[14] From these islands a large fleet of canoes and modest numbers of small outboard motor boats consistently penetrated the waterways of southern Guiné largely unchallenged and effectively extended the PAIGC distribution system and consequent combat capability well into the interior. The south of Guiné was, as a consequence, thoroughly infiltrated by the PAIGC by 1969, and this dominance posed a most serious threat to Spínola's plans. Coincident with this development was the reassignment of Alpoim Calvão as the Chief of the Special Operations Department of the Commander-in-Chief. On reporting for duty, one of his initial questions concerned the fate of Lobato. Perhaps now was the time to craft a plan to free the prisoners held by Sékou Touré. Spínola was in accord with Alpoim Calvão on most issues, and two of these included mounting an aggressive challenge to the PAIGC use of the Portuguese waterways and retrieving Lobato and the additional prisoners captured over the intervening years. The first step was Spínola's authorization of two significant operations to contest and disrupt the intense PAIGC traffic, Operation *Nebulosa* (Nebulous) and Operation *Gata Brava* (Wildcat).

It must be said that following the suspension of operations along the Camexibó, Nhafuane, and Inxanche Rivers in June 1964, the PAIGC had moved quickly and steadily to fill the vacuum. The consequent result was that Portuguese land forces were increasingly facing a well-armed and supplied PAIGC. The volume of supplies and troops moving into Guiné virtually unchallenged created a difficult and obvious problem that Tomás and Spínola would recognize instantly on their 1968 visits. This identical situation occurred in the Mekong Delta of Vietnam during the same period when the communist forces transported foodstuffs, medical supplies, arms, ammunition, and to minimal degree men on its waterways.[15] Until the U.S. Navy mounted a coordinated and consistent challenge, this enemy line of communication wreaked havoc with land security forces in the south of Vietnam. The only solution in an undeveloped country, such as Guiné or Vietnam, where the waterways act as the primary means for moving heavy cargos of munitions and foodstuffs, is to maintain a constant presence on the rivers to prevent this vital enemy traffic. This had been done successfully on the Zaire against the MPLA and the UPA/FNLA with a constant naval presence and aggressive patrolling and could have been repeated on the Inxanche.

Nebulosa was conducted between 15 and 27 August 1969 and was intended to intercept and destroy the PAIGC boats and any other enemy craft and their crews in the waters of the Inxanche River, which marked the frontier with Guiné. In preparation for this mission, Alpoim Calvão began to form an intelligence picture, and in doing so, sought the counsel of the PIDE/DGS representative in Bissau, Inspector Alberto Matos Rodrigues. The inspector was holding in detention an older sailor named Abou Camará, who had served on PAIGC vessels, including the *Patrice Lumumba*, of which we shall hear more in a minute.[16] Following some encouragement and an offer of amnesty, the prisoner became cooperative and decided to collaborate completely. He revealed several helpful facts about PAIGC operations:

- PAIGC transit of the Inxanche was always conducted at high tide. This was done to avoid grounding vessels and leaving them stranded and vulnerable to discovery and destruction by the Portuguese.
- All of the boats in Kadigné worked for the PAIGC, so any boat exiting from the village would be an enemy one.
- All of the transiting enemy boats needed to use and violate Portuguese territorial waters for their work and would thus be fair game.[17]

Given these facts, Alpoim Calvão developed the following concept of operations. He would:

- Lay an ambush using *Fuzileiros* in rubber boats hidden along the Portuguese shore.
- Make the assault when the targeted enemy boat had clearly entered Portuguese territory and was fully committed to infiltrating Guiné, for if it were sunk during the operation, then its status could not be contested.
- Reduce the number of men employed on a mission to the absolute minimum required to overcome a vessel. This minimalist approach was designed to preserve operational security and to maintain as low a profile as possible so as not to alert enemy intelligence.
- Arrange communications support to overcome the poor signal propagation and thus command and control problems along the rivers in Guiné. This would be done through radio relay by an orbiting air force aircraft at an altitude high enough to avoid daylight visual detection. A second aircraft would remain on ground alert as a backup.

In the first days of August, the LFG *Sagitário* (P 1131), whose commanding officer would act as the overall commander of *Nebuloso*, conducted a night reconnaissance of the anticipated area of operations.[18] He took *Sagitário* to the vicinity and launched a rubber boat from it to explore the Inxanche riverbank. The small force made good use of the darkness, low tide, and frequent rain showers as cover for its successful and undetected reconnaissance. The conclusion was that the small mangrove island of Calebe was the ideal ambush site. This is one of those islands created from a seedling mangrove that at some point floated into a shallow, where it took root and began growing. In a year a mangrove can grow to a meter in height. In three years it will have produced prop roots, and in five a small mangrove island will be established, assuming no natural disasters. The prop roots produce an intricately woven and formidable web that continuously expands and becomes home to a plethora of crabs, snails, barnacles, mussels, and oysters. It is also the roosting and nesting site for heron, egrets, pelicans, and other waterfowl. It was within the shelter of this densely populated ecosystem that the *Fuzileiros* would hide.

Nebulosa began on the morning of 15 August 1969 with the launching of a task group composed of the *Sagitário,* commanded by Lieutenant (*capitão tenente*) Camacho de Campos, and an assault force composed of the junior lieutenant (*segundo tenente*) Alberto Rebordão de Brito, two sergeants, and 10 *Fuzileiros,* all led by Alpoim Calvão.[19] The force embarked on *Sagitário* and waited in secretive isolation at the island of João Vieira among the offshore Bijagós Islets for opportune sea conditions. On 20 August the *Sagitário* moved to the Samba buoy and attempted to disembark four rubber boats, but the sea was running at 1.5 to 2.0 meters and frustrated the attempts. The LFG consequently returned to João Vieira to repair some damage suffered, give the crew a rest from the bad weather, and wait patiently for an opening.[20]

Finally, on 24 August at 2300 the mission began again with a return to the Samba buoy and the launching of the four rubber boats. These were guided by the LFG radar for the three miles to the mouth of the Inxanche on a flood tide, and with their motors running in "quiet," continued by compass bearing and avoided the areas where it was impossible to navigate in the darkness without grounding. The small force reached its destination of

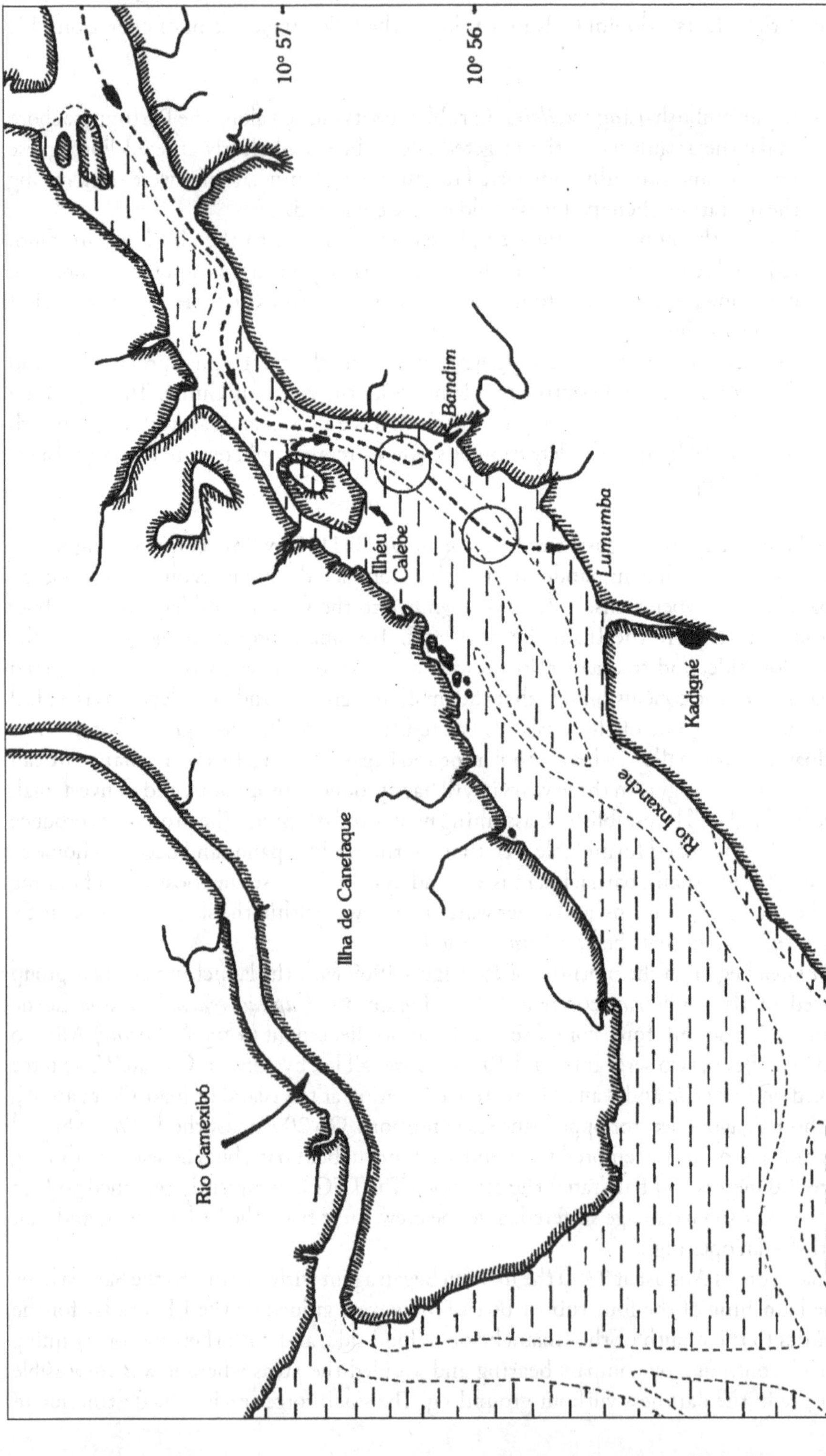

Inxanche River Showing *Bandim* and *Patrice Lumumba* Engagements. Map courtesy of Saturnino Monteiro, *Batalhas e Combates da Marinha Portuguesa*, Volume VIII, 1808–1975 (Lisbon: Livraria Sá da Costa Editora, 1997).

Calebe by 0300 on 25 August completely undetected.[21]

When the boats reached the island, which was covered with thick foliage and a confusing entanglement of mangrove trees and their tough prop roots, the *Fuzileiros* used a saw and machete to cut an opening through them and gain access to a narrow canal that would be their home for more than 54 hours. After backing the boats into the canal with their bows out, the entrance was camouflaged and closed with mangrove branches. The canal was so shallow that at low tide the boats could be completely grounded, particularly if the sea height was below normal. This was not anticipated to be a problem, as intelligence indicated the large PAIGC vessels came into the river only at high tide. As time passed, the strong rainshowers peculiar to the area resolved the drinking water problem and served to cover the noise of the outboard motors, all of which were tested routinely. During the rain the motors had to be covered, as the high humidity tended to make them unreliable. After the rain came the mosquitoes.[22] During the waiting period the *Fuzileiros* observed an intense amount of canoe traffic between the two sides of the river, principally at night. Indeed, the ambush cover was often brushed by these transiting craft, and their occupants felt wholly at home and chatted freely, oblivious to any danger. During the long and boring wait on 26 August, the *Fuzileiros* heard a motor boat from Kadigné pass very close in the dark but were not permitted to assault it amid great disappointment and much cursing.[23]

On 27 August towards 0930 as the sea was beginning to ebb, the *Fuzileiros* heard the muffled noise of a motor to the left of their position. All prepared for action, and as soon as the vessel was identified as being manned by the PAIGC and being in Portuguese territorial waters, the motors on the rubber boats were started for an attempted ambush. The interception began with a stern chase, as the long immobilization of the motors caused some to operate unevenly. Alpoin Calvão's boat took the lead and pulled even with the target, a vessel that sailed without a flag or other identification. When the *Fuzileiros* signaled for it to stop, it increased speed and veered toward the entrance canal to Kadigné. Alpoin Calvão's boat accelerated and drew to within five meters of the target, at which point he called in French and ordered it to stop. The response was some light arms fire, which was returned with a fusillade from the *Fuzileiros*.[24]

Alpoim Calvão's boat closed the gap, and the sailor Tristão flung himself at the vessel, scrambled aboard, and entered the lower deck, followed by his translator Abou Camará.[25] Meanwhile Alpoim Calvão boarded the upper deck and engaged in some hand-to-hand combat that was rapidly concluded with the arrival of the other three boats and their *Fuzileiros*. In the midst of the fray, a canister of tear gas was loosed, the helmsman of the vessel became incapacitated, and it went out of control. With its throttle wide open, it ran aground in the heavy growth lining the south bank of the river, and three or four men were tossed into the water. Petty Officer (*sargento*) André gained control of the helm, and Petty Officer (*cabo*) Abrantes Pinto, an experienced motorman mechanic, had no trouble with the engine. Between these two they refloated the vessel and set a course for the mouth of the Inxanche, all the while weeping from the effects of the gas.[26]

The vessel was identified as the *Patrice Lumumba* and carried 24 persons, who were made prisoners. It was also carrying several tons of provisions and a supply of weapons, mainly light arms. Among the passengers were three PAIGC officials, one of whom was section secretary for Kafarande. Unfortunately, he had been killed in the skirmish.

The vessel proceeded with *Fuzileiro* escort to a rendezvous with *Sagitário*, which attempted to take it in tow for a return to Bissau. Things did not go well, and despite the best efforts of the crew, the *Patrice Lumumba* was too damaged from its collision with the formidable mangroves and the exchange of fire to continue afloat. It sank in 12 meters of water while being towed across the mouth of the Cacine River.

It was some months before another such operation was mounted, as the PAIGC initially seemed to take a more cautious profile on the Inxanche following the loss of the *Patrice Lumumba*. Nevertheless, the insurgents soon recovered and moved again into the security vacuum left with the completion of *Nebulosa* and the lack of any continuous naval presence on the Inxanche to challenge them. The navy was to return on 6 March 1970, some seven months later with Operation *Gata Brava* (Wildcat). In the meantime, enemy logistic operations expanded dangerously with adverse consequences for Spínola's "A Better Guiné."

In the first days of February 1970, Spínola's staff received information that a PAIGC launch, possibly the *Bandim*, would be bringing an enemy element from Boké to Kadigné on or about the 25th of the month. Alpoim Calvão was given responsibility for planning an interception of the vessel and the capture of its personnel. Accordingly, he established an ambush with a team of eight *Fuzileiros* in two rubber boats at the entrance of the canal leading to Kadigné over the evening of the 24th and the dawn of the 25th. Unfortunately, the target did not arrive, and a thick fog developed that would have frustrated any action. Alpoim Calvão returned to other duties and was conducting operations on the Cacheu River near the northern border with Senegal, when new information indicated that the target had been delayed and would now arrive on 7 March. Alpoim Calvão had to move quickly to reestablish the operation. He met a handpicked and specially briefed team of *Fuzileiros* at Bigene, an unimproved airfield 40 miles north of Bissau, on the 5th at 1500, and within four hours all had returned to Bissau, were on board the LFG *Lira* (P 361), and underway. *Lira* arrived at its station next to the Samba buoy on the 6th in the early hours of the morning. Two rubber boats were put into the water, and eight *Fuzileiros* embarked. The first boat (Nº 1) was commanded by Alpoim Calvão, and the second (Nº 2) by the junior lieutenant (*segundo tenente*) Barbieri, and both departed *Lira* at 0300 for the mouth of the Inxanche. They were guided by its radar until contact was lost at a range of about 3,500 meters. After that, they followed the same route as in *Nebulosa* and proceeded slowly with the motors muffled to avoid detection. Guided only by compass and helped by a flood tide, the force found Calebe once more and backed the boats into the mangrove opening that had been made in August and that had remained undetected by the enemy. Indeed, there remained two sacks of combat rations left behind from *Nebulosa*.

By 0800 the sea began to ebb, and at 0810 the *Fuzileiros* contacted one of the two Aeritalia/Fiat G-91 *Gina* aircraft that were making a visual reconnaissance of the area and were informed that the *Bandim* was not in Kadigné. Alpoim Calvão resolved to wait until nightfall, and within two hours the tide had receded to the point that the two boats were grounded and immobilized. By 1600 the tide began to flood, to penetrate the channel, and to lift the boats, and by 1730 they were completely afloat. Towards 1800, as twilight came, the boats eased to the opening to be ready for action. After an hour, voices and the splash of paddles guiding a canoe were heard nearby. Minutes later at 1910, engine noise was heard coming from an upstream bearing of 070 degrees magnetic and increasing in intensity. Within twenty minutes, the unmistakable silhouette of the motor launch *Bandim* emerged from the dusk with only a dim, shielded wheelhouse light readily visible. Alpoim Calvão ordered the motors started and the boats readied to spring the ambush. When they rushed from their hiding place, boat № 1 took station astern of the target, and boat № 2, a position on its starboard amidships. Boat № 1 immediately fired a Bazooka at about 150 meters range, but it hit short of the target in the anxiety of the moment.[27] Meanwhile, the *Fuzileiros* opened fire with their MG-42 machinegun. The *Bandim* responded with light automatic weapons fire and turned sharply for the sanctuary on the Guinée side of the river. The boats maneuvered rapidly to maintain their attack positions, and on the third try the *Bazooka* rocket made solid contact with the *Bandim.*[28]

The *Fuzileiros* found themselves in the midst of a trigger-happy enemy. From a position east of the town of Kadigné, there was a near-constant fire from six antiaircraft batteries in the direction of the contact, but the aim was quite high. There were also about 20 rounds of either artillery or heavy mortar fire from the same area ranging either short or long and revealing considerable confusion in the enemy camp. Also from a PAIGC position on the Portuguese island of Canefaque a heavy machinegun fired wildly at the *Fuzileiros*, and its tracers lit the water. A PPSh-41 machinegun was fired over the boats from the earlier identified canoe as it fled the battle scene.[29]

The vicious running firefight with the *Bandim* continued with another Bazooka hit that disabled its steering and reduced it to circling. It ultimately entered a narrow estuary opposite Calebe, disappeared from view, and ran hard aground. The *Fuzileiros* pursued the *Bandim* into the firth, delivered another *Bazooka* hit, and when within 10 meters, unloosed a barrage of hand grenades. Enemy automatic weapons fire erupted from the mangroves and was returned with a blast of MG-42 fire by the *Fuzileiros* who were approaching the target.[30]

On boarding the *Bandim*, the *Fuzileiros* discovered six enemy dead. Of these, one was at the entrance to the engine room and another in the pilot house amid the destroyed engine telegraph. The *Fuzileiros* attempted to refloat the vessel, but the engine could not be reversed. The gear lever was blocked with debris from the damage, and a broken fuel line gushed gasoline everywhere. The engine was then stopped, and the *Fuzileiros* considered the idea of towing the prize back to the *Lira*. Theoretically, a line could be attached to the *Bandim* with the two rubber boats acting as tugs. Unfortunately, events conspired against such a plan, as the tide would turn shortly at 2030 and leave the vessel hard aground before the *Fuzileiros* could act. Facing mounting obstacles to the preservation option, Alpoim Calvão decided to destroy the *Bandim*. Accordingly gasoline was liberally spread throughout the vessel and lit as the *Fuzileiros* departed. It began burningly slowly, and it was only when the *Fuzileiros* had reached the center of the river that a muffled explosion was heard, and flames began to reach high into the night. When the *Fuzileiros* reached the appointed rendezvous point for *Lira* at 2200, the burning *Bandim* remained clearly visible. Disconcertingly, the *Lira* was nowhere to be found. The *Fuzileiros* attempted radio contact for two hours without success and finally located the *Lira* anchored 12 miles southwest of the rendezvous with a broken engine. It was not until 0100 the next morning that recovery was made.[31] The destruction of the *Bandim* and the death of its six crewmen threw the enemy into confusion, as judged by its intercepted and deciphered radio traffic.

In the space of six months, two key PAIGC motor vessels had been destroyed, and its logistical capability on the frontier dealt a substantial blow. The reduced PAIGC ability to supply its operations in Guiné would perforce reduce its military activity. These missions had exposed a glaring PAIGC vulnerability. Its logistical sea lines of communication from Conakry to the frontier were open to aggressive interdiction, as traffic was not protected en route by either armed escort or air cover and simply relied on international law and crewmen with small arms to defend it. This method was based on a naïve premise for parties at war and merited further examination. If interdiction operations had been successful in the frontier zone, might they not be extended to Conakry proper, as a raid there had the potential of destroying the entire PAIGC fleet. The *Fuzileiros* had proven themselves capable of conducting local strikes successfully, and thus with some imaginative and thorough planning, a long-range strike on Conakry was a realistic possibility.

Following *Nebulosa,* Alpoim Calvão had conceived the idea of neutralizing the PAIGC sea operations by sinking its key vessels in Conakry harbor with limpet mines. If the *Fuzileiros* were going to go to Conakry, then perhaps rescuing Lobato in the same stroke was also possible. The aviator's freedom had over the years become a personal commitment of Alpoim Calvão. In principle Spínola approved the bold proposal, although it remained largely in the conceptual stage, as the details had yet to be resolved. Alpoim Calvão next sought the advice of Reboredo. He was in concert with the proposed plan and agreed to support it logistically. In this vein, he authorized Alpoim Calvão to undertake an exploratory trip to the Republic of South Africa in the first days of September 1969 to review the latest demolition techniques.[32] Here, he was given a number of limpet mines and instructed in their use, returning to Portugal on a TAP commercial flight from Jan Smuts Airport with two 30-kilo handbags full of explosives.[33] This trip, however, occurred over a year before the envisioned operation, and much preparation lay ahead.

The concept of the mission, which came to be codenamed *Mar Verde* (Green Sea), was to send a raiding party from Guiné by sea to Conakry under cover of darkness and to undertake such operations there that would shatter both the ability of the PAIGC to continue its assault on Guiné and the ability of Sékou Touré to support the PAIGC. Its primary objectives were to free Lobato and twenty-five other prisoners, destroy the fast patrol boats of the PAIGC and Republic of Guinée in the port, and disable the six to eight Guinean MIG-15 and MIG-17 jet fighter aircraft at the airport. Secondary objectives would be addressed as opportunity allowed. Destruction of the fast patrol boats and the aircraft was necessary primarily as a defensive measure, because the Portuguese task force would be vulnerable returning to Guiné in daylight on the open ocean. The Portuguese vessels were considerably slower than the enemy boats, were more lightly armed, and lacked effective anti-air defenses against hostile aircraft. Portuguese air cover from its primary base of Bissau in Guiné did not extend to Conakry, and thus the returning vessels could not be protected during their exposed daylight leg. Consequently, to preempt enemy pursuit and a sure disaster, its offensive capability must be neutralized in the port and at the airfield of Conakry. The entire operation relied on the shock of complete initial surprise to enable the relatively small and unprotected Portuguese force to gain the immediate initiative and realize these three vital objectives.

As planning proceeded, the scope of the raid increased. It was decided that as a plausible cover the mission would include some 147 ex-Guinean soldiers who would stage a coup and replace Sékou Touré. These men were recruited largely from the National Front for the Liberation of Guinée (*Front National de Liberation de Guinée* or FNLG), which was the external organization seeking to overthrow the Guinean dictator through insurgent activity. Up to this time it had not been a success largely because of the tight security in Sékou Touré's repressive police state and his paranoid murdering of opponents and advocates alike.[34] Most of these recruits were veterans of the old French colonial army and were gathered from Senegal, The Gambia, Sierra Leone, and Ivory Coast. They were to be trained and supported by the Portuguese troops, and once ashore in Conakry, aided in their objectives until the Portuguese withdrew. The key in this process was the capture of Sékou Touré and his neutralization, so that the coup could be successful. Hand in glove with Sékou Touré's seizure was that of Amílcar Cabral. Cabral would be forcefully returned to Guiné and incarcerated there, while Sékou Touré would be delivered to the ex-Guinean soldiers. If either resisted, they were to be shot. The capture of both of these individuals would effectively disrupt PAIGC warfighting capabilities in Guiné and remove considerable pressure from the Portuguese war effort there. So in the words of Alpoim Calvão:

> The concept was not bad, but it was dangerous. Especially because the international community would not forgive us when it learned that we were behind an offensive intended to topple the regime by force of arms. On the other hand, the surprise attack that we proposed was not compatible with the guerrilla operation that FNLG pursued – inevitably prolonged. And it was a choice between two concepts – ours and theirs – which reinforced the idea, to be precise, of inventing a coup d'état in the Republic of Guinea as cover for the real strike that we envisioned.[35]

The Portuguese intelligence picture on the Republic of Guinée was inexact at best. Most tactical information was developed by monitoring PAIGC radio transmissions, and as the Portuguese had broken the PAIGC codes, all signals traffic was readily accessible. While this information was helpful, a more precise and tailored picture needed to be developed. Indeed, there was not even a map of the port of Conakry available to the planners. Discrete inquires were initiated with the national and foreign merchant ships that called at Bissau, and eventually an out-of-date chart was located. In order to revise it, Alpoim Calvão received permission from Spínola to conduct a reconnaissance mission in Conakry and consequently proceeded to the strategically propitious and isolated island of João Vieira in the LFG *Cassiopeia* (P 373) to plan the mission under the appropriate security conditions. There the launch was disguised as a PAIGC vessel, complete with an enemy flag flying and African elements of the crew visible topside, and continued to Conakry, arriving in the first hour of 17 September without arousing suspicion. This was considered remarkable, as the ship had encountered a number of Guinean fishermen during the daylight leg of the voyage, and all waved in greeting.[36] Indeed, Petty Officer (*cabo Fuzileiro*) António Augusto da Silva-Touré, posing as a Guinean and wearing the kepi of a major, returned each greeting with an impeccable salute.[37] Conditions were such that the lights of the city were clearly visible, and the ship maneuvered in a large turn, reconnoitering the port in an approach from the south and entering the channel between the Islands of Los and the Conakry peninsula at two in the morning. The patrol boat reduced speed, and the radar made a detailed scan of the harbor to record the modifications to the port that were not reflected on the chart. These were primarily new cargo piers. By three in the morning the work was completed, and as the patrol boat was exiting the channel, its generators failed. The anchor was dropped, and repairs made under nerve-wracking conditions.

On returning to Soga, intelligence work continued. The chart was revised, and details of the city completed as information was gathered. A model of the port area was constructed with reasonable exactness; however, other unknowns were legion. The national intelligence service had distressingly little information on the Republic of Guineé. The Ministry of Foreign Affairs did not permit national intelligence service representatives at embassies, so there was no opportunity to fill the void from this traditional source. There was some political and some strategic intelligence available, but there was virtually nothing at the operational or tactical level. Alpoim Calvão consequently established an *ad hoc* intelligence organization devoted to the mission and to the collection of every piece of information, including open sources in books, tourist brochures, and testimony from former PAIGC elements and exiled Guineans. Most data was over two years old and thus quite stale and inaccurate. In early October 1970, a most important break occurred when a former Portuguese cabin boy and deserter escaped from Conakry, crossed the border, and surrendered to the authorities. In exchange for his cooperation, he was spared punishment. Not only was his help invaluable in completing the intelligence gaps, but he was also to return to Conakry and lead the raiding party to the prisoners. This timely and valuable development enabled Alpoim Calvão to complete his intelligence on the city, which proved to be 95 percent accurate during the operation.[38]

The complexity of the *Mar Verde* is reflected in its planning. Originally Alpoim Calvão identified 52 objectives on his map of Conakry; however, this number was reduced to a more manageable 25, as the raid would be over a weekend when many public services were shut. In turn each of these objectives required certain specific equipment, armament, and training for a reasonable assurance of success. The sequencing of operations was matched with the required support and a complicated plan evolved. Still there were many unresolved operational questions. For instance, the airfield was some 45 minutes march from the harbor. If the troops had to fight their way to the field, then destruction of the MIGs would be a difficult assignment, if not an impossible one. Failure to destroy the aircraft would obviously hazard the successful withdrawal of the force. There were also political questions that may have gone unanswered. A review of the modified target list indicated that about half were critical civil infrastructure and not important military objectives. If indeed Portugal seriously intended to topple Sékou Touré and install a new government, then destroying key infrastructure would certainly generate unwanted problems for the incoming leaders. A city without electricity and an inconvenienced population, for instance, would hardly be an auspicious introduction. Further, the international community, whose condemnation was so feared, would understand a surgical strike to rescue prisoners and destroy military capability far more easily than any vindictive or wanton havoc.

The task force to transport the troops by sea consisted of the LFGs *Orion* (P 362), *Cassiopeia* (P 373), *Dragão* (P 374), and *Hidra* (P 376), and the LDGs *Bombarda* and *Montante*. The maximum speed of the force was 17 knots, so the unknowns of sea state, wind, and tide could change the speed of advance and thus the length of the voyage. Surprise could thus be jeopardized by these simple natural forces and any mistiming caused by them. The weekend of 22 November proved ideal, given the moon phase, predicted tide height, anticipated seasonal winds, and other local conditions. These circumstances would not again be propitious for some months.

For deceptive cover, radio traffic would be conducted in French, and the ships would disperse to appear as fishing vessels during a portion of their approach. The raiding force would be composed of approximately 400 men drawn from:

- DFE 21

- A Company of African Commandos
- Elements of FNLG
- Various personnel from *Fuzileiro* units specifically chosen for this operation.

Certain FNLG troops would be integrated with the Portuguese as guides, for they knew the target city of Conakry well. The troops would be inserted ashore from the six vessels by rubber boats and wear a specially manufactured olive drab battle dress for mutual identification as well as subterfuge. It was distinctive from both the traditional Portuguese battle dress and the Republic of Guinée uniforms and bore a light green arm band in sympathy with the predominantly Muslim population. For the purpose of deception, Soviet bloc weapons would be used rather than Western arms, and these had been purchased quietly on the international arms market.

Operational security for the mission was paramount and presented certain difficulties. In order to maintain the required low profile, the remote island of Soga was chosen for training the force and launching the raid. By early November there were almost two hundred men on Soga comprised largely of FNLG elements and their instructors. These men required considerable training and fieldwork to become a credible fighting unit. Adding to this obstacle was the need to keep the ex-Guineans politically organized and comforted, as tribal rivalries among them were a continuing problem. The other troops scheduled to participate would not be brought to Soga until the final days and would not know of the mission or their assignments until then. This process was dictated by a number of factors. First, the troops could not be relieved from their current duties for a long run-up to *Mar Verde*, as Portugal had few men to spare. Second, many of the African *Fuzileiros* and commandos had relatives who were fighting for the PAIGC, and leaks through familial channels would jeopardize operational security. Their fears of reprisal would also work against troop preparation. So to reduce these risks to manageable levels, Alpoim Calvão made the conscious decision to rely on their known fighting capabilities rather than specific mission training. His intent was to minimize their pre-operation exposure and thus opportunity for compromise through outside contact.

At the beginning of November, when the concentration of forces began on Soga, a diversionary operation commenced on the island of Como. Four days prior to *Mar Verde*, the detachment of African *Fuzileiros* and the company of African commandos were brought to the staging point along with some European elements of *Fuzileiros*, who added leadership strength and experience to the operation. Between this time and their departure on the evening of 20 November, the troops would become familiar with the tactical plan and operational procedures necessary for the mission.

The force, designated Task Group 27.2 (TG 27.2), was generally divided into a northern, central, and southern approach. The *Cassiopeia*, *Dragão*, and *Montante* would execute the northern approach from the point of dispersion and land their forces north of the city on the mainland, which is separated from Conakry by an isthmus. *Orion* would proceed on a central approach directly to the city, and *Hidra* and *Bombarda* would approach from the south, *Bombarda* landing its forces in the southern part of the city (Conakry I), and *Hidra*, on the mainland next to the airport (Conakry II).[39]

Cassiopeia and *Dragão* together carried DFE 21, which was comprised of African *Fuzileiros* and divided into 12 squads of six men each. It was further organized into four assault groups. Group one had two of the 12 squads; group two, three squads; and groups

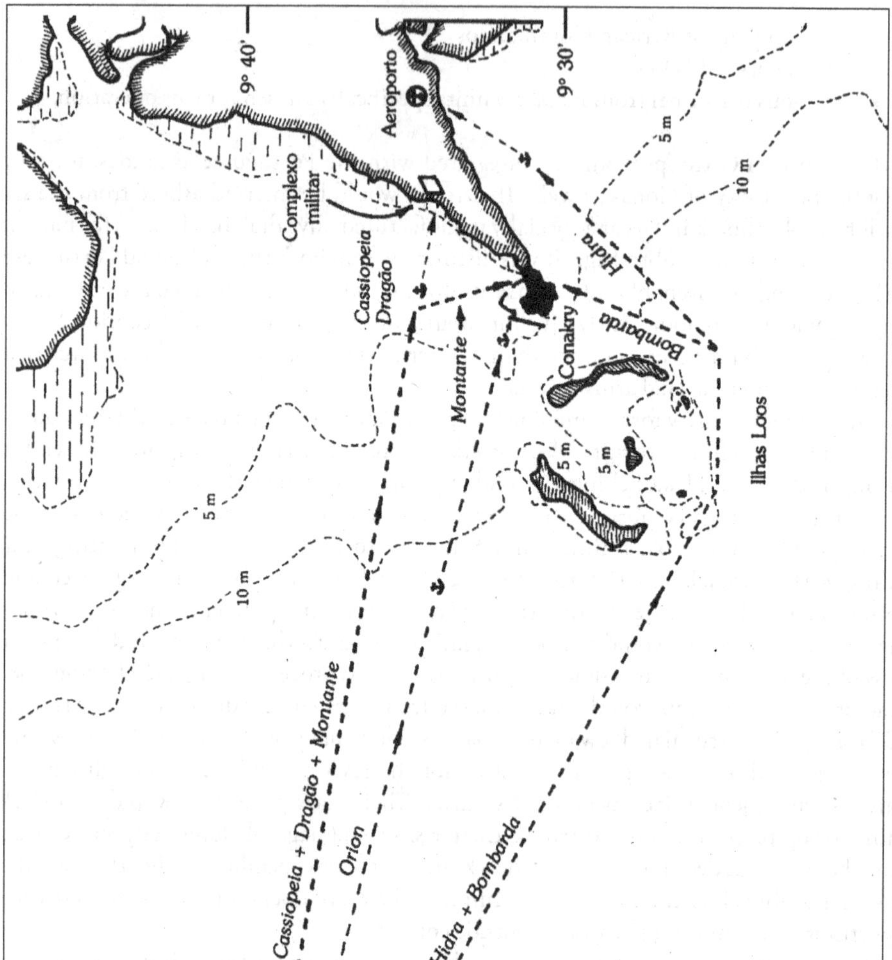

Mar Verde approaches from Point of Dispersal. Map courtesy of Saturnino Monteiro, *Batalhas e Combates da Marinha Portuguesa*, Volume VIII 1808–1975 (Lisbon: Livraria Sá da Costa Editora, 1997).

three and four, the remaining seven squads. The four groups together were known as Team Zulu and were led by the junior lieutenant (*primeiro tenente*) Raul Eugénio Dias da Cunha e Silva. Each team was designated with a letter from the NATO phonetic alphabet and given a specific assignment, as shown in Table 8.1.

Montante carried the principals of FLNG and the Company of African Commandos, a 150-man unit commanded by Captain João Bacar. These troops were divided into Teams India, Mike and Oscar.

Orion carried Team Victor, which was composed of 14 *Fuzileiros* commanded by the now promoted Lieutenant (*capitão tenente*) Rebordão de Brito. *Bombarda* carried almost 200 men of FLNG divided into Teams Alfa, Bravo, Charlie, Delta, Echo, Foxtrot, Golf, and Hotel, and Team Papa composed of African Commandos. Lastly *Hidra* carried Team Sierra composed of 44 African Commandos and led by Captain of Paratroops (*capitão pára-quedista*) Lopes Morais.

Table 8.1: *Mar Verde* Team Objectives

Sources: Alpoim Calvão, *De Conakry ao M.D.L.P.* [From Conakry to the M.D.L.P.] (Lisbon: Editorial Intervenção, 1976); and António Luís Marinho, *Operação Mar Verde* [Operation Green Sea] (Lisbon: Temas e Debates, 2006).

Ship	Team	Objective	Team Composition
Bombarda	Alfa	Presidential Palace Sékou Touré	FLING
Bombarda	Bravo	Ministry of Interior	FLING
Bombarda	Charlie	Police directorate	FLING
Bombarda	Delta	Executive residences	FLING
Bombarda	Echo	Police barracks	FLING
Bombarda	Foxtrot	La Paternelle (Cuban contingent)	FLING
Bombarda	Golf	Post office Telephone exchange	FLING
Bombarda	Hotel	National radio station	FLING
Montante	India	Electric grid	FLING & African Commandos (10 men)
Montante	Mike	Camp Samory Chief of Staff Defense	FLING & African Commandos (50 men)
Montante	Oscar	Republican Guard	FLING & African Commandos (40 men)
Bombarda	Papa	Isthmus between Conakry and airport	African Commandos
Hydra	Sierra	Airport	African Commandos (44 men)

Ship	Team	Objective	Team Composition
Orion	Victor	Fast patrol boats	*Fuzileiros* (14 men + guide)
Cassiopeia & Dragão	Zulu	Villa Silly de S. Tomé S. Touré residence	DFE 21 (22 men)
Cassiopeia & Dragão	Zulu	PAIGC Headquarters	DFE 21 (22 men)
Cassiopeia & Dragão	Zulu	La Montaigne prison	DFE 21

Each team was assigned a specific set of objectives in Conakry and began to familiarize itself with the special drills and equipment that would be required for its portion of the mission. The mission and thus the task force would be organized by vessel with each carrying one or more teams with specific assignments.

On 14 November, Alpoim Calvão flew to Lisbon with a draft plan of the operation to present to Dr. Marcello Caetano, the prime minister, on Spínola's behalf. This formal request for approval of *Mar Verde* from the highest levels of government was necessary because of the political sensitivity of the operation and the possible fallout from its execution. Caetano received Alpoim Calvão on 17 November and immediately granted permission to proceed with the caveat that no Portuguese fingerprints must be left on the operation in Conakry, a naïve condition.[40] Alpoim Calvão recalls Caetano opining that the coup attempt was problematical but if the prisoners were recovered, then the mission would be a success.[41] Alpoim Calvão returned to Guiné on the 19th and that same day continued to the island of Soga to begin final preparations for the operation. With approximately 400 men projected to be ashore in Conakry within the week, it was going to be difficult, if not impossible, to hide Portuguese complicity.

In light of the potential for diplomatic fallout, the scope of *Mar Verde* should have perhaps been reduced. Within the 25 objectives, as noted earlier, was the destruction of a great amount of Guinean infrastructure that was not critical to mission success. Also, if Sékou Touré, the head of state of a neighboring country, were killed or overthrown and imprisoned, the diplomatic repercussions for Portugal would be substantial. Further, if Amílcar Cabral, one of the most respected and prestigious leaders of any of the African liberation movements, were captured and imprisoned in Lisbon or Bissau, it would likewise prove troublesome for the Portuguese. There was also no hard intelligence on the whereabouts of either Sékou Touré or Cabral, a fact that made success problematical. Their anticipated movements were only assumed. Too much was left to luck in this area for a successful kidnapping or assassination to occur. Even Caetano felt that a favorable coup was an unrealistic expectation. Despite the despotic and murderous nature of his regime and the opposition that it generated, Sékou Touré was well guarded and had his secret police routinely identify and dispatch any hint of opposition within Guinée. The intelligence on the necessary internal opposition to support a coup was missing. A successful coup would have to overcome the difficult obstacles of decapitating Sékou Touré, neutralizing the entire leadership, and successfully installing a new leader. Such a process requires thorough planning, steadfast commitment to its execution, and subsequent extended support of the new government. Alpoim Calvão could not linger in Conakry without jeopardizing his small force and with such modest strength could not ensure that these actions would be completed. Certainly he would show the Portuguese hand, something to be avoided. All of

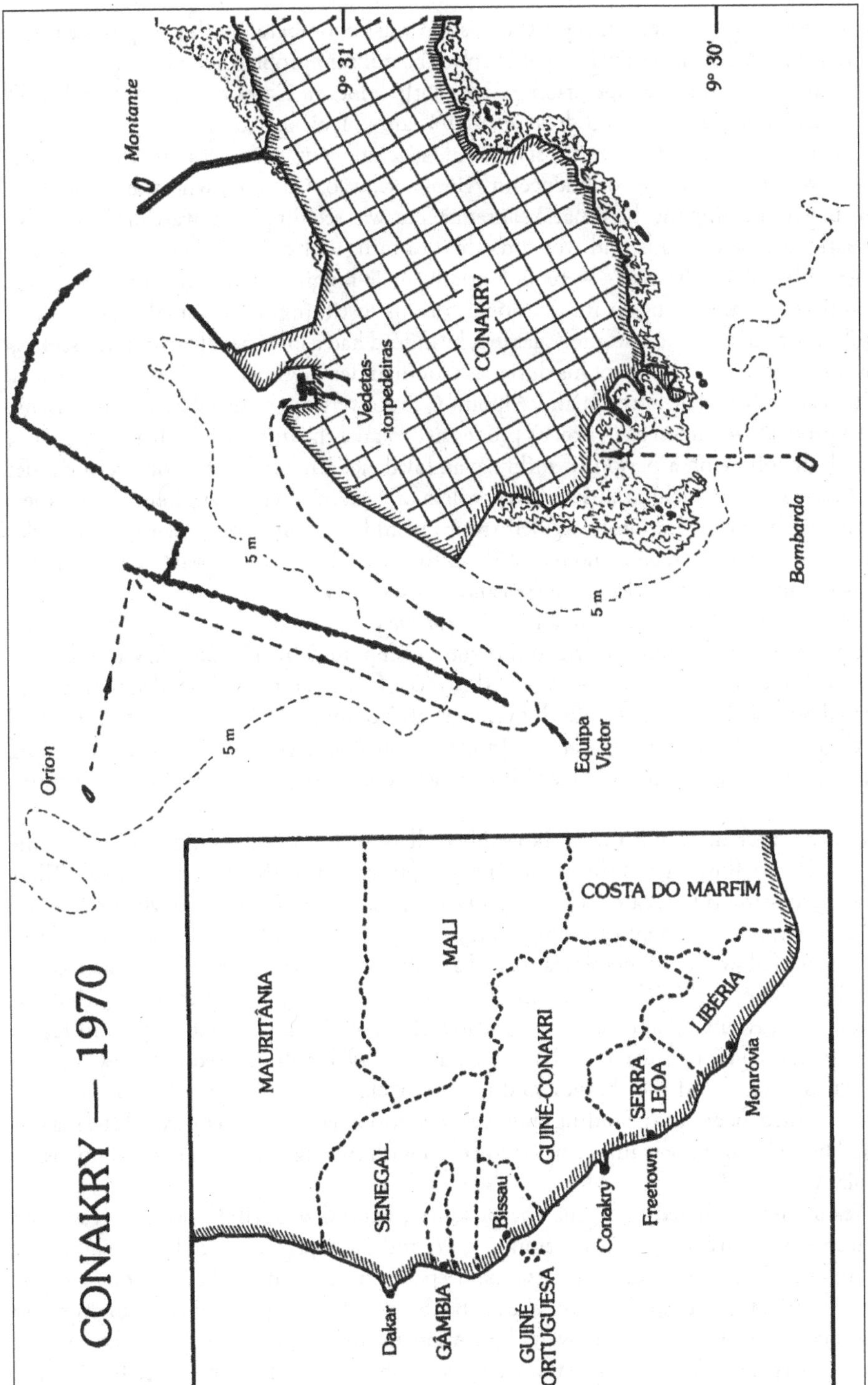

Mar Verde route of Team Victor from *Orion*. Map courtesy of Saturnino Monteiro, *Batalhas e Combates da Marinha Portuguesa*, Volume VIII 1808–1975 (Lisbon: Livraria Sá da Costa Editora).

these weaknesses were clear, and yet the mission was encumbered with this project in the hope that a risky political solution would solve the military problems of Guiné.

Local control of the operation rested with Alpoim Calvão, who was rightfully optimistic, ambitious, and confident. *Fuzileiros* are not picked to be otherwise, or their difficult missions would never be successful. Caetano put its success in the hands of Spínola, who had supreme confidence in Alpoim Calvão. Caetano, who was responsible ultimately for fielding the diplomatic consequences, was seemingly unaware of the possible international repercussions, and even today his assuming such risk is difficult to understand. The geopolitical implications were potentially wide-ranging, given the problems that Portugal was experiencing in international forums justifying its "colonial wars." While Spínola must ultimately answer to Caetano, he indeed had a local problem and was seeking a solution within the context of his duties as Commander-in-Chief and Governor-General of Guiné. The fact that both he and Alpoim Calvão were aggressive, brave, no-nonsense leaders probably fed upon each other's propensity to take the initiative with a daring move, particularly following a period of military ambivalence under the previous commander. *Mar Verde* was just such an answer. Regardless of certain obvious weaknesses, boldness and surprise in an operation by skilled troops would overcome many of these obstacles. Certainly it would overcome enough of them to attain the primary goals of rescuing the prisoners and neutralizing the enemy sea and air capability.

Preliminary to the operation, a P2V-5 *Neptune* patrol aircraft made a reconnaissance sortie on 18 November and confirmed that the warships remained in Conakry and that the sea was calm. Under this favorable omen, the force of six assault vessels loaded with troops departed Soga at 1950 hours on 20 November 1970 bound for Conakry. It rendezvoused near the island of Canhambaque at 2200 and continued south until 2020 the next evening, when the force split to enter Conakry harbor, and each vessel assumed its predetermined station.[42]

Shortly after midnight on 22 November all vessels were in position, and only the lights of the city illuminated the night. The first objective was the fast patrol boats. These were to be destroyed by Team Victor from *Orion* positioned northwest of the breakwater protecting the port of Conakry. At high tide on a calm and windless sea Rebordão de Brito and 14 of his fellow *Fuzileiros* were launched and discretely made for the breakwater *Dique Norte*. From here, the *Fuzileiros* identified their objective and moved to attack. Arriving at the naval pier, Abu Camará silently eliminated the sentry and was followed by his fellow *Fuzileiros* and a guide in three rubber boats. The *Fuzileiros* eliminated the crew on each enemy boat and placed the charges, and in a great blast and subsequent eruption of fire, seven fast patrol boats and a landing craft were destroyed. Portuguese control of the sea was secured by 0215, and the team returned to *Orion* with two lightly wounded and no loss of matérial.

Team Zulu, assigned to rescue the prisoners, neutralize PAIGC headquarters, and capture Sékou Touré, was launched from *Dragão* and *Cassiopeia* anchored in five meters of water in a small bay to the north of the Conakry peninsula next to the shoals of *La Prudente* and three miles from its landing site. The rubber boats, 10 in number, left the two ships and experienced some difficulty. They were slightly late in landing, as the propellers on some of their outboard motors had become fouled by local fishing nets. The element led by Cunha e Silva went immediately to *La Montaigne*, a two story building surrounded by a wall about three meters high. The prison guards began firing light weapons about 0215, causing one soldier to be gravely wounded. Fire was returned with a bazooka to the upper floor, which began to burn furiously. The momentum of the exchange shifted to the attackers, and this allowed them to move forward, breach the wall with another bazooka round, and enter the prison compound. As the team moved through the building freeing the 26 prisoners, eight enemy bodies were discovered on the upper floor with an assortment of Soviet bloc weapons.[43] The element led by the junior lieutenant (junior grade) (*segundo tenente*) José Carlos Freire Falcão Lucas, headed for PAIGC headquarters and on arriving neutralized a series of sentries, destroyed five party buildings and six vehicles, and eliminated various hostile personnel. The final element, led by the junior lieutenant (*segundo tenente*) Benjamin Lopes de Abreu, attacked Villa Silly, the residence of Sékou Touré. His force of 22 men forced entry into the militia camp and overcame the 60 residence guards. The dictator was not to be found.[44] With the conclusion of their various missions, the elements of Team Zulu returned to the *Dragão* and *Cassiopeia* at about 0400 and acted as a reserve force for the remainder of the operation.

Lopes Morais, with his group of 40 Portuguese and five FNLG troops, came ashore at 0130 after some navigation difficulty and began his march to the airport. During this march, he became separated from the junior lieutenant (*segundo tenente*) Januário Lopes and 20 of his men. Lopes, as it turned out, in an act of betrayal hid and surrendered himself and his 20 men to the Guinean authorities the next day.[45] By 0215, Lopes Morais and his remaining force had breached the perimeter fencing and discovered that there were no MIGs at the field, only six commercial aircraft, two Sud-Est Aviation SE-210 *Caravelles* belonging to Air Afrique and four Fokker F-27 *Friendships*.[46] Apparently, there had been a ministerial reorganization, and the MIGs had been moved. The runway was blocked as both a defensive measure and a compromise solution, although Lobato later commented that the MIGs only flew very high, maneuvered cautiously, and were mostly for show.[47] The air threat was thus minimal in light of the Guinean aviators' elementary flying skills and the obstacle of the blocked runway.

With the freeing of the prisoners and control of the sea and air established, Alpoim Calvão turned his attention to the coup and the PAIGC leadership. Sékou Touré was not to be found anywhere. He was not in his villa and not in the presidential palace. Cabral was not at home either. Later it was discovered that Sékou Touré had been with his mistress and had remained hidden in her home, while Cabral was out of the country visiting Bulgaria, both intelligence shortcomings. Nevertheless, 400 political prisoners were released, the Guinean Minister of Defense was captured and delivered to the FNLG force, and Sékou Touré's Republican Guard alone suffered over 200 casualties. The population turned to "jello" in Alpoim Calvão's words and watched passively as his force ranged throughout Conakry destroying military vehicles and certain PAIGC and civil buildings, perhaps too much so.[48] The coup was clearly in jeopardy with Sékou Touré still in hiding and the people unwilling to be galvanized into action. Despite a plan to seize the radio station and make other coordinated efforts, the FNLG plotters seemed irresolute and confounded by the total apathy of the citizenry.[49] Sixty of them remained after Calvão and the task force had departed and eventually surrendered to the authorities only to be executed. For three months afterward Sékou Touré engaged in a witch hunt. Throughout Guinée there were more than a hundred public executions, and scores of other suspects were permanently incarcerated.[50]

Having achieved the primary objectives, Alpoim Calvão decided to terminate the operation and recovered his forces on board the vessels by 0900. One of the weaknesses encountered during the raid was the realization that a large portion of the Portuguese African troops were familiar only with fighting in the bush and jungle and, because they had never been in a city the size of Conakry, had difficulty finding their way around it. To compensate for this predicament in the closing hour of the raid, Alpoim Calvão commandeered a taxi on the waterfront and cruised the city to make certain that none were left accidentally.[51] His losses were three dead and nine wounded. Conversely, Sékou Touré had lost over 500 troops and many civilians, and presided over a partially destroyed and disorganized city.[52] By 1030, Alpoim Calvão's task force had stood out of Conakry and made its turn north.

From the strictly military point of view, *Mar Verde* was a success. It was the first of its kind ever undertaken by Portugal, and it proved once again the capabilities and effectiveness of the sailor-*Fuzileiro* team. They had stormed a bastion in a city relatively far from their base of operations and relied on surprise to achieve the success necessary for a safe withdrawal. It had been an ingenious plan that ably addressed the limited resources, the unique operational security requirements, and an incomplete intelligence picture. Of the three primary military objectives, the recovery of the prisoners and the destruction of the fast patrol boats were successful. The MIGs were missed because of deficient intelligence. In this regard intelligence failures came from a poor national intelligence organization that lacked the capability to gather sufficiently detailed and current information on a target country. The movement of the MIGs and the political will of the opposition to Sékou Touré are the most obvious. While Alpoim Calvão would describe later that "At nine in the morning I held the city in my hands," in fact with the military objectives secured for all practical purposes, he made the political decision to depart rather than further support the coup, something that he could have done.[53] The longer he stayed, the more irrefutable the evidence against Portugal would be, with the result of international condemnation and possibly isolation. This judgment was well founded.

Unfortunately, the autocratic Sékou Touré was unharmed and proceeded to interrogate the FNLG prisoners who had remained behind and surrendered. Some of them described the operation at length and identified its sponsors.[54] Sékou Touré took this evidence to the UN Security Council and earned an automatic reproval of Portuguese actions. The *pro forma* mission of inquiry was dispatched to Conakry. Sékou Touré appealed both to the Soviet Union and the United States for military aid, playing the superpowers against each other. The United States had a growing commercial investment in the Guinean bauxite mines, and thus President Richard Nixon in a confidential letter to Sékou Touré deplored the incident. It remained confidential for a day. Great Britain joined the United States in confirming that any repetition of an operation similar to *Mar Verde* might seriously endanger Washington and London support for Lisbon in its African counterinsurgency. Both feared that such adventures would unsettle the equilibrium in East-West relations. Indeed, the Soviet Union viewed the incident as an excellent opportunity to increase its influence in West Africa and as a result established a naval and air presence in Conakry. The naval presence became known as the "West African Patrol," and it made regular visits to the ports in the region and shadowed U.S. and NATO naval activity. Soviet Bear-D long-range reconnaissance aircraft were also deployed to Conakry to track U.S. naval transits to the Indian Ocean. In an attempt to gain favor with Sékou Touré and counter Soviet influence, Nixon authorized the token sum of $4.7 million as a contribution to the rebuilding of

Conakry.[55] Not surprisingly, most of this gift found its way into the bank accounts of Sékou Touré and his henchmen.

These developments made Portugal a controversial member of NATO. Caetano confided that in the case of *Mar Verde* the Republic of Guinée had not represented a problem. The real difficulty came at the international level, and in going to Conakry, Lisbon had tended to forget the broader picture.[56] Spínola did not agree, and many years later he confirmed that in his opinion it was mostly overblown.[57] *Mar Verde* had in part distracted the Nixon and Kissinger effort at *détente* with the Soviet Union, and this disturbance was not welcomed. On the local military level, the Soviet Union and its surrogate Cuba began to provide increased support for the PAIGC. Sophisticated Soviet arms and Cuban instructors appeared in Conakry, and by 1973 the military struggle had increased in intensity. New weapons were changing the military balance, and three Portuguese aircraft were downed with Soviet SA-7 *Grail* hand-held ground-to-air missiles in late March and early April 1973. *Mar Verde*, it seemed, had marked a deepening of the Portuguese military agony in Guiné.

Mar Verde, the bold, daring, and successful rescue of 26 prisoners of war and the destruction of PAIGC naval capability, thus became a catalyst for increased superpower friction. Unfortunately, the customary benefits of such a mission seemed to be largely lost in the negative diplomatic and geo-strategic fallout. Sékou Touré had rebuffed traditional efforts to negotiate the exchange of prisoners and thus left a rescue mission as the only viable alternative. The operation was kept simple in its military objectives and hence its success in this field. Its political objectives, however, clouded the picture and allowed the simple tactical mission to be termed an "invasion" in international forums. The broader risk-reward relationship was not deeply explored at any level, although Alpoim Calvão was certainly sensitive to it. The fires of international condemnation were ably fanned by Sékou Touré. He no longer held any hostages, and Portugal had handed him the wherewithal to play the injured innocent and secure the protection of the Soviet Union against future aggression. The PAIGC now had an inviolate sanctuary and the military might and sophistication of the Soviet Union fully behind its cause. As we shall see, this could be a burden as well as a boon.

Following *Mar Verde,* there were a number of developments that made the strategic resolution of Guiné vital to the success of any Portuguese solution. First Spínola believed that Cabral was his own man and despite a Marxist structure and philosophy in the PAIGC, he wished to be free of Soviet influence in establishing a new regime in Guiné.[58] One route that held the answer to this desire was the offer of independence under some sort of Portuguese federation in which Guiné would be part of a Lusophone organization similar to the British Commonwealth of Nations. With this concept in mind, Spínola began a series of overtures to Cabral through Léopold Senghor, the president of Senegal, in an attempt to end the war honorably for Portugal and to obtain independence for Guiné in a prudent way.

From 1970 onward, Spínola's objective had been to drastically reduce the military capacity of the PAIGC, tilting the balance in Portuguese favor. As time passed, Spínola's plans proved successful in checking the progress of the PAIGC and in gaining its respect to such an extent that it began to make sense to open negotiations for some form of self-government with a Portuguese alignment. By 1972 conditions were ripe for negotiations, and at the end of April, Spínola had his initial conversations with a Senegalese minister to arrange a secret meeting with Senghor. This took place on 18 May at Cap Skiring in Senegal, and Senghor took the opportunity to express great sympathy for Portugal and praise its social programs in Guiné.[59] Spínola explained his concept of Guinean independence, and Senghor indicated that he thought Cabral would be receptive to the idea and that he would act as an intermediary. This prompted Spínola to suggest that Senghor meet with Caetano in Bissau or perhaps metropolitan Portugal. Later on 26 May in Lisbon in a meeting with Silva Cunha, the Portuguese Foreign Minister, and Caetano, the proposal was rejected out of hand under the rationale that such a move could not be controlled and that it would have grave consequences for the other colonies. In Caetano's view, a military defeat was preferable. Spínola was shocked and aghast at such a warped position, and in his view a great opportunity was lost. This experience prompted him to write his book *Portugal and the Future* in which he voices his frustrations.[60]

Contact with Cabral continued through his brother Luiz Cabral until shortly before his assassination on 20 January 1973.[61] Alpoim Calvão and Spínola remain convinced that Sékou Touré had an active hand in fomenting much of the internal dissention in the PAIGC in order to weaken Cabral as a leader and a perceived competitor.[62] This activity led to Cabral's death and with it any hope of negotiating an honorable conclusion for Portugal and a prudent one for Guiné.

Operations continued throughout 1972 during the negotiations with one of the more prominent ones being Operation *Verga Latina* (Lateen Yard). It was conducted between July and December from Bolama in support of the population on the peninsula of the same name. The operation was designed to build confidence in the local population through a military presence and various civic action projects. It is difficult to gauge the success of the mission, as the PAIGC was able to lob mortar rounds into the naval encampment Tabanca Nova da Armada on an almost daily basis from varying and proximate positions.[63]

By 1972 with the exception of the more important urban centers, the entire country was threatened by insurgent action. Guiné was shaped geographically in such a way that no part of the country was more than 60 kilometers from a neighboring country, a fact that made the entire territory a virtual frontier. From Senegal and Guinée, PAIGC insurgent units would enter the country, ambush and attack Portuguese forces, intimidate the population, and retire across the border to sanctuary. When Portuguese forces were not present in the rural areas, control passed into the hands of the PAIGC. The conflict seemed to have entered what might have been called an advanced phase of revolutionary war.

Indeed, after Caetano refused to authorize negotiations with Cabral, the campaign in Guiné entered a waiting period during which there seemed to be a general expectation that some event would end the conflict. Spínola had at this point gained enough credibility to bring Cabral to the negotiating table, a situation about as propitious as one could achieve in the besieged environment of Guiné. Any conflict resolution would now have to come from another direction, and the war labored on until 25 April 1974, when middle-ranking Portuguese officers effected a coup and toppled the government in Lisbon.

Portugal ultimately granted Guiné its independence, and the PAIGC assumed control of the government in 1975. It promised amnesty to all Africans who had fought on the side of Portugal and invited them to stay as citizens of the new country. No fewer than 27,000 former Portuguese soldiers and natives of Guiné accepted the offer and remained.[64] The PAIGC leaders, however, had kept company far too long with Sékou Touré and had assumed his worst habits. Almost immediately arrests of the former soldiers, sergeants, and officers of elite units began, and their fate was inevitably execution. When questioned about these deaths, the PAIGC leaders denied any knowledge. General Almeida Bruno, a member of the Portuguese delegation to transfer the government of Guiné to the PAIGC and a former commander of the Commando Battalion there, did not accept this denial, "But this is not what happened, and the PAIGC barbarically shot the majority of my African officers from the Commando Battalion."[65] This assertion was only the beginning. Ultimately the newspaper *Nô Pintcha* published a partial list of names, and those who survived to escape estimate that at least a thousand faced firing squads, some at airfields, some at soccer fields, and many in front of the civilian population. Thus for those loyal and courageous soldiers who had participated in *Mar Verde*, *Nebulosa*, *Gata Brava*, and the other operations against the PAIGC, betrayal by their new government was a final and sad footnote.[66]

Notes

1 António Lobato, *Liberdade ou Evasão* [Freedom or Evasion] (Amadora: Erasmos Editora, 1996), 172.

2 Ibid., 172–177.

3 José Pedro Castanheira, "Ao Serviço de Spínola e Marcelo" [In the Service of Spínola and Marcelo], *Expresso* (20 September 1997), 56.

4 Ibid.

5 Willem S. van der Waals, *Portugal's War in Angola 1961–1974* (Rivonia: Ashanti, 1993), 181.

6 Ibid.

7 Douglas L. Wheeler, "The Military and Portuguese Dictatorship, 1926–1974: 'The Honor of the Army,'" in *Contemporary Portugal*, ed. Lawrence S. Graham and Harry M. Makler (Austin: University of Texas Press, 1979), 199.

8 José Pedro Castanheira, "Memórias da Guerra e da Paz: Spínola" [Memories of War and Peace: Spínola], *Expresso Revista* (30 April 1994), 26.

9 Ibid., 28.

10 António de Spínola, *Por Uma Guiné Melhor* [A Better Guiné], (Lisbon: Agência-Geral do Ultramar, 1970), 24.

11 Ibid., 231–238.

12 Ibid., 23–25.

13 Armando da Silva Saturnio Monteiro, *Batalhas e Combates da Marinha Portuguesa* [Battles and Engagements of the Portuguese Navy] (Lisbon: Livraria sá da Costa Editora, 1997), 197.

14 Guilherme Almor de Alpoim Calvão, *De Conakry ao M.D.L.P.* [From Conakry to the M.D.L.P.] (Lisbon: Editorial Intervenção, 1976), 13.

15 R. Blake Dunnavent, *Brown Water Warfare* (Gainesville: University Press of Florida, 2003), 111–112.

16 Alpoim Calvão, 57.

17 Ibid., 57–58.

18 LFG *Sagitário* (P 1131) was one of the final two vessels of the *Argos* class launches and was completed in September 1965 at the Arsenal do Alfeite, Lisbon. The other was LFG *Centauro* (P 1130).

19 Alpoim Calvão, 58.

20 Ibid.

21 Ibid., 59.

22 José Freire Antunes, *A Guerra de África 1961–1974* [The African War 1961–1974] (Lisbon: Temas e Debates, 1996), 513.

23 Alpoim Calvão, 59.

24 Ibid.

25 Abou Camaná, an ex-PAIGC sailor, was enlisted in the *Fuzileiros* as part of the Portuguese policy of rehabilitating former insurgents. He was later assigned to DFE 21, a *Destacamento de Fuzileiros Especiais Africanos* (Detachment of African Special *Fuzileiros*), which was established in February 1970. He was to participate in *Mar Verde* and be awarded the Cruz de Guerra for his heroism.

26 Alpoim Calvão, 60.

27 The M20 *Bazooka* is a World War II-vintage 88.9mm rocket-propelled grenade launcher with a maximum range of 800 meters and a recommended moving target acquisition range of 185 meters.

28 Alpoim Calvão, 62.

29 The PPSh-41 (*Pistolet-Pulemet Shpagina*, from the Russian, and *41* from the 1941 date of manufacture) was the result of two national catastrophes for the Soviet Union. The first was the Winter War with Finland in 1939–1940 when the Finns used submachine guns with devastating effect during close combat in the forests, and the second was the German invasion of 1941 when the Soviets lost in the retreats both huge quantities of small arms and much of their engineering capability. There then arose an urgent demand for a light and simple weapon capable of a high volume of fire, and the answer to this was the PPSh-41, designed by Georgii Shpagin. It was much cheaper and quicker to make than the preceding models and was finished roughly. The barrel was still chromed, however, and there was never any doubt about its effectiveness. About five million PPSh guns had been made by 1945, and the Soviets adapted their infantry tactics to take full advantage of such huge numbers. In the Soviet Union, the PPSh went out of service in the late 1950s, but it has been supplied in enormous quantities to the satellite and pro-communist countries, so that it will be seen for many years.

30 Alpoim Calvão, 63.

31 Ibid., 64.

32 Ibid., 64–65.

33 José Manuel Saraiva, "Asslto a Conakry" [Assault on Conakry], *Revista do Expresso* (23 November 1996): 97–98.

34 Jean-Paul Alata, *Prison D'Afrique* (Paris: Éditions du Seuil, 1976); Lobato, 97.

35 Saraiva, 96.

36 Saturnino Monteiro, 198.

37 Alpoim Calvão, 65.

38 Ibid., 71.

39 António Luís Marinho, *Operação Mar Verde* [Operation Green Sea] (Lisbon: Temas e Debates, 2006), 108.

40 Alpoim Calvão, 72

41 Guilherme Almor de Alpoim Calvão, interview by the author, 14 March 1997, Lisbon.

42 Alpoim Calvão, 76.

43 Raúl Eugénio Dias da Cunha e Silva, "21st Detachment of Special Marines, Operation 'Green Sea,' Relating to the Period from 170300 to 252000 November 1970," after action report written at the headquarters of DFE 21, Buba, Guiné, 30 November 1970, TMs [photocopy], 2.

44 Alpoim Calvão, 76–77.

45 Aniceto Afonso and Carlos de Matos Gomes, *Guerra Colonial* [Colonial War] (Lisbon: Notícias, 1998), 503. Januário Lopes and his men were ordered shot by Sékou Touré shortly after the UN investigative team had interviewed them.

46 Alpoim Calvão, 81.

47 Lobato, 175.

48 Guilherme Almor de Alpoim Calvão, interview and correspondence with the author, 3 February 1998, Lisbon. The force destroyed quite a number of military vehicles and damaged some official buildings and

civil infrastructure. As the force carried only small demolition charges and not the explosives needed for heavy blasting, the damage was initially light. The PAIGC buildings were very insubstantial structures, and five of them were severely damaged during the exchange of fire when looking for Amílcar Cabral. The fighting, however, continued for three or four days after the Portuguese force departed, and further damage occurred during that period.

49 Alata, 51.

50 Ibid., 89.

51 Guilherme Almor de Alpoim Calvão, correspondence with the author, 29 January 1998, Lisbon. Alpoim Calvão in his correspondence describes the adventure of one of his men, Francisco Nhanque, who arrived late at the departure rendezvous in Conakry because he had been celebrating Sékou Touré's impending fall with some bystanders. On seeing that the force had departed, he did not hesitate to leap into the sea and begin to swim westwards after the distant ships. Eventually, as he progressed about three miles out to sea, he was rescued by a passing Dutch freighter bound for Monrovia, Liberia. On arrival there, he requested and received political asylum. He located a job at a bar owned by a Brazilian, with whom he had established a rapport as a fellow Portuguese speaker. There was no Portuguese embassy or consulate in Liberia at the time. After several years, he had saved enough money to purchase an airline ticket, and he flew to the Canary Islands. He worked a further year to save for the fare to Lisbon, and when he arrived there, the airport authorities, on hearing his story, telephoned Alpoim Calvão for confirmation. Alpoim Calvão rushed to the airport to greet this fine soldier who had been reported missing in action in a war long since concluded.

52 Saraiva, 104.

53 José Freire Antunes, "Calvão evoca Conakry: «Às 9 da manhã eu tinha a cidade nas mãos» [Calvão remembers Conakry: "At 9 in the morning I held the city in my hands."], *Semanário* (10 December 1988): 16.

54 Ahmed Sékou Touré, *L'Agression Portugaise contra la Republic de Guiné* (Conakry: Livre Blanc, 1970).

55 José Freire Antunes, "Invasão de Conakry, Novembro de 1970: A 'Baía dos Porcos' do General Spínola" [Invasion of Conakry, November of 1970: The "Bay of Pigs" of General Spínola], *Semanário* (29 October 1988): 21.

56 Ibid.

57 Castanheira, 28–30.

58 Castanheira, 28.

59 There are many reports of Senegalese crossing the border into Guiné to take advantage of the medical care administered to the local population there. Senghor undoubtedly knew of this generosity.

60 Castanheira, 30–31.

61 Alpoim Calvão, 88–96.

62 Castanheira, 31; Alpoim Calvão, 89.

63 J.C. Moura da Fonseca, *Viagens e Históras da Marinha* [Voyages and Stories of the Navy] (Lisbon: Edições Culturais da Marinha, 1995), 120–121.

64 Eduardo Dâmaso and Adelino Gomes, "Falecidos por Fuzilamento" [Death by Shooting], *Pública* (30 June 1996): 48.

65 Ibid.

66 Ibid., 47.

9

Brown Water Legacy

The Portuguese "brown water" navy was the result of a wide and carefully considered naval strategy designed to address the developing threat in Africa. In the African environment waterway security was critical, as the infrastructure was universally primitive, and while there was generally a road network radiating from the colonial capital, the primary routes used clandestinely by insurgents were the isolated tracks, trails, and waterways. The principal colonial road system normally served the economically important areas of agriculture and mineral extraction. These were well traveled and policed and unsuitable for the insurgents' work of proselytizing the population, collecting taxes, seeking food and shelter, and recruiting far from the eye of the government authorities. Consequently, if the government forces were to counter the insurgent successfully, they had to operate in the more remote environment. This required that it develop the dedicated forces to do so. While there were specialized land forces to address enemy activities ashore, the navy sought to develop and deploy its own force to secure the remote river, lake and coastal systems against the enemy and to provide a complement to the army.

The navy had struggled in the wake of the overthrow of the monarchy, the establishment of the First Republic in 1910 and its chaotic 16-year rule, the 1926 coup d'état, the ensuing National Dictatorship with its fiscal ineptness, and finally the advent of Salazar's New State in 1933. During these periods it had received minimal financing, and thus with few ships and resources, had been largely absent from the *ultramar.* Following World War II, it gained ascendancy. As Salazar had played his cards uncommonly well during the war, Portugal emerged on the side of the Allies and became a charter member of NATO. This membership benefited the navy in almost every way imaginable. It received a fleet of warships, valuable Allied training, integration into the NATO naval structure, and a vast new naval infrastructure. These were indeed exciting days. The navy in its post-war expansion sought not only to maintain its NATO fleet but also to establish a national fleet to protect the *ultramar.* It began this process in the mid-1950s and, as the security situation in Africa became increasingly dangerous, began to focus seriously and urgently on the safety of the colonies.

This thinking led to the construction of a naval force tailored to the riverine and lake environments there and reflected a great many reconciliations between the concept, its budget, the actual operating environment, and the enemy. The navy was intimately familiar with the need to safeguard national interests in Africa, as the colonies from the first had been managed under its auspices and had only shifted relatively recently. When it became obvious that the security of the overseas possessions would be contested, it began a review of its "gunboat policy" of the previous century that had served it so well in the pacification of the *ultramar.* This leisurely review was accelerated in January 1957 and developed a sense of urgency with events in the Belgian Congo. By design the new naval program was to avoid any infringement on the important NATO commitment, and yet effectively respond to the developing threat in Africa. Originally it was conceived simply as the nucleus of a specialized force and would consist of a few vessels of each of several agreed classes. The force could then be flexibly expanded in a number of directions to address any localized security requirement, as the need arose. The ability to do this quickly enough to meet the threat successfully was immediately thrown into question, as the debate over the force structure and manning questions raged for some two years. Eventually enough questions were answered satisfactorily to warrant proceeding, and finally ship designs, budget projections, and construction and deployment schedules were tentatively set. Despite the apparent agreement, debate continued, as complications arose with nearly every aspect of the enterprise. Ultimately there was a blend of corvettes, large and small patrol boats, and landing craft of varying sizes to address the mix of requirements. These vessels were procured at various times from a number of sources in the United States, Britain, France, and Germany, depending on the geopolitical shifts in colonial views and national self-interest, and subsequently also manufactured in Portugal. Manning of this fleet would draw heavily and competitively on the national manpower pool, and imaginative and inventive recruiting measures would play a vital role in answering the naval needs. Thus in addition to its primary "blue water" or oceanic navy, Portugal developed an equally impressive "brown water" one with an orientation toward inland seas, rivers, and lakes. This was a remarkable achievement, in that Portugal not only learned to fight a new kind of war, it built a navy to accomplish this and did so while shouldering additional NATO commitments and new responsibilities occasioned by the French withdrawal from the NATO Military Wing in 1960.

The later needs of the colonial conflict not only expanded the navy but took it more deeply in an amphibious direction to address the African littoral and riverine environment. The coastal and riverine fleet in Africa grew from 15 patrol ships, 10 patrol boats, and a gunboat in 1960 to 17 patrol ships, 43 patrol boats, and no less than 83 landing craft of various types and sizes in 1970, an expansion from 26 to 143 units without any rigid plan. The vessels ranged from small patrol craft of 30 tons to considerably more capable craft of 200 tons. Its amphibious force of landing craft in three different sizes of increasing capability was literally created from scratch. This development was loosely guided and rather followed the demonstrated needs of each theater commander. Unfortunately, there were continuing requests from each for additional ships that resulted in an almost inexorable expansion across Africa. This constant augmentation caused the Minister of the Navy in September 1970 to declare that there would be no more ships without a "full justification." The African navy consequently stabilized, and at the end of 1973 it stood at 137 units, with which it had to provide security over approximately 920 miles of navigable rivers, 120 miles of the Lake Niassa coast, and the ocean exposure of the three colonies.

The Portuguese Navy in developing such a naval force had clearly understood the paramount economic, military, and psychological importance of controlling the interior waterways of Africa. These sometimes represented primary commercial routes, as in the case of the Zaire, but were predominantly the smaller, more remote waterways that were key avenues for insurgent logistic support. The insurgent himself was invariably limited to what he could carry and thus his range and lethality was circumscribed, unless he had a supporting logistic system. More often than not such a system rested on a riverine network over which he transported foodstuffs, medical supplies, arms, and ammunition. The job of the navy was to foreclose this support.

In operating on and securing these waterways, the Portuguese Navy developed an informal doctrine that embodied a number of successful and proven practices based on the collective experiences of its officers and men. This body of theory or accumulation of ideas rested on common sense as refined from practical knowledge. It addressed such useful concepts as mutual support in a river convoy, blacked-out launches at night, use of illuminating flares instead of searchlights, closing targets at an angle so that the maximum number of weapons could be brought to bear, and the techniques of mutual support of riverine ground forces by riverine naval forces. These latter schemes of maneuver involved fixing the enemy, entrapping, and finally destroying him.

Waterway security operations were characterized by such irregular patterns as weaving, drifting, temporary anchoring, double-tracking over areas already patrolled, varying between fixed and mobile patrols, and so on to prevent ambushes and to interdict the enemy. Personal discipline was stressed in such practices as watch rotation, minimal talking, and loaded weapons. These practices or informal doctrine consisted of personal experiences, oral communication, letters, and reports, all shared among the "brown water" sailors. This exchange produced an effective force with high morale. Even today when veterans of the "battle of the rivers" speak of their units and their former comrades, it is with great pride. They had a clear idea of their duties and knew that they were succeeding.

The very nature of a war fought with small teams of *Fuzileiros* and boat crews bred loyalty. Loyalty to the team was in turn a very effective motivator in combat. Reinforcing this was the knowledge that the overall naval strategy was working. These *Fuzileiros* and sailors executed their missions with courage and efficiency, and the fact that their achievements were to be sacrificed at the negotiating table is part of the tragedy of the colonial wars.

While little of what these men did was codified in a written doctrine, there are important lessons, nevertheless, from their collective experiences that bear preserving for those who will fight such a battle in future years. With the demise of the Soviet Union and superpower bipolarity, an insurgency or "war of the weak" remains the most obvious and easy way to challenge conventionally powerful government forces. With the clear fact that industrialized countries will win in any conventional conflict with the Third World, the only remaining options lie in either nuclear war or insurgency. While countries like North Korea, Iraq, and Iran have attempted to develop a nuclear capability as their perceived answer to regional hegemony or survival, insurgency by far remains the easiest and most readily achievable route to gaining the political ends sought by both non-industrialized countries and aggrieved factions. Because insurgency is a fact of life, knowing how to fight it is vital. The Portuguese experience in Africa consequently holds valuable lessons in how to achieve success in this difficult medium.

The navy had spent considerable effort in producing detailed hydrographic and littoral charts of the operating areas, and each individual became intimately familiar with them on his arrival. These would be corrected and annotated from experience and used as a framework in which to fit every new piece of knowledge acquired. Through this process the sailors would come to know the operating environment intimately and have a sound mental model of this battleground. Detailed notes would include likely insurgent routes and crossings, vulnerable and secure settlements, historical and cultural factors, economic, health, and social grievances, and other pertinent factors. This was extremely important, as positive contact with the population was vital in this type of war. Knowing this battleground was the key to surviving and winning.

This preparation leads to the next step, which is to understand the overall problem and work to counter it. The boat crews, through contact with the population, gained an understanding of the enemy, his agenda and motivations. He proved to be adaptive and resourceful, and able to operate with ease among the population. He was neither misled nor naïve, and much of his success was due to inept government policies or earlier heavy-handed treatment of the population by security forces. The sailors and *Fuzileiros* became expert in countering the insurgent arguments and in calming the population through regular and frequent positive actions and engagement. In this regard, the enemy was attacked largely when he got in the way of this developing relationship. The strategy was not only to gain the confidence of the population but also to co-opt segments of the enemy. As most of the population had relatives fighting with the insurgents, it was believed that a defection was better than surrender, a surrender better than a capture, and a capture better than a kill. The aim was to do as little harm as possible.

As all successful counterinsurgency operations rest on sound intelligence, and both are complementary, the navy found that it had to develop its own approach to integrating the two because of the nature of its task. The traditional naval intelligence organization was aimed at supporting open ocean operations and was thus not responsive to activities in the remoteness of the river systems. It hence fell upon the sailors and *Fuzileiros* to develop their own sources and build an intelligence system tailored to process specialized information and sustain their operations. This was done thorough intensive patrolling day and night on both the rivers and their littorals and the constant contact this brought with the local population. While the information from these activities was shared up the chain of command, local assessment and the ability to act independently and quickly were vital features of this process. The constant gathering of information and turning it into actionable intelligence locally thus proved to be the key to operational success on the rivers, such as the effort on the Zaire.

One of the most important and successful features of Portuguese riverine operations in the overall context of counterinsurgency was presence. This was the first order of business on the Zaire, in the east of Angola, and in all of the other theaters. On the Zaire, it was begun by establishing the system of bases along the river and having the launch crews and *Fuzileiros* live in close proximity to the population and operating environment. The philosophy precluded the notion of raids into an area from distant and secure bases. The force lived in the remoteness of the Zaire and conducted patrols that landed *Fuzileiros* who moved on foot at night and maintained contact with the local people. These locals knew them as real individuals who could be trusted and not as aliens from afar. It also had the advantage of maintaining situational awareness and making the enemy the target and not the navy.

This practice of constant patrolling also deterred the enemy from attacking by keeping him off balance. He was never certain about the timing or the appearance of naval forces, and this unpredictable yet constant activity deterred attacks and reassured the population, producing a permissive environment. The numerous deception techniques practiced by the launch crews and *Fuzileiros* in patrolling reinforced this enemy uncertainty. On the Zaire, for instance, the navy made modifications in its operating methods to enhance this uncertainty by closing the land bases in large part and putting the crews and *Fuzileiros* on mobile bases. The enemy now could no longer watch a base and note the departure of patrols. This positive change not only reduced the cost of maintaining a network of fixed bases but also had the effect of keeping upwards of two-thirds of the naval force on patrol at any one time.

The navy in each situation sought to stamp its dominance in its area of operations by seeking an early victory. This victory would not necessarily be in combat, unless the enemy was foolish enough to present an easy target, a rare occurrence in counterinsurgency. It would most likely be a shift in allegiance and confidence within the local population. On the Zaire, for example, it was the clearing of the Bulicoco archipelago in October 1962 that produced naval dominance. This was followed by steady progress with the population over several years and ultimately with the extraordinary enemy appeal to the army doctor in Noqui to come across the Congo border to its base in Kinkusu to care for one of its wounded commanders.

The navy was prepared to be patient in conducting its counterinsurgency. Clearly there were setbacks, but failures are normal in this type of warfare, and local commanders as a rule were given the latitude and autonomy to adjust their posture to local conditions. This created an elasticity that helped strengthen the naval approach in adjusting to an innovative enemy and in competing for the mobilization of popular support.

Counterinsurgency is essentially armed social work, and this makes civil affairs a central activity. While the navy offered medical care and other forms of help, it was most noted for its commercial support. It did this in Guiné, on the Zaire, in the east of Angola, and on Lake Niassa, for example, by initiating and operating regular transport services that carried produce to market and brought needed supplies to isolated elements of the population. These were tailored to specific local conditions and were inexpensive, sustainable, and low-key. These communication links proved critical to both the military and civil dimensions of the conflict.

The navy set its sights on doing what was achievable with its resources. It developed in each theater a flexible and adaptive plan to increase security in the areas assigned and gain the initiative and maintain it. In counterinsurgency initiative is everything. If the enemy is reacting to you, then you are controlling the fight. If you can mobilize the population, then you will win. In this fight the enemy will initiate most attacks, target you unpredictably, and then withdraw too rapidly for you to react, such as the ambushes along the rivers of Guiné. The navy tended not to be drawn into reactive operations but rather to build its own solution to gain and maintain the initiative, as in the multi-year strategy in the east of Angola.

The lessons from Portuguese riverine operations and its naval experience in Africa fighting insurgency tend to be forgotten by all but the veterans of the conflict and the occasional naval historian. The experience of the U.S. Navy in Vietnam and the French in Indochina, for instance, has suffered the same fate, and yet today riverine operations are experiencing a renaissance in reaction to the "war of the weak." The U.S. Navy-Marine Corps team and the Royal Navy and Marines are moving inshore and up river in search of new enemies. Increasingly, terrorist agents and cells are combining with criminal elements, such as in the Nigerian Delta, along the Shatt-al-Arab between Iran and Iraq, and off the coast of Somalia, drawing attention to these waterways. There is now an increasing emphasis on naval operations in the green water of the littoral and the brown waters of the riverine environment, where there is an apparent convergence of evil forces. New craft, specially trained troops, and associated tactics are being developed to address the increasingly sophisticated threats on these coastal waters, estuaries, and inland waterways. Interestingly, the same capabilities developed so well by the Portuguese Navy over thirty years ago are sought today to counter threats in similar environments. The boats are more technologically advanced, and the crews use newer and better equipment and weapons, but the problems and their solutions remain largely the same. The operating environment remains the rivers, bayous, salt pans, canals, lakes, and deltas extending inland from the coast. The population remains a vulnerable target, and the need to establish a permissive environment continues as the primary goal. U.S. Chief of Naval Operations, Admiral Michael G. Mullen, in a speech at the Naval War College at Newport, Rhode Island, in August 2005, noted that a naval force floating off the continental shelf with no impact onshore is not decisive. "We cannot sit out in the deep blue waiting for the enemy to come to us. Think of the vast areas of the world covered by shallow water, those connected to the oceans by rivers and harbors and rugged shorelines. These are the decisive strips of sea that make all the difference, and we need to be there. I believe our Navy is missing a great opportunity to influence events by not having a riverine force. We're going to have one."[1] Clearly the legacy of the Portuguese "brown water navy" remains relevant today and continues to influence the shape of current and future navies.

Notes

1 Cale A. Hanie, "Riverine Craft, Crews Visit Naval Academy," *Navy Newsstand* (U.S. Naval Academy, Annapolis), 10 April 2006, story number NNS060410-03, http://www.navy.mil/search/display.asp?story_id=23074 (accessed 21 October 2011).

Selected Bibliography

Portuguese Government Publications and Documents

Alpoim Calvão, Guilherme Almor de. "Introducão as Operações na Guiné." [Introduction to Operations in Guiné]. In the unpublished collection *Participação da Armada na Defesa das Províncias Ultramarinas.* [Participation of the Navy in the Defense of the Overseas Provinces]. TMs [photocopy]. Lisbon: Ministério de Marinha, 1972.

Corpo de *Fuzileiros. Corpo de Fuzileiros, Part II: Fuzileiros Especiais.* [Marine Corps, Part II: Special Marines]. TMs [photocopy]. Lisbon: Ministério da Marinha, 1987.

Cruz Júnior, Abílio Freire da. "Evolução das Infra-estructuras da Armada no Ultramar." [Evolution of Naval Infrastructure in the *Ultramar*]. In the unpublished collection *Participação da Armada na Defesa das Províncias Ultramarinas.* [Participation of the Navy in the Defense of the Overseas Provinces]. TMs [photocopy]. Lisbon: Ministério de Marinha 1972.

Cunha e Silva, Raúl Eugénio Dias da. "21st Detachment of Special Marines, Operation 'Green Sea,' Relating to the Period from 170300 to 252000 November 1970," after action report written at the headquarters of DFE 21, Buba, Guiné, 30 November 1970. TMs [photocopy].

Estado-Maior da Armada, IV Divisão. *Características Principais das Novas Unidades Navais e do Material das Unidades de Fuzileiros.* [Principal Characteristics of New Naval and Marine Units]. TMs [photocopy]. Lisbon: Estado-Maior da Armada, 1969.

Estado-Maior do Exército. *Resenha Histórico-Militar das Campanhas de África, Vols. I–V.* [Historical Military Report of the African Campaigns, Vol. I–V]. Lisbon: Estado-Maior do Exército, 1989.

Lopes Carvalheira, José Alberto. "Acção da Marinha em Águas Interiores (1961–1971)." [Naval Operations in Inland Waters (1961–1971)]. In the unpublished collection *Participação da Armada na Defesa das Províncias Ultramarinas.* [Participation of the Navy in the Defense of the Overseas Provinces]. TMs [photocopy]. Lisbon: Ministério de Marinha, 1972.

______. "Guiné: Esquadrilha de Lanchas e Outros Navios." [Guiné: Squadron of Patrol Boats and Other Ships]. In the unpublished collection *Participação da Armada na Defesa das Províncias Ultramarinas.* [Participation of the Navy in the Defense of the Overseas Provinces]. TMs [photocopy]. Lisbon: Ministério de Marinha 1972.

Malheiro García, António José. "Particiação da Armada na Defesa das Provincias Ultramarinas, Actividade Oceânica, Breve Retrospectiva da Actividade Naval na Década de 50." [Participation of the Navy in the Defense of the Overseas Provinces, Oceanic Role, Retrospective Brief of the Naval Role in the Decade of the 50s]. In the unpublished collection *Participação da Armada na Defesa das Províncias Ultramarinas.* [Participation of the Navy in the Defense of the Overseas Provinces] TMs [photocopy]. Lisbon: Ministério de Marinha, 1972

______. "A Operação *Santa Maria.*" [Operation *Santa Maria*]. In the unpublished collection *Participação da Armada na Defesa das Províncias Ultramarinas.* [Participation of the Navy in the Defense of the Overseas Provinces]. TMs [photocopy]. Lisbon: Ministério de Marinha, 1972

Mouzinho, Captain (Engineer) Pedro da Conceição. "Relatório sobre a Operação Atum." [Report on Operation Tuna]. TMs [photocopy]. Naval Headquarters, Lourenço Marques, Mozambique, 14 January 1966.

Interviews and Correspondence

Alpoim Calvão, Guilherme Almor de. Correspondence with the author, 22 June 2005, Cascais. Correspondence with the author, 9 May 2005, Cascais. Interview and correspondence with the author, 3 February 1998, Lisbon. Interview by the author, 14 March 1997, Lisbon. *Comandante* Alpoim Calvão served as commanding officer of DFE 8 and led Operation *Mar Verde* or Green Sea.

Campos. Ricardo Manuel Migães de. Interview with the author, 30 January 2003, Lisbon. Dr. Campos was a naval doctor at Metangula on Lake Niassa.

Costa Matos, Carlos Augusto Pereira da. Interview with the author, 15 April 2000, Lisbon. Colonel Costa Matos was the governor of Niassa between 1962 and 1966.

Gomes, Carlos Encaração. Interview by the author, 5 February 2003, Lisbon. *Comandante* Gomes commanded DFE 10 in Guiné during the early years of the war.

Ferraz Sacchetti, António Emílio. Interview by the author, 18 May 2006, Lisbon. Vice Admiral Sacchetti served in a number of capacities as a junior officer during the conflict.

Leitão, Raul Patrício. Interview with the author, 10 April 2000, Lisbon. *Comandante* Leitão was a *fuzileiro* on Lake Niassa in the early years of the war.

Marques, Paulo Lownes. Interview by the author, 5 February 2003, Lisbon. Lieutenant (junior grade) Marques is a graduate of the 7th Naval Reserve course (CEORN 7°) and served in Angola between 1965 and 1967.

Marinho de Castro, António Luís. Interview by the author, 30 January 2003, Lisbon. Lieutenant (junior grade) Marinho de Castro was graduated in April 1966 in the 8th Naval Reserve course (CEORN 8°) as a *fuzileiro.*

Matos, Luís Jorge. Interview with the author, 10 February 2003, Bélem. *Comandante* Matos is an historian specializing in the *Fuzileiros.*

Mesquita Dias. Luiz C. Interview by the author, 10 February 2003, Lisbon. Rear Admiral Mesquita Dias as a junior officer was the engineer responsible for the naval yard in Guiné in the early years of the war.

Quevedo Pessanha. Vasco. Interview by the author, 5 February 2003, Lisbon. Lieutenant (junior grade) Pessanha is a graduate of the 8th Naval Reserve course (CEORN 8°) and served in Angola between 1965 and 1967.

Torres Sobral, José Deolindo. Interview with the author, 31 January and 10 April 2000, Lisbon. Vice Admiral Torres Sobral when he was a junior officer served as the commanding officer of LFP *Mercúrio* (P 1135) on Lake Niassa.

Background Literature

Abshire, David M., and Michael A. Samuels. *Portuguese Africa, A Handbook.* New York: Praeger Publishers, 1969.

Afonso, Aniceto, and Carlos de Matos Gomes. *Guerra Colonial.* [Colonial War]. Lisbon: Notícias, 1998.

Agullar, Teixeira de, Reis Arenga, Silva Ribeiro, Santos Serafim, Albuquerque e Silva, and Melo e Sousa. *A Marinha na Investigação do Mar 1800–1999.* [The Navy in the Investigation of the Sea 1800–1999]. Lisbon: Instituto Hidrográfico, 2001.

Alpoim Calvão, Guilherme Almor de. *De Conakry ao M.D.L.P.* [From Conakry to the M.D.L.P.]. Lisbon: Editorial Intervenção, 1976.

Antunes, José Freire. *Jorge Jardim Agente Secreto.* [Jorge Jardim Secret Agent]. Venda Nova: Bertrand Editora, 1996.

______. *A Guerra de África 1961–1974.* [The African War 1961–1974]. Lisbon: Temas e Debates, 1996.

______. "Calvão evoca Conakry: «Às 9 da manhã eu tinha a cidade nas mãos». [Calvão remembers Conakry: "At 9 in the morning I held the city in my hands"]. *Semanário,* 10 December 1988, 16.

______. "Invasão de Conakry, Novembro de 1970: A 'Baía dos Porcos' do General Spínola". [Invasion of Conakry, November of 1970: The "Bay of Pigs" of General Spínola]. *Semanário,* 29 October 1988, 21.

Alata, Jean-Paul. *Prison D'Afrique.* Paris: Éditions du Seuil, 1976.

Armstrong, Sue. *In Search of Freedom.* Gibraltar: Ashanti Publishing, 1989.

Arriaga, Kaúlza de. *Sinteses.* [Synthesis]. Lisbon: Privately printed, 1992.

Baêna, Luís Sanches de. *Fuzileiros: Factos e Feitos na Guerra de África, 1961/1974.* [Marines: Deeds and Feats in the African War, 1961/1974]. 4 vols. Lisbon: Comissão Cultural da Marinha–INAPA, 2006.

Barreiros, Delmar. "Cobué: A zona mais pachola..." [Cobué: The prouder zone...]. *Revista da Armada* (November 1984): 16–17.

Beckett, Ian F. W. "The Portuguese Army: The Campaign in Mozambique, 1964–1974." In *Armed Forces and Modern Counterinsurgency* ed. I. F. W. Beckett and J. Pimlott, 136–162. London: Croom Helm, 1985.

Bender, Gerald J. "The Limits of Counterinsurgency: An African Case." *Comparative Politics* 4 (April 1972): 331–360.

Borges Coelho, João Paulo. "African Troops in the Portuguese Colonial Army, 1961–1974: Angola, Guinea-Bissau and Mozambique." *Portuguese Studies Review* (Spring-Summer 2002): 129–150.

Brandão Ferreira, João José. *A Evolução do Conceito Estratégico Ultramarino Português.* [Evolution of the Portuguese *Ultramar* Strategic Concept]. Lisbon: Hugin Editores, 2002.

Bruce, Neil. "Portugal's African Wars." *Conflict Studies* 34 (March 1973): 1–22.

Cabeçadas, João Soares. "'Navegando' do Índico ao Lago Niassa." ["Navigating" from the Indian (Ocean) to Lake Niassa]. *Revista da Armada* (May 1974): 9.

Cabral, Amílcar. *Guiné-Bissau–Nação Africana Forjada na Luta.* [Guiné-Bissau–African Nation Forged in Struggle]. Lisbon: Publicações Nova Auora, 1974.

______. *Textos Políticos.* [Political Texts]. Porto: Edições Afrontamento, 1974.

______. *Palavras de Ordem Gerais.* [Speeches on Overall Methods]. Bissau: PAIGC/Secretariado Geral, 1976.

Cann, John P. *Contra-Subversão em África.* [Counterinsurgency in Africa]. Lisbon: Prefácio, 2005.

Castanheira, José Pedro. "Ao Serviço de Spínola e Marcelo." [In the Service of Spínola e Marcelo]. *Expresso,* 20 September 1997, 56.

______. "Memórias da Guerra e da Paz: Spínola." [Memories of War and Peace: Spínola]. *Expresso Revista,* 30 April 1994, 26.

Caetano, Marcello. *Depoimento.* [Deposition]. Rio de Janeiro: Distribuidora Record, 1974.

Chabal, Patrick. *Amílcar Cabral.* Cambridge: Cambridge University Press, 1983.

Clarence-Smith, W. Gervase. *The Third Portuguese Empire 1825–1975: A Study in Economic Imperialism.* Manchester: Manchester University Press, 1985.

Clegg, Robert H., ed. *Riverine Warfare.* Quantico: Marine Corps Command and Staff College, 1997.

Collins, John M. *Military Geography.* Washington: National Defense University Press, 1998.

Comacho, Francisco. "Baixa do Cassange." *Grande Reportagem* 137 (August 2002): 62–77.

Crespo, Manuel Pereira. "As Missões das Forcas Navais na Guerra Revolucionária." [The Mission of Naval Forces in Revolutionary War]. *Anais do Club Militar Naval* (June–September 1960): 537–550.

Croizat, Victor. *The Brown Water Navy*. Poole: Blanford Press, 1984.

Cutler, Thomas J. *Brown Water, Black Berets*. Annapolis: Naval Institute Press, 1988.

Dâmaso, Eduardo, and Adelino Gomes. "Falecidos por Fuzilamento." [Death by Shooting]. *Pública*, 30 June 1996, 48.

Davezies, Robert. *Les Angolais*. Paris: Éditions de Minuit, 1965.

Dunnavent, R. Blake. *Brown Water Warfare*. Gainesville: University Press of Florida, 2003.

Ellert, Henrik. *The Rhodesian Front War, Counter-insurgency and Guerrilla Warfare 1962–1980*. Gweru, Zimbabwe: Mambo Press, 1993.

Estival, Bernard. "The French Navy and the Algerian War." Translated by Paul Leahy. In *France and the Algerian War, 1954–62: Strategy, Operations and Diplomacy*, ed. Martin S. Alexander and J. F. V. Keiger, 79–96. London: Frank Cass, 2002.

Felgas, Hélio. *Os Movimentos Terroristas*. [The Terrorist Movements]. Lisbon: Privately printed, 1966.

______. *O Clima do Congo Português*. [The Climate of Portuguese Congo]. Carmona: Imprensa Angolana, 1959.

Forbes, John, and Robert Williams. *Riverine Force*. New York: Bantam, 1987.

Forbath, Peter. *The River Congo*. New York: Harper & Row, 1977.

Gomes, Adelino. "Exército e UNITA Colaboraram antes de 74." [Army and UNITA Collaborate before 74]. *Público* (19 December 1995): 2-4.

Guest, Robert. *The Shackled Continent: Power, Corruption, and African Lives*. Washington: Smithsonian Books, 2004.

Hipólito, Abel Barroso. *A Pacificação do Niassa: Um Caso Concreto de Contraguerrilha*. [The Pacification of Niassa: A Concrete Case of Counterguerrilla War]. Lisbon: privately published, 1970.

Hoar, Mike. *Congo Warriors*. London: Robert Hale, 1991.

Hochschild, Adam. *King Leopold's Ghost*. New York: Houghton Mifflin, 1998.

Kay, Hugh. *Salazar and Modern Portugal*. London: Eyre and Spottswoode, 1970.

Kilian, Robert. *Les Fusiliers Marins en Indochine*. Paris: Éditions Berger-Levrault, 1951.

Lobato, António. *Liberdade ou Evasão*. [Freedom or Evasion]. Amadora: Erasmos Editora, 1996.

Lorch, Carlos, ed. *Fuzileiros Navais, Brazil's Amphibious Warriors*. Rio de Janeiro: Action Editora, 1997.

Lima Bacelar, Sérgio Augusto Margarido. *A Guerra em África 1961–1974: Estratégias Adoptadas pelas Forças Armadas*. [The War in Africa 1961–1974: Strategies Adopted by the Armed Forces]. Porto: Liga dos Amigos do Museu Militar do Porto and Universidade Portucalenese Infante D. Henrique, 2000.

Machado. Manuel Pinto. "Postais do Ultramar: Angola – Postal № 3, Lungué-Bungo fins do octobro 68." [Overseas Postcards: Angola – Postcard № 3, Lungué-Bungo End of October '68]. *Anais do Clube Militar Naval* (October/December 1968): 695–696.

Marcum, John. *The Angolan Revolution. Volume 1, The Anatomy of an Explosion (1950–1962)*. Cambridge: M.I.T. Press, 1969.

Marinho, António Luís. *Operação Mar Verde*. [Operation Green Sea]. Lisbon: Temas e Debates, 2006.

Mateus, Dalila Cabrita. *A PIDE/DGS na Guerra Colonial 1961–1974*. [The PIDE/DGS in the Colonial War 1961–1974]. Lisbon: Terramar, 2004.

Matos Gomes, Carlos de. *Moçambique 1970, Operação Nó Górdio.* [Mozambique 1970, Operation Gordian Knot]. Lisbon: Prefácio, 2002.

Meredith, Martin. *The Fate of Africa.* New York: Public Affairs, 2005.

Ministério da Marinha. *A Marinha nos Últimos 40 Anos, 1926–1966.* [The Navy in the Last 40 Years, 1926–1966]. Lisbon: Ministério da Marinha, 1966.

Mondlane, Eduardo. *The Struggle for Mozambique.* London: Zed Press, 1969.

Moura da Fonseca, José da Cruz. *Viagens e Históras da Marinha.* [Voyages and Stories of the Navy]. Lisbon: Edições Culturais da Marinha, 1995.

Moura da Fonseca, José da Cruz. "A Marinha no Leste e no Sueste de Angola." [The Navy in the East and Southeast of Angola]. *Anais do Clube Militar Naval* (October-December 1981): 619–629.

Newett, Malyn. *A History of Mozambique.* London: Hurst & Company, 1995.

______. *Portugal in Africa: The Last Hundred Years.* London: C. Hurst & Co., 1981.

Pélissier, René. *Naissance de la Guiné, Portugais et Africains en Sénégambie (1841–1936).* Orgeval: Pélissier, 1989.

______. *Naissance du Mozambique: Résistance et Révoltes Anticoloniales (1854–1918).* Orgeval: Pélissier, 1984.

______. *Le Naufrage des Caravelles, Etudes sur la Fin de l'Empire Portugais (1961–1975).* Orgeval: Editions Pélissier, 1979.

______. *La Colonie du Minotaure, Nationalismes et Révoltes en Angola (1926–1961).* Orgeval: Editions Pélissier, 1978.

Petter-Bowyer, Peter J. H. *Winds of Destruction.* Victoria: Trafford, 2003.

Pires Nunes, António. *Angola 1966–1974, Vitória Militar no Leste.* [Angola 1966–1974, Military Victory in the East]. Lisbon: Prefácio, 2002.

Porch, Douglas. *The Portuguese Armed Forces and the Revolution.* Stanford: The Hoover Institution Press, 1977.

Ramos, Gomes. "Por Terras Nunca de Antes..." [Over Lands Never Before...]. *Anais do Clube Militar Naval* (April–June 1966): 292.

Robinson, Richard. *Contemporary Portugal.* London: George Allen & Unwin, 1979.

Roboredo, Armando de. "Subsídios para Definir uma Política Naval Portuguesa." [Aids in Defining a Portuguese Naval Policy]. *Anais de Marinha* (September–December 1956): 5–10.

Rodrigues, Luís Nuno. *Salazar–Kennedy: A Crise de uma Aliança.* [Salazar–Kennedy: The Crisis of an Alliance]. Lisbon: Editorial Notícias, 2002.

Rodrigues da Costa, A.B., and Manuel Pinto Machado. *O Anuário da Reserva Naval 1958–1975.* [The Annual of the Naval Reserve 1958–1975]. Lisbon: Associação dos Oficiais da Reserva Naval, 1992.

Ferraz Sacchetti, António Emílio. "A Armada nas Campanhas de África." [The Navy in the African Campaigns]. *Revista da Armada* (June 1997): 7.

Saraiva, José Manuel. "Asslto a Conakry." [Assault on Conakry]. *Revista do Expresso,* 23 November 1996, 97–98.

Saraiva, A. Pimentel. "Postais do Ultramar: Angola – Postal Nº 2, Luanda, Zaire, Cabinda e Leste de Angola." [Overseas Postcards: Angola – Postcard Nº 2, Luanda, Zaire, Cabinda and the East of Angola]. *Anais do Clube Militar Naval* (April/June 1968): 312.

Saturnio Monteiro, Armando da Silva. *Batalhas e Combates da Marinha Portuguesa.* [Battles and Engagements of the Portuguese Navy]. Lisbon: Livraria sá da Costa Editora, 1997.

Sékou Touré, Ahmed. *L'Agression Portugaise contra la Republic de Guiné.* Conakry: Livre Blanc, 1970.

Serras Pires, Adelino, and Fiona Claire Capstick. *The Winds of Havoc.* New York: St. Martin's Press, 2001.

Shankland, Peter. *The Phantom Flotilla.* London: Collins, 1968.

Silva Cunha, Joaquim Moreira da. *O Ultramar, a Nação e o "25 de Abril."* [The Overseas Provinces, the Nation and the "25th of April"]. Coimbra: Atlântida Editora, 1977.

Spínola, António de. *País sem Rumo.* [Country without Direction]. Lisbon: Editorial SCIRE, 1978.

______. *Portugal e o Futuro.* [Portugal and the Future]. Lisbon: Editoria Arcádia, 1974.

______. *Por Uma Guiné Melhor.* [For a Better Guiné]. Lisbon: Agência-Geral do Ultramar, 1970.

Teixeira da Mota, Avelino. *Mar, Além Mar, Estudos e Ensaios de História e Geografia.* [The Sea, Beyond the Sea, Studies and Essays on History and Geography]. Lisbon: Junta de Investigações do Ultramar, 1972.

______. *Guiné Portuguesa.* [Portuguese Guiné]. Lisbon: Agência Geral do Ultramar, 1954.

______. *Guiné Portuguesa, II Volume.* [Portuguese Guiné, Volume II]. Lisbon: Agência Geral do Ultramar, 1954.

Telo, António José. *História da Marinha Portuguesa: Homens, Doutrinas e Organização, 1824–1974* (Tomo I) [History of the Portuguese Navy: Men, Doctrine and Organization, 1824–1974 (Volume I)]. Lisbon: Academia de Marinha, 1999.

Thomas, Hugh. *The Slave Trade.* New York: Simon & Schuster, 1997.

van der Waals, W. S.. *Portugal's War in Angola 1961–1974.* Rivonia: Ashanti, 1993.

Venter, Al J. *The Zambesi Salient: Conflict in Southern Africa.* Cape Town: Howard Timmins, 1974.

______. *Portugal's Insurgent War, The Campaign for Africa.* Cape Town: John Malherbe, 1973.

Verdasca dos Santos, José. *Memórias de um Captão.* [Memories of a Captain]. Lisbon: Universitária Editoria, 2004.

Vigo, Milan N. *Naval Strategy and Operations in Narrow Seas.* London: Frank Cass, 1999.

Wheeler, Douglas L. "The Military and the Portuguese Dictatorship, 1926–1974: 'The Honor of the Army.'" In *Contemporary Portugal* ed. Lawrence S. Graham and Harry M. Makler, 191–219. Austin: University of Texas Press, 1979.

______. "African Elements in Portugal's Armies in Africa (1961–1974)." *Armed Forces and Society* 2 (February 1976): 233–250.

______, and René Pélissier. *Angola.* London: Pall Mall Press, 1971.

______. "The Portuguese Army in Angola." *Modern African Studies* 7 (October 1969): 425–439.

Index

Helion Studies in Military History

No 1 *Learning from Foreign Wars. Russian Military Thinking 1859-73* Gudrun Persson (ISBN 978-1-906033-61-3)
No 2 *A Military Government in Exile. The Polish Government-in-Exile 1939-45, a Study of Discontent* Evan McGilvray (ISBN 978-1-906033-58-3)
No 3 *From Landrecies to Cambrai. Case Studies of German Offensive and Defensive Operations on the Western Front 1914-17* Capt G.C. Wynne (ISBN 978-1-906033-76-7)
No 4 *Playing the Game. The British Junior Infantry Officer on the Western Front 1914-18* Christopher Moore-Bick (ISBN 978-1-906033-84-2)
No 5 *The History of the British Army Film & Photographic Unit in the Second World War* Dr Fred McGlade (ISBN 978-1-906033-94-1)
No 6 *Making Waves. Admiral Mountbatten's Radio SEAC 1945-49* Eric Hitchcock (ISBN 978-1-906033-95-8)
No 7 *Abolishing the Taboo. Dwight D. Eisenhower and American Nuclear Doctrine 1945-1961* Brian Madison Jones (ISBN 978-1-907677-31-1)
No 8 *The Turkish Brigade in the Korean War Volume 1. Kunu-Ri Heroes (November-December 1950)* Dr Ali Denizli (ISBN 978-1-907677-32-8)
No 9 *The Diaries of Ronnie Tritton, War Office Publicity Officer 1940-45* Edited by Dr Fred McGlade (ISBN 978-1-907677-44-1)
No 10 *The Thinking Man's Soldier. The Life and Career of General Sir Henry Brackenbury 1837-1914* Christopher Brice (ISBN 978-1-907677-69-4)
No 11 *War Surgery 1914-18* Edited by Thomas Scotland and Steven Heys (ISBN 978-1-907677-70-0)
No 12 *Counterinsurgency in Africa. The Portuguese Way of War 1961-74* John P. Cann (ISBN 978-1-907677-73-1)
No 13 *The Armed Forces of Poland in the West 1939-46* Michael Alfred Peszke (ISBN 978-1-908916-54-9)
No 14 *The Role of the Soviet Union in the Second World War* Boris Sokolov (ISBN 978-1-908916-55-6)
No 15 *Generals of the Danish Army in the First and Second Schleswig-Holstein Wars, 1848-50 and 1864* Nick B. Svendsen (ISBN 978-1-908916-46-4)
No 16 *A Considerable Achievement. The Tactical Development of the 56th (London) Division on the Western Front, 1916-1918* Matt Brosnan (ISBN 978-1-908916-47-1)
No 17 *Brown Waters of Africa. Portuguese Riverine Warfare 1961-1974* John P. Cann (ISBN 978-1-908916-56-3)
No 18 *Man of Steel and Honour. General Stanislaw Maczek. Soldier of Poland, Commander of the 1st Polish Armoured Division in North-West Europe 1944-45* Evan McGilvray (ISBN 978-1-908916-53-2)
No 19 *The Gaysh. A History of the Aden Protectorate Levies 1927-61 and the Federal Regular Army of South Arabia 1961-67* Frank Edwards (ISBN 978-1-908916-87-7)
No 20 *The Whole Armour of God. Anglican Army Chaplains in the Great War* Linda Parker (ISBN 978-1-908916-96-9)